Everyman, I will go with thee,
and be thy guide

William James

SELECTED WRITINGS

Edited by
G. H. BIRD
University of Manchester

EVERYMAN
J. M. DENT · LONDON
CHARLES E. TUTTLE
VERMONT

Introduction and other critical material © J. M. Dent, 1995

First published in Everyman in 1995

All rights reserved

J. M. Dent
Orion Publishing Group
Orion House, 5 Upper St Martin's Lane,
London WC2H 9EA
and
Charles E. Tuttle Co. Inc.
28 South Main Street,
Rutland, Vermont 05701, USA

Typeset in Sabon by CentraCet Ltd, Cambridge
Printed in Great Britain by
The Guernsey Press Co. Ltd, Guernsey, C.I.

British Library Cataloguing-in-Publication Data
is available upon request.

ISBN 0 460 87557 4

CONTENTS

NOTE ON THE AUTHOR AND EDITOR

WILLIAM JAMES was born in New York on 11 January 1842, one year before the birth of his brother Henry James, the future novelist. He spent substantial parts of his childhood at schools in Europe and spent a year training as an artist before embarking on a university career at Harvard in 1861. After his graduation in 1869 he suffered a period of ill health and depression but took up teaching posts successively in psychology and philosophy at Harvard. He was appointed a full Professor of Philosophy at Harvard in 1880. During the 1870s and 1880s he published a number of papers on psychology and philosophy which were later incorporated in a major work *The Principles of Psychology* published in 1890. The work earned him an international reputation. It offered a unified account of the methods of investigation in psychology at a time when it was beginning to free itself from its philosophical origins. After 1890 his work veered more towards philosophy. He published a collection of articles on free-will and moral philosophy in *The Will to Believe* in 1896, the Edinburgh Gifford lectures on *The Varieties of Religious Experience* in 1902, and the famous lectures on *Pragmatism* in 1907. A collection of articles which supplemented his pragmatist views was published as *The Meaning of Truth* in 1909, and in the same year he published *A Pluralistic Universe*. James provides a rounded philosophy which covers epistemology, moral philosophy and philosophy of religion and was governed throughout by pragmatic principles and his own wish to reconcile empiricism with the claims of religion. During his lifetime it influenced many philosophers, including Bertrand Russell, and it has continued to exert an influence through others as diverse as W. V. O. Quine and Richard Rorty. He died – after travelling to Europe to see Henry James – on his return to America on 26 August 1910.

GRAHAM BIRD is at present Sir Samuel Hall Professor of Philosophy at the University of Manchester. His published books include *Kant's Theory of Knowledge* (1962) and *William James* (1986).

CHRONOLOGY OF JAMES'S LIFE

Year	Age	Life
1842		Born in New York, 11 January
1843	1	Family visits England and France. Birth of Henry James junior
1844	2	Henry James senior's illness at Windsor
1845	3	Family return to New York. Birth of Wilkinson James
1846	4	Birth of Robertson James
1848	6	Family settle in New York at 58 West 14th Street. Birth of Alice James
1852	10	Henry James senior publishes *Lectures and Miscellanies*
1855–6	13–14	Travels in Europe. Attends schools in Switzerland and France
1857	15	Attends atelier of painter Leon Coigniet in Paris
1858	16	Returns to America. Attends school in Newport, Rhode Island
1859	17	Returns to Geneva and attends a Swiss school
1860	18	Returns to New York. Works with painter William Morris Hunt at Newport
1861	19	Signs of ill health. Enters Lawrence Scientific School at Harvard
1862	20	Wilkinson James joins 44th Massachusetts Regiment, Boston
1863	21	Robertson James joins 55th Massachusetts Regiment, Boston. Enters Harvard Medical School

CHRONOLOGY OF HIS TIMES

Year	Artistic and Scientific Events	Historical Events
1843	J. S. Mill, *System of Logic*	
1844	Schopenhauer, *The World as Will and Idea*, vol. 2 Emerson, *Essays*, second series	
1845–7		Irish potato famine
1848		Revolutions in Europe End of French monarchy Californian Gold Rush
1850	Hawthorne, *The Scarlet Letter*	
1851	Melville, *Moby Dick*	Great Exhibition, London
1852	Comte, *Positivist Catechism*	Louis Napoleon proclaimed Emperor of France
1854	Riemann lectures on non-Euclidean geometry	
1854–6		Crimean War
1855	Bain, *The Senses and the Intellect*	
1857		Indian 'Mutiny'
1858	Taine, *Critical and Historical Essays*	
1859	Darwin, *The Origin of Species*	
1860	Fechner, *Elements of Psychophysics*	
1861		Abraham Lincoln becomes President Slavery abolished
1861–5		American Civil War

Year	Age	Life
1864	22	Henry James senior moves to Boston
1865	23	Joins Louis Agassiz's eleven-month expedition to Brazil. Suffers from smallpox-type illness
1866	24	Returns to Boston. Intern at Massachusetts General Hospital. Alice James suffers first period of serious illness. Henry senior moves to Quincy Street, Boston
1867–8	25–6	Visits Germany. Receives treatment for back pain
1869	27	Graduates from Harvard Medical School
1870	28	Period of ill health and depression
1873	31	Teaches physiology at Harvard
1875	33	Teaches psychology at Harvard
1876	34	Appointed Assistant Professor of Physiology at Harvard
1878	36	Marries Alice Howe Gibbens
1879	37	Travels in Europe. Meets Herbert Spencer, Croom Robertson, Shadworth Hodgson and Alexander Bain
1880	38	Appointed Assistant Professor of Philosophy at Harvard
1882	40	Travels to Europe. Meets Ernst Mach, Carl Stumpf and Leslie Stephen
1884	42	'The Dilemma of Determinism'
1885	43	Appointed Professor of Philosophy at Harvard. Has first meeting with medium Mrs Piper. Founds American Society for Psychical Research
1886	44	Buys farm at Chocorua, New Hampshire
1889	47	Visits London, Dublin and Edinburgh. Attends Paris Congress of Physiological Psychology. Builds house at Irving Street, Cambridge

Year	Artistic and Scientific Events	Historical Events
1864	T. H. Huxley, *Man's Place in Nature* Maxwell, *The Electro-Magnetic Theory of Light*	
1865	Dühring, *Capital and Work*	Lincoln assassinated Prussian victory over Austria at Sadowa
1867	Karl Marx, *Das Kapital*, vol. 1	Paris Exhibition
1869	Renouvier, *Science of Morals*	Suez Canal opened
1870		Start of Franco-Prussian War
1871		Siege of Paris; Paris Commune
1873	Cantor publishes works on trans-finite numbers	
1874	Wundt, *Principles of Physiological Psychology*	
1875		Invention of telephone Disraeli buys shares in the Suez Canal
1876	Bradley, *Ethical Studies*	
1878	Helmholtz, *The Facts of Perception*	Congress of Berlin
1881	Henry James, *Washington Square*	
1882		Phoenix Park murders, Dublin
1883	Green, *Prolegomena to Ethics*	
1884	Frege, *Foundations of Arithmetic*	
1885	Royce, *The Religious Aspects of Philosophy*	Death of Gordon at Khartoum
1886	Mach, *Essay on the Analysis of Sensations*	
1887	Nietzsche, *The Genealogy of Morals*	
1889		Eiffel Tower completed

Year	Artistic and Scientific Events	Historical Events
1890	Lloyd Morgan, *Animal Life and Intelligence* Ehrenfels, 'On Gestalt Qualities' Frazer, *The Golden Bough*	Chancellor Bismarck dismissed by the Kaiser
1891		Death of Charles Stewart Parnell
1893	Death of Jean Charcot	
1894		Beginning of Dreyfus Affair
1895	Freud and Breuer, *Studies on Hysteria* Röntgen discovers X-rays	Trial of Oscar Wilde
1896	Bergson, *Matter and Memory* Müller-Lyer, 'Concerning the Theory of Optical Illusions'	Klondike Gold Rush
1897		Queen Victoria's Diamond Jubilee
1898	Thorndike, *Animal Intelligence* The Curies discover radium	Death of Bismarck
1899		Start of Boer War
1900	Freud, *The Interpretation of Dreams*	
1901		Death of Queen Victoria
1901–9		Presidency of Theodore Roosevelt
1902	Henry James, *The Wings of a Dove*	
1903		The Wright brothers' flight, Kittyhawk, North Carolina
1904	Henry James, *The Golden Bowl*	
1905	Einstein proposes Special Theory of Relativity Simon devises standardized intelligence test	First Russian Revolution Sinn Fein party founded in Dublin

Year	Age	Life
1906	64	Lectures at Stanford. Experiences San Francisco earthquake. Gives Lowell Institute Lectures on pragmatism
1907	65	Resigns post at Harvard. Lectures at Columbia University. *Pragmatism* published.
1908	66	Visits England. Gives Hibbert Lectures at Manchester College, Oxford. Writes 'The Pragmatic Account of Truth and its Misunderstanders' and 'The Meaning of the Word 'Truth'
1909	67	Experiences symptoms of angina. *The Meaning of Truth* and *A Pluralistic Universe* published
1910	68	Visits Henry in Europe. Becomes ill, returns to Quebec and Chocorua. Dies at Chocorua 26 August

Year	Artistic and Scientific Events	Historical Events
1906	Pavlov publishes results of work on conditional reflexes Sherrington, *The Integrative Action of the Nervous System* Planck publishes work on quantum theory	Suffragette campaign begins in Britain
1907	Janet, *The Major Symptoms of Hysteria* Bergson, *Creative Evolution*	Pius X condemns modernism
1908	McDougall, *An Introduction to Social Psychology*	Austria annexes Bosnia and Herzegovina
1909	Titchener, *Lectures on the Experimental Psychology of the Thought Processes*	First Ford Model T car
1910	Russell and Whitehead, *Principia Mathematica*, vol. 1	Death of Edward VII

INTRODUCTION

William James was born in 1842, into a remarkable family, and died in 1910. His family acquired a large financial legacy from his grandfather's estate. This grandfather had emigrated from Ireland in 1789 and established a successful career in Albany, New York state, in the developing American economy of the early nineteenth century. William James's father, Henry senior, devoted his life to religious and philosophical speculation and strongly influenced William's own dominant interest in those areas. Though William and his father evidently disagreed on some religious and philosophical issues their shared interests run like a thread through William's own work. Both endured a psychological crisis early in their lives, which had a dramatic effect on their intellectual interests. It led Henry senior towards a personal commitment to Swedenborg's mysticism, and led William to indulge in highly personal speculations about free-will and religious belief. Henry senior's family — with the two older sons William and Henry junior (the future novelist) — travelled extensively in Europe during the mid-nineteenth century, and these visits no doubt provided the experience of interaction between American and European families subtly recorded in Henry junior's novels. Their sister, Alice, suffered persistent medical problems and acquired a literary reputation on the publication of her diaries in 1934.[1] Two younger brothers, Wilkinson and Robertson, perhaps overshadowed by the public eminence of the older brothers, led colourful but less successful lives.

William James experimented as an artist with William Hunt in Newport, but after a year decided, with his father's strong approval, to give up art for science. He enrolled in the Lawrence Scientific School in 1861, in the Harvard Medical School in 1863, and graduated in 1869. He visited Europe both before and after graduating, and came to know something of the work of psychologists such as Charcot, Janet and Wundt. In 1869 and

1870, and to some degree throughout the 1870s, he suffered from depression. He took up a teaching post as an instructor in physiology at Harvard from 1873, and in 1878 married Alice Gibbens. Although he continued to suffer from bad health, and complained that he could not for that reason undertake laboratory work, he nevertheless began to establish a psychology department at Harvard and to publish his own work, partly in psychology and partly in philosophy.

The publication in 1890 of *The Principles of Psychology* made him famous. This two-volume work might be regarded as the first popular – and accessible – treatise on psychology, but it also deals with numerous issues of a more philosophical, even metaphysical, kind. Although James frequently expressed a strong wish to keep psychology, as an experimental and naturalistic science, distinct from philosophy, his own interests and the current development of psychology compelled him to connect the two. This is true of many of the chapters in the *Principles*, but also of the articles and lectures in which he outlines his pragmatism, his radical empiricism, his views on moral philosophy and on philosophy of religion. In 1901–2 he gave the Gifford lectures at Edinburgh University (published as *The Varieties of Religious Experience*), and in 1906 gave a series of lectures in Boston (published as *Pragmatism*). Other published collections of essays, such as *The Will to Believe*, *The Meaning of Truth* and *Essays in Radical Empiricism*, spell out his philosophical views. He published also *A Pluralistic Universe*, based on lectures given at Oxford in 1908, and left behind an incomplete work, *Some Problems of Philosophy*, published posthumously in 1911. Two collections of more general essays, *Memories and Studies* and *Collected Essays and Reviews*, were also published after his death.

James's philosophy is wide-ranging, covering epistemology, radical empiricism, his own version of pragmatism, and philosophy of psychology, as well as moral philosophy and philosophy of religion. Although his writings may seem fragmented, and contain some apparent changes of view, his philosophy nevertheless contains a cluster of central themes all of which mark a radical change from a nineteenth-century philosophical paradigm, derived in large part from Hegel and the early nineteenth-century metaphysicians, towards a less abstract twentieth-century model.

The period in which James did his major work – from the late nineteenth century to the first decade of the twentieth – witnessed radical changes in many disciplines. In physics James Clerk Maxwell helped develop a theory of wave phenomena and electro-magnetic forces. In mathematics Riemann developed non-Euclidean geometries and Cantor and Weierstrass introduced trans-finite methods into number theory. New ideas were being canvassed in the social sciences, some influenced by Darwinian theories of evolution. James knew of many of these developments, even though he professed ignorance of mathematics. He mentions Maxwell in *Pragmatism*, and refers to Cantor in *Some Problems of Philosophy*. He was himself strongly influenced by Darwin, although he criticized Darwin's views on emotions, and was even more critical of the social applications of evolutionary theory in Herbert Spencer's work.

Perhaps the clearest expression of James's recognition of the need to encourage radical change appears, quite typically, in the images he uses to mark the new directions of his own philosophy. He represents the change from nineteenth-century traditional metaphysics to pragmatism as a parallel to the change from monarchies, with their deferential 'courtier' style, to republics and democratic societies. This no doubt echoed his own sentiments about the merits of republicanism and democracy in America, though he was critical of some aspects of American society, but it marks a recognition of the need for change in philosophy itself. In *Pragmatism* it is clear that the doctrine is recommended not purely on intellectual but also on moral grounds. Pragmatism is part of an unstiffening liberation from the pompous, hidebound and ultimately immoral influence of the prevailing monistic metaphysics as James conceived it.

These radical attitudes are expressed in James's claim that 'in every genuine metaphysical dispute some practical issue, however remote or conjectural, is involved', and that under the guidance of his own philosophical republicanism 'science and metaphysics . . . would work absolutely hand in hand'.[2] These claims represent a stark divergence from the abstract pretensions of much nineteenth-century metaphysics, which tended to celebrate its distance from – and rivalry to – science. It scarcely needs saying that James applied these tenets in attacking a metaphysics which – because of its distance from science and practical life –

he believed did not contain genuine disputes, and which it was a part of his pragmatic method to unmask as spurious.

Although James fits naturally into that end of century process of radical change, it is important to recognize that he differed significantly from other radical philosophers. He did not share an interest in logic with Frege, Russell or the Logical Positivists, and in other respects, too, James either did, or would have wanted to, repudiate their views. Two related aspects of his work demonstrate this. On one side is his insistence on a non-intellectual, temperamental, root in all philosophical positions, combined with his own temperamental suspicion of intellectual theorizing and preference for practical life. His choice of a quotation from Goethe's *Faust* in 'The Sentiment of Rationality' captures his own attitude very clearly: 'Grey, dear friend, is all your theory; Life's golden tree alone is green.' On the other side is his ultimate desire to provide some justification, within empiricism, for religious – even supernatural – belief. Neither of these tendencies would have been acceptable to Russell, to the Logical Positivists or to 'tough-minded' empiricism in general.

James wished ultimately to present a philosophy which reconciled such 'tough-minded' attitudes with a 'tender-minded' recognition of the importance of our 'passional' nature and of the role religious beliefs may play in it. This represents a uniquely Jamesian turn which can be pursued further in certain of James's own unorthodox – or apparently unpragmatic – interests, such as his determined advocacy of investigation into 'psychic phenomena', or his frequent references to significant items on the 'fringe' of conscious experience. These trends are best exemplified, in philosophical terms, in his book *A Pluralistic Universe*, and in his deeply felt defence of mystical religious experiences in *The Varieties of Religious Experience*. The former contains a number of interesting comments on empiricism, in the discussion of Thomas Green's sensationalism, but it also reflects other aspects of his thought in the discussions of Gustav Fechner's mystical views and the philosophy of Henri Bergson, to which James was strongly drawn but which Russell equally strongly rejected.[3] The latter contains James's mature views of religious mysticism and an advocacy of what he calls 'crass supernaturalism' – neither of which would have been acceptable to Russell.

It is these aspects of his work which have encouraged philosophers to assimilate James to a quite different tradition from that of Russell or the Logical Positivists – that of twentieth-century postmodern Continental philosophy. Richard Rorty's enthusiastic approval[4] of both Jamesian pragmatism and postmodern philosophers, such as Derrida, is an example of such an assimilation. There is no doubt that these aspects of James's philosophy distance his views from those of the more logically oriented philosophers who followed him and also wished to break with the past. But in other respects James's down-to-earth tough-mindedness, and his intention in several issues not to reject traditional philosophy but to update or renovate it, count against his direct assimilation to post-modernism. The truth is that James, who himself disliked labels, cannot be simply labelled. What he disparagingly refers to as a 'solving name' is precisely this type of labelling, which conceals rather than resolves genuine intellectual problems. One of the most congenial aspects of his thought is the extent to which it subverts many of the standard classifications in philosophy; and this holds true even in those areas where he wished to improve on, rather than simply reject, previous philosophical traditions. He has come down to later generations as one of the major figures of American philosophy and – along with Charles Sanders Peirce and John Dewey – as one of the three founding fathers of pragmatism. He exerted a strong influence on many later philosophers, including Bertrand Russell in the early twentieth century and W. V. O. Quine in the later twentieth century.

Pragmatism

James says that pragmatism is both a method and a theory of truth. The method is outlined in this edition in the lecture 'What Pragmatism Means', from *Pragmatism*, and the theory of truth in the extracts from *The Meaning of Truth*. The second extract, 'The Sentiment of Rationality', gives a more general picture of the place that pragmatism holds in James's overall philosophy. It demonstrates James's hostility to over-intellectualism, his emphasis on a temperamental factor in intellectual and philosophical matters, and a consequent appeal to religious and moral conviction. It covers virtually the whole of James's philosophical interests, and acts as a link between the epistemological and the moral or religious aspects of that philosophy.

Pragmatic method is closely associated with James's account of meaning, which he borrowed, along with the title 'pragmatism', from Charles Sanders Peirce. In that account the meaning of some expression for an object is linked to the effects which that object produces. It is, broadly, a functional account of the meaning of concepts, and James saw those linguistic devices, and the more complex theories built up from them, as instruments. The method was designed to establish procedures in which we could become clearer about the scope of the concepts we used. The meaning of expressions has to be explained in terms of their 'practical effects'; if some expression has no such practical effects, then it has no meaning. If two hypotheses, apparently different, nevertheless share the same practical effects, then they have the same meaning. James believed that by using such guidelines we could clarify our thoughts and, most importantly, could locate the testable basis which lay at the heart of philosophical disputes. In that way the method implements James's belief that every metaphysical dispute rests on some practical, testable hypothesis. Pragmatic method, then, yields a clear picture of the practical meaning, the 'cash-value', of blurred, distorted or unclear concepts. It reduces those concepts to their 'fighting weight' and so strips them down to their essentials. The need for such a method in philosophy implies that philosophical views may become bloated or inflated, and mislead us about their practical cash-value. James makes it clear that he thinks that this has tended to happen in the prevailing monistic doctrines.

James offers little in the way of theoretical elucidation for such an account of meaning. In this context he does less well than his contemporary Gottlob Frege[5], who was already, unknown to James, providing a more powerful and more adequate account of meaning based on his formal logic and his analysis of mathematics. Nevertheless James, true to his own pragmatic instincts, offers innumerable examples of the use for such a method. Like Wittgenstein in *Philosophical Investigations*, James implies that the examples carry the weight of the account, and it can scarcely be denied that they have a real value. His discussion of the complex issues behind the apparently simple conflict between materialism and spiritualism provides a good example of his technique. Such illustrations show James's own skill in analysing complex philosophical issues, but the lack of a more developed theory of meaning to support his practice creates problems for him in other parts of his philosophy.

One of the first concepts to be subjected to a pragmatic analysis is that of truth. It is necessary for James to provide an account of truth since the notion of 'belief' lies at the heart of his philosophy and the predicate 'is true' stands as the essential evaluation for beliefs. It would be no exaggeration to say that the pivot on which his philosophy turns − the attempt to reconcile a tough-minded empiricism with a tender-minded justification for religious belief − requires a conception of truth which can cover all kinds of belief, moral and religious as well as factual. James contrasts his own pragmatic account with that of a monistic appeal to absolute truth − exemplified, for example, by F. H. Bradley − in which 'truth' can signify only a final, definitive, and unrevisable establishment of fact.[6] For James that was an understandable and tempting, but finally useless, appeal whose drawback was that it attracted attention away from the genuine issues. For him 'truth' was a 'working' notion which had to be understood in the context of our own basic beliefs; it stands as a general name for the ways in which we come to accept, reject, revise and amend beliefs in every aspect of our lives. It marks, especially, the potential conflict between a new belief and the previous stock of beliefs, which requires us to make some decision between them. We may reject the new belief, or amend our old stock to accommodate it. James thought that in such conflicts there was always a tendency to favour the older stock, but that the resulting conflict illustrated a kind of intellectual Darwinism in which an evolutionary survival value was the ultimate factor. The fitter beliefs will survive, and these will have a survival value for the human species. A theory of truth, consequently, should outline the structure of those conflicts and the guidelines which properly determine their outcome. James spoke of a 'logic of science' as the title for such guidelines, though he admitted that such a logic did not exist in his day. He also took the view that the older 'absolutist' conception of truth − 'in the singular and with a capital T' − was no more than a residual hypostatization of those complex 'workings of belief'.

James's theory of truth is epistemic in its insistence that pragmatic analysis should focus on what truth is 'known as', i.e., how it functions, but it also deals with the acceptance of belief in both cognitive and non-cognitive contexts. 'Truth' and 'falsity' are simply generic names for the adjustments we continually make to our belief systems in the hope of arriving at knowledge, or at least of achieving guides for action which have survival value. James's pragmatism links belief and action quite generally in just that intimate way. James notoriously captured these ideas in the provocative claim that the true is no more than what is useful or expedient, and so encouraged a hostility which he then sought to mitigate. In *The Meaning of Truth* he attempts to guard against some of the standard misunderstandings which he believed the theory had unfairly attracted. In particular, even though his provocative claim had seemed to suggest that anyone may believe what they please, he now makes clear that this is not so and that his account of truth is realistic. There is a real world against which our beliefs, our actions, and our survival, have to be measured. We are entitled to believe what gives us satisfaction, or what provides a survival value, only in general and in the long run. It is as if that kind of satisfaction approximates closer to some ultimate truth in the end, although James was also sceptical of the belief that there was just one final, ultimate truth.

Two deeper anxieties remain. One is that a pragmatic account of truth leaves out what truth actually 'consists in'; instead it offers only an account of the way the notion functions. A second concerns the use James makes of the account in his overall project of reconciliation. One of the merits James claimed for his account was that it unified the evaluations we make of factual and moral or religious claims. In the latter sphere, for example, there is no doubt that James wished to claim that truth ascription depended upon a personal satisfaction which the religious belief might yield. He also thought that such satisfactions attended the acceptance of belief in science, but that in religious contexts the satisfaction was linked to the 'strenuous and energetic' attitude with which it allowed us to confront moral dilemmas. A part of that attitude again linked the ideas of moral conviction with a motive for action. These ideas are present in 'The Sentiment of Rationality' and achieve their more extensive discussion in *The Will to Believe*. It is, however, worth noting now that James answered these more serious objections. He recognized that his account of truth focussed on the practical ways in which we come to ascribe truth, or to accept beliefs, and that the monistic theory might claim to address the issue of what truth consisted in. But his view was that the working of belief is prior to that general notion, and that once a concession has been made to the 'solving name' of an ultimate or final truth there is nothing more to be done with it. The whole value of an account of truth lies, for him, in the detailed workings of belief.

Radical Empiricism

James's pragmatism is claimed to be strictly independent of any substantive philosophy such as empiricism, although it is quite clear that James is drawn towards that doctrine and an associated utilitarianism. His concise summary of his own form of 'radical empiricism' represents it as a philosophy concerned only with what is experienceable, including not only the substantive parts of experience but also the relations between those substantive parts. Pragmatism itself gestures towards such views, but neither its method nor its putative theory of meaning entail them. Empiricism needs some formulation in terms of a theory of meaning but James's account is too imprecise to cover that lack. The very notion of what is experienceable needs stricter definition, especially since James's own conception of experience constitutes his primary objection to the traditional empiricists. For he believed that traditional empiricists misdescribed the nature of our basic experience, and had over-emphasized certain parts of experience at the expense of others. They had emphasized the separate and substantive parts to the exclusion of what he called 'conjunctive relations'. He thought that an empiricist like Hume had admitted 'disjunctive relations', that is relations which mark a division between substantive items, but had not recognized the positive conjunctive relations which hold those parts of experience together. He thought it psychologically unrealistic to think of experience as a succession of discrete items, and preferred the image of a continuous stream. That view forms part of his psychological account of the stream of consciousness in the *Principles of Psychology*, and leads him to reject the traditional empiricists' simple sensations as the basic building-blocks of experience. His own view is expanded in the critique of Green's 'sensationalism' in *A Pluralistic Universe*.

James offers a more detailed view of the radical empiricist

account of experience and knowledge in his paper 'Does Consciousness Exist?' Central to that view, and a part of what must have made the paper seem subversive in its time, is the idea that philosophers and psychologists had misunderstood the notion of 'consciousness'. James makes it clear that he is not simply denying any role or significance to such a notion; rather he rejects the significance and role which earlier philosophers and psychologists had given it. 'Consciousness', as he says, is not the name of some elusive *entity* but rather of a *function*, and the function is precisely that of relating parts of our experience to each other when we are said to know something. Just as he had taken a 'functional' view of the meaning of expressions, so he now takes a 'functional' view of the nature of consciousness. The upshot is that for James the fundamental division which we make between the physical and the mental is to be understood properly not as a distinction between two fundamentally different kinds of entity, but rather as two different ways of categorizing one and the same entity. To that basic item, or 'stuff', he gives the name 'pure experience' – to mark the point that it is so far undifferentiated into the physical or the mental. Those two categories are, for him, simply two different ways of counting one and the same material which, since it is undifferentiated, can be regarded as 'neutral' with regard to these derived categories. This aspect of James's view led to the label for his doctrine of 'neutral monism', although James himself seems never to have used the term. The doctrine influenced Russell and was extensively discussed in his *Logical Atomism* and *The Analysis of Mind*.[7]

James's view of pure experience is tantalizing but unclear. It is unclear in the status attached to pure experience itself, which is sometimes treated as a kind of basic 'stuff', sometimes rather as a device for gaining a proper understanding of the relation between the mental and the physical. There is no doubt that James wished to use the account as a means of rejecting traditional 'representationalist' views of perception or knowledge, and the associated sharp division between mind and body in Descartes' version of such a theory. But the postulation of a neutral material from which both mind and body derive is not the best way to express that rejection. It is better to treat James's doctrine rather as a way of avoiding any commitment to a fundamentally real stuff whether physical, as in materialism, or mental, as in spiritualism. Viewed in that better way James's claim is that mental and physical items cannot be wholly divorced from each other. Nothing is, then, *purely* mental or *purely* physical, and all items in experience have some kind of a dual aspect which links them on one side with a physical history and on another with a mental sequence. James takes the opportunity to map these relationships in noting the resemblances which make a judgment 'adequate' to its 'object', and in drawing attention to a class of what he calls 'appreciations' which show in the clearest way the dual aspect of certain of our concepts. An adequate representation of a spatially extended world, for example, must have that extension. The world represented and its mental representation differ, according to James, not in the presence or absence of extension but in the differing relations which extension has to its context in each case. Among 'appreciations' would be the concept of a 'painful object' which points on one side to the property of an object and on the other to an experience of pain. James's account here anticipates more recent views. It invokes the relation between 'content' and 'consciousness' in such propositional attitudes as that of belief. For the notion of a belief connects a mental attitude necessarily with a content which points beyond that particular consciousness. That idea of a mental representation directed towards something beyond is implicit in Brentano's appeal to intentionality,[8] as James acknowledged, and is part of a current interest in propositional attitudes in the philosophy of mind.

Philosophical Psychology

Although James had a lively sense of the boundary between psychology and philosophy his work, even in the *Principles of Psychology*, often straddles that boundary. This is not surprising given the state of development of psychology at the time, and James's own interest in philosophy. In the *Principles* there is much of philosophical interest, and not just in those sections where he addresses issues with an overt philosophical history. His accounts of attention and the will, of habits, and of the emotions, are all of interest, but it is not possible to include them all in this edition. Instead I have selected four chapters which deal with related issues about the mind–body problem, the stream of consciousness, and the associated analysis of personal identity. Even there are too long to reproduce in full, and Chapters 9 and 10 of the *Principles* have been abbreviated in order to focus on the philosophical discussion. I have also included James's short first chapter in which he outlines his conception of psychology, and Chapter 6, 'Methods and Snares of Psychology', which adds some cautionary detail to that conception.

In the opening chapter of the *Principles* James offers a definition of psychology, a survey of its immediate history, and a methodological principle for the discipline. Psychology is neatly characterized as 'the science of mental life', but James points out that two different historical conceptions of psychology lie concealed behind the phrase 'mental life'. In one, a 'spiritualist' conception, mental life consists of a range of faculties, such as memory, belief or desire, which are attributed to a central agency, the 'self'. In the other, 'associationist' conception, these powers are to be explained by means of their ideas, or contents, and the relations between them. The former might be identified as a rationalist, or Kantian, conception and the latter as predominantly empiricist, so that the division echoes James's general contrast between a rationalist monism and an empiricist pluralism. It is an issue which reappears in his discussions of the mind–body problem in Chapters 5 and 6 of the *Principles* and in his account of personal identity in Chapters 9 and 10. At this point, however, James is content merely to distinguish between questions about the *nature* of these mental aptitudes and questions about the *conditions* under which they operate, and this leads him to formulate his own important guiding principle. For psychology has to deal with the latter question of the operating conditions of the mind, and among these are pre-eminently the physiological conditions of the brain. James is sometimes regarded as a paradigm example of a humanist psychologist for whom the personal feeling of experience is the essential datum for psychology, but it is evident, even in these early pages, that his own physiological training has had a profound effect upon the way he approaches psychological investigation. It is even more evident when he formulates the guiding principle: that there is no mental modification without bodily change.

That dependence of the mind on the brain is compatible with

either a strict reduction of the mental to the physical, or a weaker relation in which the mental supervenes on the physical. The stronger claim is that mental events are nothing but physical events in the brain, but it becomes clear that James rejects that reductive view. In Chapter 5 of the *Principles* he discusses a materialist, 'automaton' theory and dismisses its advocacy on 'quasi-metaphysical' grounds as an 'unwarrantable impertinence'. By contrast he accepts the common-sense notion of mental causes, and supports this with an evolutionary argument for the role of consciousness as a 'selecting agency' and a 'fighter for ends'. This marks an initial commitment to some form of dualism, but the commitment is so far ill-defined, and is discussed further in Chapter 6.

One alternative to the 'automaton' theory is an appeal to a distinctive 'mind-stuff', a version of Cartesian dualism. In Chapter 6 James rejects some corollaries of such a theory, in particular the idea that just as physical states, such as motion, may be resultants of other aggregated physical states, namely the separate masses and velocities of other bodies, so mental states may be regarded as resultants of mental vectors. James also pursues the associated idea that such an hypothesis might be preserved at the expense of treating the basic mental vectors as unconscious, for in such cases we are conscious only of the resultant mental state and not of the separate vector properties on which it depends. That latter postulation of unconscious mental states is dismissed, however, as a 'sovereign means for believing what one likes in psychology'. The former is robustly attacked on the grounds that such mental aggregation, or fusion, requires some independent medium in which the vector quantities operate. In the physical sphere resultant forces and motions are dependent upon the aggregate effects of vector properties of other bodies within the medium of the spatial–causal nexus. James thinks that the mental sphere lacks that independent medium, and so he accepts aggregation at the physiological level, but treats the mental experience as emerging from that aggregated physical effect. His solution to the problem is the more economical view that aggregation of the physical effects in the brain is all that we need to accept. Although the mental experience results from that combined physical event there is no need to suppose that any further aggregation takes place at the mental level. This reinforces the claim that for him mental states supervene upon, and do not reduce to, the underlying physical states, and it distances his own view from Cartesian dualism. In later writings, however, particularly *A Pluralistic Universe*, James seems to modify this view and to accept some kind of mental fusion.

It might be thought that these criticisms of 'mind-stuff' would lead James to adopt a monistic materialism, but at the end of the chapter he makes it clear that he has no decisive ground to reject spiritualism. He recommends a materialist and positivist heuristic for psychology but allows that it is open even to psychologists to admit a spiritual 'self' as an enduring mystery, 'which must one day be cleared up'. The discussion ends somewhat inconclusively, but nevertheless has real merits. It outlines the requirements for an acceptable dualism which would reject both a crude materialist theory and a substance-dualism of a Cartesian kind. It contains illuminating criticism of 'unconscious mental states' and of mental states as resultants, and is honest in its attempt to steer a path through these rejected traditional views towards some better account. If no such clear account is provided at this stage James at least points to important factors in any adequate account, such as the representational power of propositional attitudes, the explanatory appeal to brain physiology, and the over-riding biological reference to evolutionary factors in selection mechanisms and the choice of ends. That latter appeal to evolution reflects James's conception of psychology as a biological science.

James's acute criticisms of such a notion as that of 'unconscious mental states' reflect a self-critical attitude to psychology which is further elaborated in his chapter 'Methods and Snares of Psychology'. There he outlines a number of tempting errors which he thinks psychologists are prone to, and associates these with the standard methods of investigation in the discipline. It is no surprise that he is sceptical of detailed numerical or statistical processing when he says of contemporary German psychology: 'This method taxes patience to the utmost, and could hardly have arisen in a country whose natives could be *bored*'. Although he here reflects his own temperamental distaste for technical or formal methods, his view also cautions against an unthinking use of them which may be technically subtle but lack genuine psychological insight. He makes interesting comments on introspective and behavioural data, but his central point is the temptation of what he calls 'the psychologist's fallacy', that is, an error in which the theorist's descriptions of the mind are thought to match exactly the subject's own consciousness as he experiences it. In part James here underlines his own methodological preference for introspection as a basic method; in part it reflects his own preference for the practical realities of life and his suspicion of intellectual theory. But it reflects also a genuine problem, which runs through the nineteenth-century view of social, or behavioural, sciences – namely, how to reconcile the theorists' 'external', third-person view of a subject's consciousness with an 'internal', first-person view. Thus James recommends caution in accepting psychological theories as comprehensive accounts of psychological reality.

That issue is specifically present in his later discussions of the stream of consciousness and its relation to personal identity in Chapters 9 and 10 of the *Principles*. In these chapters it is not just a question of the general relation of mind to body but a specific application of that issue to personal consciousness and identity. Chapter 9 explores, with the exposure of the psychologist's fallacy in mind, the basic datum of the stream of consciousness. In its phenomenology and its vivid rhetorical terminology it has become a classic text in its own right; but it deserves inclusion here as a preliminary to the account of personal identity in Chapter 10. The account of a stream of consciousness fits easily into James's radical empiricism. It emphasizes the extent to which he thinks the traditional empiricists had erred in focussing on the disjunctive elements of consciousness at the expense of the conjunctive.

The traditional empiricists commit the psychologist's fallacy, but James offers a further diagnosis of their mistake. For he thinks that they were misled by our language – in which the nouns signify the substantive and interesting parts of experience – into thinking that consciousness consisted of nothing else. Consciousness for those empiricists appears like a set of beads which need to be strung, but where the string itself is invisible and so far inexplicable. At some points James seems to fall into a similar trap, when he suggests that the words, typically prepositions, which mark the relational, conjunctive string in our consciousness, have as good a right to be treated as names of discrete objects. But his better attitude is to reject, like Wittgenstein,[9] the idea that all words function as the names of objects.

In all this he shows some anticipation of later doctrines, and the same is true of his consequent discussion of personal identity. His contribution to that problem is already anticipated in Chapter 9 of the *Principles*, where he indicates that a stream of consciousness is inseparable from the idea of an 'owner' which is itself linked to the 'appropriation' of other ideas and their associated 'warmth and intimacy' and bodily feelings. His solution also attempts to remedy defects which he thought belonged to a traditional empiricist view such as that of Hume. Throughout the chapter, however, he draws a sharp distinction between an empiricist view which locates a sense of personal identity within the stream of consciousness and one which locates an owner outside that stream as an 'arch-ego' or 'transcendental ego', as he puts it. That contrast presents an obvious dilemma. To locate a person's identity at some point in the stream of consciousness seems to fail to do justice to the continuing identity *throughout* that stream. To locate it *outside* the stream, however, seems to make it absurdly unverifiable and unrelated to the experiences which it owns. James's resolution seeks to improve on the former empiricist account without making any concessions to the latter Kantian arch-ego. It is a resolution which holds out the hope of a reconciliation between the 'spiritualist' and the 'positivist' accounts of the mind–body problem which he had failed to reconcile in Chapter 6.

The solution links the sense of personal identity firmly to each 'passing thought' in the stream of consciousness. Our sense of identity is no more than the connectedness which we feel between our present experience, with its immediate predecessors and its imminent expected successors, and others which we associate with it and with that bodily warmth and intimacy. It is as if, to use James's own striking imagery, the title to ownership of a herd of cattle was passed from one cow to another. The owner is not, then, to be found outside the herd, as in a transcendental ego, but is in each case in a functional relationship to the remainder of the herd. Such a solution fits naturally with the earlier account of consciousness in radical empiricism as the name of a function rather than of an object, but it is not clear whether the solution is entirely satisfactory. In particular it will be objected that James has offered only a plausible account of the phenomenology of personal identity rather than any adequate criterion with which to establish it. The point might be elaborated in either of two ways. In one it will be said that even if the account suffices to explain how it is that at *each* moment in our consciousness we think of 'ourselves' as a person of such and such a kind, still it provides no guarantee that we have remained the same throughout the *whole* of our experience. The point might be reinforced by noting James's own psychological reflection that our memories are imperfect and change significantly with age, so that the range of 'appropriated' experiences will itself vary, perhaps quite substantially, from time to time. One who looks for some further way of identifying all these variable classes of experience together into a full stream of consciousness over time will not find it in James's account. Or again, it will be said that the central problem of personal identity is to find some objective, third-person criterion which can determine when two streams of consciousness can be identified as belonging to one and the same person. Since James's account offers only a first-person, phenomenological picture of our sense of identity at particular points in our total consciousness, it seems unable to resolve that problem.

James might reply that he restricts himself to a first-person account, to an account of our felt sense of identity. He might also claim that his account, while focussing at any point on one particular set of appropriated experiences, nevertheless provides us with the truth about appropriation and our sense of identity at all such stages. For at *any* such point in our experience the sense of identity which we feel may amount to nothing more. This would be to argue that there simply is no other resource to appeal to, and to add that there is no need for any other resource since the supposed additional problems are spurious. Although he clearly believes that any appeal to a transcendental 'arch-ego' outside the stream of consciousness is spurious, he may not satisfy his critics that he has not left something out. As in the case of his account of truth, however, it is not easy to say clearly what that additional item may be. Certainly traditional empiricists such as Hume had failed to identify it.

Moral Philosophy

James's moral philosophy is less well known than his pragmatism or his radical empiricism, yet it is an integral part of his philosophy. In the moral philosophy, as in his epistemology, there is a bias towards practical considerations, and many of his papers comment on contemporary social issues. But the selection given here displays a more theoretical and philosophical account of moral and religious belief than appears in James's other writings. As in the epistemology, his account is influenced by a psychological approach to the issues, and this is nowhere more apparent than in his discussion of free-will. It was the free-will issue which preoccupied him during his depressive period in the 1870s, and it is the solution to that problem, in such papers as 'The Will to Believe' and 'The Dilemma of Determinism', which demonstrates the pivotal role for the notion of belief.

'The Will to Believe' argues – against the criticism of W. K. Clifford – for a legitimate place for what James calls a 'volitional' or 'passional' factor in all belief. Clifford's own view was directed against the acceptance of religious belief in the absence of any evidence or rational ground. He claimed that such attitudes were not merely rationally unwarranted, but positively immoral, and recommends the suspension of belief in these cases. James's whole attitude to morality, religion and life reacted against such an 'intellectual' and neurotically cautious view; his paper constitutes both a defence of religious belief and more generally an explanation of the way in which the will is related to belief. For James there always *is* such a volitional factor in any belief; the traditional separation between cognitive and volitional factors simply cannot be sharply drawn. His position is, as he notes, similar to that in Pascal's Wager, in which the hope of an after-life, even though the outcome is unknowable beforehand, is nevertheless something it would be unwise to gamble against. Such a hope, along with other moral and religious beliefs, is an example of what James calls 'voluntarily adopted faiths'.

James does not hold that a volitional factor in belief entitles us to belief what we please, any more than his account of truth commits him to the view that we may regard as true anything which gives us personal emotional satisfaction. He takes the view that there are well-defined circumstances in which we are justified in accepting beliefs for which we have no intellectual or evidential warrant. These circumstances, which justify our voluntarily adopted faiths, are explained in terms of options which are for us 'forced, live and momentous', or, as he puts it, 'genuine'. In those cases, he thinks, we may choose a bold strategy and accept the relevant belief, since the benefits of such a decision, as in Pascal's Wager, may be obtainable in no other way. James distinguishes the institutional caution which science imposes on its practitioners from the bolder strategy in which, when faced with a hazard, it may be rational to take the gamble. The issue may turn, of course, on personal temperament; the constitutionally nervous person may be unable to take the gamble and may consequently fail to survive. What is needed in order to obtain the beneficial outcome is some encouragement to be bold, and James is prepared, unlike Clifford, to give that encouragement.

James thinks that it is irrational to adopt the attitude of science towards religious belief and so cautiously to wait until some evidence is available, for there may be no possibility of providing evidence for religious beliefs however long we wait. In the meantime such caution may lose us any benefits we may otherwise gain, just as a nervous suitor who delays any expression of love may fail to arouse a reciprocal feeling. James seems willing to allow that religious beliefs may confer benefits just in virtue of supplying the believer with personal consolation or satisfaction, but he recommends the adoption of such faiths primarily on moral and altruistic grounds. He holds that religion provides a uniquely powerful motive for moral action, and measures the prospective benefits of such beliefs in terms of the beneficial consequences of that action. His personal experience in the 1870s seems to have made him aware of the apathy which may arise without such motivation. The remedy is, as he says in a quotation from Carlyle, to 'Hang your sensibilities. Stop your snivelling complaints and your equally snivelling raptures. Leave off your general emotional tomfoolery and get to WORK like men.' Some may find such a degree of robustness insensitive, but it matches James's own less vehement appeals to what he calls a 'strenuous and energetic life' in morality.

One of the first, and personally most important, manifestations of a voluntarily adopted faith was James's own response to the free-will problem. He makes the point that the first action of a free-will should be to affirm its freedom,[10] and so indicates that a volitional gamble may overcome a depressive apathy. That response was both practical and personal, but in 'The Dilemma of Determinism' James attempts to deal more philosophically with the determinist threat to freedom. His discussion is bounded by two assumptions: first, that in this context there is no possibility of proof, so that all that can be done is to 'deepen our theoretical sense' of the conflict; and second, that determinism and indeterminism are the only options. Determinism traditionally claims that all events are made necessary by causal laws, while indeterminism claims that some events – such as those involving human consciousness – are not subject to such laws. Determinism, in James's account, amounts to the claim that the universe contains only necessities, while indeterminism claims by contrast that there are real possibilities, or real novelties, in human behaviour which mark our free-will. James disregards a third strategy, in which it is claimed that causal necessity and human free-will are compatible, so that we do not need to make a choice between them. He disparages such a view as 'soft determinism' and pursues it no further.

Within those limits his discussion concentrates on our temperamental attitudes to events which we think ought not to have happened and profoundly regret. We may approach them with a deep pessimism in the face of their supposed necessity or simply adopt a romantic optimism, but both attitudes seem to conflict with any feeling of regret. The former makes it incomprehensible that we should feel regret when the event could not have been avoided; and the latter is in conflict with the very pessimism of regret itself. Other objections to a variety of related attitudes are made, but in the end James's view is that we should hold a different position, neither pessimistic nor optimistic but melioristic. Such an attitude frankly recognizes the problems of moral life, and robustly accepts a strenuous and energetic response to those problems in order to improve our lives. That attitude, however, rests on an acceptance of genuine chances, real possibilities and novelty, which alone provide the zest or excitement of individual and collective endeavour.

The same appeal to a strenuous – as opposed to an easy-going – mood is made in 'The Moral Philosopher and the Moral Life', but there James outlines a more philosophical ground for moral values. His view rejects any absolute moral truth, as he rejects any absolutist account of truth, and instead accepts an ultimately subjective basis for moral judgment. James refuses to enshrine any general formula for what is morally good or right, but his own positive account veers clearly towards some version of utilitarianism. In the early part of his paper James identifies what he calls a 'psychological' question about the origin of moral values; but his later discussion can be linked with a more philosophical question about the ontology of such values. For what he considers is the question of the *way* in which moral values and judgments can arise. The view is that moral values emerge from subjective properties of sentient agents, especially their feelings and desires, and it is in that limited way that James regards moral values as ultimately subjective. Although they ultimately rest on, and arise out of, subjective feelings, he does not think that this entitles us to hold any moral views we choose. Moreover, he is well aware that the central problems of a social morality arise from the competing demands or desires of sentient agents and the need to reconcile them. It is in the light of that background that he formulates his own general principle that what is good or right is whatever satisfies any desire, and that the least sum of dissatisfactions should resolve competition between those desires. James's principle, like his claim that the true and the right are in the end no different from the useful or expedient, is agreeably subversive, but it is clear that for him such a principle has a restricted value. It does not by itself resolve practical conflicts in applied ethics, for these can be decided only in a historical context in which he believes that philosophers' principles neither have, nor should have, much force. Rather what he also insists on is the relevance to such moral conflicts of what he calls 'metaphysical and theological' facts, and at this point he returns to the earlier claims about the unique strength of motivation in moral action provided by religious belief. As he puts it: 'the strenuous type of character will on the battlefield of human history always outwear the easy-going type, and religion will drive irreligion to the wall'.

The final essay in this section, 'On a Certain Blindness', reverts to a more practical theme. It is an eloquent plea for tolerance of others' moral views and practices even in the face of their apparent incomprehensibility. It rightly emphasizes the ease with which we may regard others' views as unintelligible from our own standpoint. James offers two striking illustrations of this danger, one from a story by Robert Louis Stevenson, and another from his own experience of walking in the North Carolina hills. In the former a group of Scottish schoolboys engage in a harmless but seemingly pointless ritual to strengthen their group solidarity, and give real expression to a secret joy.

In the latter James rebukes himself for responding unfavourably to the environmental damage caused by some settlers in the mountains without appreciating their way of looking at their activities. What to him, as a privileged rambler, is a scene of devastation, is to the settlers an expression of their triumph over intolerably harsh living conditions. The discussion testifies to the practical pluralism which James canvassed in both moral philosophy and epistemology. It expresses a relativism of an unobjectionable kind which warns against forms of colonialism, or group superiority, resulting from a blinkered belief that our own moral standpoint is the only intelligible or rational point of view.

Religion and Religious Belief

James makes extensive reference to his views on religious belief throughout his moral essays and in *Pragmatism*. His interest in mystical religious experiences is evident even in the *Principles* where he speaks of a 'fringe', 'suffusion' or 'more', attached to our thoughts, and their expression of which we are unconscious. His developed view of these beliefs and experiences is expressed in the Edinburgh Gifford lectures published as *The Varieties of Religious Experience*. It might be said that his whole philosophy looks hopefully towards that topic as a terminus which itself depends on the central notions of belief and the satisfactory workings of belief. At the end of the Gifford lectures his views about the nature and role of religious, mystical and supernatural belief become more explicit.

Although James was critical of appeals to unconscious mental states he nevertheless admits a significant reference to such unconscious influences in psychology and in religion. Part of the underlying motive here is, again, a wish not to be dogmatic in rejecting dubious ideas out of hand. James thought it unprofessionally intolerant of scientists to reject the evidence for 'psychic' phenomena without a proper scientific examination of that evidence. In a similar way he canvasses, in *The Varieties of Religious Experience*, the idea of a science of religion based on a psychological investigation of those claimed mystical experiences. He recognized that few people claim to have had, or even to understand, mystical experiences but wanted in the lectures to survey the available reports in order to find any common elements, and to assess the significance that might be placed on them.

That psychological survey has continued subsequently in a fragmentary way with investigations of card-guessing telepathy, and of 'out-of-body' or 'near-death' experiences. But the principal philosophical interest in James's account comes from the concluding sections of his book where he sums up his position, and measures it against other standard philosophical views. It is to those sections, above all, that we may look for the success of his attempted reconciliation of tough-minded empiricism and tender-minded religious conviction.

James identifies the essence of mystical religious views in two related claims. In the first it is claimed that there are dimensions of reality of which we are not normally or fully aware, but to which we become open in subliminal fringe experiences; and in the second it is claimed that we may feel 'secure' and 'healthy' just insofar as we achieve a harmonious relationship to such abnormal realities. James derives these features from his own survey of mystical experiences. Despite his confession that he has never had such experiences, it is difficult not to associate the account with his own attempt to overcome depression and to achieve that secure and healthy outlook in an energetic and strenuous life. It is clear that for him the strongest motives for such a life derive precisely from religious beliefs. In the Postscript to his lectures James faces the issue directly and advocates what he calls a 'crass supernaturalism' against the more intellectually refined but practically feeble ways of accommodating mystical belief. That advocacy constitutes a final example of the voluntarily adopted faiths which he had defended against Clifford in 'The Will to Believe'.

These passages mark something of a climax to his philosophy and express views which are strongly in tune with his moral philosophy, his pragmatism and his pluralism. At the same time, however, they contain an unresolved conflict which finally shows the handicap of not formulating a clear theory of meaning. For those views indicate a conflict in James's account of the meaning of religious beliefs. On one side James's account of the meaning of such beliefs points to the practical effects which they may have, including, as we have seen, their effects in terms of moral motives and actions. From that point of view the meaning of religious beliefs is determinedly immanent, that is, it points to the ordinary world of individual and social action and is to be valued according to the degree to which the actions it generates are beneficial in the long run. Insofar as those consequences are beneficial then the beliefs will be rightly regarded as true. It is in that way that James represents truth as a sub-species of the good in *Pragmatism*. On the other side, however, James's crass supernaturalism suggests that the content, and so the meaning, of mystical beliefs refer not to an immanent natural world – even with its moral properties and beneficial actions – but to a supernatural, or transcendent, reality. There remains, consequently, the difficulty of explaining how the meaning of such beliefs can accommodate both of these conflicting requirements. Perhaps it would be possible to reformulate James's account of the moral and supernatural content of such beliefs so as to mitigate the conflict, but that could be done only by means of a more developed account of meaning than James himself offers. He provides a robust attitude to religious mysticism but leaves it to later philosophers to resolve its central difficulty.

G. H. BIRD

References

1 The diaries were privately printed in 1894, published in an edited version in 1934, and published in full in 1964.

2 *Pragmatism*, Cambridge, Mass.: Harvard University Press, 1978, pp. 31 and 52.

3 Bertrand Russell, *History of Western Philosophy*, London: Allen and Unwin, 1946, Chapter 28.

4 Richard Rorty, *Contingency, Irony and Solidarity*, Cambridge: Cambridge University Press, 1989; *Objectivity, Relativism and Truth*, Cambridge: Cambridge University Press, 1991.

5 Gottlob Frege, 'On Sense and Reference', in P. T. Geach and M. Black (eds) *Frege's Philosophical Writings*, Oxford: Blackwell, 1960.

6 See, for example, F. H. Bradley, *Appearance and Reality*, Oxford: Oxford University Press, 1893.

7 Bertrand Russell, 'The Philosophy of Logical Atomism', in R. C. Marsh (ed.) *Logic and Knowledge*, London: Allen and Unwin, 1956; *The Analysis of Mind*, London: Allen and Unwin, 1921.

8 Franz von Brentano, *Psychology from an Empirical Standpoint*, translated and edited by L. L. McAlister, London: Routledge, 1973.

9 Ludwig Wittgenstein, *Philosophical Investigations*, Oxford: Blackwell, 1954, paras 1–3, 26–30, 37–9, 43.

10 For example in *The Principles of Psychology*, vol. 2, New York: Holt, 1890, p. 573.

NOTE ON THE TEXTS

The texts of the separate contributions appear as they did in book form. James frequently reprinted papers from journals in several different collections. Sometimes, as in the case of 'The Sentiment of Rationality', he combined earlier papers to form the contribution to a collection. That essay which appeared originally in *The Will to Believe* in 1897 is a combination of two earlier papers, one with the same title from 1879 and another entitled 'Rationality, Activity and Faith' from 1882.

Each contribution is dated from its appearance in book form. In some cases, such as some reprinted chapters from *The Principles of Psychology* where the earlier publications account only for a few pages, references to those publications have not been made. The numbering of footnotes has been changed in all the texts; some footnotes have been deleted. In particular I have followed Professor Bakewell's earlier Everyman edition, *William James: Selected Papers on Philosophy* (1917), in deleting some footnotes to the texts from *The Varieties of Religious Experience*, but there I have reverted to the original organization of the text. In Bakewell's earlier edition the final two sections of *The Varieties of Religious Experience* were combined into one under the title 'The Positive Content of Religious Experience', but here they are reproduced in their original form as Lecture 20 and Postscript.

Significant deletions from the original chapters have been made in the case of the extracts from *The Principles of Psychology*. Some of them, especially Chapter 10 of the *Principles*, are very long and some of the material is of more strictly psychological than philosophical interest. I have tried to focus on the central philosophical themes in those chapters, not least because they have been selected to complement epistemological themes from James's radical empiricism. This has meant that other chapters have had to be excluded, but my belief is that those chosen are more relevant to current debates about the mind–body problem and the nature of psychology both in philosophy and in cognitive science. Beyond that, the discussions of the stream of consciousness and of personal identity are classic texts which it would be wrong to omit. It would have been possible to reproduce more of *Pragmatism*, and of course to include more items from any of the collections of essays. But what is included here corresponds to the somewhat fragmentary nature of James's own publications in separate journal papers, and invites readers to go to the originals for a more extensive acquaintance with James's own writings.

The contributions have been grouped under five headings: Pragmatism, Radical Empiricism, Philosophical Psychology, Moral Philosophy and Philosophy of Religion. The five sections themselves, and the separate contributions within each of them, are grouped thematically rather than chronologically.

Sources

The following list provides information on the source of each chapter, and also provides information on where the contribution was first published.

Chapter 1, 'What Pragmatism Means', is from *Pragmatism* (1907), and was first published as part of 'A Defence of Pragmatism' in *Popular Science Monthly*, 70, 1907.

Chapter 2, 'The Sentiment of Rationality', is from *The Will to Believe* (1897), and was first published in part as 'The Sentiment of Rationality' in *Mind*, 4, 1879; and in part as 'Rationality, Activity and Faith' in the *Princeton Review*, 2, 1882.

Chapter 3, 'Humanism and Truth', is from *The Meaning of Truth* (1909), and was published in part as 'Humanism and Truth' in *Mind*, NS, 13, 1904; and in part as 'Humanism and Truth Once More' in *Mind*, NS, 14, 1905.

Chapter 4, 'The Pragmatist Account of Truth and its Misunderstanders', is from *The Meaning of Truth*, and was first published in The *Philosophical Review*, 17, 1908.

Chapter 5, 'The Meaning of the Word Truth', is from *The Meaning of Truth*, and was first published in *Mind*, NS, 17, 1908.

Chapter 6 contains two short statements entitled 'Radical Empiricism', which were first published in *The Will to Believe* (1897), and *The Meaning of Truth* (1909).

Chapter 7, 'Does Consciousness Exist?', is from *Essays in Radical Empiricism* (1912), and was first published in the *Journal of Philosophical, Psychological and Scientific Methods*, 1, 1904.

Chapter 8, 'The Scope of Psychology', is Chapter 1 of *The Principles of Psychology* (1890).

Chapter 9, 'The Automaton-theory', is Chapter 5 of the *Principles*.

Chapter 10, 'The Mind-stuff Theory', is Chapter 6 of the *Principles*.

Chapter 11, 'The Stream of Thought', is Chapter 9 of the *Principles*.

Chapter 12, 'The Consciousness of Self', is Chapter 10 of the *Principles*.

Chapter 13, 'The Methods and Snares of Psychology', is Chapter 7 of the *Principles*.

Chapter 14, 'The Will to Believe', is from *The Will to Believe* (1897), and was first published in *New World*, 5, 1896.

Chapter 15, 'The Dilemma of Determinism', is from *The Will to Believe*, and was first published in the *Unitarian Review*, 22, 1884.

Chapter 16, 'The Moral Philosopher and the Moral Life', is from *The Will to Believe*, and was first published in the *International Journal of Ethics*, 1, 1891.

Chapter 17, 'On a Certain Blindness in Human Beings', first appeared in *Talks to Teachers* (1899).

Chapters 18–19, 'Lecture 20: Conclusions' and 'Postscript', first appeared in *The Varieties of Religious Experience* (1902).

PRAGMATISM

What Pragmatism Means

Some years ago, being with a camping party in the mountains, I returned from a solitary ramble to find everyone engaged in a ferocious metaphysical dispute. The *corpus* of the dispute was a squirrel – a live squirrel supposed to be clinging to one side of a tree-trunk; while over against the tree's opposite side a human being was imagined to stand. This human witness tries to get sight of the squirrel by moving rapidly round the tree, but no matter how fast he goes, the squirrel moves as fast in the opposite direction, and always keeps the tree between himself and the man, so that never a glimpse of him is caught. The resultant metaphysical problem now is this: *Does the man go round the squirrel or not?* He goes round the tree, sure enough, and the squirrel is on the tree; but does he go round the squirrel? In the unlimited leisure of the wilderness, discussion had been worn threadbare. Everyone had taken sides, and was obstinate; and the numbers on both sides were even. Each side, when I appeared, therefore appealed to me to make it a majority. Mindful of the scholastic adage that whenever you meet a contradiction you must make a distinction, I immediately sought and found one, as follows: 'Which party is right', I said, 'depends on what you *practically mean* by "going round" the squirrel. If you mean passing from the north of him to the east, then to the south, then to the west, and then to the north of him again, obviously the man does go round him, for he occupies these successive positions. But if on the contrary you mean being first in front of him, then on the right of him, then behind him, then on his left, and finally in front again, it is quite as obvious that the man fails to go round him, for by the compensating movements the squirrel makes, he keeps his belly turned towards the man all the time, and his back turned away. Make the distinction, and there is no occasion for any farther dispute. You are both right and both wrong according as you conceive the verb "to go round" in one practical fashion or the other.'

Although one or two of the hotter disputants called my speech a shuffling evasion, saying they wanted no quibbling or scholastic hair-splitting, but meant just plain honest English 'round', the majority seemed to think that the distinction had assuaged the dispute.

I tell this trivial anecdote because it is a peculiarly simple example of what I wish now to speak of as *the pragmatic method*. The pragmatic method is primarily a method of settling metaphysical disputes that otherwise might be interminable. Is the world one or many? – fated or free? – material or spiritual? – here are notions either of which may or may not hold good of the world; and disputes over such notions are unending. The pragmatic method in such cases is to try to interpret each notion by tracing its respective practical consequences. What difference would it practically make to anyone if this notion rather than that notion were true? If no practical difference whatever can be traced, then the alternatives mean practically the same thing, and all dispute is idle. Whenever a dispute is serious, we ought to be able to show some practical difference that must follow from one side or the other's being right.

A glance at the history of the idea will show you still better what pragmatism means. The term is derived from the same Greek word πράγμα, meaning action, from which our words 'practice' and 'practical' come. It was first introduced into philosophy by Mr Charles Peirce in 1878. In an article entitled 'How to Make Our Ideas Clear', in the *Popular Science Monthly* for January of that year,[1] Mr Peirce, after pointing out that our beliefs are really rules for action, said that, to develop a thought's meaning, we need only determine what conduct it is fitted to produce: that conduct is for us its sole significance. And the tangible fact at the root of all our thought-distinctions, however subtle, is that there is no one of them so fine as to consist in anything but a possible difference of practice. To attain perfect clearness in our thoughts of an object, then, we need only consider what conceivable effects of a practical kind the object may involve – what sensations we are to expect from it, and what reactions we must prepare. Our conception of these effects, whether immediate or remote, is then for us the whole

[1] Translated in the *Revue Philosophique* for January 1879 (vol. 7).

of our conception of the object, so far as that conception has positive significance at all.

This is the principle of Peirce, the principle of pragmatism. It lay entirely unnoticed by anyone for twenty years, until I, in an address before Professor Howison's philosophical union at the University of California, brought it forward again and made a special application of it to religion. By that date (1898) the times seemed ripe for its reception. The word 'pragmatism' spread, and at present it fairly spots the pages of the philosophic journals. On all hands we find the 'pragmatic movement' spoken of, sometimes with respect, sometimes with contumely, seldom with clear understanding. It is evident that the term applies itself conveniently to a number of tendencies that hitherto have lacked a collective name, and that it has 'come to stay'.

To take in the importance of Peirce's principle, one must get accustomed to applying it to concrete cases. I found a few years ago that Ostwald, the illustrious Leipzig chemist, had been making perfectly distinct use of the principle of pragmatism in his lectures on the philosophy of science, though he had not called it by that name.

'All realities influence our practice,' he wrote me, 'and that influence is their meaning for us. I am accustomed to put questions to my classes in this way: In what respects would the world be different if this alternative or that were true? If I can find nothing that would become different, then the alternative has no sense.'

That is, the rival views mean practically the same thing, and meaning, other than practical, there is for us none. Ostwald in a published lecture gives this example of what he means. Chemists have long wrangled over the inner constitution of certain bodies called 'tautomerous'. Their properties seemed equally consistent with the notion that an unstable hydrogen atom oscillates inside of them, or that they are unstable mixtures of two bodies. Controversy raged; but never was decided. 'It would never have begun,' says Ostwald, 'if the combatants had asked themselves what particular experimental fact could have been made different by one or the other view being correct. For it would then have appeared that no difference of fact could possibly ensue; and the quarrel was as unreal as if, theorizing in primitive times about the raising of dough by yeast, one party shoul invoked a "brownie", while another insisted on an "elf" as the true cause of the phenomenon.'[2]

It is astonishing to see how many philosophical disputes collapse into insignificance the moment you subject them to this simple test of tracing a concrete consequence. There can *be* no difference anywhere that doesn't *make* a difference elsewhere – no difference in abstract truth that doesn't express itself in a difference in concrete fact and in conduct consequent upon that fact, imposed on somebody, somehow, somewhere and some-when. The whole function of philosophy ought to be to find out what definite difference it will make to you and me, at definite instants of our life, if this world-formula or that world-formula be the true one.

There is absolutely nothing new in the pragmatic method. Socrates was an adept at it. Aristotle used it methodically. Locke, Berkeley and Hume made momentous contributions to truth by its means. Shadworth Hodgson keeps insisting that realities are only what they are 'known-as'. But these forerunners of pragmatism used it in fragments: they were preluders only. Not until in our time has it generalized itself, become conscious of a universal mission, pretended to a conquering destiny. I believe in that destiny, and I hope I may end by inspiring you with my belief.

Pragmatism represents a perfectly familiar attitude in philosophy, the empiricist attitude, but it represents it, as it seems to me, both in a more radical and in a less objectionable form than it has ever yet assumed. A pragmatist turns his back resolutely and once for all upon a lot of inveterate habits dear to professional philosophers. He turns away from abstraction and insufficiency, from verbal solutions, from bad *a priori* reasons, from fixed principles, closed systems, and pretended absolutes and origins. He turns towards concreteness and adequacy, towards facts, towards action, and towards power. That means the empiricist temper regnant, and the rationalist temper sin-

---

[2] 'Theorie und Praxis', *Zeitsch. des Oesterreichischen Ingenieur u. Architecten-Vereines*, 1905, 4 and 6. I find a still more radical pragmatism than Ostwald's in an address by Professor W. S. Franklin: 'I think that the sickliest notion of physics, even if a student gets it, is that it is "the science of masses, molecules and the ether". And I think that the healthiest notion, even if a student does not wholly get it, is that physics is the science of the ways of taking hold of bodies and pushing them!' (*Science*, 2 January 1903)

cerely given up. It means the open air and possibilities of nature, as against dogma, artificiality and the pretence of finality in truth.

At the same time it does not stand for any special results. It is a method only. But the general triumph of that method would mean an enormous change in what I called in my last lecture the 'temperament' of philosophy. Teachers of the ultra-rationalistic type would be frozen out, much as the courtier type is frozen out in republics, as the ultramontane type of priest is frozen out in Protestant lands. Science and metaphysics would come much nearer together, would in fact work absolutely hand in hand.

Metaphysics has usually followed a very primitive kind of quest. You know how men have always hankered after unlawful magic, and you know what a great part, in magic, *words* have always played. If you have his name, or the formula of incantation that binds him, you can control the spirit, genie, afrite, or whatever the power may be. Solomon knew the names of all the spirits, and having their names, he held them subject to his will. So the universe has always appeared to the natural mind as a kind of enigma, of which the key must be sought in the shape of some illuminating or power-bringing word or name. That word names the universe's *principle*, and to possess it is, after a fashion, to possess the universe itself. 'God', 'matter', 'reason', 'the absolute', 'energy', are so many solving names. You can rest when you have them. You are at the end of your metaphysical quest.

But if you follow the pragmatic method, you cannot look on any such word as closing your quest. You must bring out of each word its practical cash-value, set it at work within the stream of your experience. It appears less as a solution, then, than as a programme for more work, and more particularly as an indication of the ways in which existing realities may be *changed*.

Theories thus become instruments, not answers to enigmas, in which we can rest. We don't lie back upon them, we move forward, and, on occasion, make nature over again by their aid. Pragmatism unstiffens all our theories, limbers them up and sets each one at work. Being nothing essentially new, it harmonizes with many ancient philosophic tendencies. It agrees with nominalism for instance, in always appealing to particulars; with utilitarianism in emphasizing practical aspects; with positivism in its disdain for verbal solutions, useless questions, and meta-physical abstractions.

All these, you see, are *anti-intellectualist* tendencies. Against rationalism as a pretension and a method, pragmatism is fully armed and militant. But, at the outset, at least, it stands for no particular results. It has no dogmas, and no doctrines save its method. As the young Italian pragmatist Papini has well said, it lies in the midst of our theories, like a corridor in a hotel. Innumerable chambers open out of it. In one you may find a man writing an atheistic volume; in the next someone on his knees praying for faith and strength; in a third a chemist investigating a body's properties. In a fourth a system of idealistic metaphysics is being excogitated; in a fifth the impos-sibility of metaphysics is being shown. But they all own the corridor, and all must pass through it if they want a practicable way of getting into or out of their respective rooms.

No particular results then, so far, but only an attitude of orientation, is what the pragmatic method means. *The attitude of looking away from first things, principles, 'categories', sup-posed necessities; and of looking towards last things, fruits, consequences, facts.*

So much for the pragmatic method! You may say that I have been praising it rather than explaining it to you, but I shall presently explain it abundantly enough by showing how it works on some familiar problems. Meanwhile the word prag-matism has come to be used in a still wider sense, as meaning also a certain *theory of truth*. I mean to give a whole lecture to the statement of that theory, after first paving the way, so I can be very brief now. But brevity is hard to follow, so I ask for your redoubled attention for a quarter of an hour. If much remains obscure, I hope to make it clearer in the later lectures.

One of the most successfully cultivated branches of philos-ophy in our time is what is called inductive logic, the study of the conditions under which our sciences have evolved. Writers on this subject have begun to show a singular unanimity as to what the laws of nature and elements of fact mean, when formulated by mathematicians, physicists and chemists. When the first mathematical, logical and natural uniformities, the first *laws*, were discovered, men were so carried away by the clearness, beauty and simplification that resulted that they believed themselves to have deciphered authentically the eternal

thoughts of the Almighty. His mind also thundered and rever-
berated in syllogisms. He also thought in conic sections, squares
and roots and ratios, and geometrized like Euclid. He made
Kepler's Laws for the planets to follow; he made velocity
increase proportionally to the time in falling bodies; he made
the law of the sines for light to obey when refracted; he
established the classes, orders, families and genera of plants and
animals, and fixed the distances between them. He thought the
archetypes of all things, and devised their variations; and when
we rediscover any one of these his wondrous institutions, we
seize his mind in its very literal intention.

But as the sciences have developed farther, the notion has
gained ground that most, perhaps all, of our laws are only
approximations. The laws themselves, moreover, have grown so
numerous that there is no counting them; and so many rival
formulations are proposed in all the branches of science that
investigators have become accustomed to the notion that no
theory is absolutely a transcript of reality, but that any one of
them may from some point of view be useful. Their great use is
to summarize old facts and to lead to new ones. They are only a
man-made language, a conceptual shorthand, as someone calls
them, in which we write our reports of nature; and languages,
as is well known, tolerate much choice of expression and many
dialects.

Thus human arbitrariness has driven divine necessity from
scientific logic. If I mention the names of Sigwart, Mach,
Ostwald, Pearson, Milhaud, Poincaré, Duhem, Ruyssen, those
of you who are students will easily identify the tendency I speak
of, and will think of additional names.

Riding now on the front of this wave of scientific logic, Messrs
Schiller and Dewey appear with their pragmatistic account of
what truth everywhere signifies. Everywhere, these teachers say,
'truth' in our ideas and beliefs means the same thing that it
means in science. It means, they say, nothing but this, *that ideas
(which themselves are but parts of our experience) become true
just in so far as they help us to get into satisfactory relation with
other parts of our experience*, to summarize them and get about
among them by conceptual short-cuts instead of following the
interminable succession of particular phenomena. Any idea
upon which we can ride, so to speak; any idea that will carry us
prosperously from any one part of our experience to any other

part, linking things satisfactorily, working securely, simplifying, saving labour; is true for just so much, true in so far forth, true *instrumentally*. This is the 'instrumental' view of truth taught so successfully at Chicago, the view that truth in our ideas means their power to 'work', promulgated so brilliantly at Oxford.

Messrs Dewey, Schiller and their allies, in reaching this general conception of all truth, have only followed the example of geologists, biologists and philologists. In the establishment of these other sciences, the successful stroke was always to take some simple process actually observable in operation – as denudation by weather, say, or variation from parental type, or change of dialect by incorporation of new words and pronunciations – and then to generalize it, making it apply to all times, and produce great results by summating its effects through the ages.

The observable process which Schiller and Dewey particularly singled out for generalization is the familiar one by which any individual settles into *new opinions*. The process here is always the same. The individual has a stock of old opinions already, but he meets a new experience that puts them to a strain. Somebody contradicts them; or in a reflective moment he discovers that they contradict each other; or he hears of facts with which they are incompatible; or desires arise in him which they cease to satisfy. The result is an inward trouble to which his mind till then had been a stranger, and from which he seeks to escape by modifying his previous mass of opinions. He saves as much of it as he can, for in this matter of belief we are all extreme conservatives. So he tries to change first this opinion, and then that (for they resist change very variously), until at last some new idea comes up which he can graft upon the ancient stock with a minimum of disturbance of the latter, some idea that mediates between the stock and the new experience and runs them into one another most felicitously and expediently.

This new idea is then adopted as the true one. It preserves the older stocks of truths with a minimum of modification, stretching them just enough to make them admit the novelty, but conceiving that in ways as familiar as the case leaves possible. An *outrée* explanation, violating all our preconceptions, would never pass for a true account of a novelty. We should scratch round industriously till we found something less eccentric. The most violent revolutions in an individual's beliefs leave most of his old order standing. Time and space, cause and effect, nature and history, and one's own biography remain untouched. New truth is always a go-between, a smoother-over of transitions. It marries old opinion to new fact so as ever to show a minimum of jolt, a maximum of continuity. We hold a theory true just in proportion to its success in solving this 'problem of maxima and minima'. But success in solving this problem is eminently a matter of approximation. We say this theory solves it on the whole more satisfactorily than that theory; but that means more satisfactorily to ourselves, and individuals will emphasize their points of satisfaction differently. To a certain degree, therefore, everything here is plastic.

The point I now urge you to observe particularly is the part played by the older truths. Failure to take account of it is the source of much of the unjust criticism levelled against pragmatism. Their influence is absolutely controlling. Loyalty to them is the first principle – in most cases it is the only principle; for by far the most usual way of handling phenomena so novel that they would make for a serious rearrangement of our preconceptions is to ignore them altogether, or to abuse those who bear witness for them.

You doubtless wish examples of this process of truth's growth, and the only trouble is their superabundance. The simplest case of new truth is of course the mere numerical addition of new kinds of facts, or of new single facts of old kinds, to our experience – an addition that involves no alteration in the old beliefs. Day follows day, and its contents are simply added. The new contents themselves are not true, they simply *come* and *are*. Truth is *what we say about* them, and when we say that they have come, truth is satisfied by the plain additive formula.

But often the day's contents oblige a rearrangement. If I should now utter piercing shrieks and act like a maniac on this platform, it would make many of you revise your ideas as to the probable worth of my philosophy. 'Radium' came the other day as part of the day's content, and seemed for a moment to contradict our ideas of the whole order of nature, that order having come to be identified with what is called the conservation of energy. The mere sight of radium paying heat away indefinitely out of its own pocket seemed to violate that conservation. What to think? If the radiations from it were nothing but an escape of unsuspected 'potential' energy, pre-existent inside of the atoms, the principle of conservation would be saved. The discovery of 'helium' as the radiation's outcome, opened a way to this belief. So Ramsay's view is generally held to be true, because, although it extends our old ideas of energy, it causes a minimum of alteration in their nature.

I need not multiply instances. A new opinion counts as 'true' just in proportion as it gratifies the individual's desire to assimilate the novel in his experience to his beliefs in stock. It must both lean on old truth and grasp new fact; and its success (as I said a moment ago) in doing this, is a matter for the individual's appreciation. When old truth grows, then, by new truth's addition, it is for subjective reasons. We are in the process and obey the reasons. That new idea is truest which performs most felicitously its function of satisfying our double urgency. It makes itself true, gets itself classed as true, by the way it works; grafting itself then upon the ancient body of truth, which thus grows much as a tree grows by the activity of a new layer of cambium.

Now Dewey and Schiller proceed to generalize this observation and to apply it to the most ancient parts of truth. They also once were plastic. They also were called true for human reasons. They also mediated between still earlier truths and what in those days were novel observations. Purely objective truth, truth in whose establishment the function of giving human satisfaction in marrying previous parts of experience with newer parts played no role whatever, is nowhere to be found. The reasons why we call things true is the reason why they *are* true, for 'to be true' *means* only to perform this marriage-function.

The trail of the human serpent is thus over everything. Truth independent; truth that we *find* merely; truth no longer malleable to human need; truth incorrigible, in a word; such truth exists indeed superabundantly − or is supposed to exist by rationalistically minded thinkers; but then it means only the dead heart of the living tree, and its being there means only that truth also has its paleontology and its 'prescription', and may grow stiff with years of veteran service and petrified in men's regard by sheer antiquity. But how plastic even the oldest truths nevertheless really are has been vividly shown in our day by the transformation of logical and mathematical ideas, a transformation which seems even to be invading physics. The ancient formulas are reinterpreted as special expressions of much wider principles, principles that our ancestors never got a glimpse of in their present shape and formulation.

Mr Schiller still gives to all this view of truth the name of 'humanism', but, for this doctrine too, the name of pragmatism seems fairly to be in the ascendant, so I will treat it under the name of pragmatism in these lectures.

Such then would be the scope of pragmatism – first, a method; and second, a genetic theory of what is meant by truth. And these two things must be our future topics.

What I have said of the theory of truth will, I am sure, have appeared obscure and unsatisfactory to most of you by reason of its brevity. I shall make amends for that hereafter. In a lecture on 'common-sense' I shall try to show what I mean by truths grown petrified by antiquity. In another lecture I shall expatiate on the idea that our thoughts become true in proportion as they successfully exert their go-between function. In a third I shall show how hard it is to discriminate subjective from objective factors in Truth's development. You may not follow me wholly in these lectures; and if you do, you may not wholly agree with me. But you will, I know, regard me at least as serious, and treat my effort with respectful consideration.

You will probably be surprised to learn, then, that Messrs Schiller's and Dewey's theories have suffered a hailstorm of contempt and ridicule. All rationalism has risen against them. In influential quarters Mr Schiller, in particular, has been treated like an impudent schoolboy who deserves a spanking. I should not mention this, but for the fact that it throws so much sidelight upon that rationalistic temper to which I have opposed the temper of pragmatism. Pragmatism is uncomfortable away from facts. Rationalism is comfortable only in the presence of abstractions. This pragmatist talks about truths in the plural, about their utility and satisfactoriness, about the success with which they 'work', etc., suggests to the typical intellectual mind a sort of coarse lame second-rate makeshift article of truth. Such truths are not real truth. Such tests are merely subjective. As against this, objective truth must be something non-utilitarian, haughty, refined, remote, august, exalted. It must be an absolute correspondence of our thoughts with an equally absolute reality. It must be what we *ought* to think, unconditionally. The conditioned ways in which we *do* think are so much irrelevance and matter for psychology. Down with psychology, up with logic, in all this question!

See the exquisite contrast of the types of mind! The pragmatist clings to facts and concreteness, observes truth at its work in particular cases, and generalizes. Truth, for him, becomes a class-name for all sorts of definite working values in experience. For the rationalist it remains a pure abstraction, to the bare name of which we must defer. When the pragmatist undertakes to show in detail just *why* we must defer, the rationalist is unable to recognize his concretes from which his own abstraction is taken. He accuses us of *denying* truth; whereas we have only sought to trace exactly why people follow it and always ought to follow it. Your typical ultra-abstractionist fairly shudders at concreteness: other things equal, he positively prefers the pale and spectral. If the two universes were offered, he would always choose the skinny outline rather than the rich thicket of reality. It is so much purer, clearer, nobler.

I hope that as these lectures go on, the concreteness and closeness to facts of the pragmatism which they advocate may be what approves itself to you as its most satisfactory peculiarity. It only follows here the example of the sister sciences, interpreting the unobserved by the observed. It brings old and new harmoniously together. It converts the absolutely empty notion of a static relation of 'correspondence' (what that may mean we must ask later) between our minds and reality, into that of a rich and active commerce (that anyone may follow in detail and understand) between particular thoughts of ours, and the great universe of other experiences in which they play their parts and have their uses.

But enough of this at present? The justification of what I say must be postponed. I wish now to add a word in further explanation of the claim I made at our last meeting, that pragmatism may be a happy harmonizer of empiricist ways of thinking, with the more religious demands of human beings.

Men who are strongly of the fact-loving temperament, you may remember me to have said, are liable to be kept at a distance by the small sympathy with facts which that philosophy from the present-day fashion of idealism offers them. It is far too intellectualistic. Old fashioned theism was bad enough, with its notion of God as an exalted monarch, made up of a lot of unintelligible or preposterous 'attributes'; but, so long as it held strongly by the argument from design, it kept some touch with concrete realities. Since, however, Darwinism has once for all displaced design from the minds of the 'scientific', theism has lost that foothold; and some kind of an immanent or pantheistic deity working *in* things rather than above them is, if any, the kind recommended to our contemporary imagination. Aspirants to a philosophic religion turn, as a rule, more hopefully nowadays towards idealistic pantheism than towards the older dualistic theism, in spite of the fact that the latter still counts able defenders.

But, as I said in my first lecture, the brand of pantheism offered is hard for them to assimilate if they are lovers of facts, or empirically minded. It is the absolutistic brand, spurning the dust and reared upon pure logic. It keeps no connection whatever with concreteness. Affirming the absolute mind, which is its substitute for God, to be the rational presupposition of all particulars of fact, whatever they may be, it remains supremely indifferent to what the particular facts in our world actually are. Be they what they may, the absolute will father them. Like the sick lion in Aesop's fable, all footprints lead into his den, but *nulla vestigia retrorsum*. You cannot redescend into the world of particulars by the absolute's aid, or deduce any necessary consequences of detail important for your life from your idea of his nature. He gives you indeed the assurance that all is well with *Him*, and for his eternal way of thinking; but thereupon he leaves you to be finitely saved by your own temporal devices.

Far be it from me to deny the majesty of this conception, or its capacity to yield religious comfort to a most respectable class of minds. But from the human point of view, no one can pretend that it doesn't suffer from the faults of remoteness and abstractness. It is eminently a product of what I have ventured to call the rationalistic temper. It disdains empiricism's needs. It substitutes a pallid outline for the real world's richness. It is dapper; it is noble in the bad sense, in the sense in which to be noble is to be inapt for humble service. In this real world of sweat and dirt, it seems to me that when a view of things is 'noble', that ought to count as a presumption against its truth, and as a philosophic disqualification. The prince of darkness may be a gentleman, as we are told he is, but whatever the God of earth and heaven is, he can surely be no gentleman. His menial services are needed in the dust of our human trials, even more than his dignity is needed in the empyrean.

Now pragmatism, devoted though she be to facts, has no such materialistic bias as ordinary empiricism labours under. Moreover, she has no objection whatever to the realizing of abstractions, so long as you get about among particulars with their aid and they actually carry you somewhere. Interested in no conclusions but those which our minds and our experiences work out together, she has no *a priori* prejudices against theology. *If theological ideas prove to have a value for concrete life, they will be true, for pragmatism, in the sense of being good for so much. For how much more they are true, will depend entirely on their relations to the other truths that also have to be acknowledged.*

What I said just now about the absolute of transcendental idealism is a case in point. First, I called it majestic and said it yielded religious comfort to a class of minds, and then I accused it of remoteness and sterility. But so far as it affords such comfort, it surely is not sterile; it has that amount of value; it performs a concrete function. As a good pragmatist, I myself ought to call the absolute true 'in so far forth', then; and I unhesitatingly now do so.

But what does *true in so far forth* mean in this case? To answer, we need only apply the pragmatic method. What do believers in the absolute mean by saying that their belief affords them comfort? They mean that since in the absolute finite evil is 'overruled' already, we may, therefore, whenever we wish, treat the temporal as if it were potentially the eternal, be sure that we can trust its outcome, and, without sin, dismiss our fear and drop the worry of our finite responsibility. In short, they mean that we have a right ever and anon to take a moral holiday, to let the world wag in its own way, feeling that its issues are in better hands than ours and are none of our business.

The universe is a system of which the individual members may relax their anxieties occasionally, in which the don't-care mood is also right for men, and moral holidays in order – that, if I mistake not, is part, at least, of what the absolute is 'known-as', that is the great difference in our particular experiences when his being true makes for us, that is part of his cash-value when he is pragmatically interpreted. Farther than that the ordinary lay-reader in philosophy who thinks favourably of absolute idealism does not venture to sharpen his conceptions. He can use the absolute for so much and so much is very precious. He is pained at hearing you speak incredulously of the absolute, therefore, and disregards your criticisms because they deal with aspects of the conception that he fails to follow.

If the absolute means this, and means no more than this, who can possibly deny the truth of it? To deny it would be to insist that men should never relax, and that holidays are never in order.

I am well aware how odd it must seem to some of you to hear me say that an idea is 'true' so long as to believe it is profitable to our lives. That it is *good*, for as much as it profits, you will gladly admit. If what we do by its aid is good, you will allow the idea itself to be good in so far forth, for we are the better for possessing it. But is it not a strange misuse of the word 'truth', you will say, to call ideas also 'true' for this reason?

To answer this difficulty fully is impossible at this stage of my account. You touch here upon the very central point of Messrs Schiller's, Dewey's and my own doctrine of truth, which I cannot discuss with detail until my sixth lecture. Let me now say only this, that truth is *one species of good*, and not, as is usually supposed, a category distinct from good, and co-ordinate with it. *The true is the name of whatever proves itself to be good in the way of belief, and good, too, for definite, assignable reasons.* Surely you must admit this, that if there were *no* good for life in true ideas, or if the knowledge of them were positively disadvantageous and false ideas the only useful ones, then the current notion that truth is divine and precious, and its pursuit a duty, could never have grown up or become a dogma. In a world like that, our duty would be to *shun* truth, rather. But in this world, just as certain foods are not only agreeable to our taste, but good for our teeth, our stomach and our tissues; so certain ideas are not only agreeable to think about, or agreeable as supporting other ideas that we are fond of, but they are also helpful in life's practical struggles. If there be any life that it is really better we should lead, and if there be any idea which, if believed in, would help us to lead that life, then it would be really *better for us* to believe in that idea, *unless, indeed, belief in it incidentally clashed with other greater vital benefits.*

'What would be better for us to believe'! This sounds very like a definition of truth. It comes very near to saying 'what *we ought* to believe': and in *that* definition none of you would find any oddity. Ought we ever not to believe what it is *better for us* to believe? And can we then keep the notion of what is better for us, and what is true for us, permanently apart?

Pragmatism says no, and I fully agree with her. Probably you also agree, so far as the abstract statement goes, but with a suspicion that if we practically did believe everything that made for good in our own personal lives, we should be found indulging all kinds of fancies about this world's affairs, and all kinds of sentimental superstitions about a world hereafter. Your suspicion here is undoubtedly well founded, and it is evident that something happens when you pass from the abstract to the concrete, that complicates the situation.

I said just now that what is better for us to believe is true *unless the belief incidentally clashes with some other vital benefit.* Now in real life what vital benefits is any particular belief of ours most liable to clash with? What indeed except the vital benefits yielded by *other beliefs* when these prove incompatible with the first ones? In other words, the greatest enemy of any one of our truths may be the rest of our truths. Truths have once for all this desperate instinct of self-preservation and of desire to extinguish whatever contradicts them. My belief in the absolute, based on the good it does me, must run the gauntlet of all my other beliefs. Grant that it may be true in giving me a moral holiday. Nevertheless, as I conceive it – and let me speak now confidentially, as it were, and merely in my own private person – it clashes with other truths of mine whose benefits I hate to give up on its account. It happens to be associated with a kind of logic of which I am the enemy, I find that it entangles me in metaphysical paradoxes that are unacceptable, etc., etc. But as I have enough trouble in life already without adding the trouble of carrying these intellectual unconsistencies, I personally just give up the absolute. I just *take* my moral holidays; or else as a professional philosopher, I try to justify them by some other principle.

If I could restrict my notion of the absolute to its bare holiday-giving value, it wouldn't clash with my other truths. But we cannot easily thus restrict our hypotheses. They carry supernumerary features, and these it is that clash so. My disbelief in the absolute means then disbelief in those other supernumerary features, for I fully believe in the legitimacy of taking moral holidays.

You see by this what I meant when I called pragmatism a mediator and reconciler and said, borrowing the word from Papini, that she 'unstiffens' our theories. She has in fact no prejudices whatever, no obstructive dogmas, no rigid canons of what shall count as proof. She is completely genial. She will entertain any hypothesis, she will consider any evidence. It follows that in the religious field she is at a great advantage both over positivistic empiricism, with its anti-theological bias, and over religious rationalism, with its exclusive interest in the remote, the noble, the simple, and the abstract in the way of conception.

In short, she widens the field of search for God. Rationalism sticks to logic and the empyrean. Empiricism sticks to the external senses. Pragmatism is willing to take anything, to follow either logic or the senses, and to count the humblest and most personal experiences. She will count mystical experiences if they have practical consequences. She will take a god who lives in the very dirt of private fact — if that should seem a likely place to find him.

Her only test of probable truth is what works best in the way of leading us, what fits every part of life best and combines with the collectivity of experience's demands, nothing being omitted. If theological ideas should do this, if the notion of God, in particular, should prove to do it, how could pragmatism possibly deny God's existence? She could see no meaning in treating as 'not true' a notion that was pragmatically so successful. What other kind of truth could there be, for her, than all this agreement with concrete reality?

In my last lecture I shall return again to the relations of pragmatism with religion. But you see already how democratic she is. Her manners are as various and flexible, her resources as rich and endless, and her conclusions as friendly as those of mother nature.

The Sentiment of Rationality

What is the task which philosophers set themselves to perform; and why do they philosophize at all? Almost everyone will immediately reply: They desire to attain a conception of the frame of things which shall on the whole be more rational than that somewhat chaotic view which everyone by nature carries about with him under his hat. But suppose this rational conception attained, how is the philosopher to recognize it for what it is, and not let it slip through ignorance? The only answer can be that he will recognize its rationality as he recognizes everything else, by certain subjective marks with which it affects him. When he gets the marks, he may know that he has got the rationality.

What, then, are the marks? A strong feeling of ease, peace, rest, is one of them. The transition from a state of puzzle and perplexity to rational comprehension is full of lively relief and pleasure.

But this relief seems to be a negative rather than a positive character. Shall we then say that the feeling of rationality is constituted merely by the absence of any feelings of irrationality? I think there are very good grounds for upholding such a view. All feeling whatever, in the light of certain recent psychological speculations, seems to depend for its physical condition not on simple discharge of nerve-currents, but on their discharge under arrest, impediment or resistance. Just as we feel no particular pleasure when we breathe freely, but a very intense feeling of distress when the respiratory motions are prevented – so any unobstructed tendency to action discharges itself without the production of much cogitative accompaniment, and any perfectly fluent course of thought awakens but little feeling; but when the movement is inhibited, or when the thought meets with difficulties, we experience distress. It is only when the distress is upon us that we can be said to strive, to crave or to aspire. When enjoying plenary freedom either in the way of motion or of thought, we are in a sort of anaesthetic state in which we might say with Walt Whitman, if we cared to say anything about ourselves at such times, 'I am sufficient as I am.' This feeling of the sufficiency of the present moment, of its absoluteness – this absence of all need to explain it, account for it, or justify it – is what I call the sentiment of rationality. As soon, in short, as we are enabled from any cause whatever to think with perfect fluency, the thing we think of seems to us *pro tanto* rational.

Whatever modes of conceiving the cosmos facilitate this fluency, produce the sentiment of rationality. Conceived in such modes, being vouches for itself and needs no further philosophic formulation. But this fluency may be obtained in various ways; and first I will take up the theoretic way.

The facts of the world in their sensible diversity are always before us, but our theoretic need is that they should be conceived in a way that reduces their manifoldness to simplicity. Our pleasure at finding that a chaos of facts is the expression of a single underlying fact is like the relief of the musician at resolving a confused mass of sound into melodic or harmonic order. The simplified result is handled with far less mental effort than the original data; and a philosophic conception of nature is thus in no metaphorical sense a labour-saving contrivance. The passion for parsimony, for economy of means in thought, is the philosophic passion *par excellence*, and any character or aspect of the world's phenomena which gathers up their diversity into monotony will gratify that passion, and in the philosopher's mind stand for that essence of things compared with which all their other determinations may by him be overlooked.

More universality or extensiveness is, then, one mark which the philosopher's conceptions must possess. Unless they apply to an enormous number of cases they will not bring him relief. The knowledge of things by their causes, which is often given as a definition of rational knowledge, is useless to him unless the causes converge to a minimum number, while still producing the maximum number of effects. The more multiple then are the instances, the more flowingly does his mind rove from fact to fact. The phenomenal transitions are no real transitions; each item is the same old friend with a slightly altered dress.

Who does not feel the charm of thinking that the moon and

the apple are, as far as their relation to the earth goes, identical; of knowing respiration and combustion to be one; of understanding that the balloon rises by the same law whereby the stone sinks; of feeling that the warmth in one's palm when one rubs one's sleeve is identical with the motion which the friction checks; of recognizing the difference between beast and fish to be only a higher degree of that between human father and son; of believing our strength when we climb the mountain or fell the tree to be no other than the strength of the sun's rays which made the corn grow out of which we got our morning meal?

But alongside of this passion for simplification there exists a sister passion, which in some minds – though they perhaps form the minority – is its rival. This is the passion for distinguishing; it is the impulse to be *acquainted* with the parts rather than to comprehend the whole. Loyalty to clearness and integrity of perception, dislike of blurred outlines, of vague identifications, are its characteristics. It loves to recognize particulars in their full completeness, and the more of these it can carry the happier it is. It prefers any amount of incoherence, abruptness and fragmentariness (so long as the literal details of the separate facts are saved) to an abstract way of conceiving things that, while it simplifies them, dissolves away at the same time their concrete fullness. Clearness and simplicity thus set up rival claims, and make a real dilemma for the thinker.

A man's philosophic attitude is determined by the balance in him of these two cravings. No system of philosophy can hope to be universally accepted among men which grossly violates either need, or entirely subordinates the one to the other. The fate of Spinoza, with his barren union of all things in one substance, on the one hand; that of Hume, with his equally barren 'looseness and separateness' of everything, on the other – neither philosopher owning any strict and systematic disciples today, each being to posterity a warning as well as a stimulus – show us that the only possible philosophy must be a compromise between an abstract monotony and a concrete heterogeneity. But the only way to mediate between diversity and unity is to class the diverse items as cases of a common essence which you discover in them. Classification of things into extensive 'kinds' is thus the first step; and classification of their relations and conduct into extensive 'laws' is the last step, in their philosophic unification.

A completed theoretic philosophy can thus never be anything more than a completed classification of the world's ingredients; and its results must always be abstract, since the basis of every classification is the abstract essence embedded in the living fact – the rest of the living fact being for the time ignored by the classifier. This means that none of our explanations are complete. They subsume things under heads wider or more familiar; but the last heads, whether of things or of their connections, are mere abstract genera, data which we just find in things and write down.

When, for example, we think that we have rationally explained the connection of the facts A and B by classing both under their common attribute x, it is obvious that we have really explained only so much of these items as is x. To explain the connection of choke-damp and suffocation by the lack of oxygen is to leave untouched all the other pecularities both of choke-damp and suffocation – such as convulsions and agony on the one hand, density and explosibility on the other. In a word, so far as A and B contain l, m, n, and o, p, q, respectively, in addition to x, they are not explained by x. Each additional particularity makes its distinct appeal. A single explanation of a fact only explains it from a single point of view. The entire fact is not accounted for until each and all of its characters have been classed with their likes elsewhere. To apply this now to the case of the universe, we see that the explanation of the world by molecular movements explains it only so far as it actually *is* such movements. To invoke the 'unknowable' explains only so much as is unknowable, 'thought' only so much as is thought, 'God' only so much as is God. *Which* thought? *Which* god – are questions that have to be answered by bringing in again the residual data from which the general term was abstracted. All those data that cannot be analytically identified with the attribute invoked as universal principle, remain as independent kinds or natures, associated empirically with the said attribute but devoid of rational kinship with it.

Hence the unsatisfactoriness of all our speculations. On the one hand, so far as they retain any multiplicity in their terms, they fail to get us out of the empirical sand-heap world; on the other, so far as they eliminate multiplicity the practical man despises their empty barrenness. The most they can say is that the elements of the world are such and such, and that each is identical with itself wherever found; but the question Where is it found? the practical man is left to answer by his own wit. Which, of all the essences, shall here and now be held the essence of this concrete thing, the fundamental philosophy never attempts to decide. We are thus led to the conclusion that the simple classification of things is, on the one hand, the best possible theoretic philosophy, but is, on the other, a most miserable and inadequate substitute for the fullness of the truth. It is a monstrous abridgement of life, which, like all abridgements is got by the absolute loss and casting out of real matter. This is why so few human beings truly care for philosophy. The particular determinations which she ignores are the real matter exciting needs, quite as potent and authoritative as hers. What does the moral enthusiast care for philosophical ethics? Why does the *Aesthetik* of every German philosopher appear to the artist an abomination of desolation?

> *Grau, theurer Freund, ist alle Theorie*
> *Und grün des Lebens goldner Baum.*
> [Grey, dear friend, is all your theory
> Life's golden tree alone is green.]

The entire man, who feels all needs by turns, will take nothing as an equivalent for life but the fullness of living itself. Since the essences of things are as a matter of fact disseminated through the whole extent of time and space, it is in their spread-outness and alternation that he will enjoy them. When weary of the concrete clash and dust and pettiness, he will refresh himself by a bath in the eternal springs, or fortify himself by a look at the immutable natures. But he will only be a visitor, not a dweller in the region; he will never carry the philosophic yoke upon his shoulders, and when tired of the grey monotony of her problems and insipid spaciousness of her results, will always escape gleefully into the teeming and dramatic richness of the concrete world.

So our study turns back here to its beginning. Every way of classifying a thing is but a way of handling it for some particular purpose. Conceptions, 'kinds', are teleological instruments. No abstract concept can be a valid substitute for a concrete reality except with reference to a particular interest in the conceiver. The interest of theoretic rationality, the relief of identification, is but one of a thousand human purposes. When others rear their heads, it must pack up its little bundle and retire till its turn recurs. The exaggerated dignity and value that philosophers have claimed for their solutions is thus greatly reduced. The only virtue their theoretic conception need have is simplicity, and a simple conception is an equivalent for the world only so far as the world is simple – the world meanwhile, whatever simplicity it may harbour, being also a mightily complex affair. Enough simplicity remains, however, and enough urgency in our craving to reach it, to make the theoretic function one of the most invincible of human impulses. The quest of the fewest elements of things is an ideal that some will follow, as long as there are men to think at all.

But suppose the goal attained. Suppose that at last we have a system unified in the sense that has been explained. Our world can now be conceived simply, and our mind enjoys the relief. Our universal concept has made the concrete chaos rational. But now I ask, Can that which is the ground of rationality in all else be itself properly called rational? It would seem at first sight that it might. One is tempted at any rate to say that, since the craving for rationality is appeased by the identification of one thing with another, a datum which left nothing else outstanding might quench that craving definitively, or be rational *in se*. No otherness being left to annoy us, we should sit down at peace. In other words, as the theoretic tranquillity of the boor results from his spinning no further considerations about his chaotic universe, so any datum whatever (provided it were simple, clear and ultimate) ought to banish puzzle from the universe of the philosopher and confer peace, inasmuch as there would then be for him absolutely no further considerations to spin.

This in fact is what some persons think. Professor Bain says—

A difficulty is solved, a mystery unriddled, when it can be shown to resemble something else; to be an example of a fact already known. Mystery is isolation, exception, or it may be apparent contradiction: the resolution of the mystery is found in assimilation, identity, fraternity. When all things are assimilated, so far as assimilation can go, so far as likeness holds, there is an end to explanation; there is an end to what the mind can do, or can intelligently desire . . . The path of science as exhibited in modern ages is toward generality, wider and wider, until we reach the highest, the widest laws of every department of things; there explanation is finished, mystery ends, perfect vision is gained.

But, unfortunately, this first answer will not hold. Our mind is so wedded to the process of seeing an *other* beside every item of its experience, that when the notion of an absolute datum is presented to it, it goes through its usual procedure and remains pointing at the void beyond, as if in that lay further matter for contemplation. In short, it spins for itself the further positive consideration of a nonentity enveloping the being of its datum; and as that leads nowhere, back recoils the thought towards its datum again. But there is no natural bridge between nonentity and this particular datum, and the thought stands oscillating to and fro, wondering 'Why was there anything but nonentity; why just this universal datum and not another?' and finds no end, in wandering mazes lost. Indeed, Bain's words are so untrue that in reflecting men it is just when the attempt to fuse the manifold into a single totality has been most successful, when the conception of the universe as a unique fact is nearest its perfection, that the craving for further explanation, the ontological wonder-sickness, arises in its extremest form. As Schopenhauer says, {The uneasiness which keeps the never-resting clock of metaphysics in motion, is the consciousness that the nonexistence of this world is just as possible as its existence.' }

The notion of nonentity may thus be called the parent of the philosophic craving in its subtlest and profoundest sense. Absolute existence is absolute mystery, for its relations with the nothing remain unmediated to our understanding. One philosopher only has pretended to throw a logical bridge over this chasm. Hegel, by trying to show that nonentity and concrete being are linked together by a series of identities of a synthetic kind, binds everything conceivable into a unity, with no outlying notion to disturb the free rotary circulation of the mind within its bounds. Since such unchecked movement gives the feeling of rationality, he must be held, if he has succeeded, to have eternally and absolutely quenched all rational demands.

But for those who deem Hegel's heroic effort to have failed, nought remains but to confess that when all things have been unified to the supreme degree, the notion of a possible other than the actual may still haunt our imagination and prey upon our system. The bottom of being is left logically opaque to us, as something which we simply come upon and find, and about which (if we wish to act) we should pause and wonder as little as possible. The philosopher's logical tranquillity is thus in essence no other than the boor's. They differ only as to the point at which each refuses to let further considerations upset the absoluteness of the data he assumes. The boor does so immediately, and is liable at any moment to the ravages of many kinds of doubt. The philosopher does not do so till the unity has been reached, and is warranted against the inroads of those considerations, but only practically, not essentially, secure from the blighting breath of the ultimate Why? If he cannot exorcise this question, he must ignore or blink it, and, assuming the data of his system as something given, and the gift as ultimate, simply proceed to a life of contemplation or of action based on it. There is no doubt that this acting on an opaque necessity is accompanied by a certain pleasure. See the reverence of Carlyle for brute fact: 'There is an infinite significance in fact.' 'Necessity,' says Dühring, and he means not rational but given necessity, 'is the last and highest point that we can reach . . . It is not only the interest of ultimate and definitive knowledge, but also that of the feelings, to find a last response and an ideal equilibrium in an uttermost datum which can simply not be other than it is.'

Such is the attitude of ordinary men in their theism. God's fiat being in physics and morals such an uttermost datum. Such also is the attitude of all hard-minded analysts and *Verstandesmenschen*. Lotze, Renouvier and Hodgson promptly say that of experience as a whole no account can be given, but neither seek to soften the abruptness of the confession nor to reconcile us with our impotence.

But mediating attempts may be made by more mystical minds. The peace of rationality may be sought through ecstasy when logic fails. To religious persons of every shade of doctrine moments come when the world, as it is, seems so divinely orderly, and the acceptance of it by the heart so rapturously complete, that intellectual questions vanish; nay, the intellect itself is hushed to sleep – as Wordsworth says, 'thought is not; in enjoyment it expires.' Ontological emotion so fills the soul that ontological speculation can no longer overlap it and put her girdle of interrogation-marks round existence. Even the least religious of men must have felt with Walt Whitman, when loafing on the grass on some transparent summer morning, that 'swiftly arose and spread round him the peace and knowledge that pass all the argument of the earth'. At such moments of energetic living we feel as if there were something diseased and contemptible, yea vile, in theoretic grubbing and brooding. In the eye of healthy sense the philosopher is at best a learned fool.

Since the heart can thus wall out the ultimate irrationality which the head ascertains, the erection of its procedure into a systematized method would be a philosophic achievement of first-rate importance. But as used by mystics hitherto it has lacked universality, being available for few persons and at few times, and even in these being apt to be followed by fits of reaction and dryness; and if men should agree that the mystical method is a subterfuge without logical pertinency, a plaster but no cure, and that the idea of nonentity can never be exorcised, empiricism will be the ultimate philosophy. Existence then will be a brute fact to which as a whole the emotion of ontologic wonder shall rightfully cleave, but remain eternally unsatisfied. Then wonderfulness or mysteriousness will be an essential attribute of the nature of things, and the exhibition and emphasizing of it will continue to be an ingredient in the philosophic industry of the race. Every generation will produce its Job, its Hamlet, its Faust, or its Sartor Resartus.

With this we seem to have considered the possibilities of purely theoretic rationality. But we saw at the outset that rationality meant only unimpeded mental function. Impediments that arise in the theoretic sphere might perhaps be avoided if the stream of mental action should leave that sphere betimes and pass into the practical. Let us therefore inquire what constitutes the feeling of rationality in its *practical* aspect. If thought is not to stand forever pointing at the universe in wonder, if its movement is to be diverted from the issueless channel of purely theoretic contemplation, let us ask what conception of the universe will awaken active impulses capable of effecting this diversion. A definition of the world which will give back to the mind the free motion which had been blocked in the purely contemplative path may so far make the world seem rational again.

Well, of two conceptions equally fit to satisfy the logical demand, that one which awakens the active impulses, or satisfies other aesthetic demands better than the other, will be accounted the more rational conception, and will deservedly prevail.

There is nothing improbable in the supposition that an analysis of the world may yield a number of formulae, all consistent with the facts. In physical science different formulae may explain the phenomena equally well — the one-fluid and the two-fluid theories of electricity, for example. Why may it not be so with the world? Why may there not be different points of view for surveying it, within each of which all data harmonize, and which the observer may therefore either choose between, or simply cumulate one upon another? A Beethoven string quartet is truly, as someone has said, a scraping of horses' tails on cats' bowels, and may be exhaustively described in such terms; but the application of this description in no way precludes the simultaneous applicability of an entirely different description. Just so a thoroughgoing interpretation of the world in terms of mechanical sequence is compatible with its being interpreted teleologically, for the mechanism itself may be designed.

If, then, there were several systems excogitated, equally satisfying to our purely logical needs, they would still have to be passed in review, and approved or rejected by our aesthetic and practical nature. Can we define the tests of rationality which these parts of our nature would use?

Philosophers long ago observed the remarkable fact that mere familiarity with things is able to produce a feeling of their rationality. The empiricist school has been so much struck by this circumstance as to have laid it down that the feeling of rationality and the feeling of familiarity are one and the same thing, and that no other kind of rationality than this exists. The daily contemplation of phenomena juxtaposed in a certain order begets an acceptance of their connection, as absolute as the repose engendered by theoretic insight into their coherence. To explain a thing is to pass easily back to its antecedents; to know it is easily to foresee its consequents. Custom, which lets us do both, is thus the source of whatever rationality the thing may gain in our thought.

In the broad sense in which rationality was defined at the outset of this essay, it is perfectly apparent that custom must be one of its factors. We said that any perfectly fluent and easy thought was devoid of the sentiment of irrationality. Inasmuch

ie there is a history

then as custom acquaints us with all the relations of a thing, it teaches us to pass fluently from that thing to others, and *pro tanto* tinges it with the rational character.

Now, there is one particular relation of greater practical importance than all the rest – I mean the relation of a thing to its future consequences. So long as an object is unusual, our expectations are baffled; they are fully determined as soon as it becomes familiar. I therefore propose this as the first practical requisite which a philosophic conception must satisfy: *It must, in a general way at least, banish uncertainty from the future.* The permanent presence of the sense of futurity in the mind has been strangely ignored by most writers, but the fact is that our consciousness at a given moment is never free from the ingredient of expectancy. Everyone knows how when a painful thing has to be undergone in the near future, the vague feeling that it is impending penetrates all our thought with uneasiness and subtly vitiates our mood even when it does not control our attention; it keeps us from being at rest, at home in the given present. The same is true when a great happiness awaits us. But when the future is neutral and perfectly certain, 'we do not mind it', as we say, but give an undisturbed attention to the actual. Let now this haunting sense of futurity be thrown off its bearings or left without an object, and immediately uneasiness takes possession of the mind. But in every novel or unclassified experience this is just what occurs; we do not know what will come next; and novelty *per se* becomes a mental irritant, while custom *per se* is a mental sedative, merely because the one baffles while the other settles our expectations.

Every reader must feel the truth of this. What is meant by coming 'to feel at home' in a new place, or with new people? It is simply that, at first, when we take up our quarters in a new room, we do not know what draughts may blow in upon our back, what doors may open, what forms may enter, what interesting objects may be found in cupboards and corners. When after a few days we have learned the range of all these possibilities, the feeling of strangeness disappears. And so it does with people, when we have got past the point of expecting any essentially new manifestations from their character.

The utility of this emotional effect of expectation is perfectly obvious; 'natural selection', in fact, was bound to bring it about sooner or later. It is of the utmost practical importance to an animal that he should have prevision of the qualities of the objects that surround him, and especially that he should not come to rest in presence of circumstances that might be fraught either with peril or advantage – go to sleep, for example, on the brink of precipices, in the dens of enemies, or view with indifference some new-appearing object that might, if chased, prove an important addition to the larder. Novelty *ought* to irritate him. All curiosity has thus a practical genesis. We need only look at the physiognomy of a dog or a horse when a new object comes into his view, his mingled fascination and fear, to see that the element of conscious insecurity or perplexed expectation lies at the root of his emotion. A dog's curiosity about the movements of his master or a strange object only extends as far as the point of deciding what is going to happen next. That settled, curiosity is quenched. The dog quoted by Darwin, whose behaviour in presence of a newspaper moved by the wind seemed to testify to a sense 'of the supernatural', was merely exhibiting the irritation of an uncertain future. A newspaper which could move spontaneously was in itself so unexpected that the poor brute could not tell what new wonders the next moment might bring forth.

To turn back now to philosophy. An ultimate datum, even though it be logically unrationalized, will, if its quality is such as to define expectancy, be peacefully accepted by the mind; while if it leave the least opportunity for ambiguity in the future, it will to that extent cause mental uneasiness if not distress. Now, in the ultimate explanations of the universe which the craving for rationality has elicited from the human mind, the demands of expectancy to be satisfied have always played a fundamental part. The term set up by philosophers as primordial has been one which banishes the incalculable. 'Substance', for example, means, as Kant says, *das Beharrliche*, which will be as it has been, because its being is essential and eternal. And although we may not be able to prophesy in detail the future phenomena to which the substance shall give rise, we may set our minds at rest in a general way, when we have called the substance God, perfection, love, or reason, by the reflection that whatever is in store for us can never at bottom be inconsistent with the character of this term; so that our attitude even toward the unexpected is in a general sense defined. Take again the notion of immortality, which for common people seems to be the touchstone of every philosophic or religious creed: what is this but a way of saying that the determination of expectancy is the essential factor of rationality? The wrath of science against miracles, of certain philosophers against the doctrine of free-will, has precisely the same root – dislike to admit any ultimate factor in things which may rout our prevision or upset the stability of our outlook.

Anti-substantialist writers strangely overlook this function in the doctrine of substance: 'If there be such a *substratum*,' says Mill,

> suppose it at this instant miraculously annihilated, and let the sensations continue to occur in the same order, and how would the *substratum* be missed? By what signs should we be able to discover what its existence had terminated? Should we not have as much reason to believe that it still existed as we now have? And if we should not then be warranted in believing it, how can we be so now?'

Truly enough, if we have already securely bagged our facts in a certain order, we can dispense with any further warrant for that order. But with regard to the facts yet to come the case is far different. It does not follow that if substance may be dropped from our conception of the irrecoverably past, it need be an equally empty complication to our notions of the future. Even if it were true that, for aught we know to the contrary, the substance might develop at any moment a wholly new set of attributes, the mere logical form of referring things to a substance would still (whether rightly or wrongly) remain accompanied by a feeling of rest and future confidence. In spite of the acutest nihilistic criticism, men will therefore always have a liking for any philosophy which explains things *per substantiam*.

A very natural reaction against the theosophizing conceit and hidebound confidence in the upshot of things, which vulgarly optimistic minds display, has formed one factor of the scepticism of empiricists, who never cease to remind us of the reservoir of possibilities alien to our habitual experience which the cosmos may contain, and which, for any warrant we have to the contrary, may turn it inside out tomorrow. Agnostic substantialism like that of Mr Spencer, whose unknowable is not merely the unfathomable but the absolute-irrational, on which, if consistently represented in thought, it is of course impossible to count, performs the same function of rebuking a certain stagnancy and smugness in the manner in which the ordinary philistine feels his security. But considered as anything else than as reactions against an opposite excess, these philosophies of uncertainty cannot be acceptable; the general mind will fail to come to rest in their presence, and will seek for solutions of a more reassuring kind.

We may then, I think, with perfect confidence lay down as a first point gained in our inquiry, that a prime factor in the philosophic craving is the desire to have expectancy defined; and that no philosophy will definitively triumph which in an emphatic manner denies the possibility of gratifying this need.

We pass with this to the next great division of our topic. It is not sufficient for our satisfaction merely to know the future as determined, for it may be determined in either of many ways, agreeable or disagreeable. For a philosophy to succeed on a universal scale it must define the future *congruously with our spontaneous powers*. A philosophy may be unimpeachable in other respects, but either of two defects will be fatal to its universal acceptance. First, its ultimate principle must not be one that essentially baffles and disappoints our dearest desires and most cherished powers. A pessimistic principle like Schopenhauer's incurably vicious will-substance, or Hartmann's wicked jack-of-all-trades the unconscious, will perpetually call forth essays at other philosophies. Incompatability of the future with their desires and active tendencies is, in fact, to most men a source of more fixed disquietude than uncertainty itself. Witness the attempts to overcome the 'problem of evil', the 'mystery of pain'. There is no 'problem of good'.

But a second and worse defect in a philosophy than that of contradicting our active propensities is to give them no object whatever to press against. A philosophy whose principle is so incommensurate with our most intimate powers as to deny them all relevancy in universal affairs, as to annihilate their motives at one blow, will be even more unpopular than pessimism. Better face the enemy than the eternal void! This is why materialism will always fail of universal adoption, however well it may fuse things into an atomistic unity, however clearly it may prophesy the future eternity. For materialism denies reality to the objects of almost all the impulses which we most cherish.

The real *meaning* of the impulses, it says, is something which has no emotional interest for us whatever. Now, what is called 'extradition' is quite as characteristic of our emotions as of our senses: both point to an object as the cause of the present feeling. What an intensely objective reference lies in fear! In like manner an enraptured man and a dreary feeling man are not simply aware of their subjective states; if they were, the force of their feelings would all evaporate. Both believe there is outward cause why they should feel as they do: either, 'It is a glad world! how good life is!', or, 'What a loathsome tedium is existence!' Any philosophy which annihilates the validity of the reference by explaining away its objects or translating them into terms of no emotional pertinency, leaves the mind with little to care or act for. This is the opposite condition from that of nightmare, but when acutely brought home to consciousness it produces a kindred horror. In nightmare we have motives to act, but no power; here we have powers, but no motives. A nameless *unheimlichkeit* comes over us at the thought of there being nothing eternal in our final purposes, in the objects of those loves and aspirations which are our deepest energies. The monstrously lopsided equation of the universe and its knower, which we postulate as the ideal of cognition, is perfectly paralleled by the no less lopsided equation of the universe and the *doer*. We demand in it a character for which our emotions and active propensities shall be a match. Small as we are, minute as is the point by which the cosmos impinges upon each one of us, each one desires to feel that his reaction at that point is congruous with the demands of the vast whole – that he balances the latter, so to speak, and is able to do what it expects of him. But as his abilities to do lie wholly in the line of his natural propensities; as he enjoys reacting with such emotions as fortitude, hope, rapture, admiration, earnestness, and the like; and as he very unwillingly reacts with fear, disgust, despair or doubt – a philosophy which should only legitimate emotions of the latter sort would be sure to leave the mind a prey to discontent and craving.

It is far too little recognized how entirely the intellect is built up of practical interests. The theory of evolution is beginning to do very good service by its reduction of all mentality to the type of reflex action. Cognition, in this view, is but a fleeting moment, a cross-section at a certain point, of what in its totality is a motor phenomenon. In the lower forms of life no one will pretend that cognition is anything more than a guide to appropriate action. The germinal question concerning things brought for the first time before consciousness is not the theoretic 'What is that?' but the practical 'Who goes there?' or rather, as Horwicz has admirably put it, 'What is to be done?' – '*Was fang' ich an?*' In all our discussions about the intelligence of lower animals, the only test we use is that of their *acting* as if for a purpose. Cognition, in short, is incomplete until discharged in act; and although it is true that the later mental development, which attains its maximum through the hypertrophied cerebrum of man, gives birth to a vast amount of theoretic activity over and above that which is immediately ministerial to practice, yet the earlier claim is only postponed, not effaced, and the active nature asserts its rights to the end.

When the cosmos in its totality is the object offered to consciousness, the relation is in no whit altered. React on it we must in some congenial way. It was a deep instinct in Schopenhauer which led him to reinforce his pessimistic argumentation by a running volley of invective against the practical man and his requirements. No hope for pessimism unless he is slain!

Helmholtz's immortal works on the eye and ear are to a great extent little more than a commentary on the law that practical utility wholly determines which parts of our sensations we shall be aware of, and which parts we shall ignore. We notice or discriminate an ingredient of sense only so far as we depend upon it to modify our actions. We *comprehend* a thing when we synthesize it by identity with another thing. But the other great department of our understanding, *acquaintance* (the two departments being recognized in all languages by the antithesis of such words as *wissen* and *kennen*; *scire* and *noscere*, etc.), what is that also but a synthesis – a synthesis of a passive perception with a certain tendency to reaction? We are acquainted with a thing as soon as we have learned how to behave towards it, or how to meet the behaviour which we expect from it. Up to that point it is still 'strange' to us.

If there be anything at all in this view, it follows that however vaguely a philosopher may define the ultimate universal datum, he cannot be said to leave it unknown to us so long as he in the slightest degree pretends that our emotional or active attitude toward it should be of one sort rather than another. He who

Ecclesiastics
the Teacher.

says 'life is real, life is earnest', however much he may speak of
the fundamental mysteriousness of things, gives a distinct definition to that mysteriousness by ascribing to it the right to claim
from us the particular mood called seriousness – which means
the willingness to live with energy, though energy bring pain.
The same is true of him who says that all is vanity. For
indefinable as the predicate 'vanity' may be *in se*, it is clearly
something that permits anaesthesia, mere escape from suffering,
to be our rule of life. There can be no greater incongruity than
for a disciple of Spencer to proclaim with one breath that the
substance of things is unknowable, and with the next that the
thought of it should inspire us with awe, reverence and a
willingness to add our co-operative push in the direction toward
which its manifestations seem to be drifting. The unknowable
may be unfathomed, but if it make such distinct demands upon
our activity we surely are not ignorant of its essential quality.

If we survey the field of history and ask what feature all great
periods of revival, of expansion of the human mind, display in
common, we shall find, I think, simply this: that each and all of
them have said to the human being, 'The inmost nature of the
reality is congenial to *powers* which you possess.' In what did
the emancipating message of primitive Christianity consist but
in the announcement that God recognizes those weak and tender
impulses which paganism had so rudely overlooked? Take
repentance: the man who can do nothing rightly can at least
repent of his failures. But for paganism this faculty of repentance
was a pure supernumerary, a straggler too late for the fair.
Christianity took it, and made it the one power within us which
appealed straight to the heart of God. And after the night of the
Middle Ages had so long branded with obloquy even the
generous impulses of the flesh, and defined the reality to be such
that only slavish natures could commune with it, in what did
the *sursum corda* of the Platonizing renaissance lie but in the
proclamation that the archetype of verity in things laid claim on
the widest activity of our whole aesthetic being? What were
Luther's mission and Wesley's but appeals to powers which even
the meanest of men might carry with them – faith and self-
despair – but which were personal, requiring no priestly inter-
mediation, and which brought their owner face to face with
God? What caused the wildfire influence of Rousseau but the

assurance he gave that man's nature was in harmony with the nature of things, if only the paralysing corruptions of custom would stand from between? How did Kant and Fichte, Goethe and Schiller, inspire their time with cheer, except by saying, 'Use all your powers; that is the only obedience the universe exacts'? And Carlyle with his gospel of work, of fact, of veracity, how does he move us except by saying that the universe imposes no tasks upon us but such as the most humble can perform? Emerson's creed that everything that ever was or will be is here in the enveloping now; that man has but to obey himself – 'He who will rest in what he *is*, is a part of destiny' – is in like manner nothing but an exorcism of all scepticism as to the pertinency of one's natural faculties.

In a word, 'Son of Man, *stand upon thy feet* and I will speak unto thee!' is the only revelation of truth to which the solving epochs have helped the disciple. But that has been enough to satisfy the greater part of his rational need. *In se* and *per se* the universal essence has hardly been more defined by any of these formulas than by the agnostic x; but the mere assurance that my powers, such as they are, are not irrelevant to it, but pertinent; that it speaks to them and will in some way recognize their reply; that I can be a match for it if I will, and not a footless waif – suffices to make it rational to my feelings in the sense given above. Nothing could be more absurd than to hope for the definitive triumph of any philosophy which should refuse to legitimate, and to legitimate in any emphatic manner, the more powerful of our emotional and practical tendencies. Fatalism, whose solving word in all crises of behaviour is 'all striving is vain', will never reign supreme, for the impulse to take life strivingly is indestructible in the race. Moral creeds which speak to that impulse will be widely successful in spite of inconsistency, vagueness and shadowy determination of expectancy. Man needs a rule for his will, and will invent one if one be not given him.

But now observe a most important consequence. Men's active impulses are so differently mixed that a philosophy fit in this respect for Bismarck will almost certainly be unfit for a valetudinarian poet. In other words, although one can lay down in advance the rule that a philosophy which utterly denies all fundamental ground for seriousness, for effort, for hope, which says the nature of things is radically alien to human nature, can never succeed – one cannot in advance say what particular dose of hope, or of gnosticism of the nature of things, the definitely successful philosophy shall contain. In short, it is almost certain that personal temperament will here make itself felt, and that although all men will insist on being spoken to by the universe in some way, few will insist on being spoken to in just the same way. We have here, in short, the sphere of what Matthew Arnold likes to call *Aberglaube*, legitimate, inexpurgable, yet doomed to eternal variations and disputes.

Take idealism and materialism as examples of what I mean, and suppose for a moment that both give a conception of equal theoretic clearness and consistency, and that both determine our expectations equally well. Idealism will be chosen by a man of one emotional constitution, materialism by another. At this very day all sentimental natures, fond of conciliation and intimacy, tend to an idealistic faith. Why? Because idealism gives to the nature of things such kinship with our personal selves. Our own thoughts are what we are most at home with, what we are least afraid of. To say then that the universe essentially is thought, is to say that I myself, potentially at least, am all. There is no radically alien corner, but an all-pervading *intimacy*. Now, in certain sensitively egotistic minds this conception of reality is sure to put on a narrow, close, sick-room air. Everything sentimental and priggish will be consecrated by it. That element in reality which every strong man of common-sense willingly feels there because it calls forth powers that he owns – the rough, harsh, sea-wave, north-wind element, the denier of persons, the democratizer – is banished because it jars too much on the desire for communion. Now, it is the very enjoyment of this element that throws many men upon the materialistic or agnostic hypothesis, as a polemic reaction against the contrary extreme. They sicken at a life wholly constituted of intimacy. There is an overpowering desire at moments to escape personality, to revel in the action of forces that have no respect for our ego, to let the tides flow, even though they flow over us. The strife of these two kinds of mental temper will, I think, always be seen in philosophy. Some men will keep insisting on the reason, the atonement, that lies in the heart of things, and that we can act *with*; others, on the opacity of brute fact that we must react *against*.

*

Now, there is one element of our active nature which the Christian religion has emphatically recognized, but which philosophers as a rule have with great insincerity tried to huddle out of sight in their pretension to found systems of absolute certainty. I mean the element of faith. Faith means belief in something concerning which doubt is still theoretically possible; and as the test of belief is willingness to act, one may say that faith is the readiness to act in a cause the prosperous issue of which is not certified to us in advance. It is in fact the same moral quality which we call courage in practical affairs; and there will be a very widespread tendency in men of vigorous nature to enjoy a certain amount of uncertainty in their philosophic creed, just as risk lends a zest to worldly activity. Absolutely certified philosophies seeking the *inconcussum* are fruits of mental natures in which the passion for identity (which we saw to be but one factor of the rational appetite) plays an abnormally exclusive part. In the average man, on the contrary, the power to trust, to risk a little beyond the literal evidence, is an essential function. Any mode of conceiving the universe which makes an appeal to this generous power, and makes the man seem as if he were individually helping to create the actuality of the truth whose metaphysical reality he is willing to assume, will be sure to be responded to by large numbers.

The necessity of faith as an ingredient in our mental attitude is strongly insisted on by the scientific philosophers of the present day; but by a singularly arbitrary caprice they say that it is only legitimate when used in the interests of one particular proposition – the proposition, namely, that the course of nature is uniform. That nature will follow tomorrow the same laws that she follows today is, they all admit, a truth which no man can *know*; but in the interests of cognition as well as of action we must postulate or assume it. As Helmholtz says: '*Hier gilt nur der eine Rath: vertraue und handle!*' And Professor Bain urges: 'Our only error is in proposing to give any reason or justification of the postulate, or to treat it as otherwise than begged at the very outset.'

With regard to all other possible truths, however, a number of our most influential contemporaries think that an attitude of faith is not only illogical but shameful. Faith in a religious dogma for which there is no outward proof, but which we are tempted to postulate for our emotional interests, just as we postulate the uniformity of nature for our intellectual interests, is branded by Professor Huxley as 'the lowest depth of immorality'. Citations of this kind from leaders of the modern *Aufklärung* might be multiplied almost indefinitely. Take Professor Clifford's article on the 'Ethics of Belief'. He calls it 'guilt' and 'sin' to believe even the truth without 'scientific evidence'. But what is the use of being a genius, unless *with the same scientific evidence* as other men, one can reach more truth than they? Why does Clifford fearlessly proclaim his belief in the conscious-automaton theory, although the 'proofs' before him are the same which make Mr Lewes reject it? Why does he believe in primordial units of 'mind-stuff' on evidence which would seem quite worthless to Professor Bain? Simply because, like every human being of the slightest mental originality, he is peculiarly sensitive to evidence that bears in some one direction. It is utterly hopeless to try to exorcise such sensitiveness by calling it the disturbing subjective factor, and branding it as the root of all evil. 'Subjective' be it called! and 'disturbing' to those whom it foils! But if it helps those who, as Cicero says, *'vim naturae magis sentiunt'*, it is good and not evil. Pretend what we may, the whole man within us is at work when we form our philosophical opinions. Intellect, will, taste and passion co-operate just as they do in practical affairs; and lucky it is if the passion be not something as petty as a love of personal conquest over the philosopher across the way. The absurd abstraction of an intellect verbally formulating all its evidence and carefully estimating the probability thereof by a vulgar fraction by the size of whose denominator and numerator alone it is swayed, is ideally as inept as it is actually impossible. It is almost incredible that men who are themselves working philosophers should pretend that any philosophy can be, or ever has been, constructed without the help of personal preference, belief or divination. How have they succeeded in so stultifying their sense for the living facts of human nature as not to perceive that every philosopher, or man of science either, whose initiative counts for anything in the evolution of thought, has taken his stand on a sort of dumb conviction that the truth must lie in one direction rather than another, and a sort of preliminary assurance that his notion can be made to work; and has borne his best fruit in trying to make it work? These mental instincts in different men are the spontaneous variations upon which the intellectual struggle for existence is based. The fittest conceptions survive, and with them the names of their champions shining to all futurity.

The coil is about us, struggle as we may. The only escape from faith is mental nullity. What we enjoy most in a Huxley or a Clifford is not the professor with his learning, but the human personality ready to go in for what it feels to be right, in spite of all appearances. The concrete man has but one interest – to be right. That for him is the art of all arts, and all means are fair which help him to it. Naked he is flung into the world, and between him and nature there are no rules of civilized warfare. The rules of the scientific game, burdens of proof, presumptions, *experimenta crucis*, complete inductions, and the like, are only binding on those who enter that game. As a matter of fact we all more or less do enter it, because it helps us to our end. But if the means presume to frustrate the end and call us cheats for being right in advance of their slow aid, by guesswork or by hook or crook, what shall we say of them? Were all of Clifford's works, except the 'Ethics of Belief', forgotten, he might well figure in future treatises on psychology in place of the somewhat threadbare instance of the miser who has been led by the association of ideas to prefer his gold to all the goods he might buy therewith.

In short, if I am born with such a superior general reaction to evidence that I can guess right and act accordingly, and gain all that comes of right action, while my less gifted neighbour (paralysed by his scruples and waiting for more evidence which he dares not anticipate, much as he longs to) still stands shivering on the brink, by what law shall I be forbidden to reap the advantages of my superior native sensitiveness? Of course I yield to my belief in such a case as this or distrust it, alike at my peril, just as I do in any of the great practical decisions of life. If my inborn faculties are good, I am a prophet; if poor, I am a failure: nature spews me out of her mouth, and there is an end of me. In the total game of life we stake our persons all the while; and if in its theoretic part our persons will help us to a conclusion, surely we should also stake them there, however inarticulate they may be.[1]

---

[1] At most, the command laid upon us by science to believe nothing not yet verified by the senses is a prudential rule intended to maximize our right thinking and

But in being myself so very articulate in proving what to all readers with a sense for reality will seem a platitude, am I not wasting words? We cannot live or think at all without some degree of faith. Faith is synonymous with working hypothesis. The only difference is that while some hypotheses can be refuted in five minutes, others may defy ages. A chemist who conjectures that a certain wallpaper contains arsenic, and has faith enough to lead him to take the trouble to put some of it into a hydrogen bottle, finds out by the results of his action whether he was right or wrong. But theories like that of Darwin, or that of the kinetic constitution of matter, may exhaust the labours of generations in their corroboration, each tester of the truth proceeding in this simple way – that he acts as if it were true, and expects the result to disappoint him if his assumption is false. The longer disappointment is delayed, the stronger grows his faith in his theory.

Now, in such questions as god, immortality, absolute morality and free-will, no non-papal believer at the present day pretends his faith to be of an essentially different complexion; he can always doubt his creed. But his intimate persuasion is that the odds in its favour are strong enough to warrant him in acting all along on the assumption of its truth. His corroboration or repudiation by the nature of things may be deferred until the day of judgment. The uttermost he now means is something like this: 'I *expect* then to triumph with tenfold glory; but if it should turn out, as indeed it may, that I have spent my days in a fool's paradise, why, better have been the dupe of *such* a dreamland than the cunning reader of a world like that which then beyond all doubt unmasks itself to view.' In short, we *go in* against materialism very much as we should *go in*, had we a chance,

---

minimize our errors *in the long run*. In the particular instance we must frequently lose truth by obeying it; but on the whole we are safer if we follow it consistently, for we are sure to cover our losses with our gains. It is like those gambling and insurance rules based on probability, in which we secure ourselves against losses in detail by hedging on the total run. But this hedging philosophy requires that long run should be there; and this makes it inapplicable to the question of religious faith as the latter comes home to the individual man. He plays the game of life not to escape losses, for he brings nothing with him to lose; he plays it for gains; and it is now or never with him, for the long run which exists indeed for humanity, is not there for him. Let him doubt, believe, or deny, he runs the risk, and has the natural right to choose which one it shall be.

against the second French empire or the Church of Rome, or any other system of things toward which our repugnance is vast enough to determine energetic action, but too vague to issue in distinct argumentation. Our reasons are ludicrously incommensurate with the volume of our feeling, yet on the latter we unhesitatingly act.

Now, I wish to show what to my knowledge has never been clearly pointed out, that belief (as measured by action) not only does and must continually outstrip scientific evidence, but that there is a certain class of truths of whose reality belief is a factor as well as a confessor; and that as regards this class of truths faith is not only licit and pertinent, but essential and indispensable. The truths cannot become true till our faith has made them so.

Suppose, for example, that I am climbing in the Alps, and have had the ill luck to work myself into a position from which the only escape is by a terrible leap. Being without similar experience, I have no evidence of my ability to perform it successfully; but hope and confidence in myself make me sure I shall not miss my aim, and nerve my feet to execute what without those subjective emotions would perhaps have been impossible. But suppose that, on the contrary, the emotions of fear and mistrust preponderate; or suppose that, having just read the 'Ethics of Belief', I feel it would be sinful to act upon an assumption unverified by previous experience – why, then I shall hesitate so long that at last, exhausted and trembling, and launching myself in a moment of despair, I miss my foothold and roll into the abyss. In this case (and it is one of an immense class) the part of wisdom clearly is to believe what one desires; for the belief is one of the indispensable preliminary conditions of the realization of its object. *There are then cases where faith creates its own verification.* Believe, and you shall be right, for you shall save yourself; doubt, and you shall again be right, for you shall perish. The only difference is that to believe is greatly to your advantage.

The future movements of the stars or the facts of past history are determined now once for all, whether I like them or not. They are given irrespective of my wishes, and in all that concerns truths like these subjective preference should have no part; it can only obscure the judgment. But in every fact into which there enters an element of personal contribution on my part, as soon as this personal contribution demands a certain degree of subjective energy which, in its turn, calls for a certain amount of faith in the result – so that, after all, the future fact is conditioned by my present faith in it – how trebly asinine would it be for me to deny myself the use of the subjective method, the method of belief based on desire!

In every proposition whose bearing is universal (and such are all the propositions of philosophy), the acts of the subject and their consequences throughout eternity should be included in the formula. If M represent the entire world *minus* the reaction of the thinker upon it, and if $M + x$ represent the absolutely total matter of philosophic propositions (x standing for the thinker's reaction and its results) – what would be a universal truth if the term x were of one complexion might become egregious error if x altered its character. Let it not be said that x is too infinitesimal a component to change the character of the immense whole in which it lies embedded. Everything depends on the point of view of the philosophic proposition in question. If we have to define the universe from the point of view of sensibility, the critical material for our judgment lies in the animal kingdom, insignificant as that is, quantitatively considered. The moral definition of the world may depend on phenomena more restricted still in range. In short, many a long phrase may have its sense reversed by the addition of three letters, *n–o–t*; many a monstrous mass have its unstable equilibrium discharged one way or the other by a feather weight that falls.

Let us make this clear by a few examples. The philosophy of evolution offers us today a new criterion to serve as an ethical test between right and wrong. Previous criteria, it says, being subjective, have left us still floundering in variations of opinion and the *status belli*. Here is a criterion which is objective and fixed: *That is to be called good which is destined to prevail or survive*. But we immediately see that this standard can only remain objective by leaving myself and my conduct out. If what prevails and survives does so by my help, and cannot do so without that help; if something else will prevail in case I alter my conduct – how can I possibly now, conscious of alternative courses of action open before me, either of which I may suppose capable of altering the path of events, decide which course to take by asking what path events will follow? If they follow my direction, evidently my direction cannot wait on them. The only possible manner in which an evolutionist can use his standard is the obsequious method of forecasting the course society would take *but for him*, and then putting an extinguisher on all personal idiosyncracies of desire and interest, and with bated breath and tiptoe tread following as straight as may be at the tail, and bringing up the rear of everything. Some pious creatures may find a pleasure in this; but not only does it violate our general wish to lead and not to follow (a wish which is surely not immoral if we but lead aright), but if it be treated as every ethical principle must be treated — namely, as a rule good for all men alike — its general observance would lead to its practical refutation by bringing about a general deadlock. Each good man hanging back and waiting for orders from the rest, absolute stagnation would ensue. Happy, then, if a few unrighteous ones contribute an initiative which sets things moving again!

All this is no caricature. That the course of destiny may be altered by individuals no wise evolutionist ought to doubt. Everything for him has small beginnings, has a bud which may be 'nipped', and nipped by a feeble force. Human races and tendencies follow the law, and have also small beginnings. The best, according to evolution, is that which has the biggest endings. Now, if a present race of men, enlightened in the evolutionary philosophy, and able to forecast the future, were able to discern in a tribe arising near them the potentiality of future supremacy; were able to see that their own race would eventually be wiped out of existence by the newcomers if the expansion of these were left unmolested — these present sages would have two courses open to them, either perfectly in harmony with the evolutionary test: Strangle the new race *now*, and ours survives; help the new race, and *it* survives. In both cases the action is right as measured by the evolutionary standard — it is action for the winning side.

Thus the evolutionist foundation of ethics is purely objective only to the herd of nullities whose votes count for zero in the march of events. But for others, leaders of opinion or potentates, and in general those to whose actions position or genius gives a far-reaching import, and to the rest of us, each in his measure — whenever we espouse a cause we contribute to the determination of the evolutionary standard of right. The truly wise disciple of this school will then admit faith as an ultimate ethical factor. Any philosophy which makes such questions as, What is the ideal type of humanity? What shall be reckoned virtues? What conduct is good? depend on the question, What is going to succeed? – must needs fall back on personal belief as one of the ultimate conditions of the truth. For again and again success depends on energy of act; energy again depends on faith that we shall not fail; and that faith in turn on the faith that we are right – which faith thus verifies itself.

Take as an example the question of optimism or pessimism, which makes so much noise just now in Germany. Every human being must sometime decide for himself whether life is worth living. Suppose that in looking at the world and seeing how full it is of misery, of old age, of wickedness and pain, and how unsafe is his own future, he yields to the pessimistic conclusion, cultivates disgust and dread, ceases striving, and finally commits suicide. He thus adds to the mass M of mundane phenomena, independent of his subjectivity, the subjective complement x, which makes of the whole an utterly black picture illumined by no gleam of good. Pessimism completed, verified by his moral reaction and the deed in which this ends, is true beyond a doubt. $M + x$ expresses a state of things totally bad. The man's belief supplied all that was lacking to make it so, and now that it is made so the belief was right.

But now suppose that with the same evil facts M, the man's reaction x is exactly reversed; suppose that instead of giving way to the evil he braves it, and finds a sterner, more wonderful joy than any passive pleasure can yield in triumphing over pain and defying fear; suppose he does this successfully, and however thickly evils crowd upon him proves his dauntless subjectivity to be more than their match – will not everyone confess that the bad character of the M is here the *conditio sine qua non* of the good character of the x? Will not everyone instantly declare a world fitted only for fairweather human beings susceptible of every passive enjoyment, but without independence, courage or forti-tude, to be from a moral point of view incommensurably inferior to a world framed to elicit from the man every form of triumphant endurance and conquering moral energy? As James Hinton says,

Little inconveniences, exertions, pains – these are the only things in which we rightly feel our life at all. If these be not there, existence becomes worthless, or worse; success in putting them all away is fatal. So it is men engage in athletic sports, spend their holidays in climbing up mountains, find nothing so enjoyable as that which taxes their endurance and their energy. This is the way we are made, I say. It may or may not be a mystery or a paradox; it is a fact. Now, this enjoyment in endurance is just according to the intensity of life: the more physical vigour and balance, the more endurance can be made an element of satisfaction. A sick man cannot stand it. The line of enjoyable suffering is not a fixed one; it fluctuates with the perfectness of the life. That our pains are, as they are, unendurable, awful, overwhelming, crushing, not to be borne save in misery and dumb impatience, which utter exhaustion alone makes patient – that our pains are thus unendurable, means not that they are too great, but that we *are* sick. We have not got our proper life. So you perceive pain is no more necessarily an evil, but an essential element of the highest good.[2]

But the highest good can be achieved only by our getting our proper life; and that can come about only by help of a moral energy born of the faith that in some way or other we shall succeed in getting it if we try pertinaciously enough. This world *is* good, we must say, since it is what we make it – and we shall make it good. How can we exclude from the cognition of a truth a faith which is involved in the creation of the truth? M has its character indeterminate, susceptible of forming part of a thoroughgoing pessimism on the one hand, or of a meliorism, a moral (as distinguished from a sensual) optimism on the other. All depends on the character of the personal contribution x. Wherever the facts to be formulated contain such a contribution, we may logically, legitimately and inexpugnably believe what we desire. The belief creates its verification. The thought becomes literally father to the fact, as the wish was father to the thought.[3]

Let us now turn to the radical question of life – the question

---

[2] *Life of James Hinton*, pp. 172 and 173. See also the excellent chapter on 'Faith and Sight' in *The Mystery of Matter*, by J. Allanson Picton. Hinton's *Mystery of Pain* will undoubtedly always remain the classical utterance on this subject.

[3] Observe that in all this not a word has been said of free-will. It all applies as well to a predetermined as to an indeterminate universe. If $M + x$ is fixed in advance, the belief which leads to x and the desire which prompts the belief are also fixed. But fixed or not, these subjective states form a phenomenal condition necessarily preceding the facts; necessarily constitutive, therefore, of the truth $M + x$ which we seek. If, however, free acts be possible, a faith in their possibility, by augmenting the moral energy which gives them birth, will increase their frequency in a given individual.

whether this be at bottom a moral or an unmoral universe – and see whether the method of faith may legitimately have a place there. It is really the question of materialism. Is the world a simple brute actuality, an existence *de facto* about which the deepest thing that can be said is that it happens so to be; or is the judgment of *better* or *worse*, of *ought*, as intimately pertinent to phenomena as the simple judgment *is* or *is not?* The materialistic theorists say that judgments of worth are themselves mere matters of fact; that the words 'good' and 'bad' have no sense apart from subjective passions and interests which we may, if we please, play fast and loose with at will, so far as any duty of ours to the non-human universe is concerned. Thus, when a materialist says it is better for him to suffer great inconvenience than to break a promise, he only means that his social interests have become so knit up with keeping faith that, those interests once being granted, it *is* better for him to keep the promise in spite of everything. But the interests themselves are neither right nor wrong, except possibly with reference to some ulterior order of interests, which themselves again are mere subjective data without character, either good or bad.

For the absolute moralists, on the contrary, the interests are not there merely to be felt – they are to be believed in and obeyed. Not only is it best for my social interests to keep my promise, but best for me to have those interests, and best for the cosmos to have this me. Like the old woman in the story who described the world as resting on a rock, and then explained that rock to be supported by another rock, and finally when pushed with questions said it was rocks all the way down – he who believes this to be a radically moral universe must hold the moral order to rest either on an absolute and ultimate *should*, or on a series of *shoulds* all the way down.[4]

The practical difference between this objective sort of moralist and the other one is enormous. The subjectivist in morals, when his moral feelings are at war with the facts about him, is always free to seek harmony by toning down the sensitiveness of the feelings. Being mere data, neither good nor evil in themselves, he may pervert them or lull them to sleep by any means at his

[4] In either case, as a later essay explains, the *should* which the moralist regards as binding upon *him* must be rooted in the feeling of some other thinkers, or collection of thinkers, to whose demands he individually bows.

command. Truckling, compromise, time-serving, capitulations of conscience, are conventionally opprobrious names for what, if successfully carried out, would be on his principles by far the easiest and most praiseworthy mode of bringing about that harmony between inner and outer relations which is all that he means by good. The absolute moralist, on the other hand, when his interests clash with the world, is not free to gain harmony by sacrificing the ideal interests. According to him, these latter should be as they are and not otherwise. Resistance then, poverty, martyrdom if need be, tragedy in a word – such are the solemn feasts of his inward faith. Not that the contradiction between the two men occurs every day; in commonplace matters all moral schools agree. It is only in the lonely emergencies of life that our creed is tested: then routine maxims fail, and we fall back on our gods. It cannot then be said that the question, Is this a moral world? is a meaningless and unverifiable question because it deals with something non-phenomenal. Any question is full of meaning to which, as here, contrary answers lead to contrary behaviour. And it seems as if in answering such a question as this we might proceed exactly as does the physical philosopher in testing an hypothesis. He deduces from the hypothesis an experimental action, x; this he adds to the facts M already existing. It fits them if the hypothesis be true; if not, there is discord. The results of the action corroborate or refute the idea from which it flowed. So here: the verification of the theory which you may hold as to the objectively moral character of the world can consist only in this – that if you proceed to act upon your theory it will be reversed by nothing that later turns up as your action's fruit; it will harmonize so well with the entire drift of experience that the latter will, as it were, adopt it, or at most give it an ampler interpretation, without obliging you in any way to change the essence of its formulation. If this be an objectively moral universe, all acts that I make on that assumption, all expectations that I ground on it, will tend more and more completely to interdigitate with the phenomena already existing. $M + x$ will be in accord; and the more I live, and the more the fruits of my activity come to light, the more satisfactory the consensus will grow. While if it be not such a moral universe, and I mistakenly assume that it is, the course of experience will throw ever new impediments in the way of my belief, and become more and more difficult to express in its language.

Epicycle upon epicycle of subsidiary hypothesis will have to be invoked to give to the discrepant terms a temporary appearance of squaring with each other; but at last even this resource will fail.

If, on the other hand, I rightly assume the universe to be not moral, in what does my verification consist? It is that by letting moral interests sit lightly, by disbelieving that there is any duty about *them* (since duty obtains only as *between* them and other phenomena), and so throwing them over if I find it hard to get them satisfied – it is that by refusing to take up a tragic attitude, I deal in the long run most satisfactorily with the facts of life. 'All is vanity' is here the last word of wisdom. Even though in certain limited series there may be a great appearance of seriousness, he who in the main treats things with a degree of good-natured scepticism and radical levity will find that the practical fruits of his epicurean hypothesis verify it more and more, and not only save him from pain but do honour to his sagacity. While, on the other hand, he who contrary to reality stiffens himself in the notion that certain things absolutely should be, and rejects the truth that at bottom it makes no difference what is, will find himself evermore thwarted and perplexed and bemuddled by the facts of the world, and his tragic disappointment will, as experience accumulates, seem to drift farther and farther away from that final atonement or reconciliation which certain partial tragedies often get.

Anaesthesia is the watchword of the moral sceptic brought to bay and put to his trumps. *Energy* is that of the moralist. Act on my creed, cries the latter, and the results of your action will prove the creed true, and that the nature of things is earnest infinitely. Act on mine, says the epicurean, and the results will prove that seriousness is but a superficial glaze upon a world of fundamentally trivial import. You and your acts and the nature of things will be alike enveloped in a single formula, a universal *vanitas vanitatum*.

For the sake of simplicity I have written as if the verification might occur in the life of a single philosopher – which is manifestly untrue, since the theories still face each other, and the facts of the world give countenance to both. Rather should we expect, that, in a question of this scope, the experience of the entire human race must make the verification, and that all the evidence will not be 'in' till the final integration of things, when the last man has had his say and contributed his share to the still unfinished x. Then the proof will be complete; then it will appear without doubt whether the moralistic x has filled up the gap which alone kept the M of the world from forming an even and harmonious unity, or whether the non-moralistic x has given the finishing touches which were alone needed to make the M appear outwardly as vain as it inwardly was.

But if this be so, is it not clear that the facts M, taken *per se*, are inadequate to justify a conclusion either way in advance of my action? My action is the complement which, by proving congruous or not, reveals the latent nature of the mass to which it is applied. The world may in fact be likened unto a lock, whose inward nature, moral or unmoral, will never reveal itself to our simply expectant gaze. The positivists, forbidding us to make any assumptions regarding it, condemn us to eternal ignorance, for the 'evidence' which they wait for can never come so long as we are passive. But nature has put into our hands two keys, by which we may test the lock. If we try the moral key *and it fits*, it is a moral lock. If we try the unmoral key and *it* fits, it is an unmoral lock. I cannot possibly conceive of any other sort of 'evidence' or 'proof' than this. It is quite true that the co-operation of generations is needed to educe it. But in these matters the solidarity (so called) of the human race is a patent fact. The essential thing to notice is that our active preference is a legitimate part of the game – that it is our plain business as men to try one of the keys, and the one in which we most confide. If then the proof exist not till I have acted, and I must needs in acting run the risk of being wrong, how can the popular science professors be right in objurgating in me as infamous a 'credulity' which the strict logic of the situation requires? If this really be a moral universe; if by my acts I be a factor of its destinies; if to believe where I may doubt be itself a moral act analogous to voting for a side not yet sure to win – by what right shall they close in upon me and steadily negate the deepest conceivable function of my being by their preposterous command that I shall stir neither hand nor foot, but remain balancing myself in eternal and insoluble doubt? Why, doubt itself is a decision of the widest practical reach, if only because we may miss by doubting what goods we might be gaining by espousing the winning side. But more than that! it is often practically impossible to distinguish doubt from dogmatic negation. If I refuse to stop a murder because I am in doubt whether it be not justifiable homicide, I am virtually abetting the crime. If I refuse to bale out a boat because I am in doubt whether my efforts will keep her afloat, I am really helping to sink her. If in the mountain precipice I doubt my right to risk a leap, I actively connive at my destruction. He who commands himself not to be credulous of God, of duty, of freedom, of immortality, may again and again be indistinguishable from him who dogmatically denies them. Scepticism in moral matters is an active ally of immorality. Who is not for is against. The universe will have no neutrals in these questions. In theory as in practice, dodge or hedge, or talk as we like about a wise scepticism, we are really doing volunteer military service for one side or the other.

Yet obvious as this necessity practically is, thousands of innocent magazine readers lie paralysed and terrified in the network of shallow negations which the leaders of opinion have thrown over their souls. All they need to be free and hearty again in the exercise of their birthright is that these fastidious vetoes should be swept away. All that the human heart wants is its chance. It will willingly forego certainty in universal matters if only it can be allowed to feel that in them it has that same inalienable right to run risks, which no one dreams of refusing to it in the pettiest practical affairs. And if I, in these last pages, like the mouse in the fable, have gnawed a few of the strings of the sophistical net that has been binding down its lion-strength, I shall be more than rewarded for my pains.

To sum up: No philosophy will permanently be deemed rational by all men which (in addition to meeting logical demands) does not to some degree pretend to determine expectancy, and in a still greater degree make a direct appeal to all those powers of our nature which we hold in highest esteem. Faith, being one of these powers, will always remain a factor not to be banished from philosophic constructions, the more so since in many ways it brings forth its own verification. In these points, then, it is hopeless to look for literal agreement among mankind.

The ultimate philosophy, we may therefore conclude, must not be too straitlaced in form, must not in all its parts divide heresy from orthodoxy by too sharp a line. There must be left over and above the propositions to be subscribed, *ubique*, *semper*, *et ab omnibus*, another realm into which the stifled soul may escape from pedantic scruples and indulge its own faith at its own risks; and all that can here be done will be to mark out distinctly the questions which fall within faith's sphere.

Humanism and Truth[1]

Receiving from the editor of *Mind* an advance proof of Mr Bradley's article on 'Truth and Practice', I understand this as a hint to me to join in the controversy over 'pragmatism' which seems to have seriously begun. As my name has been coupled with the movement, I deem it wise to take the hint, the more so as in some quarters greater credit has been given me than I deserve, and probably undeserved discredit in other quarters falls also to my lot.

First, as to the word 'pragmatism', I myself have only used the term to indicate a method of carrying on abstract discussion. The serious meaning of a concept, says Mr Peirce, lies in the concrete difference to someone which its being true will make. Strive to bring all debated conceptions to that 'pragmatic' test, and you will escape vain wrangling: if it can make no practical difference which of two statements be true, then they are really one statement in two verbal forms; if it can make no practical difference whether a given statement be true or false, then the statement has no real meaning. In neither case is there anything fit to quarrel about: we may save our breath, and pass to more important things.

All that the pragmatic method implies, then, is that truths should *have* practical consequences. In England the word has been used more broadly still, to cover the notion that the truth of any statement *consists* in the consequences, and particularly in their being good consequences. Here we get beyond affairs of method altogether; and since my pragmatism and this wider pragmatism are so different, and both are important enough to have different names, I think that Mr Schiller's proposal to call the wider pragmatism by the name of 'humanism' is excellent

---

[1] Reprinted, with slight verbal revision, from *Mind*, vol. 13, NS, p. 457 (October 1904). A couple of interpolations from another article in *Mind*, 'Humanism and Truth Once More', in vol. 14, have been made.

and ought to be adopted. The narrower pragmatism may still be spoken of as the 'pragmatic method'.

I have read in the past six months many hostile reviews of Schiller's and Dewey's publications; but with the exception of Mr Bradley's elaborate indictment, they are out of reach where I write, and I have largely forgotten them. I think that a free discussion of the subject on my part would in any case be more useful than a polemic attempt at rebutting these criticisms in detail. Mr Bradley in particular can be taken care of by Mr Schiller. He repeatedly confesses himself unable to comprehend Schiller's views, he evidently has not sought to do so sympathetically, and I deeply regret to say that his laborious article throws, for my mind, absolutely no useful light upon the subject. It seems to me on the whole an *ignoratio elenchi*, and I feel free to disregard it altogether.

The subject is unquestionably difficult. Messrs Dewey's and Schiller's thought is eminently an induction, a generalization working itself free from all sorts of entangling particulars. If true, it involves much restatement of traditional notions. This is a kind of intellectual product that never attains a classic form of expression when first promulgated. The critic ought therefore not to be too sharp and logic-chopping in his dealings with it, but should weigh it as a whole, and especially weigh it against its possible alternatives. One should also try to apply it first to one instance, and then to another to see how it will work. It seems to me that it is emphatically not a case for instant execution, by conviction of intrinsic absurdity of self-contradiction, or by caricature of what it would look like if reduced to skeleton shape. Humanism is in fact much more like one of those secular changes that come upon public opinion overnight, as it were, borne upon tides 'too deep for sound or foam', that survive all the crudities and extravagances of their advocates, that you can pit to no one absolutely essential statement, nor kill by any one decisive stab.

Such have been the changes from aristocracy to democracy, from classic to romantic taste, from theistic to pantheistic feeling, from static to evolutionary ways of understanding life – changes of which we all have been spectators. Scholasticism still opposes to such changes the method of confutation by single decisive reasons, showing that the new view involves self-contradiction, or traverses some fundamental principle. This is like stopping a river by planting a stick in the middle of its bed. Round your obstacle flows the water and 'gets there all the same'. In reading some of our opponents, I am not a little reminded of those Catholic writers who refute Darwinism by telling us that higher species cannot come from lower because *minus nequit gignere plus*, or that the notion of transformation is absurd, for it implies that species tend to their own destruction, and that would violate the principle that every reality tends to persevere in its own shape. The point of view is too myopic, too tight and close to take in the inductive argument. Wide generalizations in science always meet with these summary refutations in their early days; but they outlive them, and the refutations then sound oddly antiquated and scholastic. I cannot help suspecting that the humanistic theory is going through this kind of would-be refutation at present.

The one condition of understanding humanism is to become inductive minded oneself, to drop rigorous definitions, and follow lines of least resistance 'on the whole'. 'In other words', an opponent might say, 'resolve your intellect into a kind of slush.' 'Even so,' I make reply – 'if you will consent to use no politer word.' For humanism, conceiving the more 'true' as the more 'satisfactory' (Dewey's term), has sincerely to renounce rectilinear arguments and ancient ideals of rigour and finality. It is in just this temper of renunciation, so different from that of pyrrhonistic scepticism, that the spirit of humanism essentially consists. Satisfactoriness has to be measured by a multitude of standards, of which some, for aught we know, may fail in any given case; and what is more satisfactory than any alternative in sight, may to the end be a sum of *pluses* and *minuses*, concerning which we can only trust that by ulterior corrections and improvements a maximum of the one and a minimum of the other may some day be approached. It means a real change of heart, a break with absolutistic hopes, when one takes up this inductive view of the conditions of belief.

As I understand the pragmatist way of seeing things, it owes its being to the breakdown which the last fifty years have brought about in the older notions of scientific truth. 'God geometrizes,' it used to be said; and it was believed that Euclid's elements literally reproduced his geometrizing. There is an eternal and unchangeable 'reason'; and its voice was supposed to reverberate in *Barbara* and *Celarent*. So also of the 'laws of

nature', physical and chemical, so of natural history classifications – all were supposed to be exact and exclusive duplicates of
pre-human archetypes buried in the structure of things, to which
the spark of divinity hidden in our intellect enables us to
penetrate. The anatomy of the world is logical, and its logic is
that of a university professor, it was thought. Up to about 1850
almost everyone believed that sciences expressed truths that
were exact copies of a definite code of non-human realities. But
the enormously rapid multiplication of theories in these latter
days has well-nigh upset the notion of any one of them being a
more literally objective kind of thing than another. There are so
many geometries, so many logics, so many physical and chemical
hypotheses, so many classifications, each one of them good for
so much and yet not good for everything, that the notion that
even the truest formula may be a human device and not a literal
transcript has dawned upon us. We hear scientific laws now
treated as so much 'conceptual shorthand', true so far as they
are useful but no farther. Our mind has become tolerant of
symbol instead of reproduction, of approximation instead of
exactness, of plasticity instead of rigour. 'Energetics', measuring
the bare face of sensible phenomena so as to describe in a single
formula all their changes of 'level', is the last word of this
scientific humanism, which indeed leaves queries enough outstanding as to the reason for so curious a congruence between
the world and the mind, but which at any rate makes our whole
notion of scientific truth more flexible and genial than it used
to be.

It is to be doubted whether any theorizer today, either in
mathematics, logic, physics or biology, conceives himself to be
literally re-editing processes of nature or thoughts of God. The
main forms of our thinking, the separation of subjects from
predicates, the negative, hypothetic and disjunctive judgments,
are purely human habits. The ether, as Lord Salisbury said, is
only a noun for the verb to undulate; and many of our
theological ideas are admitted, even by those who call them
'true', to be humanistic in like degree.

I fancy that these changes in the current notions of truth
are what originally gave the impulse to Messrs Dewey's and
Schiller's views. The suspicion is in the air nowadays that
the superiority of one of our formulas to another may not consist so much in its literal 'objectivity', as in subjective qualities

like its usefulness, its 'elegance' or its congruity with our residual beliefs. Yielding to these suspicions, and generalizing, we fall into something like the humanistic state of mind. Truth we conceive to mean everywhere, not duplication, but addition; not the constructing of inner copies of already complete realities, but rather the collaborating with realities so as to bring about a clearer result. Obviously this state of mind is at first full of vagueness and ambiguity. 'Collaborating' is a vague term; it must at any rate cover conceptions and logical arrangements. 'Clearer' is vaguer still. Truth must bring clear thoughts, as well as clear the way to action. 'Reality' is the vaguest term of all. The only way to test such a programme at all is to apply it to the various types of truth, in the hope of reaching an account that shall be more precise. Any hypothesis that forces such a review upon one has one great merit, even if in the end it prove invalid: it gets us better acquainted with the total subject. To give the theory plenty of 'rope' and see if it hangs itself eventually is better tactics than to choke it off at the outset by abstract accusations of self-contradiction. I think therefore that a decided effort at sympathetic mental play with humanism is the provisional attitude to be recommended to the reader.

When I find myself playing sympathetically with humanism, something like what follows is what I end by conceiving it to mean.

Experience is a process that continually gives us new material to digest. We handle this intellectually by the mass of beliefs of which we found ourselves already possessed, assimilating, rejecting or rearranging in different degrees. Some of the apperceiving ideas are recent acquisitions of our own, but most of them are common-sense traditions of the race. There is probably not a common-sense tradition, of all those which we now live by, that was not in the first instance a genuine discovery, an inductive generalization like those more recent ones of the atom, of inertia, of energy, of reflex action, or of fitness to survive. The notions of one time and of one space as single continuous receptacles; the distinction between thought and things, matter and mind; between permanent subjects and changing attributes; the conception of classes with sub-classes within them; the separation of fortuitous from regularly caused connections; surely all these were once definite conquests made at historic dates by our ancestors in their attempts to get the chaos of their crude individual experiences into a more shareable and manageable shape. They proved of such sovereign use as *denkmittel* that they are now a part of the very structure of our mind. We cannot play fast and loose with them. No experience can upset them. On the contrary, they apperceive every experience and assign it to its place.

To what effect? That we may the better foresee the course of our experiences, communicate with one another, and steer our lives by rule. Also that we may have a cleaner, clearer, more inclusive mental view.

The greatest common-sense achievement, after the discovery of one time and one space, is probably the concept of permanently existing things. When a rattle first drops out of the hand of a baby, he does not look to see where it has gone. Non-perception he accepts as annihilation until he finds a better belief. That our perceptions mean *beings*, rattles that are there whether we hold them in our hands or not, becomes an interpretation so luminous of what happens to us that, once employed, it never gets forgotten. It applies with equal felicity to things and persons, to the objective and to the ejective realm. However a Berkeley, a Mill or a Cornelius may criticize it, it *works*; and in practical life we never think of 'going back' upon it, or reading our incoming experiences in any other terms. We may, indeed, speculatively imagine a state of 'pure' experience before the hypothesis of permanent objects behind its flux had been framed; and we can play with the idea that some primeval genius might have struck into a different hypothesis. But we cannot positively imagine today what the different hypothesis could have been, for the category of trans-perceptual reality is now one of the foundations of our life. Our thoughts must still employ it if they are to possess reasonableness and truth.

This notion of a *first* in the shape of a most chaotic pure experience which sets us questions, of a *second* in the way of fundamental categories, long ago wrought into the structure of our consciousness and practically irreversible, which define the general frame within which answers must fall, and of a *third* which gives the detail of the answers in the shapes most congruous with all our present needs, is, as I take it, the essence of the humanistic conception. It represents experience in its pristine purity to be now so enveloped in predicates historically worked out that we can think of it as little more than an *other*, of a *that*, which the mind, in Mr Bradley's phrase, 'encounters', and to whose stimulating presence we respond by ways of thinking which we call 'true' in proportion as they facilitate our mental or physical activities and bring us outer power and inner peace. But whether the other, the universal *that*, has itself any definite inner structures, or whether, if it have any, the structure resembles any of our predicated *whats*, this is a question which humanism leaves untouched. For us, at any rate, it insists, reality is an accumulation of our own intellectual inventions, and the struggle for 'truth' in our progressive dealings with it is always a struggle to work in new nouns and adjectives while altering as little as possible the old.

It is hard to see why either Mr Bradley's own logic or his metaphysics should oblige him to quarrel with this conception. He might consistently adopt it *verbatim et literatim*, if he would, and simply throw his peculiar absolute round it, following in this the good example of Professor Royce. Bergson in France, and his disciples, Wilbois the physicist and Leroy, are thoroughgoing humanists in the sense defined. Professor Milhaud also appears to be one; and the great Poincaré misses it by only the breadth of a hair. In Germany the name of Simmel offers itself as that of a humanist of the most radical sort. Mach and his school, and Hertz and Ostwald must be classed as humanists. The view is in the atmosphere and must be patiently discussed.

The best way to discuss it would be to see what the alternative might be. What is it indeed? Its critics make no explicit statement, Professor Royce being the only one so far who has formulated anything definite. The first service of humanism to philosophy accordingly seems to be that it will probably oblige those who dislike it to search their own hearts and heads. It will force analysis to the front and make it the order of the day. At present the lazy tradition that truth is *adaequatio intellectus et rei* seems all there is to contradict it with. Mr Bradley's only suggestion is that true thought 'must correspond to a determinate being which it cannot be said to make', and obviously that sheds no new light. What is the meaning of the word to 'correspond'? Where is the 'being'? What sort of things are 'determinations', and what is meant in this particular case by 'not to make'?

Humanism proceeds immediately to refine upon the looseness of these epithets. We correspond in *some* way with anything with which we enter into any relations at all. If it be a thing, we may produce an exact copy of it, or we may simply feel it as an existent in a certain place. If it be a demand, we may obey it without knowing anything more about it than its push. If it be a proposition, we may agree by not contradicting it, by letting it pass. If it be a relation between things, we may act on the first thing so as to bring ourselves out where the second will be. If it be something inaccessible, we may substitute a hypothetical object for it, which, having the same consequences, will cipher out for us real results. In a general way we may simply *add our thought to it*; and if it *suffers the addition*, and the whole situation harmoniously prolongs and enriches itself, the thought will pass for true.

As for the whereabouts of the beings thus corresponded to, although they may be outside of the present thought as well as in it, humanism sees no ground for saying they are outside of finite experience itself. Pragmatically, their reality means that we submit to them, take account of them, whether we like to or not, but this we must perpetually do with experiences other than our own. The whole system of what the present experience must correspond to 'adequately' may be continuous with the present experience itself. Reality, so taken as experience other than the present, might be either the legacy of past experience or the content of experience to come. Its determinations for *us* are in any case the adjectives which our acts of judging fit to it, and those are essentially humanistic things.

To say that our thought does not 'make' this reality means pragmatically that if our own particular thought were annihilated the reality would still be there in some shape, though possibly it might be a shape that would lack something that our thought supplies. That reality is 'independent' means that there is something in every experience that escapes our arbitrary control. If it be a sensible experience it coerces our attention; if a sequence, we cannot invert it; if we compare two terms we can come to only one result. There is a push, an urgency, within our very experience, against which we are on the whole powerless, and which drives us in a direction that is the destiny of our

belief. That this drift of experience itself is in the last resort due
to something independent of all possible experience may or may
not be true. There may or may not be an extra-experiential '*ding
an sich*' that keeps the ball rolling, or an 'absolute' that lies
eternally behind all the successive determinations which human
thought has made. But within our experience *itself* at any rate,
humanism says, some determinations show themselves as being
independent of others; some questions, if we ever ask them, can
only be answered in one way; some beings, if we ever suppose
them, must be supposed to have existed previously to the
supposing; some relations, if they exist ever, must exist as long
as their terms exist.

Truth thus means, according to humanism, the relation of less
fixed parts of experience (predicates) to other relatively more
fixed parts (subjects); and we are not required to seek it in a
relation of experience as such to anything beyond itself. We can
stay at home, for our behaviour as experients is hemmed in on
every side. The forces both of advance and of resistance are
exerted by our own objects, and the notion of truth as something
opposed to waywardness or licence inevitably grows up solips-
istically inside of every human life.

So obvious is all this that a common charge against the
humanistic authors 'makes me tired'. 'How can a Deweyite
discriminate sincerity from bluff?' was a question asked at a
philosophic meeting where I reported on Dewey's *Studies*. 'How
can the mere[2] pragmatist feel any duty to think truly?' is the
objection urged by Professor Royce. Mr Bradley in turn says
that if a humanist understands his own doctrine, he 'must hold
. . . any idea however mad to be the truth if any one will have it
so.' And Professor Taylor describes pragmatism as believing
anything one pleases and calling it truth.

Such a shallow sense of the condition under which men's
thinking actually goes on seems to me most surprising. These
critics appear to suppose that, if left to itself, the rudderless raft
of our experience must be ready to drift anywhere or nowhere.
Even though there were compasses on board, they seem to say,
there would be no pole for them to point to. There must be

---

[2] I know of no 'mere' pragmatist, if *mereness* here means, as it seems to, the denial
of all concreteness to the pragmatist's thought.

absolute sailing directions, they insist, decreed from outside, and an independent chart of the voyage added to the 'mere' voyage itself, if we are ever to make a port. But is it not obvious that even though there be such absolute sailing directions in the shape of pre-human standards of truth that we *ought* to follow, the only guarantee that we shall in fact follow them must lie in our human equipment. The 'ought' would be a *brutum fulmen* unless there were a felt grain inside of our experience that conspired. As a matter of fact the devoutest believers in absolute standards must admit that men fail to obey them. Waywardness is here, in spite of the eternal prohibitions, and the existence of any amount of reality *ante rem* is no warrant against unlimited error *in rebus* being incurred. The only *real* guarantee we have against licentious thinking is the circumpressure of experience itself, which gets us sick of concrete errors, whether there be a trans-empirical reality or not. How does the partisan of absolute reality know what this orders him to think? He cannot get direct sight of the absolute; and he has no means of guessing what it wants of him except by following the humanistic clues. The only truth that he himself will ever practically *accept* will be that to which his finite experiences lead him of themselves. The state of mind which shudders at the idea of a lot of experiences left to themselves, and that augurs protection from the sheer name of an absolute, as if, however inoperative, that might still stand for a sort of ghostly security, is like the mood of those good people who, whenever they hear of a social tendency that is damnable, begin to redden and to puff, and say 'Parliament or Congress ought to make a law against it', as if an impotent decree would give relief.

All the *sanctions* of a law of truth lie in the very texture of experience. Absolute or no absolute, the concrete truth for *us* will always be that way of thinking in which our various experiences most profitably combine.

And yet, the opponent obstinately urges, your humanist will always have a greater liberty to play fast and loose with truth than will your believer in an independent realm of reality that makes the standard rigid. If by this latter believer he means a man who pretends to know the standard and who fulminates it, the humanist will doubtless prove more flexible; but no more flexible than the absolutist himself if the latter follows (as fortunately our present-day absolutists do follow) empirical methods of inquiry in concrete affairs. To consider hypotheses is surely always better than to dogmatize *ins blaue hinein*.

Nevertheless this probable flexibility of temper in him has been used to convict the humanist of sin. Believing as he does, that truth lies *in rebus*, and is at every moment our own line of most propitious reaction, he stands forever debarred, as I have heard a learned colleague say, from trying to convert opponents, for does not their view, being *their* most propitious momentary reaction, already fit the bill? Only the believer in the *ante-rem* brand of truth can on this theory seek to make converts without self-stultification. But can there be self-stultification in urging any account whatever of truth? Can the definition ever contradict the deed? 'Truth is what I feel like saying' – suppose that to be the definition. 'Well, I feel like saying that, and I want you to feel like saying it, and shall continue to say it until I get you to agree.' Where is there any contradiction? Whatever truth may be said to be, that is the kind of truth which the saying can be held to carry. The *temper* which a saying may comport is an extra-logical matter. It may indeed be hotter in some individual absolutist than in a humanist, but it need not be so in another. And the humanist, for his part, is perfectly consistent in compassing sea and land to make one proselyte, if his nature be enthusiastic enough.

'But how *can* you be enthusiastic over any view of things which you know to have been partly made by yourself, and which is liable to alter during the next minute? How is any heroic devotion to the ideal of truth possible under such paltry conditions?'

This is just another of those objections by which the anti-humanists show their own comparatively slack hold on the realities of the situation. If they would only follow the pragmatic method and ask: 'What is truth *known-as*? What does its existence stand for in the way of concrete goods?' – they would see that the name of it is in the *inbegriff* of almost everything that is valuable in our lives. The true is the opposite of whatever is unstable, of whatever is practically disappointing, of whatever is useless, of whatever is lying and unreliable, of whatever is unverifiable and unsupported, of whatever is inconsistent and contradictory, of whatever is artificial and eccentric, of whatever is unreal in the sense of being of no practical account. Here are pragmatic reasons with a vengeance why we should turn to truth – truth saves us from a world of that complexion. What wonder that its very name awakens loyal feeling! In particular what wonder that all little provisional fool's paradises of belief should appear contemptible in comparison with its bare pursuit! When absolutists reject humanism because they feel it to be untrue, that means that the whole habit of their mental needs is wedded already to a different view of reality, in comparison with which the humanistic world seems but the whim of a few irresponsible youths. Their own subjective apperceiving mass is what speaks here in the name of the eternal natures and bids them reject our humanism – as they apprehend it. Just so with us humanists, when we condemn all noble, clean-cut, fixed, eternal, rational, temple-like systems of philosophy. These contradict the *dramatic temperament* of nature, as our dealings with nature and our habits of thinking have so far brought us to conceive it. They seem oddly personal and artificial, even when not bureaucratic and professional in an absurd degree. We turn from them to the great unpent and unstayed wilderness of truth as we feel it to be constituted, with as good a conscience as rationalists are moved by when they turn from our wilderness into their neater and cleaner intellectual abodes.

This is surely enough to show that the humanist does not ignore the character of objectivity and independence in truth. Let me turn next to what his opponents mean when they say that to be true, our thoughts must 'correspond'.

The vulgar notion of correspondence here is that the thoughts must *copy* the reality – *cognitio fit per* assimiliationem *cogniti et cognoscentis*; and philosophy, without having ever fairly sat down to the question, seems to have instinctively accepted this idea: propositions are held true if they copy the eternal thought; terms are held true if they copy extra-mental realities. Implicitly, I think that the copy-theory has animated most of the criticisms that have been made on humanism.

A priori, however, it is not self-evident that the sole business of our mind with realities should be to copy them. Let my reader suppose himself to constitute for a time all the reality there is in the universe, and then to receive the announcement that another being is to be created who shall know him truly. How will he represent the knowing in advance? What will he hope it to be? I doubt extremely whether it could ever occur to him to fancy it as a mere copying. Of what use to him would an imperfect second edition of himself in the newcomer's interior be? It would seem pure waste of a propitious opportunity. The demand would more probably be for something absolutely new. The reader would conceive the knowing humanistically, 'the newcomer', he would say, 'must *take account of my presence by reacting on it in such a way that good would accrue to us both.* If copying be requisite to that end, let there be copying; otherwise not.' The essence in any case would not be the copying, but the enrichment of the previous world.

I read the other day, in a book of Professor Eucken's, a phrase '*Die erhöhung des vorgefundenen daseins*', which seems to be pertinent here. Why may not thought's mission be to increase and elevate, rather than simply to imitate and reduplicate, existence? No one who has read Lotze can fail to remember his striking comment on the ordinary view of the secondary qualities of matter, which brands them as 'illusory' because they copy nothing in the thing. The notion of a world complete in itself, to which thought comes as a passive mirror, adding nothing to fact, Lotze says is irrational. Rather is thought itself a most momentous part of fact, and the whole mission of the pre-existing and insufficient world of matter may simply be to provoke thought to produce its far more precious supplement.

'Knowing', in short, may, for aught we can see beforehand to the contrary, be *only one way of getting into fruitful relations with reality*, whether copying be one of the relations or not.

It is easy to see from what special type of knowing the copy-theory arose. In our dealings with natural phenomena the great point is to be able to foretell. Foretelling, according to such a writer as Spencer, is the whole meaning of intelligence. When Spencer's 'law of intelligence' says that inner and outer relations must 'correspond', it means that the distribution of terms in our inner time-scheme and space-scheme must be an exact copy of the distribution in real time and space of the real terms. In strict theory the mental terms themselves need not answer to the real terms in the sense of severally copying them, symbolic mental terms being enough, if only the real dates and places be copied. But in our ordinary life the mental terms are images and the real ones are sensations, and the images so often copy the sensations, that we easily take copying of terms as well as of relations to be the natural significance of knowing. Meanwhile much, even of this common descriptive truth, is couched in verbal symbols. If our symbols *fit* the world, in the sense of determining our expectations rightly, they may even be the better for not copying its terms.

It seems obvious that the pragmatic account of all this routine of phenomenal knowledge is accurate. Truth here is a relation, not of our ideas to non-human realities, but of conceptual parts of our experience to sensational parts. Those thoughts are true which guide us to *beneficial interaction* with sensible particulars as they occur, whether they copy these in advance or not.

From the frequency of copying in the knowledge of phenomenal fact, copying has been supposed to be the essence of truth in matters rational also. Geometry and logic, it has been supposed, must copy archetypal thoughts in the Creator. But in these abstract spheres there is no need of assuming archetypes. The mind is free to carve so many figures out of space, to make so many numerical collections, to frame so many classes and series, and it can analyse and compare so endlessly, that the very superabundance of the resulting ideas makes us doubt the 'objective' pre-existence of their models. It would be plainly wrong to suppose a god whose thought consecrated rectangular but not polar co-ordinates, or Jevons's notation but not Boole's. Yet if, on the other hand, we assume God to have thought in advance of every *possible* flight of human fancy in these directions, his mind becomes too much like a Hindu idol with three heads, eight arms and six breasts, too much made up of superfoetation and redundancy for us to wish to copy it, and the whole notion of copying tends to evaporate from these sciences. Their objects can be better interpreted as being created step by step by men, as fast as they successively conceive them.

If now it be asked how, if triangles, squares, square roots, genera, and the like, are but improvised human 'artefacts', their properties and relations can be so promptly known to be 'eternal', the humanistic answer is easy. If triangles and genera are of our own production we can keep them invariant. We can make them 'timeless' by expressly decreeing that on *the things we mean* time shall exert no altering effect, that they are intentionally and it may be fictitiously abstracted from every corrupting real associate and condition. But relations between invariant objects will themselves be invariant. Such relations cannot be happening, for by hypothesis nothing shall happen to the objects. I have tried to show in the last chapter of my *Principles of Psychology*[3] that they can only be relations of comparison. No one so far seems to have noticed my suggestion, and I am too ignorant of the development of mathematics to feel very confident of my own view. But if it were correct it would solve the difficulty perfectly. Relations of comparison are matters of direct inspection. As soon as mental objects are mentally compared, they are perceived to be either like or unlike. But once the same, always the same, once different, always different, under these timeless conditions. Which is as much as to say that truths concerning these man-made objects are necessary and eternal. We can change our conclusions only by changing our data first.

The whole fabric of the *a priori* sciences can thus be treated as a man-made project. As Locke long ago pointed out, these sciences have no immediate connection with fact. Only *if* a fact can be humanized by being identified with any of these ideal objects, is what was true of the objects now true also of the facts. The truth itself meanwhile was originally a copy of nothing; it was only a relation directly perceived to obtain between two artificial mental things.

We may now glance at some special types of knowing, so as to see better whether the humanistic account fits. On the mathematical and logical types we need not enlarge further, nor need we return at much length to the case of our descriptive knowledge of the course of nature. So far as this involves anticipation, though that *may* mean copying, it need, as we saw, mean little more than 'getting ready' in advance. But with many distant and future objects, our practical relations are to the last degree potential and remote. In no sense can we now get ready for the arrest of the earth's revolution by the tidal brake, for instance; and with the past, though we suppose ourselves to know it truly, we have no practical relations at all. It is obvious that, although interests strictly practical have been the original starting point of our search for true phenomenal descriptions, yet an intrinsic interest in the bare describing function has grown up. We wish accounts that shall be true, whether they bring

---

[3] Vol. 2, pp. 641ff.

collateral profit or not. The primitive function has developed its demand for mere exercise. This theoretic curiosity seems to be the characteristically human *differentia*, and humanism recognizes its enormous scope. A true idea now means not only one that prepares us for an actual perception. It means also one that might prepare us for a merely possible perception, or one that, if spoken, would suggest possible perceptions to others, or suggest actual perceptions which the speaker cannot share. The *ensemble* of perceptions thus thought of as either actual or possible forms a system which it is obviously advantageous to us to get into a stable and consistent shape; and here it is that the common-sense notion of permanent beings finds triumphant use. Beings acting outside of the thinker explain, not only his actual perceptions, past and future, but his possible perceptions and those of everyone else. Accordingly they gratify our theoretic need in a supremely beautiful way. We pass from our immediate actual through them into the foreign and the potential, and back again into the future actual, accounting for innumerable particulars by a single cause. As in those circular panoramas, where a real foreground of dirt, grass, bushes, rocks and a broken-down cannon is enveloped by a canvas picture of sky and earth and of a raging battle, continuing the foreground so cunningly that the spectator can detect no joint; so these conceptual objects, added to our present perceptual reality, fuse with it into the whole universe of our belief. In spite of all Berkeleyan criticism, we do not doubt that they are really there. Though our discovery of any one of them may only date from now, we unhesitatingly say that it not only *is*, but *was* there, if, by so saying, the past appears connected more consistently with what we feel the present to be. This is historic truth. Moses wrote the Pentateuch, we think, because if he didn't, all our religious habits will have to be undone. Julius Caesar was real, or we can never listen to history again. Trilobites were once alive, or all our thought about the strata is at sea. Radium, discovered only yesterday, must always have existed, or its analogy with other natural elements, which are permanent, fails. In all this, it is but one portion of our beliefs reacting on another so as to yield the most satisfactory total state of mind. That state of mind, we say, sees truth, and the content of its deliverances we believe.

Of course, if you take the satisfactoriness concretely, as

something felt by you now, and if, by truth, you mean truth taken abstractly and verified in the long run, you cannot make them equate, for it is notorious that the temporarily satisfactory is often false. Yet at each and every concrete moment, truth for each man is what the man 'troweth' at that moment with the maximum of satisfaction to himself; and similarly, abstract truth, truth verified by the long run, and abstract satisfactoriness, long-run satisfactoriness, coincide. If, in short, we compare concrete with concrete and abstract with abstract, the true and the satisfactory do mean the same thing. I suspect that a certain muddling of matters hereabouts is what makes the general philosophic public so impervious to humanism's claims.

The fundamental fact about our experience is that it is a process of change. For the 'trower' at any moment, truth, like the visible area round a man walking in a fog, or like what George Eliot calls 'the wall of dark seen by small fishes' eyes that pierce a span in the wide ocean', is an objective field which the next moment enlarges and of which it is the critic, and which then either suffers alteration or is continued unchanged. The critic sees both the first trower's truth and his own truth, compares them with each other, and verifies or confutes. *His* field of view is the reality independent of that early trower's thinking with which that thinking ought to correspond. But the critic is himself only a trower; and if the whole process of experience should terminate at that instant, there would be no otherwise known independent reality with which *his* thought might be compared.

The immediate in experience is always provisionally in this situation. The humanism, for instance, which I see and try so hard to defend, is the completest truth attained from my point of view up to date. But, owing to the fact that all experience is a process, no point of view can ever be *the* last one. Every one is insufficient and off its balance, and responsible to later points of view than itself. You, occupying some of these later points in your own person, and believing in the reality of others, will not agree that my point of view sees truth positive, truth timeless, truth that counts, unless they verify and confirm what it sees.

You generalize this by saying that any opinion, however satisfactory, can count positively and absolutely as true only so far as it agrees with a standard beyond itself; and if you then forget that this standard perpetually grows up endogenously inside the web of the experiences, you may carelessly go on to say that what distributively holds of each experience, holds also collectively of all experience, and that experience as such and in its totality owes whatever truth it may be possessed of to its correspondence with absolute realities outside of its own being. This evidently is the popular and traditional position. From the fact that finite experiences must draw support from one another, philosophers pass to the notion that experience *überhaupt* must need an absolute support. The denial of such a notion by humanism lies probably at the root of most of the dislike which it incurs.

But is this not the globe, the elephant and the tortoise over again? Must not something end by supporting itself? Humanism is willing to let finite experience be self-supporting. Somewhere being must immediately breast nonentity. Why may not the advancing front of experience, carrying its immanent satisfactions and dissatisfactions, cut against the black inane as the luminous orb of the moon cuts the caerulean abyss? Why should anywhere the world be absolutely fixed and finished? And if reality genuinely grows, why may it not grow in these very determinations which here and now are made?

In point of fact it actually seems to grow by our mental determinations, be these never so 'true'. Take the 'Great Bear' or 'Dipper' constellation in the heavens. We call it by that name, we count the stars and call them seven, we say they were seven before they were counted, and we say that whether anyone had ever noted the fact or not, the dim resemblance to a long-tailed (or long-necked?) animal was always truly there. But what do we mean by this projection into past eternity of recent human ways of thinking? Did an 'absolute' thinker actually do the counting, tell off the stars upon his standing number-tally, and make the bear-comparison, silly as the latter is? Were they explicitly seven, explicitly bear-like, before the human witness came? Surely nothing in the truth of the attributions drives us to think this. They were only implicitly or virtually what we call them, and we human witnesses first explicated them and made them 'real'. A fact virtually pre-exists when every condition of its realization save one is already there. In this case the condition lacking is the act of the counting and comparing mind. But the stars (once the mind considers them) themselves dictate the result. The counting in no wise modifies their previous nature, and, they being what and where they are, the count cannot fall out differently. It could then *always* be made. *Never* could the number seven be questioned, *if the question once were raised*.

We have here a quasi-paradox. Undeniably something comes by the counting that was not there before. And yet that something was *always true*. In one sense you create it, and in another sense you *find* it. You have to treat your count as being true beforehand, the moment you come to treat the matter at all.

Our stellar attributes must always be called true, then; yet none the less are they genuine additions made by our intellect to the world of fact. Not additions of consciousness only, but additions of 'content'. They copy nothing that pre-existed, yet they agree with what pre-existed, fit it, amplify it, relate and connect it with a 'wain', a number-tally, or what not, and build it out. It seems to me that humanism is the only theory that builds this case out in the good direction, and this case stands for innumerable other kinds of case. In all such cases, odd as it may sound, our judgment may actually be said to retroact and to enrich the past.

Our judgments at any rate change the character of *future* reality by the acts to which they lead. Where these acts are acts expressive of trust – trust, e.g., that a man is honest, that our health is good enough, or that we can make a successful effort – which acts may be a needed antecedent of the trusted things becoming true, Professor Taylor says[4] that our trust is at any rate *untrue when it is made*, i.e., before the action; and I seem to remember that he disposes of anything like a faith in the general excellence of the universe (making the faithful person's part in it at any rate more excellent) as a 'lie in the soul'. But the pathos of this expression should not blind us to the complication of the facts. I doubt whether Professor Taylor would himself be in favour of practically handling trusters of these kinds as liars. Future and present really mix in such emergencies, and one can always escape lies in them by using hypothetic forms. But Mr Taylor's attitude suggests such absurd possibilities of practice that it seems to me to illustrate beautifully how self-stultifying

[4] In an article criticizing pragmatism (as he conceives it) in the *McGill University Quarterly* published at Montreal, for May 1904.

the conception of a truth that shall merely register a standing fixture may become. Theoretic truth, truth of passive copying, sought in the sole interests of copying as such, not because copying is *good for something*, but because copying ought *schlechthin* to be, seems, if you look at it coldly, to be an almost preposterous ideal. Why should the universe, existing in itself, also exist in copies? How *can* it be copied in the solidity of its objective fullness? And even if it could, what would the motive be? 'Even the hairs of your head are numbered.' Doubtless they are, virtually; but why, as an absolute proposition, *ought* the number to become copied and known? Surely knowing is only one way of interacting with reality and adding to its effect.

The opponent here will ask: 'Has not the knowing of truth any substantive value on its own account, apart from the collateral advantages it may bring? And if you allow theoretic satisfaction to exist at all, do they not crowd the collateral satisfactions out of house and home, and must not pragmatism go into bankruptcy, if she admits them at all?' The destructive force of such talk disappears as soon as we use words concretely instead of abstractly, and ask, in our quality of good pragmatists, just what the famous theoretic needs are known – as and in what the intellectual satisfactions consist.

Are they not all mere matters of *consistency* – and emphatically *not* of consistency between an absolute reality and the mind's copies of it, but of actually felt consistency among judgments, objects, and habits of reacting, in the mind's own experienceable world? And are not both our need of such consistency and our pleasure in it conceivable as outcomes of the natural fact that we are beings that do develop mental *habits* – habit itself proving adaptively beneficial in an environment where the same objects, or the same kinds of objects, recur and follow 'law'? If this were so, what would have come first would have been the collateral profits of habit as such, and the theoretic life would have grown up in aid of these. In point of fact, this seems to have been the probable case. At life's origin, any present perception may have been 'true' – if such a word could then be applicable. Later, when reactions became organized, the reactions became 'true' whenever expectation was fulfilled by them. Otherwise they were 'false' or 'mistaken' reactions. But the same class of objects needs the same kind of reaction, so the impulse to react consistently must gradually have been established, and a disappointment felt whenever the results frustrated expectation. Here is a perfectly plausible germ for all our higher consistencies. Nowadays, if an object claims from us a reaction of the kind habitually accorded only to the opposite class of objects, our mental machinery refuses to run smoothly. The situation is intellectually unsatisfactory.

Theoretic truth thus falls *within* the mind, being the accord of some of its processes and objects with other processes and objects – 'accord' consisting here in well-definable relations. So long as the satisfaction of feeling such an accord is denied us, whatever collateral profits may seem to inure from what we believe in are but as dust in the balance – provided always that we are highly organized intellectually, which the majority of us are not. The amount of accord which satisfies most men and women is merely the absence of violent clash between their usual thoughts and statements and the limited sphere of sense perceptions in which their lives are cast. The theoretic truth that most of us think we 'ought' to attain to is thus the possession of a set of predicates that do not explicitly contradict their subjects. We preserve it as often as not by leaving other predicates and subjects out.

In some men theory is a passion, just as music is in others. The form of inner consistency is pursued far beyond the line at which collateral profits stop. Such men systematize and classify and schematize and make synoptical tables and invent ideal objects for the pure love of unifying. Too often the results, glowing with 'truth' for the inventors, seem pathetically personal and artificial to bystanders. Which is as much as to say that the purely theoretic criterion of truth can leave us in the lurch as easily as any other criterion, and that the absolutists, for all their pretensions, are 'in the same boat' concretely with those whom they attack.

I am well aware that this paper has been rambling in the extreme. But the whole subject is inductive, and sharp logic is hardly yet in order. My great trammel has been the non-existence of any definitely stated alternative on my opponents' part. It may conduce to clearness if I recapitulate, in closing, what I conceive the main points of humanism to be. They are these:

1 An experience, perceptual or conceptual, must conform to reality in order to be true.

2 By 'reality' humanism means nothing more than the other conceptual or perceptual experiences with which a given present experience may find itself in point of fact mixed up.[5]

3 By 'conforming', humanism means taking account of in such a way as to gain any intellectually and practically satisfactory result.

4 To 'take account of' and to be 'satisfactory' are terms that admit of no definition, so many are the ways in which these requirements can practically be worked out.

5 Vaguely and in general, we take account of a reality by *preserving* it in as unmodified a form as possible. But, to be then satisfactory, it must not contradict other realities outside of it which claim also to be preserved. That we must preserve all the experience we can and minimize contradiction in what we preserve, is about all that can be said in advance.

6 The truth which the conforming experience embodies may be a positive addition to the previous reality, and later judgments may have to conform to *it*. Yet, virtually at least, it may have been true previously. Pragmatically, virtual and actual truth mean the same thing: the possibility of only one answer, *when once the question is raised*.

[5] This is meant merely to exclude reality of an 'unknowable' sort, of which no account in either perceptual or conceptual terms can be given. It includes of course any amount of empirical reality independent of the knower. Pragmatism is thus 'epistemologically' realistic in its account.

4

The Pragmatist Account of Truth and its Misunderstanders[1]

The account of truth given in my volume entitled *Pragmatism*, continues to meet with such persistent misunderstanding that I am tempted to make a final brief reply. My ideas may well deserve refutation, but they can get none till they are conceived of in their proper shape. The fantastic character of the current misconceptions shows how unfamiliar is the concrete point of view which pragmatism assumes. Persons who are familiar with a conception move about so easily in it that they understand each other at a hint, and can converse without anxiously attending to their Ps and Qs. I have to admit, in view of the results, that we have assumed too ready an intelligence, and consequently in many places used a language too slipshod. We should never have spoken elliptically. The critics have boggled at every word they could boggle at, and refused to take the spirit rather than the letter of our discourse. This seems to show a genuine unfamiliarity in the whole point of view. It also shows, I think, that the second stage of opposition, which has already begun to express itself in the stock phrase that 'what is new is not true, and what is true not new', in pragmatism, is insincere. If we said nothing in any degree new, why was our meaning so desperately hard to catch? The blame cannot be laid wholly upon our obscurity of speech, for in other subjects we have attained to making ourselves understood. But recriminations are tasteless; and, as far as I personally am concerned, I am sure that some of the misconception I complain of is due to my doctrine of truth being surrounded in that volume of popular lectures by a lot of other opinions not necessarily implicated with it, so that a reader may very naturally have grown confused. For this I am to blame – likewise for omitting certain explicit cautions, which the pages that follow will now in part supply.

[1] Reprint from the *Philosophical Review*, January 1908 (vol. 17, p. 1).

First misunderstanding: Pragmatism is only a re-editing of positivism

This seems the commonest mistake. Scepticism, positivism and agnosticism agree with ordinary dogmatic rationalism in presupposing that everybody knows what the word 'truth' means, without further explanation. But the former doctrines then either suggest or declare that real truth, absolute truth, is inaccessible to us, and that we must fain put up with relative or phenomenal truth as its next best substitute. By scepticism this is treated as an unsatisfactory state of affairs, while positivism and agnosticism are cheerful about it, call real truth sour grapes, and consider phenomenal truth quite sufficient for all our 'practical' purposes.

In point of fact, nothing could be farther from all this than what pragmatism has to say of truth. Its thesis is an altogether previous one. It leaves off where these other theories begin, having contented itself with the word truth's *definition*. 'No matter whether any mind extant in the universe possess truth or not', it asks, 'what does the notion of truth signify *ideally*?' 'What kind of things would true judgments be *in case* they existed?' The answer which pragmatism offers is intended to cover the most complete truth that can be conceived of, 'absolute' truth if you like, as well as truth of the most relative and imperfect description. This question of what truth would be like if it did exist, belongs obviously to a purely speculative field of inquiry. It is not a psychological, but rather a logical question. It is not a theory about any sort of reality, or about what kind of knowledge is actually possible; it abstracts from particular terms altogether, and defines the nature of a possible relation between two of them.

As Kant's question about synthetic judgments had escaped previous philosophers, so the pragmatist question is not only so subtle as to have escaped attention hitherto, but even so subtle, it would seem, that when openly broached now, dogmatists and sceptics alike fail to apprehend it, and deem the pragmatist to be treating of something wholly different. He insists, they say (I quote an actual critic), 'that the greater problems are insoluble by human intelligence, that our need of knowing truly is artificial and illusory, and that our reason, incapable of reaching the foundations of reality, must turn itself exclusively towards *action*.' There could not be a worse misapprehension.

Second misunderstanding: Pragmatism is primarily an appeal to action.

The name 'pragmatism', with its suggestions of action, has been an unfortunate choice, I have to admit, and has played into the hands of this mistake. But no word could protect the doctrine from critics so blind to the nature of the inquiry that, when Dr Schiller speaks of ideas 'working' well, the only thing they think of is their immediate workings in the physical environment, their enabling us to make money, or gain some similar 'practical' advantage. Ideas do work thus, of course, immediately or remotely; but they work indefinitely inside of the mental world also. Not crediting us with this rudimentary insight, our critics treat our view as offering itself exclusively to engineers, doctors, financiers, and men of action generally, who need some sort of a rough and ready *weltanschauung*, but have no time or wit to study genuine philosophy. It is usually described as a character-istically American movement, a sort of bobtailed scheme of thought, excellently fitted for the man on the street, who naturally hates theory and wants cash returns immediately.

It is quite true that, when the refined theoretic question that pragmatism begins with is once answered, secondary corollaries of a practical sort follow. Investigation shows that, in the function called truth, previous realities are not the only indepen-dent variables. To a certain extent our ideas, being realities, are also independent variables, and, just as they follow other reality and fit it, so, in a measure, does other reality follow and fit them. When they add themselves to being, they partly redeter-mine the existent, so that reality as a whole appears incompletely definable unless ideas also are kept account of. This pragmatist doctrine, exhibiting our ideas as complemental factors of reality, throws open (since our ideas are instigators of our action) a wide window upon human action, as well as a wide licence to originality in thought. But few things could be sillier than to ignore the prior epistemological edifice in which the window is built, or to talk as if pragmatism began and ended at the window. This, nevertheless, is what our critics do almost without exception. They ignore our primary step and its motive, and make the relation to action, which is our secondary achievement, primary.

Third misunderstanding: Pragmatists cut themselves off from the right to believe in ejective realities

They do so, according to the critics, by making the truth of our beliefs consist in their verifiability, and their verifiability in the way in which they do work for us. Professor Stout, in his otherwise admirable and helpful review of Schiller in *Mind* for October, 1907, considers that this ought to lead Schiller (could he sincerely realize the effects of his own doctrine) to the absurd consequence of being unable to believe genuinely in another man's headache, even were the headache there. He can only 'postulate' it for the sake of the working value of the postulate to himself. The postulate guides certain of his acts and leads to advantageous consequences; but the moment he understands fully that the postulate is true *only*(!) in this sense, it ceases (or should cease) to be true for him that the other man really *has* a headache. All that makes the postulate most precious then evaporates: his interest in his fellow-man 'becomes a veiled form of self-interest, and his world becomes cold, dull and heartless'.

Such an objection makes a curious muddle of the pragmatist's universe of discourse. Within that universe the pragmatist finds someone with a headache or other feeling, and someone else who postulates that feeling. Asking on what condition the postulate is 'true', the pragmatist replies that, for the postulator at any rate, it is true just in proportion as to believe in it works in him the fuller sum of satisfactions. What is it that is satisfactory here? Surely to *believe* in the postulated object, namely, in the really existing feeling of the other man. But how (especially if the postulator were himself a thoroughgoing pragmatist) could it ever be satisfactory to him *not* to believe in that feeling, so long as, in Professor Stout's words, disbelief 'made the world seem to him cold, dull, and heartless'? Disbelief would seem, on pragmatist principles, quite out of the question under such conditions, unless the heartlessness of the world were made probable already on other grounds. And since the belief in the headache, true for the subject assumed in the pragmatist's universe of discourse, is also true for the pragmatist who for his epistemologizing purposes has assumed that entire universe, why is it not true in that universe absolutely? The headache believed in is a reality there, and no extant mind disbelieves it, neither the critic's mind nor his subject's! Have our opponents any better brand of truth in this real universe of ours that they can show us?[2]

So much for the third misunderstanding, which is but one specification of the following still wider one.

Fourth misunderstanding: No pragmatist can be a realist in his epistemology

This is supposed to follow from his statement that the truth of our beliefs consists in general in their giving satisfaction. Of course satisfaction *per se* is a subjective condition; so the conclusion is drawn that truth falls wholly inside of the subject who then may manufacture it at his pleasure. True beliefs become thus wayward affections, severed from all responsibility to other parts of experience.

It is difficult to excuse such a parody of the pragmatist's opinion, ignoring as it does every element but one of his universe of discourse. The terms of which that universe consists positively forbid any non-realistic interpretation of the function of knowledge defined there. The pragmatizing epistemologist posits there

[2] I see here a chance to forestall a criticism which someone may make on Lecture 3 of my *Pragmatism*, where I said that 'God' and 'matter' might be regarded as synonymous terms, so long as no differing future consequences were deducible from the two conceptions. The passage was transcribed from my address at the California Philosophical Union, reprinted in the *Journal of Philosophy*, vol. 1, p. 673. I had no sooner given the address than I perceived a flaw in that part of it; but I have left the passage unaltered ever since, because the flaw did not spoil its illustrative value. The flaw was evident when, as a case analogous to that of a godless universe, I thought of what I called an 'automatic sweetheart', meaning a soulless body which should be absolutely indistinguishable from a spiritually animated maiden, laughing, talking, blushing, nursing us, and performing all feminine offices as tactfully and sweetly as if a soul were in her. Would anyone regard her as a full equivalent? Certainly not, and why? Because, framed as we are, our egoism craves above all things inward sympathy and recognition, love and admiration. The outward treatment is valued mainly as an expression, as a manifestation of the accompanying consciousness believed in. Pragmatically, then, belief in the automatic sweetheart would not *work*, and in point of fact no one treats it as a serious hypothesis. The godless universe would be exactly similar. Even if matter could do every outward thing that God does, the idea of it would not work as satisfactorily, because the chief call for a god on modern men's part is for a being who will inwardly recognize them and judge them sympathetically. Matter disappoints this craving of our ego, so God remains for most men the true hypothesis, and indeed remains so for definite pragmatic reasons.

a reality and a mind with ideas. What, now, he asks, can make those ideas true of that reality? Ordinary epistemology contents itself with the vague statement that the ideas must 'correspond' or 'agree'; the pragmatist insists on being more concrete, and asks what such 'agreement' may mean in detail. He finds first that the ideas must point to or lead towards *that* reality and no other, and then that the pointings and leadings must yield satisfaction as their result. So far the pragmatist is hardly less abstract than the ordinary slouchy epistemologist; but as he defines himself farther, he grows more concrete. The entire quarrel of the intellectualist with him is over his concreteness, intellectualism contending that the vaguer and more abstract account is here the more profound. The concrete pointing and leading are conceived by the pragmatist to be the work of other portions of the same universe to which the reality and the mind belong, intermediary verifying bits of experience with which the mind at one end, and the reality at the other, are joined. The 'satisfaction', in turn, is no abstract satisfaction *überhaupt*, felt by an unspecified being, but is assumed to consist of such satisfactions (in the plural) as concretely existing men actually do find in their beliefs. As we humans are constituted in point of fact, we find that to believe in other men's minds, in independent physical realities, in past events, in eternal logical relations, is satisfactory. We find hope satisfactory. We often find it satisfactory to cease to doubt. Above all we find *consistency* satisfactory, consistency between the present idea and the entire rest of our mental equipment, including the whole order of our sensations, and that of our intuitions of likeness and difference, and our whole stock of previously acquired truths.

The pragmatist, being himself a man, and imagining in general no contrary lines of truer belief than ours about the 'reality' which he has laid at the base of his epistemological discussion, is willing to treat our satisfaction as possibly really true guides to it, not as guides true solely for *us*. It would seem here to be the duty of his critics to show with some explictness why, being our subjective feelings, these satisfactions can *not* yield 'objective' truth. The beliefs which they accompany 'posit' the assumed reality, 'correspond' and 'agree' with it, and 'fit' it in perfectly definite and assignable ways, through the sequent trains of thought and action which form their verification, so merely to insist on using these words abstractly instead of concretely is no way of driving the pragmatist from the field – his more concrete account virtually includes his critic's. If our critics have any definite idea of a truth more objectively grounded than the kind we propose, why do they not show it more articulately? As they stand, they remind one of Hegel's man who wanted 'fruit', but rejected cherries, pears and grapes, because they were not fruit in the abstract. We offer them the full quart-pot, and they cry for the empty quart-capacity.

But here I think I hear some critic retort as follows: 'If satisfactions are all that is needed to make truth, how about the notorious fact that errors are so often satisfactory? And how about the equally notorious fact that certain true beliefs may cause the bitterest dissatisfaction? Isn't it clear that not the satisfaction which it gives, but the relation of the belief *to the reality* is all that makes it true? Suppose there were no such reality, and that the satisfactions yet remained: would they not then effectively work falsehood? Can they consequently be treated distinctively as the truth-builders? It is the *inherent relation to reality* of a belief that gives us that specific *truth*-satisfaction, compared with which all other satisfactions are the hollowest humbug. The satisfaction of *knowing truly* is thus the only one which the pragmatist ought to have considered. As a *psychological sentiment*, the anti-pragmatist gladly concedes it to him, but then only as a concomitant of truth, not as a constituent. What *constitutes* truth is not the sentiment, but the purely logical or objective function of rightly cognizing the reality, and the pragmatist's failure to reduce this function to lower values is patent.'

Such anti-pragmatism as this seems to me a tissue of confusion. To begin with, when the pragmatist says 'indispensable', it confounds this with 'sufficient'. The pragmatist calls satisfactions indispensable for truth-building, but I have everywhere called them insufficient unless reality be also incidentally led to. If the reality assumed were cancelled from the pragmatist's universe of discourse, he would straightaway give the name of falsehoods to the beliefs remaining, in spite of all their satisfactoriness. For him, as for his critic, there can be no truth if there is nothing to be true about. Ideas are so much flat psychological surface unless some mirrored matter gives them cognitive lustre. This is why as a pragmatist I have so carefully posited 'reality' *ab initio*, and why, throughout my whole discussion, I remain an epistemological realist.[3]

The anti-pragmatist is guilty of the further confusion of imagining that, in undertaking to give him an account of what truth formally means, we are assuming at the same time to provide a warrant for it, trying to define the occasions when he can be sure of materially possessing it. Our making it hinge on a reality so 'independent' that when it comes, truth comes, and when it goes, truth goes with it, disappoints this naive expectation, so he deems our description unsatisfactory. I suspect that under this confusion lies the still deeper one of not discriminating sufficiently between the two notions, truth and reality. Realities are not *true*, they *are*; and beliefs are true *of* them. But I suspect that in the anti-pragmatist mind the two notions sometimes swap their attributes. The reality itself, I fear, is treated as if 'true', and conversely. Who so tells us of the one, it is then supposed, must also be telling us of the other; and a true idea must in a manner *be*, or at least *yield* without extraneous aid, the reality it cognitively is possessed of.

To this absolute-idealistic demand pragmatism simply opposes its *non possumus*. If there is to be truth, it says, both realities and beliefs about them must conspire to make it; but whether there ever is such a thing, or how anyone can be sure that his own beliefs possess it, it never pretends to determine. That truth-satisfaction *par excellence* which may tinge a belief unsatisfactory in other ways, it easily explains as the feeling of consistency with the stock of previous truths, or supposed truths, of which one's whole past experience may have left one in possession.

But are not all pragmatists sure that their own belief is right? their enemies will ask at this point; and this leads me to the

Fifth misunderstanding: What pragmatists say is inconsistent with their saying so

A correspondent puts this objection as follows: 'When you say to your audience, "pragmatism is the truth concerning truth", the first truth is different from the second. About the first you

---

[3] I need hardly remind the reader that both sense-percepts and percepts of ideal relation (comparisons, etc.) should be classed among the realities. The bulk of our mental 'stock' consists of truths concerning these terms.

and they are not to be at odds; you are not giving them liberty to take or leave it according as it works satisfactorily or not for their private uses. Yet the second truth, which ought to describe and include the first, affirms this liberty. Thus the *intent* of your utterance seems to contradict the *content* of it.'

General scepticism has always received the same classic refutation. 'You have to dogmatize', the rationalists say to the sceptics, 'whenever you express the sceptical position; so your lives keep contradicting your thesis.' One would suppose that the impotence of so hoary an argument to abate in the slightest degree the amount of general scepticism in the world might have led some rationalists themselves to doubt whether these instantaneous logical refutations are such fatal ways, after all, of killing off live mental attitudes. General scepticism is the live mental attitude of refusing to conclude. It is a permanent torpor of the will, renewing itself in detail towards each successive thesis that offers, and you can no more kill it off by logic than you can kill off obstinacy or practical joking. This is why it is so irritating. Your consistent sceptic never puts his scepticism into a formal proposition – he simply chooses it as a habit. He provokingly hangs back when he might so easily join us in saying yes, but he is not illogical or stupid – on the contrary, he often impresses us by his intellectual superiority. This is the *real* scepticism that rationalists have to meet, and their logic does not even touch it.

No more can logic kill the pragmatist's behaviour: his act of utterance, so far from contradicting, accurately exemplifies the matter which he utters. What is the matter which he utters? In part, it is this, that truth, concretely considered, is an attribute of our beliefs, and that these are attitudes that follow satisfactions. The ideas around which the satisfactions cluster are primarily only hypotheses that challenge or summon a belief to come and take its stand upon them. The pragmatist's idea of truth is just such a challenge. He finds it ultra-satisfactory to accept it, and takes his own stand accordingly. But, being gregarious as they are, men seek to spread their beliefs, to awaken imitation, to infect others. Why should not *you* also find the same belief satisfactory? thinks the pragmatist, and forthwith endeavours to convert you. You and he will then believe similarly; you will hold up your subject-end of a truth, which will be a truth objective and irreversible if the reality holds up the object-end by being itself present simultaneously. What there is of self-contradiction in all this I confess I cannot discover. The pragmatist's conduct in his own case seems to me on the contrary admirably to illustrate his universal formula; and of all epistemologists, he is perhaps the only one who is irreproachably self-consistent.

Sixth misunderstanding: Pragmatism explains not what truth is, but only how it is arrived at

In point of fact it tells us both, tells us what it is incidentally to telling us how it is arrived at – for what *is* arrived at except just what the truth is? If I tell you how to get to the railroad station, don't I implicitly introduce you to the *what*, to the being and nature of that edifice? It is quite true that the abstract *word* 'how' hasn't the same meaning as the abstract *word* 'what', but in this universe of concrete facts you cannot keep hows and whats asunder. The reasons why I find it satisfactory to believe that any idea is true, the *how* of my arriving at that belief, may be among the very reasons why the idea *is* true in reality. If not, I summon the anti-pragmatist to explain the impossibility articulately.

His trouble seems to me mainly to arise from his fixed inability to understand how a concrete statement can possibly mean as much, or be as valuable, as an abstract one. I said above that the main quarrel between us and our critics was that of concreteness *versus* abstractness. This is the place to develop that point farther.

In the present question, the links of experience sequent upon an idea, which mediate between it and a reality, form and for the pragmatist indeed *are*, the *concrete* relation of truth that may obtain between the idea and that reality. They, he says, are all that we mean when we speak of the idea 'pointing' to the reality, 'fitting' it, 'corresponding' with it, or 'agreeing' with it – they or other similar mediating trains of verification. Such mediating events *make* the idea 'true'. The idea itself, if it exists at all, is also a concrete event: so pragmatism insists that truth in the singular is only a collective name for truths in the plural, these consisting always of series of definite events; and that what intellectualism calls *the* truth, the *inherent* truth, of any one such series is only the abstract name for its truthfulness in act, for the fact that the ideas there do lead to the supposed reality in a way that we consider satisfactory.

The pragmatist himself has no objection to abstractions. Elliptically, and 'for short', he relies on them as much as anyone, finding upon innumerable occasions that their comparative emptiness makes of them useful substitutes for the overfullness of the facts he meets with. But he never ascribes to them a higher grade of reality. The full reality of a truth for him is always some process of verification, in which the abstract property of connecting ideas with objects truly is workingly embodied. Meanwhile it is endlessly serviceable to be able to talk of properties abstractly and apart from their working, to find them the same in innumerable cases, to take them 'out of time', and to treat of their relations to other similar abstractions. We thus form whole universes of Platonic ideas *ante rem*, universes *in posse*, though none of them exists effectively except *in rebus*. Countless relations obtain there which nobody experiences as obtaining – as, in the eternal universe of musical relations, for example, the notes of Aennchen von Tharau were a lovely melody long ere mortal ears ever heard them. Even so the music of the future sleeps now, to be awakened hereafter. Or, if we take the world of geometrical relations, the thousandth decimal of pi sleeps there, though no one may ever try to compute it. Or, if we take the universe of 'fitting', countless coats 'fit' backs, and countless boots 'fit' feet, on which they are not practically *fitted*; countless stones 'fit' gaps in walls into which no one seeks to fit them actually. In the same way countless opinions 'fit' realities, and countless truths are valid, though no thinker ever thinks them.

For the anti-pragmatist these prior timeless relations are the presupposition of the concrete ones, and possess the profounder dignity and value. The actual workings of our ideas in verification processes are as naught in comparison with the 'obtainings' of this discarnate truth within them.

For the pragmatist, on the contrary, all discarnate truth is static, impotent, and relatively spectral, full truth being the truth that energizes and does battle. Can anyone suppose that the sleeping quality of truth would ever have been abstracted or have received a name, if truths had remained forever in that storage vault of essential timeless 'agreements' and had never been embodied in any panting struggle of men's live ideas for verification? Surely no more than the abstract property of 'fitting' would have received a name, if in our world there had been no backs or feet or gaps in walls to be actually fitted. *Existential* truth is incidental to the actual competition of opinions. *Essential* truth, the truth of the intellectualists, the truth with no one thinking it, is like the coat that fits though no one has ever tried it on, like the music that no ear has listened to. It is less real, not more real, than the verified article; and to attribute a superior degree of glory to it seems little more than a piece of perverse abstraction-worship. As well might a pencil insist that the outline is the essential thing in all pictorial representation, and chide the paintbrush and the camera for omitting it, forgetting that *their* pictures not only contain the whole outline, but a hundred other things in addition. Pragmatist truth contains the whole of intellectualist truth and a hundred other things in addition. Intellectualist truth is then only pragmatist truth *in posse*. That on innumerable occasions men do substitute truth *in posse* or verifiability, for verification or truth in act, is a fact to which no one attributes more importance than the pragmatist: he emphasizes the practical utility of such a habit. But he does not on that account consider truth *in posse* – truth not alive enough ever to have been asserted or questioned or contradicted – to be the metaphysically prior thing, to which truths in act are tributary and subsidiary. When intellectualists do this, pragmatism charges them with inverting the real relation. Truth *in posse means* only truths in act; and he insists that these latter take precedence in the order of logic as well as in that of being.

Seventh misunderstanding: Pragmatism ignores the theoretic interest

This would seem to be an absolutely wanton slander, were not a certain excuse to be found in the linguistic affinities of the word 'pragmatism', and in certain offhand habits of speech of ours which assumed too great a generosity on our reader's part. When we spoke of the meaning of ideas consisting in their 'practical' consequences, or of the 'practical' differences which our beliefs make to us; when we said that the truth of a belief consists in its 'working' value, etc.; our language evidently was too careless, for by 'practical' we were almost unanimously held to mean *opposed* to theoretical or genuinely cognitive, and the consequence was punctually drawn that a truth in our eyes could have no relation to any independent reality, or to any other truth, or to anything whatever but the acts which we might ground on it or the satisfactions they might bring. The mere existence of the idea, all by itself, if only its results were satisfactory, would give full truth to it, it was charged, in our absurd pragmatist epistemology. The solemn attribution of this rubbish to us was also encouraged by two other circumstances. First, ideas are practically useful in the narrow sense, false ideas sometimes, but most often ideas which we can verify by the sum total of all their leadings, and the reality of whose objects may thus be considered established beyond doubt. That these ideas should be true in advance of and apart from their utility, that, in other words, their objects should be really there, is the very condition of their having that kind of utility – the objects they connect us with are so important that the ideas which serve as the objects' substitutes grow important also. This manner of their practical working was the first thing that made truths good in the eyes of primitive men; and buried among all the other good workings by which true beliefs are characterized, this kind of subsequential utility remains.

The second misleading circumstance was the emphasis laid by Schiller and Dewey on the fact that, unless a truth be relevant to the mind's momentary predicament, unless it be germane to the 'practical' situation – meaning by this the quite particular perplexity – it is no good to urge it. It doesn't meet our interests any better than a falsehood would under the same circumstances. But why our predicaments and perplexities might not be theoretical here as well as narrowly practical, I wish that our critics would explain. They simply assume that no pragmatist *can* admit a genuinely theoretic interest. Having used the phrase 'cash-value' of an idea, I am implored by one correspondent to alter it, 'for everyone thinks you mean only pecuniary profit and loss'. Having said that the true is 'the expedient in our thinking', I am rebuked in this wise by another learned correspondent: 'The word expedient has no other meaning than that of self-interest. The pursuit of this has ended by landing a number of officers of national banks in penitentiaries. A philosophy that leads to such results must be unsound.'

But the word 'practical' is so habitually loosely used that

more indulgence might have been expected. When one says that a sick man has now practically recovered, or that an enterprise has practically failed, one usually means just the opposite of practically in the literal sense. One means that, although untrue in strict practice, what one says is true in theory, true virtually, *certain to be* true. Again, by the practical one often means the distinctively concrete, the individual, particular and effective, as opposed to the abstract, general and inert. To speak for myself, whenever I have emphasized the practical nature of truth, this is mainly what has been in my mind. 'Pragmata' are things in their plurality; and in that early California address, when I described pragmatism as holding that 'the meaning of any proposition can always be brought down to some particular consequence, in our future practical experience, whether active or passive', I expressly added these qualifying words: 'the point lying rather in the fact that the experience must be particular, than the fact that it must be active' – by 'active' meaning here 'practical' in the narrow literal sense.[4] But particular consequences can perfectly well be of a theoretic nature. Every remote fact which we infer from an idea is a particular theoretic consequence which our mind practically works towards. The loss of every old opinion of ours which we see that we shall have to give up if a new opinion be true, is a particular theoretic as well as a particular practical consequence. After man's interest in breathing freely, the greatest of all his interests (because it never fluctuates or remits, as most of his physical interests do) is his interest in *consistency*, in feeling that what he now thinks goes with what he thinks on other occasions. We tirelessly compare truth with truth for this sole purpose. Is the present candidate for belief perhaps contradicted by principle number one? Is it compatible with fact number two? and so forth. The particular operations here are the purely logical ones of analysis, deduction, comparison, etc., and although general terms may be used

[4] The ambiguity of the word 'practical' comes out well in these words of a recent would-be reporter of our views: 'Pragmatism is an Anglo-Saxon reaction against the intellectualism and rationalism of the Latin mind ... Man, each individual man, is the measure of things. He is able to conceive none but relative truths, that is to say, illusions. What these illusions are worth is revealed to him, not by general theory, but by individual practice. Pragmatism, which consists in experiencing these illusions of the mind and obeying them by acting them out, is a *philosophy without words*, a philosophy of *gestures and of acts*, which abandons what is general and holds only to what is *particular*.' (Bourdeau, in *Journal des Débats*, 29 October 1907.)

ad libitum, the satisfactory *practical working* of the candidate-idea consists in the consciousness yielded by each successive theoretic consequence in particular. It is therefore simply idiotic to repeat that pragmatism takes no account of purely theoretic interests. All it insists on is that verity in act means *verifications*, and that these are always particulars. Even in exclusively theoretic matters, it insists that vagueness and generality serve to verify nothing.

Eighth misunderstanding: Pragmatism is shut up to solipsism

I have already said something about this misconception under the third and fourth heads, above, but a little more may be helpful. The objection is apt to clothe itself in words like these: 'You make truth to consist in every value except the cognitive value proper; you always leave your knower at many removes (or, at the uttermost, at one remove) from his real object; the best you do is to let his ideas carry him towards it; it remains forever outside of him', etc.

I think that the leaven working here is the rooted intellectualist persuasion that, to know a reality, an idea must in some inscrutable fashion possess or be it.[5] For pragmatism this kind of coalescence is inessential. As a rule our cognitions are only processes of mind off their balance and in motion towards real termini; and the reality of the termini, believed in by the states of mind in question, can be *guaranteed* only by some wider knower.[6] But if there is no reason extant in the universe why

[5] Sensations may, indeed, possess their objects or coalesce with them, as common-sense supposes that they do; and intuited differences between concepts may coalesce with the 'eternal' objective differences; but to simplify our discussion here we can afford to abstract from these very special cases of knowing.

[6] The transcendental idealist thinks that, in some inexplicable way, the finite states of mind are identical with the transfinite all-knower which he finds himself obliged to postulate in order to supply a *fundamentum* for the relation of knowing, as he apprehends it. Pragmatists can leave the question of identity open; but they cannot do without the wider knower any more than they can do without the reality, if they want to *prove* a case of knowing. They themselves play the part of the absolute knower for the universe of discourse which serves them as material for epistemologizing. They warrant the reality there, and the subject's true knowledge, there, of it. But whether what they themselves say about that whole universe is objectively true, i.e., whether the pragmatic theory of truth is true *really*, they cannot warrant – they can only believe it. To their hearers they can only *propose* it, as I propose it to my readers, as something to be verified *ambulando*, or by the way in which its consequences may confirm it.

they should be doubted, the beliefs are true in the only sense in which anything can be true anyhow: they are practically and concretely true, namely. True in the mystical mongrel sense of an *identitäts-philosophie* they need not be; nor is there any intelligible reason why they ever need be true otherwise than verifiably and practically. It is reality's part to possess its own existence; it is thought's part to get into 'touch' with it by innumerable paths of verification.

I fear that the 'humanistic' development of pragmatism may cause a certain difficulty here. We get at one truth only through the rest of truth; and the reality, everlastingly postulated as that which all our truth must keep in touch with, may never be given to us save in the form of truth other than that which we are now testing. But since Dr Schiller has shown that all our truths, even the most elemental, are affected by race inheritance with a human coefficient, reality *per se* thus may appear only as a sort of limit; it may be held to shrivel to the mere *place* for an object, and what is known may be held to be only matter of our psyche that we fill the place with.

It must be confessed that pragmatism, worked in this humanistic way, is *compatible* with solipsism. It joins friendly hands with the agnostic part of Kantism, with contemporary agnosticism, and with idealism generally. But worked thus, it is a metaphysical theory about the matter of reality, and flies far beyond pragmatism's own modest analysis of the nature of the knowing function, which analysis may just as harmoniously be combined with less humanistic accounts of reality. One of pragmatism's merits is that it is so purely epistemological. It must assume realities; but it prejudges nothing as to their constitution, and the most diverse metaphysics can use it as their foundation. It certainly has no special affinity with solipsism.

As I look back over what I have written, much of it gives me a queer impression, as if the obvious were set forth so condescendingly that readers might well laugh at my pomposity. It may be, however, that concreteness as radical as ours is not so obvious. The whole originality of pragmatism, the whole point in it, is its use of the concrete way of seeing it. It begins with concreteness, and returns and ends with it. Dr Schiller, with his two 'practical' aspects of truth, (1) relevancy to situation, and (2) subsequential utility, is only filling the cup of concreteness to the brim for us.

Once seize that cup, and you cannot misunderstand pragmatism. It seems as if the power of imagining the world concretely *might* have been common enough to let our readers apprehend us better, as if they might have read between our lines, and, in spite of all our infelicities of expression, guessed a little more correctly what our thought was. But alas! this was not on fate's programme, so we can only think, with the German ditty:

> *Es wär' zu schön gewesen,*
> *Es hat nicht sollen sein.*
> [It would have been too good,
> but it was not to be.]

5

The Meaning of the Word Truth[1]

My account of truth is realistic, and follows the epistemological dualism of common-sense. Suppose I say to you 'The thing exists' – is that true or not? How can you tell? Not till my statement has developed its meaning farther is it determined as being true, false or irrelevant to reality altogether. But if now you ask 'what thing?' and I reply 'a desk'; if you ask 'where?' and I point to a place; if you ask 'does it exist materially, or only in imagination?' and I say 'materially'; if moreover I say 'I mean that desk', and then grasp and shake a desk which you see just as I have described it, you are willing to call my statement true. But you and I are commutable here; we can exchange places; and as you go bail for my desk, so I can go bail for yours.

This notion of a reality independent of either of us, taken from ordinary social experience, lies at the base of the pragmatist definition of truth. With some such reality any statement, in order to be counted true, must agree. Pragmatism defines 'agreeing' to mean certain ways of 'working', be they actual or potential. Thus, for my statement 'the desk exists' to be true of a desk recognized as real by you, it must be able to lead me to shake your desk, to explain myself by words that suggest that desk to your mind, to make a drawing that is like the desk you see, etc. Only in such ways as this is there sense in saying it agrees with *that* reality, only thus does it gain for me the satisfaction of hearing you corroborate me. Reference then to something determinate, and some sort of adaptation to it worthy of the name of agreement, are thus constituent elements in the definition of any statement of mine as 'true'.

You cannot get at either the reference or the adaptation without using the notion of the workings. *That* the thing is,

[1] Remarks at the meeting of the American Philosophical Association, Cornell University, December 1907.

what it is, and *which* it is (of all the possible things with that what) are points determinable only by the pragmatic method. The 'which' means a possibility of pointing, or of otherwise singling out the special object; the 'what' means choice on our part of an essential aspect to conceive it by (and this is always relative to what Dewey calls our own 'situation'); and the 'that' means our assumption of the attitude of belief, the reality-recognizing attitude. Surely for understanding what the world 'true' means as applied to a statement, the mention of such workings is indispensable. Surely if we leave them out the subject and the object of the cognitive relation float – in the same universe, 'tis true – but vaguely and ignorantly and without mutual contact or mediation.

Our critics nevertheless call the workings inessential. No functional possibilities 'make' our beliefs true, they say; they are true inherently, true positively, born 'true' as the Count of Chambord was born 'Henri-Cinq'. Pragmatism insists, on the contrary, that statements and beliefs are thus inertly and statically true only by courtesy: they practically pass for true; but you *cannot define what you mean* by calling them true without referring to their functional possibilities. These give its whole *logical content* to that relation to reality on a belief's part to which the name 'truth' is applied, a relation which otherwise remains one of mere coexistence or bare witness.

The foregoing statements reproduce the essential content of the lecture on Truth in my book *Pragmatism*. Schiller's doctrine of 'humanism', Dewey's *Studies in Logical Theory*, and my own 'radical empiricism', all involve this general notion of truth as 'working', either actual or conceivable. But they envelop it as only one detail in the midst of much wider theories that aim eventually at determining the notion of what 'reality' at large is in its ultimate nature and constitution.

RADICAL EMPIRICISM

6

Radical Empiricism (1897)

Were I obliged to give a short name to the attitude in question, I should call it that of *radical empiricism*, in spite of the fact that such brief nicknames are nowhere more misleading than in philosophy. I say 'empiricism', because it is contented to regard its most assured conclusions concerning matters of fact as hypotheses liable to modification in the course of future experience; and I say 'radical', because it treats the doctrine of monism itself as an hypothesis, and, unlike so much of the halfway empiricism that is current under the name of positivism or agnosticism or scientific naturalism, it does not dogmatically affirm monism as something with which all experience has got to square. The difference between monism and pluralism is perhaps the most pregnant of all the differences in philosophy. *Prima facie* the world is a pluralism; as we find it, its unity seems to be that of any collection; and our higher thinking consists chiefly of an effort to redeem it from that first crude form. Postulating more unity than the first experiences yield, we also discover more. But absolute unity, in spite of brilliant dashes in its direction, still remains undiscovered, still remains a *Grenzbegriff*. 'Ever not quite' must be the rationalistic philosopher's last confession concerning it. After all that reason can do has been done, there still remains the opacity of the finite facts as merely given, with most of their peculiarities mutually unmediated and unexplained. To the very last, there are the various 'points of view' which the philosopher must distinguish in discussing the world; and what is inwardly clear from one point remains a bare externality and datum to the other. The negative, the alogical, is never wholly banished. Something – 'call it fate, chance, freedom, spontaneity, the devil, what you will' – is still wrong and other and outside and unincluded, from *your* point of view, even though you be the greatest of philosophers. Something is always mere fact and *givenness*; and there may be in the whole universe no one point of view extant from

which this would not be found to be the case. 'Reason', as a
gifted writer says, 'is but one item in the mystery; and behind
the proudest consciousness that ever reigned, reason and wonder
blushed face to face. The inevitable stales, while doubt and hope
are sisters. Not unfortunately the universe is wild – game-
flavoured as a hawk's wing. Nature is miracle all; the same
returns not save to bring the different. The slow round of the
engraver's lathe gains but the breadth of a hair, but the
difference is distributed back over the whole curve, never an
instant true – ever not quite.'[1]

This is pluralism, somewhat rhapsodically expressed. He who
takes for his hypothesis the notion that it is the permanent form
of the world is what I call a radical empiricist. For him the
crudity of experience remains an eternal element thereof. There
is no possible point of view from which the world can appear
an absolutely single fact. Real possibilities, real indetermina-
tions, real beginnings, real ends, real evil, real crises, catas-
trophes, and escapes, a real God, and a real moral life, just as
common-sense conceives these things, may remain in empiricism
as conceptions which that philosophy gives up the attempt either
to 'overcome' or to reinterpret in monistic form.

Many of my professionally trained *confrères* will smile at the
irrationalism of this view, and at the artlessness of my essays in
point of technical form. But they should be taken as illustrations
of the radically empiricist attitude rather than as argumentations
for its validity. That admits meanwhile of being argued in as
technical a shape as anyone can desire, and possibly I may be
spared to do later a share of that work. Meanwhile these essays
seem to light up with a certain dramatic reality the attitude
itself, and make it visible alongside of the higher and lower
dogmatisms between which in the pages of philosophic history
it has generally remained eclipsed from sight.

Radical Empiricism (1909)

Radical empiricism consists first of a postulate, next of a
statement of fact, and finally of a generalized conclusion.

The postulate is that the only things that shall be debatable

[1] B. P. Blood, *The Flaw in Supremacy*, published by the author, Amsterdam, NY,
1893.

among philosophers shall be things definable in terms drawn from experience. Things of an unexperienceable nature may exist *ad libitum*, but they form no part of the material for philosophic debate.

The statement of fact is that the relations between things, conjunctive as well as disjunctive, are just as much matters of direct particular experience, neither more so nor less so, than the things themselves.

The generalized conclusion is that therefore the parts of experience hold together from next to next by relations that are themselves parts of experience. The directly apprehended universe needs, in short, no extraneous trans-empirical connective support, but possesses in its own right a concatenated or continuous structure.

Does Consciousness Exist?

'Thoughts' and 'things' are names for two sorts of objects, which common-sense will always find contrasted and will always practically oppose to each other. Philosophy, reflecting on the contrast, has varied in the past in her explanations of it, and may be expected to vary in the future. At first, 'spirit and matter', 'soul and body', stood for a pair of equipollent substances quite on a par in weight and interest. But one day Kant undermined the soul and brought in the transcendental ego, and ever since then the bipolar relation has been very much off its balance. The transcendental ego seems nowadays in rationalist quarters to stand for everything, in empiricist quarters for almost nothing. In the hands of such writers as Schuppe, Rehmke, Natorp, Münsterberg – at any rate in his earlier writings, Schubert-Soldern and others, the spiritual principle attenuates itself to a thoroughly ghostly condition, being only a name for the fact that the 'content' of experience *is known*. It loses personal form and activity – these passing over to the content – and becomes a bare *Bewusstheit* or *Bewusstsein überhaupt*, of which in its own right absolutely nothing can be said.

I believe that 'consciousness', when once it has evaporated to this estate of pure diaphaneity, is on the point of disappearing altogether. It is the name of a nonentity, and has no right to a place among first principles. Those who still cling to it are clinging to a mere echo, the faint rumour left behind by the disappearing 'soul' upon the air of philosophy. During the past year, I have read a number of articles whose authors seemed just on the point of abandoning the notion of consciousness, and substituting for it that of an absolute experience not due to two factors. But they were not quite radical enough, not quite daring enough in their negations. For twenty years past I have mistrusted 'consciousness' as an entity; for seven or eight years past I have suggested its non-existence to my students, and tried to give them its pragmatic equivalent in realities of experience. It seems to me that the hour is ripe for it to be openly and universally discarded. ←

To deny plumply that 'consciousness' exists seems so absurd on the face of it – for undeniably 'thoughts' do exist – that I fear some readers will follow me no farther. Let me then immediately explain that I mean only to deny that the word stands for an entity, but to insist most emphatically that it does stand for a <u>function.</u> There is, I mean, no aboriginal stuff or quality of being, contrasted with that of which material objects are made, out of which our thoughts of them are made; but there is a function in experience which thoughts perform, and for the performance of which this quality of being is invoked. That function is *knowing*. 'Consciousness' is supposed necessary to explain the fact that things not only are, but get reported, are known. Whoever blots out the notion of consciousness from his list of first principles must still provide in some way for that function's being carried on.

I

My thesis is that if we start with the supposition that there is only one primal stuff or material in our world, a stuff of which everything is composed, and if we call that stuff 'pure experience', then knowing can easily be explained as a particular sort of relation towards one another into which portions of pure experience may enter. The relation itself is a part of pure experience; one of its 'terms' becomes the subject or bearer of the knowledge, the knower,[1] the other becomes the object known. This will need much explanation before it can be understood. The best way to get it understood is to contrast it with the alternative view; and for that we may take the recentest alternative, that in which the evaporation of the definite soul-substance has proceeded as far as it can go without being yet complete. If neo-Kantism has expelled earlier forms of dualism, we shall have expelled all forms if we are able to expel neo-Kantism in its turn.

For the thinkers I call neo-Kantian, the word consciousness

---

[1] In my *Psychology* I have tried to show that we need no knower other than the 'passing thought'. [See Chapter 12 below.]

today does no more than signalize the fact that experience is indefeasibly dualistic in its structure. It means that not subject, not object, but object-plus-subject is the minimum that can actually be. The subject—object distinction meanwhile is entirely different from that between mind and matter, from that between body and soul. Souls were detachable, had separate destinies, things could happen to them. To consciousness as such nothing can happen, for, timeless itself, it is only a witness of happenings in time, in which it plays no part. It is, in a word, but the logical correlative of 'content' in an Experience of which the peculiarity is that *fact comes to light* in it, that *awareness of content* takes place. Consciousness as such is entirely impersonal – 'self' and its activities belong to the content. To say that I am self-conscious, or conscious of putting forth volition, means only that certain contents, for which 'self' and 'effort of will' are the names, are not without witness as they occur.

Thus, for these belated drinkers at the Kantian spring, we should have to admit consciousness as an 'epistemological' necessity, even if we had no direct evidence of its being there.

But in addition to this, we are supposed by almost everyone to have an immediate consciousness of consciousness itself. When the world of outer fact ceases to be materially present, and we merely recall it in our memory, or fancy it, the consciousness is believed to stand out and to be felt as a kind of impalpable inner flowing, which, once known in this sort of experience, may equally be detected in presentations of the outer world. 'The moment we try to fix our attention upon consciousness and to see *what*, distinctly, it is', says a recent writer, 'it seems to vanish. It seems as if we had before us a mere emptiness. When we try to introspect the sensation of blue, all we can see is the blue; the other element is as if it were diaphanous. Yet it *can* be distinguished, if we look attentively enough, and know that there is something to look for.'[2] 'Consciousness' (*Bewusstheit*), says another philosopher, 'is inexplicable and hardly describable, yet all conscious experiences have this in common that what we call their content has this peculiar reference to a centre for which "self" is the name, in virtue of which reference alone the content is subjectively given, or appears . . . While in this way consciousness, or reference to a

[2] G. E. Moore, *Mind*, vol. 12, NS, p. 450

self, is the only thing which distinguishes a conscious content from any sort of being that might be there with no one conscious of it, yet this only ground of the distinction defies all closer explanations. The existence of consciousness, although it is the fundamental fact of psychology, can indeed be laid down as certain, can be brought out by analysis, but can neither be defined nor deduced from anything but itself.'[3]

'Can be brought out by analysis', this author says. This supposes that the consciousness is one element, moment, factor – call it what you like – of an experience of essentially dualistic inner constitution, from which, if you abstract the content, the consciousness will remain revealed to its own eye. Experience, at this rate, would be much like a paint of which the world pictures were made. Paint has a dual constitution, involving, as it does, a menstruum[4] (oil, size or what not) and a mass of content in the form of pigment suspended therein. We can get the pure menstruum by letting the pigment settle, and the pure pigment by pouring off the size or oil. We operate here by physical subtraction; and the usual view is, that by mental subtraction we can separate the two factors of experience in an analogous way – not isolating them entirely, but distinguishing them enough to know that they are two.

2

Now my contention is exactly the reverse of this. *Experience, I believe, has no such inner duplicity; and the separation of it into consciousness and content comes, not by way of subtraction, but by way of addition* – the addition, to a given concrete piece of it, of other sets of experiences, in connection with which severally its use or function may be of two different kinds. The paint will also serve here as an illustration. In a pot in a paint shop, along with other paints, it serves in its entirety as so much saleable matter. Spread on a canvas, with other paints around it, it represents, on the contrary, a feature in a picture and performs a spiritual function. Just so, I maintain, does a given

[3] Paul Natorp, *Einleitung in die Psychologie*, 1888, pp. 14, 112.
[4] 'Figuratively speaking, consciousness may be said to be the one universal solvent, or menstruum, in which the different concrete kinds of psychic acts and facts are contained, whether in concealed or in obvious form.' G. T. Ladd, *Psychology, Descriptive and Explanatory*, 1894, p. 30.

undivided portion of experience, taken in one context of associates, play the part of a knower, of a state of mind, of 'consciousness'; while in a different context the same undivided bit of experience plays the part of a thing known, of an objective 'content'. In a word, in one group it figures as a thought, in another group as a thing. (And, since it can figure in both groups simultaneously we have every right to speak of it as subjective and objective both at once.) The dualism connoted by such double-barrelled terms as 'experience', 'phenomenon', 'datum', 'Vorfindung' – terms which, in philosophy at any rate, tend more and more to replace the single-barrelled terms of 'thought' and 'thing' – that dualism, I say, is still preserved in this account, but reinterpreted, so that, instead of being mysterious and elusive, it becomes verifiable and concrete. It is an affair of relations, it falls outside, not inside, the single experience considered, and can always be particularized and defined.

The entering wedge for this more concrete way of understanding the dualism was fashioned by Locke when he made the word 'idea' stand indifferently for thing and thought, and by Berkeley when he said that what common-sense means by realities is exactly what the philosopher means by ideas. Neither Locke nor Berkeley thought his truth out into perfect clearness, but it seems to me that the conception I am defending does little more than consistently carry out the 'pragmatic' method which they were the first to use.

If the reader will take his own experiences, he will see what I mean. Let him begin with a perceptual experience, the 'presentation', so called, of a physical object, his actual field of vision, the room he sits in, with the book he is reading as its centre; and let him for the present treat this complex object in the common-sense way as being 'really' what it seems to be, namely, a collection of physical things cut out from an environing world of other physical things with which these physical things have actual or potential relations. Now at the same time it is just *those self-same things* which his mind, as we say, perceives; and the whole philosophy of perception from Democritus's time downwards has been just one long wrangle over the paradox that what is evidently one reality should be in two places at once, both in outer space and in a person's mind. 'Representative' theories of perception avoid the logical paradox, but on the other hand they violate the reader's sense of life, which knows no intervening mental image but seems to see the room and the book immediately just as they physically exist.

The puzzle of how the one identical room can be in two places is at bottom just the puzzle of how one identical point can be on two lines. It can, if it be situated at their intersection; and similarly, if the 'pure experience' of the room were a place of intersection of two processes, which connected it with different groups of associates respectively, it could be counted twice over, as belonging to either group, and spoken of loosely as existing in two places, although it would remain all the time a numerically single thing.

Well, the experience is a member of diverse processes that can be followed away from it along entirely different lines. The one self-identical thing has so many relations to the rest of experience that you can take it in disparate systems of association, and treat it as belonging with opposite contexts. In one of these contexts it is your 'field of consciousness'; in another it is 'the room in which you sit', and it enters both contexts in its wholeness, giving no pretext for being said to attach itself to consciousness by one of its parts or aspects, and to outer reality by another. What are the two processes, now, into which the room-experience simultaneously enters in this way?

One of them is the reader's personal biography, the other is the history of the house of which the room is part. The presentation, the experience, the *that* in short (for until we have decided *what* it is it must be a mere *that*) is the last term of a train of sensations, emotions, decisions, movements, classifications, expectations, etc., ending in the present, and the first term of a series of similar 'inner' operations extending into the future, on the reader's part. On the other hand, the very same *that* is the *terminus ad quem* of a lot of previous physical operations, carpentering, papering, furnishing, warming, etc., and the *terminus a quo* of a lot of future ones, in which it will be concerned when undergoing the destiny of a physical room. The physical and the mental operations form curiously incompatible groups. As a room, the experience has occupied that spot and had that environment for thirty years. As your field of consciousness it may never have existed until now. As a room, attention will go on to discover endless new details in it. As your mental state merely, few new ones will emerge under attention's eye. As a room, it will take an earthquake, or a gang of men, and in any case a certain amount of time, to destroy it. As your subjective state, the closing of your eyes, or any instantaneous play of your fancy will suffice. In the real world, fire will consume it. In your mind, you can let fire play over it without effect. As an outer object, you must pay so much a month to inhabit it. As an inner content, you may occupy it for any length of time rent-free. If, in short, you follow it in the mental direction, taking it along with events of personal biography solely, all sorts of things are true of it which are false, and false of it which are true if you treat it as a real thing experienced, follow it in the physical direction, and relate it to associates in the outer world.

3

So far, all seems plain sailing, but my thesis will probably grow less plausible to the reader when I pass from percepts to concepts, or from the case of things presented to that of things remote. I believe, nevertheless, that here also the same law holds good. If we take conceptual manifolds, or memories, or fancies, they also are in their first intention mere bits of pure experience, and, as such, are single *thats* which act in one context as objects, and in another context figure as mental states. By taking them in their first intention, I mean ignoring their relation to possible perceptual experiences with which they may be connected, which they may lead to and terminate in, and which then they may be supposed to 'represent'. Taking them in this way first, we confine the problem to a world merely 'thought-of' and not directly felt or seen. This world, just like the world of percepts, comes to us at first as a chaos of experiences, but lines of order soon get traced. We find that any bit of it which we may cut out as an example is connected with distinct groups of associates, just as our perceptual experiences are, that these associates link themselves with it by different relations,[5] and that one forms the inner history of a person, while the other acts as an impersonal 'objective' world, either spatial and temporal, or else merely logical or mathematical, or otherwise 'ideal'.

The first obstacle on the part of the reader to seeing that these

[5] Here as elsewhere the relations are of course *experienced* relations, members of the same originally chaotic manifold of non-perceptual experience of which the related terms themselves are parts.

non-perceptual experiences have objectivity as well as subjectivity will probably be due to the intrusion into his mind of *percepts*, that third group of associates with which the non-perceptual experiences have relations, and which, as a whole, they 'represent', standing to them as thoughts to things. This important function of the non-perceptual experiences complicates the question and confuses it; for, so used are we to treat percepts as the sole genuine realities that, unless we keep them out of the discussion, we tend altogether to overlook the objectivity that lies in non-perceptual experiences by themselves. We treat them, 'knowing' percepts as they do, as through and through subjective, and say that they are wholly constituted of the stuff called consciousness, using this term now for a kind of entity, after the fashion which I am seeking to refute.[6]

Abstracting, then, from percepts altogether, what I maintain is, that any single non-perceptual experience tends to get counted twice over, just as a perceptual experience does, figuring in one context as an object or field of objects, in another as a state of mind: and all this without the least internal self-diremption on its own part into consciousness and content. It is all consciousness in one taking; and, in the other, all content.

I find this objectivity of non-perceptual experiences, this complete parallelism in point of reality between the presently felt and the remotely thought, so well set forth in a page of Münsterberg's *Grundzüge*, that I will quote it as it stands.

'I may only think of my objects,' says Professor Münsterberg; 'yet, in my living thought they stand before me exactly as perceived objects would do, no matter how different the two ways of apprehending them may be in their genesis. The book here lying on the table before me, and the book in the next room of which I think and which I mean to get, are both in the same sense given realities for me, realities which I acknowledge and of which I take account. If you agree that the perceptual object is not an idea within me, but that percept and thing, as indistinguishably one, are really experienced *there*, *outside*, you ought not to believe that the merely thought-of object is hid away inside of the thinking subject. The object of which I think,

---

[6] Of the representative function of non-perceptual experience as a whole, I will say a word in a subsequent article: it leads too far into the general theory of knowledge for much to be said about it in a short paper like this.

and of whose existence I take cognizance without letting it now work upon my senses, occupies its definite place in the outer world as much as does the object which I directly see.

'What is true of the here and the there, is also true of the now and the then. I know of the thing which is present and perceived, but I know also of the thing which yesterday was but is no more, and which I only remember. Both can determine my present conduct, both are parts of the reality of which I keep account. It is true that of much of the past I am uncertain, just as I am uncertain of much of what is present if it be but dimly perceived. But the interval of time does not in principle alter my relation to the object, does not transform it from an object known into a mental state ... The things in the room here which I survey, and those in my distant home of which I think, the things of this minute and those of my long-vanished boyhood, influence and decide me alike, with a reality which my experience of them directly feels. They both make up my real world, they make it directly, they do not have first to be introduced to me and mediated by ideas which now and here arise within me ... This not-me character of my recollections and expectations does not imply that the external objects of which I am aware in those experiences should necessarily be there also for others. The objects of dreamers and hallucinated persons are wholly without general validity. But even were they centaurs and golden mountains, they still would be "off there", in fairy land, and not "inside" of ourselves.'[7]

This certainly is the immediate, primary, naive or practical way of taking our thought-of world. Were there no perceptual world to serve as its 'reductive', in Taine's sense, by being 'stronger' and more genuinely 'outer' (so that the whole merely thought-of world seems weak and inner in comparison), our world of thought would be the only world, and would enjoy complete reality in our belief. This actually happens in our dreams, and in our daydreams so long as percepts do not interrupt them.

And yet, just as the seen room (to go back to our late example) is *also* a field of consciousness, so the conceived or recollected room is *also* a state of mind; and the doubling-up of the experience has in both cases similar grounds.

[7] Münsterberg, *Grundzüge der Psychologie*, vol. 1, p. 48.

The room thought-of, namely, has many thought-of couplings with many thought-of things. Some of these couplings are inconstant, others are stable. In the reader's personal history the room occupies a single date – he saw it only the once perhaps, a year ago. Of the house's history, on the other hand, it forms a permanent ingredient. Some couplings have the curious stubbornness, to borrow Royce's term, of fact; others show the fluidity of fancy – we let them come and go as we please. Grouped with the rest of its house, with the name of its town, of its owner, builder, value, decorative plan, the room maintains a definite foothold, to which, if we try to loosen it, it tends to return, and to reassert itself with force.[8] With these associates, in a word, it coheres, while to other houses, other towns, other owners, etc., it shows no tendency to cohere at all. The two collections, first of its cohesive, and, second, of its loose associates, inevitably come to be contrasted. We call the first collection the system of external realities, in the midst of which the room, as 'real', exists; the other we call the stream of our internal thinking, in which, as a 'mental image', it for a moment floats.[9] The room thus again gets counted twice over. It plays two different roles, being *Gedanke* and *Gedachtes*, the thought-of-an-object, and the object-thought-of, both in one; and all this without paradox or mystery, just as the same material thing may be both low and high, or small and great, or bad and good, because of its relations to opposite parts of an environing world.

As 'subjective' we say that the experience represents; as 'objective' it is represented. What represents and what is represented is here numerically the same; but we must remember that no dualism of being represented and representing resides in the experience *per se*. In its pure state, or when isolated, there is no self-splitting of it into consciousness and what the consciousness is 'of'. Its subjectivity and objectivity are functional attributes solely, realized only when the experience is 'taken', i.e., talked of, twice, considered along with its two differing contexts

[8] Cf. A. L. Hodder, *The Adversaries of the Sceptic*, pp. 94–9.
[9] For simplicity's sake I confine my exposition to 'external' reality. But there is also the system of ideal reality in which the room plays its part. Relations of comparison, of classification, serial order, value, also are stubborn, assign a definite place to the room, unlike the incoherence of its places in the mere rhapsody of our successive thoughts.

respectively, by a new retrospective experience, of which that whole past complication now forms the fresh content.

The instant field of the present is at all times what I call the 'pure' experience. It is only virtually or potentially either object or subject as yet. For the time being, it is plain, unqualified actuality, or existence, a simple *that*. In this immediacy it is of course *valid*; it is *there*, we *act* upon it; and the doubling of it in retrospection into a state of mind and a reality intended thereby, is just one of the acts. The 'state of mind', first treated explicitly as such in retrospection, will stand corrected or confirmed, and the retrospective experience in its turn will get a similar treatment; but the immediate experience in its passing is always 'truth',[10] practical truth, *something to act on*, at its own movement. If the world were then and there to go out like a candle, it would remain truth absolute and objective, for it would be 'the last word', would have no critic, and no one would ever oppose the thought in it to the reality intended.[11]

I think I may now claim to have made my thesis clear. Consciousness connotes a kind of external relation, and does not denote a special stuff or way of being. *The peculiarity of our experiences, that they not only are, but are known, which their 'conscious' quality is invoked to explain, is better explained by their relations — these relations themselves being experiences — to one another.*

4

Were I now to go on to treat of the knowing of perceptual by conceptual experiences, it would again prove to be an affair of external relations. One experience would be the knower, the other the reality known; and I could perfectly well define, without the notion of 'consciousness', what the knowing

[10] Note the ambiguity of this term, which is taken sometimes objectively and sometimes subjectively.

[11] In the *Psychological Review* for July [1904], Dr R. B. Perry has published a view of consciousness which comes nearer to mine than any other with which I am acquainted. At present, Dr Perry thinks, every field of experience is so much 'fact'. It becomes 'opinion' or 'thought' only in retrospection, when a fresh experience, thinking the same object, alters and corrects it. But the corrective experience becomes itself in turn corrected, and thus experience as a whole is a process in which what is objective originally forever turns subjective, turns into our apprehension of the object. I strongly recommend Dr Perry's admirable article to my readers.

actually and practically amounts to – leading-towards, namely, and terminating-in percepts, through a series of transitional experiences which the world supplies. But I will not treat of this, space being insufficient.[12] I will rather consider a few objections that are sure to be urged against the entire theory as it stands.

5

First of all, this will be asked: 'If experience has not "conscious" existence, if it be not partly made of "consciousness", of what then is it made? Matter we know, and thought we know, and conscious content we know, but neutral and simple "pure experience" is something we know not at all. Say *what* it consists of – for it must consist of something – or be willing to give it up!'

To this challenge the reply is easy. Although for fluency's sake I myself spoke early in this article of a stuff of pure experience, I have now to say that there is no *general* stuff of which experience at large is made. There are as many stuffs as there are 'natures' in the things experienced. If you ask what any one bit of pure experience is made of, the answer is always the same: 'It is made of *that*, of just what appears, of space, of intensity, of flatness, brownness, heaviness, or what not.' Experience is only a collective name for all these sensible natures, and save for time and space (and, if you like, for 'being') there appears no universal element of which all things are made.

6

The next objection is more formidable, in fact it sounds quite crushing when one hears it first.

'If it be the self-same piece of pure experience, taken twice over, that serves now as thought and now as thing' – so the objection runs – 'how comes it that its attributes should differ so fundamentally in the two takings. As thing, the experience is extended; as thought, it occupies no space or place. As thing, it is red, hard, heavy; but who ever heard of a red, hard or heavy

---

[12] I have given a partial account of the matter in *Mind*, vol. 10, p. 27, 1885, and in the *Psychological Review*, vol. 2, p. 105, 1895. See also C. A. Strong's article in the *Journal of Philosophy*, 'Psychology and Scientific Methods', vol. 1, p. 253, 12 May 1904. I hope myself very soon to recur to the matter.

thought? Yet even now you said that an experience is made of just what appears, and what appears is just such adjectives. How can the one experience in its thing-function be made of them, consist of them, carry them as its own attributes, while in its thought-function it disowns them and attributes them elsewhere. There is a self-contradiction here from which the radical dualism of thought and thing is the only truth that can save us. Only if the thought is one kind of being can the adjectives exist in it "intentionally" (to use the scholastic term); only if the thing is another kind, can they exist in it constitutively and energetically. No simple subject can take the same adjectives and at one time be qualified by it, and at another time be merely "of it", as of something only meant or known.'

The solution insisted on by this objector, like many other common-sense solutions, grows the less satisfactory the more one turns it in one's mind. To begin with, *are* thought and thing as heterogeneous as is commonly said?

No one denies that they have some categories in common. Their relations to time are identical. Both, moreover, may have parts (for psychologists in general treat thoughts as having them); and both may be complex or simple. Both are of kinds, can be compared, added and subtracted and arranged in serial orders. All sorts of adjectives qualify our thoughts which appear incompatible with consciousness, being as such a bare diaphaneity. For instance, they are natural and easy, or laborious. They are beautiful, happy, intense, interesting, wise, idiotic, focal, marginal, insipid, confused, vague, precise, rational, casual, general, particular, and many things besides. Moreover, the chapters on 'perception' in the psychology books are full of facts that make for the essential homogeneity of thought with thing. How, if 'subject' and 'object' were separated 'by the whole diameter of being', and had no attributes in common, could it be so hard to tell, in a presented and recognized material object, what part comes in through the sense organs and what part comes 'out of one's own head'? Sensations and apperceptive ideas fuse here so intimately that you can no more tell where one begins and the other ends, than you can tell, in those cunning circular panoramas that have lately been exhibited, where the real foreground and the painted canvas join together.[13]

[13] Spencer's proof of his 'transfigured realism' (his doctrine that there is an

Descartes for the first time defined thought as the absolutely unextended, and later philosophers have accepted the description as correct. But what possible meaning has it to say that, when we think of a foot-rule or a square yard, extension is not attributable to our thought? Of every extended object the *adequate* mental picture must have all the extension of the object itself. The difference between objective and subjective extension is one of relation to a context solely. In the mind the various extents maintain no necessarily stubborn order relatively to each other, while in the physical world they bound each other stably, and, added together, make the great enveloping Unit which we believe in and call real space. As 'outer', they carry themselves adversely, so to speak, to one another, exclude one another and maintain their distances; while, as 'inner', their order is loose, and they form a *durcheinander* in which unity is lost.[14] But to argue from this that inner experience is absolutely inextensive seems to me little short of absurd. The two worlds differ, not by the presence or absence of extension, but by the relations of the extensions which in both worlds exist.

Does not this case of extension now put us on the track of truth in the case of other qualities? It does; and I am surprised that the facts should not have been noticed long ago. Why, for example, do we call a fire hot, and water wet, and yet refuse to say that our mental state, when it is 'of' these objects, is either wet or hot? 'Intentionally', at any rate, and when the mental state is a vivid image, hotness and wetness are in it just as much as they are in the physical experience. The reason is this, that, as the general chaos of all our experiences gets sifted, we find that there are some fires that will always burn sticks and always warm our bodies, and that there are some waters that will always put out fires; while there are other fires and waters that will not act at all. The general group of experiences that *act*, that do not only possess their natures intrinsically, but wear

---

absolutely non-mental reality) comes to mind as a splendid instance of the impossibility of establishing radical heterogeneity between thought and thing. All his painfully accumulated points of difference run gradually into their opposites, and are full of exceptions. Cf. Spencer, *Principles of Psychology*, Part 7, ch. 19.

[14] I speak here of the complete inner life in which the mind plays freely with its materials. Of course the mind's free play is restricted when it seeks to copy real things in real space.

them adjectively and energetically, turning them against one another, comes inevitably to be contrasted with the group whose members, having identically the same natures, fail to manifest them in the 'energetic' way. I make for myself now an experience of blazing fire; I place it near my body; but it does not warm me in the least. I lay a stick upon it, and the stick either burns or remains green, as I please. I call up water, and pour it on the fire, and absolutely no difference ensues. I account for all such facts by calling this whole train of experiences unreal, a mental train. Mental fire is what won't burn real sticks; mental water is what won't necessarily (though of course it may) put out even a mental fire. Mental knives may be sharp, but they won't cut real wood. Mental triangles are pointed, but their points won't wound. With 'real' objects, on the contrary, consequences always accrue; and thus the real experiences get sifted from the mental ones, the things from our thoughts of them, fanciful or true, and precipitated together as the stable part of the whole experience-chaos, under the name of the physical world. Of this our perceptual experiences are the nucleus, they being the originally *strong* experiences. We add a lot of conceptual experiences to them, making these strong also in imagination, and building out the remoter parts of the physical world by their means; and around this core of reality the world of laxly connected fancies and mere rhapsodical objects floats like a bank of clouds. In the clouds, all sorts of rules are violated which in the core are kept. Extensions there can be indefinitely located; motion there obeys no Newton's Laws.

7

There is a peculiar class of experiences to which, whether we take them as subjective or as objective, we *assign* their several natures as attributes, because in both contexts they affect their associates actively, though in neither quite as 'strongly' or as sharply as things affect one another by their physical energies. I refer here to *appreciations*, which form an ambiguous sphere of being, belonging with emotion on the one hand, and having objective 'value' on the other, yet seeming not quite inner nor quite outer, as if a diremption had begun but had not made itself complete.

Experiences of painful objects, for example, are usually also painful experiences; perceptions of loveliness, of ugliness, tend to pass muster as lovely or as ugly perceptions; intuitions of the morally lofty are lofty intuitions. Sometimes the adjective wanders as if uncertain where to fix itself. Shall we speak of seductive visions or of visions of seductive things? Of wicked desires or of desires for wickedness? Of healthy thoughts or of thoughts of healthy objects? Of good impulses, or of impulses towards the good? Of feelings of anger, or of angry feelings? Both in the mind and in the thing, these natures modify their context, exclude certain associates and determine others, have their mates and incompatibles. Yet not as stubbornly as in the case of physical qualities, for beauty and ugliness, love and hatred, pleasant and painful can, in certain complex experiences, coexist.

If one were to make an evolutionary construction of how a lot of originally chaotic pure experiences became gradually differentiated into an orderly inner and outer world, the whole theory would turn upon one's success in explaining how or why the quality of an experience, once active, could become less so, and, from being an energetic attribute in some cases, elsewhere lapse into the status of an inert or merely internal 'nature'. This would be the 'evolution' of the psychical from the bosom of the physical, in which the aesthetic, moral and otherwise emotional experiences would represent a halfway stage.

8

But a last cry of *non possumus* will probably go up from many readers. 'All very pretty as a piece of ingenuity,' they will say, 'but our consciousness itself intuitively contradicts you. We, for our part, *know* that we are conscious. We *feel* our thought, flowing as a life within us, in absolute contrast with the objects which it so unremittingly escorts. We cannot be faithless to this immediate intuition. The dualism is a fundamental datum: Let no man join what God has put asunder.'

My reply to this is my last word, and I greatly grieve that to many it will sound materialistic. I cannot help that, however, for I, too, have my intuitions and I must obey them. Let the case be what it may in others, I am as confident as I am of anything that, in myself, the stream of thinking (which I recognize emphatically as a phenomenon) is only a careless name for what, when scrutinized, reveals itself to consist chiefly of the stream of my breathing. The 'I think' which Kant said must be able to accompany all my objects, is the 'I breathe' which actually does accompany them. There are other internal facts besides breathing (intracephalic muscular adjustments, etc., of which I have said a word in my larger *Psychology*), and these increase the assets of 'consciousness', so far as the latter is subject to immediate perception;[15] but breath, which was ever the original of 'spirit', breath moving outwards, between the glottis and the nostrils, is, I am persuaded, the essence out of which philosophers have constructed the entity known to them as consciousness. *That entity is fictitious, while thoughts in the concrete are fully real. But thoughts in the concrete are made of the same stuff as things are.*

I wish I might believe myself to have made that plausible in this article. In another article I shall try to make the general notion of a world composed of pure experiences still more clear.

[15] *Principles of Psychology*, vol. 1, pp. 213–15 below.

PHILOSOPHICAL PSYCHOLOGY

8

The Scope of Psychology

Psychology is the science of mental life, both of its phenomena and their conditions. The phenomena are such things as we call feelings, desires, cognitions, reasonings, decisions, and the like; and, superficially considered, their variety and complexity is such as to leave a chaotic impression on the observer. The most natural and consequently the earliest way of unifying the material was, first, to classify it as well as might be, and, secondly, to affiliate the diverse mental modes thus found, upon a simple entity, the personal soul, of which they are taken to be so many facultative manifestations. Now, for instance, the soul manifests its faculty of memory, now of reasoning, now of volition, or again its imagination or its appetite. This is the orthodox 'spiritualistic' theory of scholasticism and of common-sense. Another and a less obvious way of unifying the chaos is to seek common elements *in* the diverse mental facts rather than a common agent behind them, and to explain them constructively by the various forms of arrangement of these elements, as one explains houses by stones and bricks. The 'associationist' schools of Herbart in Germany, and of Hume, the Mills and Bain in Britain have thus constructed a *psychology without a soul* by taking discrete 'ideas', faint or vivid, and showing how, by their cohesions, repulsions, and forms of succession, such things as reminiscences, perceptions, emotions, volitions, passions, theories, and all the other furnishings of an individual's mind may be engendered. The very self or ego of the individual comes in this way to be viewed no longer as the pre-existing source of the representations, but rather as their last and most complicated fruit.

Now, if we strive rigorously to simplify the phenomena in either of these ways, we soon become aware of inadequacies in our method. Any particular cognition, for example, or recollection, is accounted for on the soul-theory by being referred to the spiritual faculties of cognition or of memory. These faculties themselves are thought of as absolute properties of the soul; that is, to take the case of memory, no reason is given why we should remember a fact as it happened, except that so to remember it constitutes the essence of our recollective power. We may, as spiritualists, try to explain our memory's failures and blunders by secondary causes. But its *successes* can invoke no factors save the existence of certain objective things to be remembered on the one hand, and of our faculty of memory on the other. When, for instance, I recall my graduation day, and drag all its incidents and emotions up from death's dateless night, no mechanical cause can explain this process, nor can any analysis reduce it to lower terms or make its nature seem other than an ultimate datum, which, whether we rebel or not at its mysteriousness, must simply be taken for granted if we are to psychologize at all. However the associationist may represent the present ideas as thronging and arranging themselves, still, the spiritualist insists, he has in the end to admit that *something*, be it brain, be it 'ideas', be it 'association', *knows* past time *as* past, and fills it out with this or that event. And when the spiritualist calls memory an 'irreducible faculty', he says no more than this admission of the associationist already grants.

And yet the admission is far from being a satisfactory simplification of the concrete facts. For why should this absolute God-given faculty retain so much better the events of yesterday than those of last year, and, best of all, those of an hour ago? Why, again, in old age should its grasp of childhood's events seem firmest? Why should illness and exhaustion enfeeble it? Why should repeating an experience strengthen our recollection of it? Why should drugs, fevers, asphyxia and excitement resuscitate things long since forgotten? If we content ourselves with merely affirming that the faculty of memory is so peculiarly constituted by nature as to exhibit just these oddities, we seem little the better for having invoked it, for our explanation becomes as complicated as that of the crude facts with which we started. Moreover there is something grotesque and irrational in the supposition that the soul is equipped with elementary powers of such an ingeniously intricate sort. Why *should* our memory cling more easily to the near than the remote? Why should it lose its grasp of proper sooner than of abstract names? Such peculiarities seem quite fantastic; and might, for aught we can see *a priori*, be the precise opposites of what they are. Evidently, then, *the faculty does not exist absolutely, but works under conditions*; and *the quest of the conditions* becomes the psychologist's most interesting task.

However firmly he may hold to the soul and her remembering faculty, he must acknowledge that she never exerts the latter without a *cue*, and that something must always precede and *remind* us of whatever we are to recollect. '*An idea*!' says the associationist, 'an idea associated with the remembered thing; and this explains also why things repeatedly met with are more easily recollected, for their associates on the various occasions furnish so many distinct avenues of recall.' But this does not explain the effects of fever, exhaustion, hypnotism, old age, and the like. And in general, the pure associationist's account of our mental life is almost as bewildering as that of the pure spiritualist. This multitude of ideas, existing absolutely, yet clinging together, and weaving an endless carpet of themselves, like dominoes in ceaseless change, or the bits of glass in a kaleidoscope – whence do they get their fantastic laws of clinging, and why do they cling in just the shapes they do?

For this the associationist must introduce the order of experience in the outer world. The dance of the ideas is a copy, somewhat mutilated and altered, of the order of phenomena. But the slightest reflection shows that phenomena have absolutely no power to influence our ideas until they have first impressed our senses and our brain. The bare existence of a past fact is no ground for our remembering it. Unless we have seen it, or somehow *undergone* it, we shall never know of its having been. The experiences of the body are thus one of the conditions of the faculty of memory being what it is. And a very small amount of reflection on facts shows that one part of the body, namely, the brain, is the part whose experiences are directly concerned. If the nervous communication be cut off between the brain and other parts, the experiences of those other parts are non-existent for the mind. The eye is blind, the ear deaf, the hand insensible and motionless. And conversely, if the brain be injured, consciousness is abolished or altered, even although every other organ in the body be ready to play its normal part. A blow on the head, a sudden subtraction of blood, the pressure of an apoplectic haemorrhage, may have the first effect; whilst a very few ounces of alcohol or grains of opium or hashish, or a whiff of chloroform or nitrous oxide gas, are sure to have the second. The delirium of fever, the altered self of insanity, are all due to foreign matters circulating through the brain, or to pathological changes in that organ's substance. The fact that the brain is the one immediate bodily condition of the mental operations is indeed so universally admitted nowadays that I need spend no more time in illustrating it, but will simply postulate it and pass on. The whole remainder of the book will be more or less of a proof that the postulate was correct.

Bodily experiences, therefore, and more particularly brain experiences, must take place amongst those conditions of the mental life of which psychology need take account. *The spiritualist and the associationist must both be 'cerebralists'*, to the extent at least of admitting that certain peculiarities in the way of working of their own favourite principles are explicable only by the fact that the brain laws are a codeterminant of the result.

Our first conclusion, then, is that a certain amount of brain physiology must be presupposed or included in psychology.[1]

In still another way the psychologist is forced to be something of a nerve physiologist. Mental phenomena are not only conditioned *a parte ante* by bodily processes; but they lead to them *a parte post*. That they lead to *acts* is of course the most familiar of truths, but I do not merely mean acts in the sense of voluntary and deliberate muscular performances. Mental states occasion also changes in the calibre of blood vessels, or alteration in the heart beats, or processes more subtle still, in glands and viscera. If these are taken into account, as well as acts which follow at some *remote period* because the mental state was once there, it will be safe to lay down the general law that *no mental modification ever occurs which is not accompanied or followed by a bodily change*. The ideas and feelings, e.g., which these present printed characters excite in the reader's mind not only occasion movements of his eyes and nascent movements of articulation in him, but will some day make him speak, or take sides in a discussion, or give advice, or choose a book to read, differently from what would have been the case had they never impressed his retina. Our psychology must therefore take

[1] Cf. Geo. T. Ladd, *Elements of Physiological Psychology* (1887) Pt 3, ch. 3, s. 9 and 12.

account not only of the conditions antecedent to mental states, but of their resultant consequences as well.

But actions originally prompted by conscious intelligence may grow so automatic by dint of habit as to be apparently unconsciously performed. Standing, walking, buttoning and unbuttoning, piano-playing, talking, even saying one's prayers, may be done when the mind is absorbed in other things. The performances of animal *instinct* seem semi-automatic, and the *reflex acts* of self-preservation certainly are so. Yet they resemble intelligent acts in bringing about the *same ends* at which the animals' consciousness, on other occasions, deliberately aims. Shall the study of such machine-like yet purposive acts as these be included in psychology?

The boundary-line of the mental is certainly vague. It is better not to be pedantic, but to let the science be as vague as its subject, and include such phenomena as these if by so doing we can throw any light on the main business in hand. It will ere long be seen, I trust, that we can; and that we gain much more by a broad than by a narrow conception of our subject. At a certain stage in the development of every science a degree of vagueness is what best consists with fertility. On the whole, few recent formulas have done more real service of a rough sort in psychology than the Spencerian one that the essence of mental life and of bodily life are one, namely, 'the adjustment of inner to outer relations'. Such a formula is vagueness incarnate; but because it takes into account the fact that minds inhabit environments which act on them and on which they in turn react; because, in short, it takes mind in the midst of all its concrete relations, it is immensely more fertile than the old-fashioned 'rational psychology', which treated the soul as a detached existent, sufficient unto itself, and assumed to consider only its nature and properties. I shall therefore feel free to make any sallies into zoology or into pure nerve physiology which may seem instructive for our purposes, but otherwise shall leave those sciences to the physiologists.

Can we state more distinctly still the manner in which the mental life seems to intervene between impressions made from without upon the body, and reactions of the body upon the outer world again? Let us look at a few facts.

If some iron filings be sprinkled on a table and a magnet brought near them, they will fly through the air for a certain distance and stick to its surface. A savage seeing the phenomenon explains it as the result of an attraction or love between the magnet and the filings. But let a card cover the poles of the magnet, and the filings will press forever against its surface without its ever occurring to them to pass around its sides and thus come into more direct contact with the object of their love. Blow bubbles through a tube into the bottom of a pail of water, they will rise to the surface and mingle with the air. Their action may again be poetically interpreted as due to a longing to recombine with the mother-atmosphere above the surface. But if you invert a jar full of water over the pail, they will rise and remain lodged beneath its bottom, shut in from the outer air, although a slight deflection from their course at the outset, or a re-descent towards the rim of the jar when they found their upward course impeded, would easily have set them free.

If now we pass from such actions as these to those of living things, we notice a striking difference. Romeo wants Juliet as the filings want the magnet; and if no obstacles intervene he moves towards her by as straight a line as they. But Romeo and Juliet, if a wall be built between them, do not remain idiotically pressing their faces against its opposite sides like the magnet and the filings with the card. Romeo soon finds a circuitous way, by scaling the wall or otherwise, of touching Juliet's lips directly. With the filings the path is fixed; whether it reaches the end depends on accidents. With the lover it is the end which is fixed, the path may be modified indefinitely.

Suppose a living frog in the position in which we placed our bubbles of air, namely, at the bottom of a jar of water. The want of breath will soon make him also long to rejoin the mother-atmosphere, and he will take the shortest path to his end by swimming straight upwards. But if a jar full of water be inverted over him, he will not, like the bubbles, perpetually press his nose against its unyielding roof, but will restlessly explore the neighbourhood until by re-descending again he has discovered a path round its brim to the goal of his desires. Again the fixed end, the varying means!

Such contrasts between living and inanimate performances end by leading men to deny that in the physical world final purposes exist at all. Loves and desires are today no longer imputed to particles of iron or of air. No one supposes now that the end of any activity which they may display is an ideal purpose presiding over the activity from its outset and soliciting or drawing it into being by a sort of *vis a fronte*. The end, on the contrary, is deemed a mere passive result, pushed into being *a tergo*, having had, so to speak, no voice in its own production. Alter the pre-existing conditions, and with inorganic materials you bring forth each time a different apparent end. But with intelligent agents, altering the conditions changes the activity displayed, but not the end reached; for here the idea of the yet unrealized end co-operates with the conditions to determine what the activities shall be.

The pursuance of future ends and the choice of means for their attainment are thus the mark and criterion of the presence of mentality in a phenomenon. We all use this test to discriminate between an intelligent and a mechanical performance. We impute no mentality to sticks and stones, because they never seem to move for *the sake of* anything, but always when pushed, and then indifferently and with no sign of choice. So we unhesitatingly call them senseless.

Just so we form our decision upon the deepest of all philosophic problems: Is the Kosmos an expression of intelligence rational in its inward nature, or a brute external fact pure and simple? If we find ourselves, in contemplating it, unable to banish the impression that it is a realm of final purposes, that it exists for the sake of something, we place intelligence at the heart of it and have a religion. If, on the contrary, in surveying its irremediable flux, we can think of the present only as so much mere mechanical sprouting from the past, occurring with no reference to the future, we are atheists and materialists.

In the lengthy discussions which psychologists have carried on about the amount of intelligence displayed by lower mammals, or the amount of consciousness involved in the functions of the nerve centres of reptiles, the same test has always been applied: Is the character of the actions such that we must believe them to be performed *for the sake* of their result? The result in question, as we shall hereafter abundantly see, is as a rule a useful one – the animal is, on the whole, safer under the circumstances for bringing it forth. So far the action has a teleological character; but such mere outward teleology as this might still be the blind result of *vis a tergo*. The growth and movements of plants, the processes of development, digestion, secretion, etc., in animals, supply innumerable instances of performances useful to the invididual which may nevertheless be, and by most of us are supposed to be, produced by automatic mechanism. The physiologist does not confidently assert conscious intelligence in the frog's spinal cord until he has shown that the useful result which the nervous machinery brings forth under a given irritation *remains the same when the machinery is altered*. If, to take the stock instance, the right knee of a headless frog be irritated with acid, the right foot will wipe it off. When, however, this foot is amputated, the animal will often raise the *left* foot to the spot and wipe the offending material away.

Pflüger and Lewes reason from such facts in the following way: If the first reaction were the result of mere machinery, they say; if that irritated portion of the skin discharged the right leg as a trigger discharges its own barrel of a shotgun; then amputating the right foot would indeed frustrate the wiping, but would not make the *left* leg move. It would simply result in the right stump moving through the empty air (which is in fact the phenomenon sometimes observed). The right trigger makes no effort to discharge the left barrel if the right one be unloaded; nor does an electrical machine ever get restless because it can only emit sparks, and not hem pillowcases like a sewing machine.

If, on the contrary, the right leg originally moved for the *purpose* of wiping the acid, then nothing is more natural than that, when the easiest means of effecting that purpose prove fruitless, other means should be tried. Every failure must keep the animal in a state of disappointment which will lead to all sorts of new trials and devices; and tranquillity will not ensue till one of these, by a happy stroke, achieves the wished-for end.

In a similar way Goltz ascribes intelligence to the frog's optic lobes and cerebellum. We alluded above to the manner in which a sound frog imprisoned in water will discover an outlet to the atmosphere. Goltz found that frogs deprived of their cerebral hemispheres would often exhibit a like ingenuity. Such a frog, after rising from the bottom and finding his farther upward progress checked by the glass bell which has been inverted over him, will not persist in butting his nose against the obstacle until dead of suffocation, but will often re-descend and emerge from under its rim as if, not a definite mechanical propulsion upwards, but rather a conscious desire to reach the air by hook or crook were the mainspring of his activity. Goltz concluded from this that the hemispheres are the seat of intellectual power in frogs. He made the same inference from observing that a brainless frog will turn over from his back to his belly when one of his legs is sewed up, although the movements required are then very different from those excited under normal circumstances by the same annoying position. They seem determined, consequently, not merely by the antecedent irritant, but by the final end – though the irritant of course is what makes the end desired.

Another brilliant German author, Liebmann,[2] argues against the brain's mechanism accounting for mental action, by very similar considerations. A machine as such, he says, will bring forth right results when it is in good order, and wrong results if out of repair. But both kinds of result flow with equally fatal necessity from their conditions. We cannot suppose the clock-work whose structure fatally determines it to a certain rate of speed, noticing that this speed is too slow or too fast and vainly trying to correct it. Its conscience, if it have any, should be as good as that of the best chronometer, for both alike obey equally well the same eternal mechanical laws – laws from behind. But if the *brain* be out of order and the man says, 'Twice four are two', instead of 'Twice four are eight', or else 'I must go to the coal to buy the wharf', instead of 'I must go to the wharf to buy the coal', instantly there arises a consciousness of error. The wrong performance, though it obey the same mechanical law as the right, is nevertheless condemned – condemned as contradicting the inner law – the law from in front, the purpose or ideal for which the brain *should* act, whether it does so or not.

We need not discuss here whether these writers in drawing their conclusion have done justice to all the premises involved in the cases they treat of. We quote their arguments only to show how they appeal to the principle that *no actions but such as are done for an end, and show a choice of means, can be called indubitable expressions of mind.*

I shall then adopt this as the criterion by which to circumscribe the subject matter of this work so far as action enters into

[2] *Zur Analysis der Wirklichkeit*, p. 489.

it. Many nervous performances will therefore be unmentioned, as being purely physiological. Nor will the anatomy of the nervous system and organs of sense be described anew. The reader will find in H. N. Martin's *Human Body*, in G. T. Ladd's *Physiological Psychology*, and in all the other standard anatomies and physiologies, a mass of information which we must regard as preliminary and take for granted in the present work.[3] Of the functions of the cerebral hemispheres, however, since they directly subserve consciousness, it will be well to give some little account.

[3] Nothing is easier than to familiarize oneself with the mammalian brain. Get a sheep's head, a small saw, chisel, scalpel and forceps (all three can best be had from a surgical instrument maker), and unravel its parts either by the aid of a human dissecting book, such as Holden's *Manual of Anatomy*, or by the specific directions *ad hoc* given in such books as Foster and Langley's *Practical Physiology* (Macmillan) or Morrell's *Comparative Anatomy and Dissection of Mammalia* (Longmans).

9

The Automaton Theory

In describing the functions of the hemispheres a short way back, we used language derived from both the bodily and the mental life, saying now that the animal made indeterminate and unforeseeable reactions, and anon that he was swayed by considerations of future good and evil; treating his hemispheres sometimes as the seat of memory and ideas in the psychic sense, and sometimes talking of them as simply a complicated addition to his reflex machinery. This sort of vacillation in the point of view is a fatal incident of all ordinary talk about these questions; but I must now settle my scores with those readers to whom I already dropped a word in passing and who have probably been dissatisfied with my conduct ever since.

Suppose we restrict our view to facts of one and the same plane, and let that be the bodily plane: cannot all the outward phenomena of intelligence still be exhaustively described? Those mental images, those 'considerations' whereof we spoke – presumably they do not arise without neural processes arising simultaneously with them, and presumably each consideration corresponds to a process *sui generis*, and unlike all the rest. In other words, however numerous and delicately differentiated the train of ideas may be, the train of brain events that runs alongside of it must in both respects be exactly its match, and we must postulate a neural machinery that offers a living counterpart for every shading, however fine, of the history of its owner's mind. Whatever degree of complication the latter may reach, the complication of the machinery must be quite as extreme, otherwise we should have to admit that there may be mental events to which no brain events correspond. But such an admission as this the physiologist is reluctant to make. It would violate all his beliefs. 'No psychosis without neurosis', is one form which the principle of continuity takes in his mind.

But this principle forces the physiologist to make still another step. If neural action is as complicated as mind; and if in the sympathetic system and lower spinal cord we see what, so far as we know, is unconscious neural action executing deeds that to all outward intent may be called intelligent; what is there to hinder us from supposing that even where we know consciousness to be there, the still more complicated neural action which we believe to be its inseparable companion is alone and of itself the real agent of whatever intelligent deeds may appear? 'As actions of a certain degree of complexity are brought about by mere mechanism, why may not actions of a still greater degree of complexity be the result of a more refined mechanism?' The conception of reflex action is surely one of the best conquests of physiological theory; why not be radical with it? Why not say that just as the spinal cord is a machine with few reflexes, so the hemispheres are a machine with many, and that that is all the difference? The principle of continuity would press us to accept this view.

But what on this view could be the function of the consciousness itself? *Mechanical* function it would have none. The sense organs would awaken the brain cells; these would awaken each other in rational and orderly sequence, until the time for action came; and then the last brain vibration would discharge downward onto the motor tracts. But this would be a quite autonomous chain of occurrences, and whatever mind went with it would be there only as an 'epiphenomenon', an inert spectator, a sort of 'foam, aura or melody' as Mr Hodgson says, whose opposition or whose furtherance would be alike powerless over the occurrences themselves. When talking, some time ago, we ought not, accordingly, *as physiologists*, to have said anything about 'considerations' as guiding the animal. We ought to have said 'paths left in the hemispherical cortex by former currents', and nothing more.

Now so simple and attractive is this conception from the consistently physiological point of view, that it is quite wonderful to see how late it was stumbled on in philosophy, and how few people, even when it has been explained to them, fully and easily realize its import. Much of the polemic writing against it is by men who have as yet failed to take it into their imaginations. Since this has been the case, it seems worthwhile to devote a few more words to making it plausible, before criticizing it ourselves.

To Descartes belongs the credit of having first been bold

enough to conceive of a completely self-sufficing nervous mechanism which should be able to perform complicated and apparently intelligent acts. By a singularly arbitrary restriction,
however, Descartes stopped short at man, and while contending
that in beasts the nervous machinery was all, he held that the
higher acts of man were the result of the agency of his rational
soul. The opinion that beasts have no consciousness at all was
of course too paradoxical to maintain itself long as anything
more than a curious item in the history of philosophy. And with
its abandonment the very notion that the nervous system *per se*
might work the work of intelligence, which was an integral,
though detachable part of the whole theory, seemed also to slip
out of men's conception, until, in this century, the elaboration
of the doctrine of reflex action made it possible and natural that
it should again arise. But it was not till 1870, I believe, that Mr
Hodgson made the decisive step, by saying that feelings, no
matter how intensely they may be present, can have no causal
efficacy whatever, and comparing them to the colours laid on
the surface of a mosaic, of which the events in the nervous
system are represented by the stones. Obviously the stones are
held in place by each other and not by the several colours which
they support.

About the same time Mr Spalding, and a little later Messrs
Huxley and Clifford, gave great publicity to an identical doctrine, though in their case it was backed by less refined metaphysical considerations.[1]

A few sentences from Huxley and Clifford may be subjoined
to make the matter entirely clear. Professor Huxley says:

> The consciousness of brutes would appear to be related to the
> mechanism of their body simply as a collateral product of its
> working, and to be as completely without any power of modifying
> that working as the steam whistle which accompanies the work of
> a locomotive engine is without influence on its machinery. Their

[1] The present writer recalls how in 1869, when still a medical student, he began to
write an essay showing how almost everyone who speculated about brain processes
illicitly interpolated into his account of them links derived from the entirely heterogeneous universe of feeling. Spencer, Hodgson (in his *Time and Space*), Maudsley,
Lockhart Clarke, Bain, Dr Carpenter, and other authors were cited as having been
guilty of the confusion. The writing was soon stopped because he perceived that the
view which he was upholding against these authors was a pure conception, with no
proofs to be adduced of its reality. Later it seemed to him that whatever *proofs*
existed really told in favour of their view.

volition, if they have any, is an emotion *indicative* of physical changes, not a *cause* of such changes ... The soul stands related to the body as the bell of a clock to the works, and consciousness answers to the sound which the bell gives out when it is struck ... Thus far I have strictly confined myself to the automatism of brutes ... It is quite true that, to the best of my judgment, the argumentation which applies to brutes holds equally good of men; and, therefore, that all states of consciousness in us, as in them, are immediately caused by molecular changes of the brain substance. It seems to me that in men, as in brutes, there is no proof that any state of consciousness is the cause of change in the motion of the matter of the organism. If these positions are well based, it follows that our mental conditions are simply the symbols in consciousness of the changes which take place automatically in the organism; and that, to take an extreme illustration, the feeling we call volition is not the cause of a voluntary act, but the symbol of that state of the brain which is the immediate cause of that act. We are conscious automata.

Professor Clifford writes:

All the evidence that we have goes to show that the physical world gets along entirely by itself, according to practically universal rules ... The train of physical facts between the stimulus sent into the eye, or to any one of our senses, and the exertion which follows it, and the train of physical facts which goes on in the brain, even when there is no stimulus and no exertion – these are perfectly complete physical trains, and every step is fully accounted for by mechanical conditions ... The two things are on utterly different platforms – the physical facts go along by themselves, and the mental facts go along by themselves. There is a parallelism between them, but there is no interference of one with the other. Again, if anybody says that the will influences matter, the statement is not untrue, but it is nonsense. Such an assertion belongs to the crude materialism of the savage. The only thing which influences matter is the position of surrounding matter or the motion of surrounding matter ... The assertion that another man's volition, a feeling in his consciousness that I cannot perceive, is part of the train of physical facts which I may perceive – this is neither true nor untrue, but nonsense; it is a combination of words whose corresponding ideas will not go together ... Sometimes one series is known better, and sometimes the other; so that in telling a story we speak sometimes of mental and sometimes of material facts. A feeling of chill made a man run; strictly speaking, the nervous disturbance which coexisted with that feeling of chill made him run, if we want to talk about material facts; or the feeling of chill produced the form of subconsciousness which coexists with the motion of legs, if we want to talk about mental facts . . . When, therefore, we ask: 'What is the physical link between the ingoing message from chilled skin and the outgoing message which moves the leg?' and the answer is, 'A man's will', we have as much right to be amused as if we had asked our friend with the picture what pigment was used in painting the cannon in the foreground, and received the answer, 'Wrought iron'. It will be found excellent practice in the mental operations required by this doctrine to imagine a train, the fore part of which is an engine and three carriages linked with iron couplings, and the hind part three other carriages linked with iron couplings; the bond between the two parts being made up out of the sentiments of amity subsisting between the stoker and the guard.

To comprehend completely the consequences of the dogma so confidently enunciated, one should unflinchingly apply it to the most complicated examples. The movements of our tongues and pens, the flashings of our eyes in conversation, are of course events of a material order, and as such their causal antecedents must be exclusively material. If we knew thoroughly the nervous system of Shakespeare, and as thoroughly all his environing conditions, we should be able to show why at a certain period of his life his hand came to trace on certain sheets of paper those crabbed little black marks which we for shortness' sake call the manuscript of *Hamlet*. We should understand the rationale of every erasure and alteration therein, and we should understand all this without in the slightest degree acknowledging the existence of the thoughts in Shakespeare's mind. The words and sentences would be taken, not as signs of anything beyond themselves, but as little outward facts, pure and simple. In like manner, we might exhaustively write the biography of those two hundred pounds, more or less, of warmish albuminoid matter called Martin Luther, without ever implying that it felt.

But, on the other hand, nothing in all this could prevent us from giving an equally complete account of either Luther's or Shakespeare's spiritual history, an account in which every gleam of thought and emotion should find its place. The mind-history would run alongside of the body-history of each man, and each point in the one would correspond to, but not react upon, a point in the other. So the melody floats from the harp string, but neither checks nor quickens its vibrations; so the shadow runs alongside the pedestrian, but in no way influences his steps.

Another inference, apparently more paradoxical still, needs to be made, though, as far as I am aware, Dr Hodgson is the only writer who has explicitly drawn it. That inference is that feelings, not causing nerve-actions, cannot even cause each other. To ordinary common-sense, felt pain is, as such, not only the cause of outward tears and cries, but also the cause of such inward events as sorrow, compunction, desire or inventive thought. So the consciousness of good news is the direct producer of the feeling of joy, the awareness of premises that of the belief in conclusions. But according to the automaton-theory, each of the feelings mentioned is only the correlate of some nerve movement whose *cause* lay wholly in a previous nerve movement. The first nerve movement called up the second; whatever feeling was attached to the second consequently found itself following upon the feeling that was attached to the first. If, for example, good news was the consciousness correlated with the first movement, then joy turned out to be the correlate in consciousness of the second. But all the while the items of the nerve series were the only ones in causal continuity; the items of the conscious series, however inwardly rational their sequence, were simply juxtaposed.

Reasons for the Theory

The 'conscious automaton-theory', as this conception is generally called, is thus a radical and simple conception of the manner in which certain facts may possibly occur. But between conception and belief, proof ought to lie. And when we ask, 'What proves that all this is more than a mere conception of the possible?' it is not easy to get a sufficient reply. If we start from the frog's spinal cord and reason by continuity, saying, as that acts so intelligently, *though unconscious*, so the higher centres, *though conscious*, may have the intelligence they show quite as mechanically based; we are immediately met by the exact counter argument from continuity, an argument actually urged by such writers as Pflüger and Lewes, which starts from the acts of the hemispheres, and says: 'As *these* owe *their* intelligence to the consciousness which we know to be there, so the intelligence of the spinal cord's acts must really be due to the invisible presence of a consciousness lower in degree.' All arguments from continuity work in two ways, you can either level up or down by their means; and it is clear that such arguments as these can eat each other up to all eternity.

There remains a sort of philosophic faith, bred like most faiths from an aesthetic demand. Mental and physical events are, on all hands, admitted to present the strongest contrast in the entire field of being. The chasm which yawns between them is less easily bridged over by the mind than any interval we know. Why, then, not call it an absolute chasm, and say not only that the two worlds are different, but that they are independent? This gives us the comfort of all simple and absolute formulas, and it makes each chain homogeneous to our consideration. When talking of nervous tremors and bodily actions, we may feel secure against intrusion from an irrelevant mental world. When, on the other hand, we speak of feelings, we may with equal consistency use terms always of one denomination, and never be annoyed by what Aristotle calls 'slipping into another kind'. The desire on the part of men educated in laboratories not to have their physical reasonings mixed up with such incommensurable factors as feelings is certainly very strong. I have heard a most intelligent biologist say: 'It is high time for scientific men to protest against the recognition of any such thing as consciousness in a scientific investigation.' In a word, feeling constitutes the 'unscientific' half of existence, and anyone who enjoys calling himself a 'scientist' will be too happy to purchase an untrammelled homogeneity of terms in the studies of his predilection, at the slight cost of admitting a dualism which, in the same breath that it allows to mind an independent status of being, banishes it to a limbo of causal inertness, from whence no intrusion or interruption on its part need ever be feared.

Over and above this great postulate that matters must be kept simple, there is, it must be confessed, still another highly abstract reason for denying causal efficacity to our feelings. We can form no positive image of the *modus operandi* of a volition or other thought affecting the cerebral molecules.

Let us try to imagine an idea, say of food, producing a movement, say of carrying food to the mouth . . . What is the method of its action? Does it assist the decomposition of the molecules of the gray matter, or does it retard the process, or does it alter the direction in which the shocks are distributed? Let us imagine the molecules of the gray matter combined in such a way that they will fall into simpler combinations on the impact of an incident force. Now suppose the incident force, in the shape of a shock from some other centre, to impinge upon these molecules. By hypothesis it will decompose them, and they will fall into the simpler combination. How is the idea of food to prevent this decomposition? Manifestly it can do so only by increasing the force which binds the molecules together. Good! Try to imagine the idea of a beefsteak binding two molecules together. It is impossible. Equally impossible is it to imagine a similar idea loosening the attractive force between two molecules.[2]

This passage from an exceedingly clever writer expresses admirably the difficulty to which I allude. Combined with a strong sense of the 'chasm' between the two worlds, and with a lively faith in reflex machinery, the sense of this difficulty can hardly fail to make one turn consciousness out of the door as a superfluity so far as one's explanations go. One may bow her out politely, allow her to remain as a 'concomitant', but one insists that matter shall hold all the power.

Having thoroughly recognized the fathomless abyss that separates mind from matter, and having so blended the very notion into his very nature that there is no chance of his ever forgetting it or failing to saturate with it all his meditations, the student of psychology has next to appreciate the association between these two orders of phenomena ... They are associated in a manner so intimate that some of the greatest thinkers consider them different aspects of the same process ... When the rearrangement of molecules takes place in the higher regions of the brain, a change of consciousness simultaneously occurs ... The change of consciousness never takes place without the change in the brain; the change in the brain never ... without the change in consciousness. But *why* the two occur together, or what the link is which connects them, we do not know, and most authorities believe that we never shall and never can know. Having firmly and tenaciously grasped these two notions, of the absolute separateness of mind and matter, and of the invariable concomitance of a mental change with a bodily change, the student will enter on the study of psychology with half his difficulties surmounted.[3]

[2] Chas. Mercier, *The Nervous System and the Mind*, 1888, p. 9.
[3] Op. cit., p. 11.

Half his difficulties ignored, I should prefer to say. For this 'concomitance' in the midst of 'absolute separateness' is an utterly irrational notion. It is to my mind quite inconceivable that consciousness should have *nothing to do* with a business which it so faithfully attends. And the question, 'What has it to do?' is one which psychology has no right to 'surmount', for it is her plain duty to consider it. The fact is that the whole question of interaction and influence between things is a meta-physical question, and cannot be discussed at all by those who are unwilling to go into matters thoroughly. It is truly enough hard to imagine the 'idea of a beefsteak binding two molecules together'; but since Hume's time it has been equally hard to imagine *anything* binding them together. The whole notion of 'binding' is a mystery, the first step towards the solution of which is to clear scholastic rubbish out of the way. Popular science talks of 'forces', 'attractions' or 'affinities' as binding the molecules; but clear science, though she may use such words to abbreviate discourse, has no use for the conceptions, and is satisfied when she can express in simple 'laws' the bare space-relations of the molecules as functions of each other and of time. To the more curiously inquiring mind, however, this simplified expression of the bare facts is not enough; there must be a 'reason' for them, and something must 'determine' the laws. And when one seriously sits down to consider what sort of a thing one *means* when one asks for a 'reason', one is led so far afield, so far away from popular science and its scholasticism, as to see that even such a fact as the existence or non-existence in the universe of 'the idea of a beefsteak' may not be wholly indifferent to other facts in the same universe, and in particular may have something to do with determining the distance at which two molecules in that universe shall lie apart. If this is so, then common-sense, though the intimate nature of causality and of the connection of things in the universe lies beyond her pitifully bounded horizon, has the root and gist of the truth in her hands when she obstinately holds to it that feelings and ideas are causes. However inadequate our ideas of causal efficacy may be, we are less wide of the mark when we say that our ideas and feelings have it, than the automatists are when they say they haven't it. As in the night all cats are grey, so in the darkness of metaphysical criticism all causes are obscure. But one has no right to pull the pall over the psychic half of the subject only, as the automatists do, and to say that *that* causation is unintelligible, whilst in the same breath one dogmatizes about *material* causation as if Hume, Kant and Lotze had never been born. One cannot thus blow hot and cold. One must be impartially naive or impartially critical. If the latter, the reconstruction must be thorough-going or 'metaphysical', and will probably preserve the common-sense view that ideas are forces, in some translated form. But psychology is a mere natural science, accepting certain terms uncritically as her data, and stopping short of metaphysical reconstruction. Like physics, she must be naive; and if she finds that in her very peculiar field of study ideas *seem* to be causes, she had better continue to talk of them as such. She gains absolutely nothing by a breach with common-sense in this matter, and she loses, to say the least, all naturalness of speech. If feelings are causes, of course their effects must be furtherances and checkings of internal cerebral motions, of which in themselves we are entirely without knowledge. It is probable that for years to come we shall have to infer what happens in the brain either from our feelings or from motor effects which we observe. The organ will be for us a sort of vat in which feelings and motions somehow go on stewing together, and in which innumerable things happen of which we catch but the statistical result. Why, under these circumstances, we should be asked to forswear the language of our childhood I cannot well imagine, especially as it is perfectly compatible with the language of physiology. The feelings can produce nothing absolutely new, they can only reinforce and inhibit reflex currents, and the original organization by physiological forces of these in paths must always be the groundwork of the psychological scheme.

My conclusion is that to urge the automaton theory upon us, as it is now urged, on purely *a priori* and quasi-metaphysical grounds, is an *unwarrantable impertinence in the present state of psychology.*

Reasons Against the Theory

But there are much more positive reasons than this why we ought to continue to talk in psychology as if consciousness had causal efficacy. The *particulars of the distribution of conscious-*

ness, so far as we know them, *point to its being efficacious*. Let us trace some of them.

It is very generally admitted, though the point would be hard to prove, that consciousness grows the more complex and intense the higher we rise in the animal kingdom. That of a man must exceed that of an oyster. From this point of view it seems an organ, superadded to the other organs which maintain the animal in the struggle for existence; and the presumption of course is that it helps him in some way in the struggle, just as they do. But it cannot help him without being in some way efficacious and influencing the course of his bodily history. If now it could be shown in what way consciousness *might* help him, and if, moreover, the defects of his other organs (where consciousness is most developed) are such as to make them need just the kind of help that consciousness would bring provided it *were* efficacious; why, then the plausible inference would be that it came just *because* of its efficacy – in other words, its efficacy would be inductively proved.

Now the study of the phenomena of consciousness which we shall make throughout the rest of this book will show us that consciousness is at all times primarily *a selecting agency*.[4] Whether we take it in the lowest sphere of sense, or in the highest of intellection, we find it always doing one thing, choosing one out of several of the materials so presented to its notice, emphasizing and accentuating that and suppressing as far as possible all the rest. The item emphasized is always in close connection with some *interest* felt by consciousness to be paramount at the time.

But what are now the defects of the nervous system in those animals whose consciousness seems most highly developed? Chief among them must be *instability*. The cerebral hemispheres are the characteristically 'high' nerve-centres, and we saw how indeterminate and unforeseeable their performances were in comparison with those of the basal ganglia and the cord. But this very vagueness constitutes their advantage. They allow their possessor to adapt his conduct to the minutest alterations in the environing circumstances, any one of which may be for him a sign, suggesting distant motives more powerful than any present solicitations of sense. It seems as if certain mechanical

[4] See in particular the end of Chapter 9 [*Principles of Psychology*].

conclusions should be drawn from this state of things. An organ swayed by slight impressions is an organ whose natural state is one of unstable equilibrium. We may imagine the various lines of discharge in the cerebrum to be almost on a par in point of permeability – what discharge a given small impression will produce may be called *accidental*, in the sense in which we say it is a matter of accident whether a raindrop falling on a mountain ridge descend the eastern or the western slope. It is in this sense that we may call it a matter of accident whether a child be a boy or a girl. The ovum is so unstable a body that certain causes too minute for our apprehension may at a certain moment tip it one way or the other. The natural law of an organ constituted after this fashion can be nothing but a law of caprice. I do not see how one could reasonably expect from it any certain pursuance of useful lines of reaction, such as the few and fatally determined performances of the lower centres constitute within their narrow sphere. The dilemma in regard to the nervous system seems, in short, to be of the following kind. We may construct one which will react infallibly and certainly, but it will then be capable of reacting to a very few changes in the environment – it will fail to be adapted to all the rest. We may, on the other hand, construct a nervous system potentially adapted to respond to an infinite variety of minute features in the situation; but its fallibility will then be as great as its elaboration. We can never be sure that its equilibrium will be upset in the appropriate direction. In short, a high brain may do many things, and may do each of them at a very slight hint. But its hair-trigger organization makes of it a happy-go-lucky, hit-or-miss affair. It is as likely to do the crazy as the same thing at any given moment. A low brain does few things, and in doing them perfectly forfeits all other use. The performances of a high brain are like dice thrown forever on a table. Unless they be loaded, what chance is there that the highest number will turn up oftener than the lowest?

All this is said of the brain as a physical machine pure and simple. *Can consciousness increase its efficiency by loading its dice?* Such is the problem.

Loading its dice would mean bringing a more or less constant pressure to bear in favour of *those* of its performances which make for the most permanent interests of the brain's owner; it would mean a constant inhibition of the tendencies to stray aside.

Well, just such pressure and such inhibitions are what consciousness *seems* to be exerting all the while. And the interests in whose favour it seems to exert them are *its* interests and its alone, interests which it *creates*, and which, but for it, would have no status in the realm of being whatever. We talk, it is true, when we are Darwinizing, as if the mere *body* that owns the brain had interests; we speak about the utilities of its various organs and how they help or hinder the body's survival; and we treat the survival as if it were an absolute end, existing as such in the physical world, a sort of actual *should-be*, presiding over the animal and judging his reactions, quite apart from the presence of any commenting intelligence outside. We forget that in the absence of some such superadded commenting intelligence (whether it be that of the animal itself, or only ours or Mr Darwin's), the reactions cannot be properly talked of as 'useful' or 'hurtful' at all. Considered merely physically, all that can be said of them is that *if* they occur in a certain way survival will as a matter of fact prove to be their incidental consequences. The organs themselves, and all the rest of the physical world, will, however, all the time be quite indifferent to this consequence, and would quite as cheerfully, the circumstances changed, compass the animal's destruction. In a word, survival can enter into a purely physiological discussion only as an *hypothesis made by an onlooker* about the future. But the moment you bring a conciousness into the midst, survival ceases to be a mere hypothesis. No longer is it, '*if* survival is to occur, then so and so must brain and other organs work'. It has now become an imperative decree: 'Survival *shall* occur, and therefore organs *must* so work!' *Real* ends appear for the first time now upon the world's stage. The conception of consciousness as a purely cognitive form of being, which is the pet way of regarding it in many idealistic-modern as well as ancient schools, is thoroughly anti-psychological, as the remainder of this book will show. Every actually existing consciousness seems to itself at any rate to be a *fighter for ends*, of which many, but for its presence, would not be ends at all. Its powers of cognition are mainly subservient to these ends, discerning which facts further them and which do not.

Now let consciousness only be what it seems to itself, and it will help an instable brain to compass its proper ends. The movements of the brain *per se* yield the means of attaining these ends mechanically, but only out of a lot of other ends, if so they may be called, which are not the proper ones of the animal, but often quite opposed. The brain is an instrument of possibilities, but of no certainties. But the consciousness, with its own ends present to it, and knowing also well which possibilities lead thereto and which away, will, if endowed with causal efficacy, reinforce the favourable possibilities and repress the unfavourable or indifferent ones. The nerve currents, coursing through the cells and fibres, must in this case be supposed strengthened by the fact of their awaking one consciousness and dampened by awaking another. *How* such reaction of the consciousness upon the currents may occur must remain at present unsolved: it is enough for my purpose to have shown that it may not uselessly exist, and that the matter is less simple than the brain-automatists hold.

All the facts of the natural history of consciousness lend colour to this view. Consciousness, for example, is only intense when nerve processes are hesitant. In rapid, automatic, habitual action it sinks to a minimum. Nothing could be more fitting than this, if consciousness have the teleological function we suppose; nothing more meaningless, if not. Habitual actions are certain, and being in no danger of going astray from their end, need no extraneous help. In hesitant action, there seem many alternative possibilities of final nervous discharge. The feeling awakened by the nascent excitement of each alternative nerve tract seems by its attractive or repulsive quality to determine whether the excitement shall abort or shall become complete. Where indecision is great, as before a dangerous leap, consciousness is agonizingly intense. Feeling, from this point of view, may be likened to a cross-section of the chain of nervous discharge, ascertaining the links already laid down, and groping among the fresh ends presented to it for the one which seems best to fit the case.

The phenomena of 'vicarious function' which we studied in Chapter 2 [*Principles of Psychology*] seem to form another bit of circumstantial evidence. A machine in working order acts fatally in one way. Our consciousness calls this the right way. Take out a valve, throw a wheel out of gear or bend a pivot, and it becomes a different machine, acting just as fatally in another way which we call the wrong way. But the machine itself knows nothing of wrong or right: matter has no ideals to pursue. A locomotive will carry its train through an open drawbridge as cheerfully as to any other destination.

A brain with part of it scooped out is virtually a new machine, and during the first days after the operation functions in a thoroughly abnormal manner. As a matter of fact, however, its performances become from day to day more normal, until at last a practised eye may be needed to suspect anything wrong. Some of the restoration is undoubtedly due to 'inhibitions' passing away. But if the consciousness which goes with the rest of the brain, be there not only in order to take cognizance of each functional error, but also to exert an efficient pressure to check it if it be a sin of commission, and to lend a strengthening hand if it be a weakness or sin of omission – nothing seems more natural than that the remaining parts, assisted in this way, should by virtue of the principle of habit grow back to the old teleological modes of exercise for which they were at first incapacitated. Nothing, on the contrary, seems at first sight more unnatural than that they should vicariously take up the duties of a part now lost without those *duties as such* exerting any persuasive or coercive force. At the end of Chapter 26 [*Principles of Psychology*] I shall return to this again.

There is yet another set of facts which seem explicable on the supposition that consciousness has causal efficacy. *It is a well-known fact that pleasures are generally associated with beneficial, pains with detrimental, experiences.* All the fundamental vital processes illustrate this law. Starvation, suffocation, privation of food, drink and sleep, work when exhausted, burns, wounds, inflammation, the effects of poison, are as disagreeable as filling the hungry stomach, enjoying rest and sleep after fatigue, exercise after rest, and a sound skin and unbroken bones at all times, are pleasant. Mr Spencer and others have suggested that these coincidences are due, not to any pre-established harmony, but to the mere action of natural selection which would certainly kill off in the long run any breed of creatures to whom the fundamentally noxious experience seemed enjoyable. An animal that should take pleasure in a feeling of suffocation would, if that pleasure were efficacious enough to make him immerse his head in water, enjoy a longevity of four or five minutes. But if pleasures and pains have no efficacy, one does not see (without some such *a priori* rational harmony as would be scouted by the 'scientific' champions of the automaton theory) why the most noxious acts, such as burning, might not give thrills of delight, and the most necessary ones, such as breathing, cause agony. The exceptions to the law are, it is true, numerous, but relate to experiences that are either not vital or not universal. Drunkenness, for instance, which though noxious, is to many persons delightful, is a very exceptional experience. But, as the excellent physiologist Fick remarks, if all rivers and springs ran alcohol instead of water, either all men would now be born to hate it or our nerves would have been selected so as to drink it with impunity. The only considerable attempt, in fact, that has been made to explain the *distribution* of our feelings is that of Mr Grant Allen in his suggestive little work *Physiological Aesthetics*; and his reasoning is based exclusively on that causal efficacy of pleasures and pains which the 'double-aspect' partisans so strenuously deny.

Thus, then, from every point of view the circumstantial evidence against that theory is strong. *A priori* analysis of both brain action and conscious action shows us that if the latter were efficacious it would, by its selective emphasis, make amends for the indeterminateness of the former; whilst the study *a posteriori* of the *distribution* of consciousness shows it to be exactly such as we might expect in an organ added for the sake of steering a nervous system grown too complex to regulate itself. The conclusion that it is useful, is, after all this, quite justifiable. But, if it is useful, it must be so through its causal efficaciousness, and the automaton theory must succumb to the theory of common-sense. I, at any rate (pending metaphysical reconstructions not yet successfully achieved), shall have no hesitation in using the language of common-sense throughout this book.

10

The Mind-stuff Theory

The reader who found himself swamped with too much metaphysics in the last chapter will have a still worse time of it in this one, which is exclusively metaphysical. Metaphysics means nothing but an unusually obstinate effort to think clearly. The fundamental conceptions of psychology are practically very clear to us, but theoretically they are very confused, and one easily makes the obscurest assumptions in this science without realizing, until challenged, what internal difficulties they involve. When these assumptions have once established themselves (as they have a way of doing in our very descriptions of the phenomenal facts) it is almost impossible to get rid of them afterwards or to make anyone see that they are not essential features of the subject. The only way to prevent this disaster is to scrutinize them beforehand and make them give an articulate account of themselves before letting them pass. One of the obscurest of the assumptions of which I speak is *the assumption that our mental states are composite in structure, made up of smaller states conjoined*. This hypothesis has outward advantages which make it almost irresistibly attractive to the intellect, and yet it is inwardly quite unintelligible. Of its unintelligibility, however, half the writers on psychology seem unaware. As our own aim is *to understand* if possible, I make no apology for singling out this particular notion for very explicit treatment before taking up the descriptive part of our work. *The theory of 'mind-stuff' is the theory that our mental states are compounds*, expressed in its most radical form.

Evolutionary Psychology Demands a Mind-dust

In a general theory of evolution the inorganic comes first, then the lowest forms of animal and vegetable life, then forms of life that possess mentality, and finally those like ourselves that possess it in a high degree. As long as we keep to the

consideration of purely outward facts, even the most complicated facts of biology, our task as evolutionists is comparatively
easy. We are dealing all the time with matter and its aggregations
and separations; and although our treatment must perforce be
hypothetical, this does not prevent it from being *continuous*.
The point which as evolutionists we are bound to hold fast to is
that all the new forms of being that make their appearance are
really nothing more than results of the redistribution of the
original and unchanging materials. The self-same atoms which,
chaotically dispersed, made the nebula, now, jammed and
temporarily caught in peculiar positions, form our brains; and
the 'evolution' of the brains, if understood, would be simply the
account of how the atoms came to be so caught and jammed. In
this story no new *natures*, no factors not present at the beginning, are introduced at any later stage.

But with the dawn of consciousness an entirely new nature
seems to slip in, something whereof the potency was *not* given
in the mere outward atoms of the original chaos.

The enemies of evolution have been quick to pounce upon
this undeniable discontinuity in the data of the world, and many
of them, from the failure of evolutionary explanations at this
point, have inferred their general incapacity all along the line.
Everyone admits the entire incommensurability of feeling as
such with material motion as such. 'A motion became a feeling!'
— no phrase that our lips can frame is so devoid of apprehensible
meaning. Accordingly, even the vaguest of evolutionary enthu-
siasts, when deliberately comparing material with mental facts,
have been as forward as anyone else to emphasize the 'chasm'
between the inner and the outer worlds. 'Can the oscillations of
a molecule', says Mr Spencer,

> be represented side by side with a nervous shock, and the two be
> recognized as one? No effort enables us to assimilate them. That
> a unit of feeling has nothing in common with a unit of motion
> becomes more than ever manifest when we bring the two into
> juxtaposition.[1]

And again:

> Suppose it to have become quite clear that a shock in conscious-
> ness and a molecular motion are the subjective and objective faces

[1] *Psychology*, s. 62

of the same thing; we continue utterly incapable of uniting the two, so as to conceive that reality of which they are the opposite faces.[2]

In other words, incapable of perceiving in them any common character. So Tyndall, in that lucky paragraph which has been quoted so often that everyone knows it by heart:

The passage from the physics of the brain to the corresponding facts of consciousness is unthinkable. Granted that a definite thought and a definite molecular action in the brain occur simultaneously; we do not possess the intellectual organ, nor apparently any rudiment of the organ, which would enable us to pass, by a process of reasoning, from one to the other.[3]

Or in this other passage:

We can trace the development of a nervous system and correlate with it the parallel phenomena of sensation and thought. We see with undoubting certainty that they go hand in hand. But we try to soar in a vacuum the moment we seek to comprehend the connection between them . . . There is no fusion possible between the two classes of facts – no motor energy in the intellect of man to carry it without logical rupture from the one to the other.[4]

None the less easily, however, when the evolutionary afflatus is upon them, do the very same writers leap over the breach whose flagrancy they are the foremost to announce, and talk as if mind grew out of body in a continuous way. Mr Spencer, looking back on his review of mental evolution, tells us how 'in tracing up the increase we found ourselves passing *without break* from the phenomena of bodily life to the phenomena of mental life.'[5] And Mr Tyndall, in the same Belfast Address from which we just quoted, delivers his other famous passage:

[2] Ibid., s. 272.
[3] *Fragments of Science*, 5th edn, p. 420.
[4] Belfast Address, *Nature*, 20 August 1874, p. 318. I cannot help remarking that the disparity between motions and feelings on which these authors lay so much stress, is somewhat less absolute than at first sight it seems. There are categories common to the two worlds. Not only temporal succession (as Helmholtz admits, *Physiol. Optik*, p. 445), but such attributes as intensity, volume, simplicity or complication, smooth or impeded change, rest or agitation, are habitually predicated of both physical facts and mental facts. Where such analogies obtain, the things do have something in common.
[5] *Psychology*, s. 131.

Abandoning all disguise, the confession that I feel bound to make before you is that I prolong the vision backward across the boundary of the experimental evidence, and discern in that matter which we, in our ignorance and notwithstanding our professed reverence for its Creator, have hitherto covered with opprobrium the promise and potency of every form and quality of life.[6]

— mental life included, as a matter of course.

So strong a postulate is continuity! Now this book will tend to show that mental postulates are on the whole to be respected. The demand for continuity has, over large tracts of science, proved itself to possess true prophetic power. We ought therefore ourselves sincerely to try every possible mode of conceiving the dawn of consciousness so that it may *not* appear equivalent to the irruption into the universe of a new nature, non-existent until then.

Merely to call the consciousness 'nascent' will not serve our turn.[7] It is true that the word signifies not yet *quite* born, and so

---

[6] *Nature*, as above, pp. 317–8.

[7] 'Nascent' is Mr Spencer's great word. In showing how at a certain point consciousness must appear upon the evolving scene this author fairly outdoes himself in vagueness.

'In its higher forms, instinct is probably accompanied by a rudimentary consciousness. There cannot be co-ordination of many stimuli without some ganglion through which they are all brought into relation. In the process of bringing them into relation, this ganglion must be subject to the influence of each – must undergo many changes. And the quick succession of changes in a ganglion, implying as it does perpetual experiences of differences and likenesses, constitutes the *raw material* of consciousness. The *implication* is that as fast as instinct is developed, some kind of consciousness becomes nascent.' (*Psychology*, s. 195.)

The words 'raw material' and 'implication' which I have italicized are the words which do the *evolving*. They are supposed to have all the rigour which the 'synthetic philosophy' requires. In the following passage, when 'impressions' pass through a common 'centre of communication' in succession (much as people might pass into a theatre through a turnstile) consciousness, non-existent until then, is supposed to result:

'Separate impressions are received by the senses – by different parts of the body. If they go no further than the places at which they are received, they are useless. Or if only some of them are brought into relation with one another, they are useless. That an effectual adjustment may be made, they must be all brought into relation with one another. But this implies some centre of communication common to them all, through which they severally pass; and as they cannot pass through it simultaneously, they must pass through it in succession. So that as the external phenomena responded to become greater in number and more complicated in kind, the variety and rapidity of the changes to which this common centre of communication is subject must increase – there must result an unbroken series of these changes – *there must arise a consciousness*.

'Hence the progress of the correspondence between the organism and its environment necessitates a gradual reduction of the sensorial changes to a succession; and by seems to form a sort of bridge between existence and nonentity. But that is a verbal quibble. The fact is that discontinuity comes in if a new nature comes in at all. The *quantity* of the latter is quite immaterial. The girl in *Midshipman Easy* could not excuse the illegitimacy of her child by saying, 'it was a very small one'. And consciousness, however small, is an illegitimate birth in any philosophy that starts without it, and yet professes to explain all facts by continuous evolution.

If evolution is to work smoothly, consciousness in some shape must have been present at the very origin of things. Accordingly we find that the more clear-sighted evolutionary philosophers are beginning to posit it there. Each atom of the nebula, they suppose, must have had an aboriginal atom of consciousness linked with it; and, just as the material atoms have formed bodies and brains by massing themselves together, so the mental atoms, by an analogous process of aggregation, have fused into those larger consciousnesses which we know in ourselves and suppose to exist in our fellow-animals. Some such doctrine of *atomistic hylozoism* as this is an indispensable part of a thorough-going philosophy of evolution. According to it there must be an infinite number of degrees of consciousness, following the degrees of complication and aggregation of the primordial mind-dust. To prove the separate existence of these degrees of consciousness by indirect evidence, since direct intuition of them is not to be had, becomes therefore the first duty of psychological evolutionism.

Some Alleged Proofs that Mind-dust Exists

Some of this duty we find already performed by a number of philosophers who, though not interested at all in evolution, have

---

so doing *evolves a distinct consciousness* – a consciousness that becomes higher as the succession becomes more rapid and the correspondence more complete.' (Ibid, s. 179).

It is true that in the *Fortnightly Review* (vol. 14, p. 716) Mr Spencer denies that he means by this passage to tell us anything about the origin of consciousness at all. It resembles, however, too many other places in his *Psychology* (e.g. s. 43, 110 and 244) not to be taken as a serious attempt to explain how consciousness must at a certain point be 'evolved'. That, when a critic calls his attention to the inanity of his words, Mr Spencer should say he never meant anything particular by them, is simply an example of the scandalous vagueness with which this sort of 'chromo-philosophy' is carried on.

nevertheless on independent grounds convinced themselves of the existence of a vast amount of subconscious mental life. The criticism of this general opinion and its grounds will have to be postponed for a while. At present let us merely deal with the arguments assumed to prove aggregation of bits of mind-stuff into distinctly sensible feelings. They are clear and admit of a clear reply.

The German physiologist A. Fick, in 1862, was, so far as I know, the first to use them. He made experiments on the discrimination of the feelings of warmth and of touch, when only a very small portion of the skin was excited through a hole in a card, the surrounding parts being protected by the card. He found that under these circumstances mistakes were frequently made by the patient,[8] and concluded that this must be because the number of sensations from the elementary nerve tips affected was too small to sum itself distinctly into either of the qualities of feeling in question. He tried to show how a different manner of the summation might give rise in one case to the heat and in another to the touch.

'A feeling of temperature', he says, 'arises when the intensities of the units of feeling are evenly graduated, so that between two elements a and b no other unit can spatially intervene whose intensity is not also *between* that of a and b. A feeling of contact perhaps arises when this condition is not fulfilled. Both kinds of feeling, however, are composed of the same units.'

But it is obviously far clearer to interpret such a graduation of intensities as a brain-fact than as a mind-fact. If in the brain a tract were first excited in one of the ways suggested by Prof. Fick, and then again in the other, it might very well happen, for

[8] His own words are: 'Mistakes are made in the sense that he admits having been touched, when in reality it was radiant heat that affected his skin. In our own before-mentioned experiments there was never any deception on the entire palmar side of the hand or on the face. On the back of the hand in one case in a series of 60 stimulations 4 mistakes occurred, in another case 2 mistakes in 45 stimulations. On the extensor side of the upper arm 3 deceptions out of 48 stimulations were noticed, and in the case of another individual, 1 out of 31. In one case over the spine 3 deceptions in a series of 11 excitations were observed; in another, 4 out of 19. On the lumbar spine 6 deceptions came among 29 stimulations, and again 4 out of 7. There is certainly not yet enough material on which to rest a calculation of probabilities, but anyone can easily convince himself that on the back there is no question of even a moderately accurate discrimination between warmth and a light pressure so far as but small portions of skin come into play. It has been as yet impossible to make corresponding experiments with regard to sensibility to cold.' (*Lehrb. d. Anat. u. Physiol. d. Sinnesorgane*, 1862, p. 29)

aught we can say to the contrary, that the psychic accompaniment in the one case would be heat, and in the other pain. The pain and the heat would, however, not be composed of psychic units, but would each be the direct result of one total brain process. So long as this latter interpretation remains open, Fick cannot be held to have proved psychic summation.

Later, both Spencer and Taine, independently of each other, took up the same line of thought. Mr Spencer's reasoning is worth quoting *in extenso*. He writes:

Although the individual sensations and emotions, real or ideal, of which consciousness is built up, appear to be severally simple, homogeneous, unanalysable, or of inscrutable natures, yet they are not so. There is at least one kind of feeling which, as ordinarily experienced, seems elementary, that is demonstrably not elementary. And after resolving it into its proximate components, we can scarcely help suspecting that other apparently elementary feelings are also compound, and may have proximate components like those which we can in this one instance identify.

Musical sound is the name we give to this seemingly simple feeling which is clearly resolvable into simpler feelings. Well-known experiments prove that when equal blows or taps are made one after another at a rate not exceeding some sixteen per second, the effect of each is perceived as a separate noise; but when the rapidity with which the blows follow one another exceeds this, the noises are no longer identified in separate states of consciousness, and there arises in place of them a continuous state of consciousness, called a tone. In further increasing the rapidity of the blows, the tone undergoes the change of quality distinguished as rise in pitch; and it continues to rise in pitch as the blows continue to increase in rapidity, until it reaches an acuteness beyond which it is no longer appreciable as a tone. So that out of units of feeling of the same kind, many feelings distinguishable from one another in quality result, according as the units are more or less integrated.

This is not all. The inquiries of Professor Helmholtz have shown that when, along with one series of these rapidly recurring noises, there is generated another series in which the noises are more rapid though not so loud, the effect is a change in that quality known as its timbre. As various musical instruments show us, tones which are alike in pitch and strength are distinguishable by their harshness or sweetness, their ringing or their liquid characters; and all their specific peculiarities are proved to arise from the combination of one, two, three, or more, supplementary series of recurrent noises with the chief series of recurrent noises. So that while the unlikenesses of feeling known as differences of pitch in tones are due to differences of integration among the recurrent noises of one series, the unlikenesses of feeling known as differences of timbre, are due to the simultaneous integration with this series of other series having other degrees of integration. And thus an enormous number of qualitatively contrasted kinds of consciousness that seem severally elementary prove to be composed of one simple kind of consciousness, combined and recombined with itself in multitudinous ways.

Can we stop short here? If the different sensations known as sounds are built out of a common unit, is it not to be rationally inferred that so likewise are the different sensations known as tastes, and the different sensations known as odours, and the different sensations known as colours? Nay, shall we not regard it as probable that there is a unit common to all these strongly contrasted classes of sensations? If the unlikenesses among the sensations of each class may be due to unlikenesses among the modes of aggregation of a unit of consciousness common to them all; so too may the much greater unlikenesses between the sensations of each class and those of other classes. There may be a single primordial element of consciousness, and the countless kinds of consciousness may be produced by the compounding of this element with itself and the recompounding of its compounds with one another in higher and higher degrees: so producing increased multiplicity, variety and complexity.

Have we any clue to this primordial element? I think we have. That simple mental impression which proves to be the unit of composition of the sensation of musical tone, is allied to certain other simple mental impressions differently originated. The subjective effect produced by a crack or noise that has no appreciable duration is little else than a nervous shock. Though we distinguish such a nervous shock as belonging to what we call sounds, yet it does not differ very much from nervous shocks of other kinds. An electric discharge sent through the body causes a feeling akin to that which a sudden loud report causes. A strong unexpected impression made through the eyes, as by a flash of lightning, similarly gives rise to a start or shock; and though the feeling so named seems, like the electric shock, to have the body at large for its seat, and may therefore be regarded as the correlative rather of the efferent than of the afferent disturbance yet on remembering the mental change that results from the instantaneous transit of an object across the field of vision, I think it may be perceived that the feeling accompanying the efferent disturbance is itself reduced very nearly to the same form. The state of consciousness so generated is, in fact, comparable in quality to the initial state of consciousness caused by a blow (distinguishing it from the pain or other feeling that commences the instant after); which state of consciousness caused by a blow may be taken as the primitive and typical form of the nervous shock. The fact that sudden brief disturbances thus set up by different stimuli through different sets of nerves cause feelings scarcely distinguishable in quality will not appear strange when we recollect that distinguishableness of feeling implies appreciable duration; and that when the duration is greatly abridged, nothing more is known than that some mental change has occurred and ceased. To have a sensation of redness, to know a tone as acute or grave, to be conscious of a taste as sweet, implies in each case a considerable continuity of state. If the state does not last long enough to admit of its being contemplated, it cannot be classed as of this or that kind; and becomes a momentary modification very similar to momentary modifications otherwise caused.

It is possible, then – may we not even say probable – that something of the same order as that which we call a nervous shock is the ultimate unit of consciousness; and that all the unlikenesses among our feelings result from unlike modes of integration of this ultimate unit. I say of the same order, because there are discernible differences among nervous shocks that are differently caused; and the primitive nervous shock probably differs somewhat from each of them. And I say of the same order, for the further reason that while we may ascribe to them a general likeness in nature, we must suppose a great unlikeness in degree. The nervous shocks recognized as such are violent – must be violent before they can be perceived amid the procession of multitudinous vivid feelings suddenly interrupted by them. But the rapidly recurring nervous shocks of which the different forms of feeling consist, we must assume to be of comparatively moderate, or even of very slight intensity. Were our various sensations and emotions composed of rapidly recurring shocks as strong as those ordinarily called shocks, they would be unbearable; indeed life would cease at once. We must think of them rather as successive faint pulses of subjective change, each having the same quality as the strong pulse of subjective change distinguished as a nervous shock.[9]

Refutation of these Proofs

Convincing as this argument of Mr Spencer's may appear on a first reading, it is singular how weak it really is.[10] We do, it is

[9] *Principles of Psychology*, s. 60.
[10] Oddly enough, Mr Spencer seems quite unaware of the *general* function of the theory of elementary units of mind-stuff in the evolutionary philosophy. We have

true, when we study the connection between a musical note and
its outward cause, find the note simple and continuous while the
cause is multiple and discrete. Somewhere, then, there *is* a
transformation, reduction or fusion. The question is, Where —
in the nerve-world or in the mind-world? Really we have no
experimental proof by which to decide; and if decide we must,
analogy and *a priori* probability can alone guide us. Mr Spencer
assumes that the fusion must come to pass in the mental world,
and that the physical processes get through air and ear, auditory
nerve and medulla, lower brain and hemispheres, without their
number being reduced. Figure 1 will make the point clear.

Let the line *a–b* represent the threshold of consciousness: then
everything drawn below that line will symbolize a physical
process, everything above it will mean a fact of mind. Let the
crosses stand for the physical blows, the circles for the events in
successively higher orders of nerve cells, and the horizontal
marks for the facts of feeling. Spencer's argument implies that
each order of cells transmits just as many impulses as it receives
to the cells above it; so that if the blows come at the rate of
20,000 in a second the cortical cells discharge at the same rate,
and one unit of feeling corresponds to each one of the 20,000
discharges. Then, and only then, does 'integration' occur, by the
20,000 units of feeling 'compounding with themselves' into the
'continuous state of consciousness' represented by the short line
at the top of the figure.

Now such an interpretation as this flies in the face of physical
analogy, no less than of logical intelligibility. Consider physical
analogy first.

A pendulum may be deflected by a single blow, and swing
back. Will it swing back the more often the more we multiply
the blows? No; for if they rain upon the pendulum too fast, it
will not swing at all but remain deflected in a sensibly stationary
state. In other words, increasing the cause numerically need not

---

seen it to be absolutely indispensable, if that philosophy is to work, to postulate
consciousness in the nebula — the simplest way being, of course, to suppose every
atom animated. Mr Spencer, however, will have it (e.g., *First Principles*, s. 71) that
consciousness is only the occasional result of the 'transformation' of a certain amount
of 'physical force' to which it is 'equivalent'. Presumably a brain must already be
there before any such 'transformation' can take place; and so the argument quoted in
the text stands as a mere local detail, without general bearings.

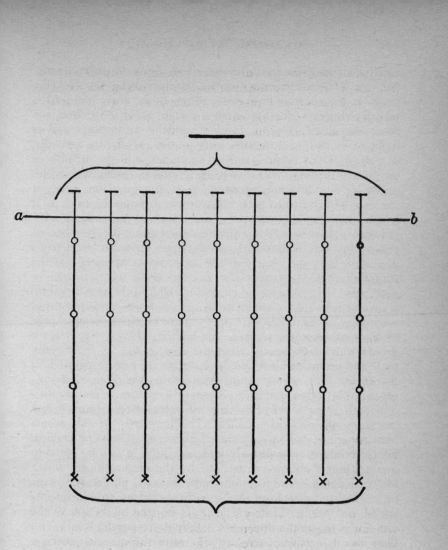

Figure 1   *One second of time*

equally increase numerically the effect. Blow through a tube: you get a certain musical note; and increasing the blowing increases for a certain time the loudness of the note. Will this be true indefinitely? No; for when a certain force is reached, the note, instead of growing louder, suddenly disappears and is replaced by its higher octave. Turn on the gas slightly and light it: you get a tiny flame. Turn on more gas, and the breadth of the flame increases. Will this relation increase indefinitely? No, again; for at a certain moment up shoots the flame into a ragged streamer and begins to hiss. Send slowly through the nerve of a frog's gastrocnemius muscle a succession of galvanic shocks: you get a succession of twitches. Increasing the number of shocks does not increase the twitching; on the contrary, it stops it, and we have the muscle in the apparently stationary state of contraction called tetanus. This last fact is the true analogue of what must happen between the nerve cell and the sensory fibre. It is certain that cells are more inert than fibres, and that rapid vibrations in the latter can only arouse relatively simple processes or states in the former. The higher cells may have even a slower rate of explosion than the lower, and so the twenty thousand supposed blows of the outer air may be 'integrated' in the cortex into a very small number of cell discharges in a second. This other diagram will serve to contrast this supposition with Spencer's. In Figure 2 all 'integration' occurs below the threshold of consciousness. The frequency of cell events becomes more and more reduced as we approach the cells to which feeling is most directly attached, until at last we come to a condition of things symbolized by the larger ellipse, which may be taken to stand for some rather massive and slow process of tension and discharge in the cortical centres, to which, *as a whole*, the feeling of musical tone symbolized by the line at the top of the diagram *simply and totally* corresponds. It is as if a long file of men were to start one after the other to reach a distant point. The road at first is good and they keep their original distance apart. Presently it is intersected by bogs each worse than the last, so that the front men get so retarded that the hinder ones catch up with them before the journey is done, and all arrive together at the goal.[11]

[11] The compounding of colours may be dealt with in an identical way. Helmholtz has shown that if green light and red light fall simultaneously on the retina, we see

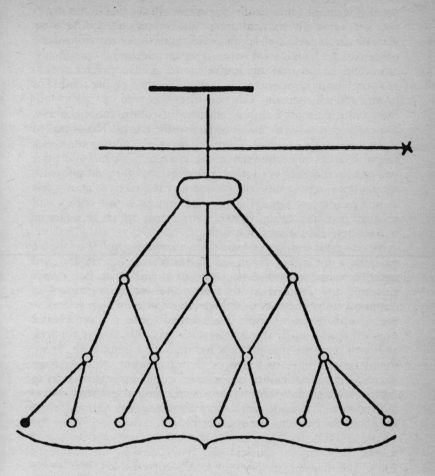

Figure 2   *One second of time*

On this supposition there *are* no unperceived units of mind-stuff preceding and composing the full consciousness. The latter is itself an immediate psychic fact and bears an immediate relation to the neural state which is its unconditional accompaniment. Did each neural shock give rise to its own psychic shock, and the psychic shocks then combine, it would be impossible to understand why severing one part of the central nervous system from another should break up the integrity of the consciousness. The cut has nothing to do with the psychic world. The atoms of mind-stuff ought to float off from the nerve-matter on either side of it, and come together over it and fuse, just as well as if it had not been made. We know, however, that they do not; that severance of the paths of conduction between a man's left auditory centre or optical centre and the rest of his cortex will sever all communication between the words which he hears or sees written and the rest of his ideas.

Moreover, if feelings can mix into a *tertium quid*, why do we not take a feeling of greenness and a feeling of redness, and make a feeling of yellowness out of them? Why has optics neglected the open road to truth, and wasted centuries in disputing about theories of colour-composition which two minutes of introspection would have settled forever?[12] We cannot mix feelings as such, though we may mix the objects we feel, and from *their* mixture get new feelings. We cannot even (as we shall later see) have two feelings in our mind at once. At most we can compare together *objects previously presented* to us in distinct feelings; but then we find each object stubbornly maintaining its separate identity before consciousness, whatever the verdict of the comparison may be.[13]

---

the colour yellow. The mind-stuff theory would interpret this as a case where the feeling green and the feeling red 'combine' into the *tertium quid* of feeling, yellow. What really occurs is no doubt that a third kind of nerve-process is set up when the combined lights impinge on the retina – not simply the process of red plus the process of green, but something quite different from both or either. Of course, then, there *are* no feelings, either of red or of green, present to the mind at all; but the feeling of yellow which *is* there, answers as directly to the nerve-process which momentarily then exists, as the feelings of green and red would answer to their respective nerve-processes did the latter happen to be taking place.

[12] Cf. Mill's *Logic*, Book 6, ch. 4, s. 3.

[13] I find in my students an almost invincible tendency to think that we can immediately perceive that feelings do combine. 'What!' they say, 'is not the taste of lemonade composed of that of lemon *plus* that of sugar?' This is taking the combining

Self-compounding of Mental Facts is Inadmissible

But there is a still more fatal objection to the theory of mental units 'compounding with themselves' or 'integrating'. It is logically unintelligible; it leaves out the essential feature of all the 'combinations' we actually know.

All the 'combinations' which we actually know are EFFECTS, wrought by the units said to be 'combined', UPON SOME ENTITY OTHER THAN THEMSELVES. Without this feature of a medium or vehicle, the notion of combination has no sense.

> A multitude of contractile units, by joint action, and by being all connected, for instance, with a single tendon, will pull at the same, and will bring about a dynamical effect which is undoubtedly the resultant of their combined individual energies ... On the whole, tendons are to muscular fibres, and bones are to tendons, combining recipients of mechanical energies. A medium of composition is indispensable to the summation of energies. To realize the complete dependence of mechanical resultants on a combining substratum, one may fancy for a moment all the individually contracting muscular elements severed from their attachments. They might then still be capable of contracting with the same energy as before, yet no co-operative result would be accomplished. The medium of dynamical combination would be wanting. The multiple energies, singly exerted on no common recipient, would lose themselves on entirely isolated and disconnected efforts.[14]

In other words, no possible number of entities (call them as you like, whether forces, material particles or mental elements) can sum *themselves* together. Each remains, in the sum, what it always was; and the sum itself exists only *for a bystander* who happens to overlook the units and to apprehend the sum as such; or else it exists in the shape of some other *effect* on an entity external to the sum itself. Let it not be objected that H_2 and O combine of themselves into 'water', and thenceforward

---

of objects for that of feelings. The physical lemonade contains both the lemon and the sugar, but its taste does not contain their tastes, for if there are any two things which are certainly *not* present in the taste of lemonade, those are the lemon-sour on the one hand and the sugar-sweet on the other. These tastes are absent utterly. The entirely new taste which is present *resembles*, it is true, both those tastes; but in Chapter 13 [*Principles of Psychology*] we shall see that resemblance cannot always be held to involve partial identity.

[14] E. Montgomery, in *Mind*, vols 18–19. See also pp. 24–5.

exhibit new properties. They do not. The 'water' is just the old atoms in the new position, H–O–H; the 'new properties' are just their combined *effects*, when in this position, upon external media, such as our sense organs and the various reagents on which water may exert its properties and be known.

> Aggregations are organized wholes only when they behave as such in the presence of other things. A statue is an aggregation of particles of marble; but as such it has no unity. For the spectator it is one; in itself it is an aggregate; just as, to the consciousness of an ant crawling over it, it may again appear a mere aggregate. No summing up of parts can make a unity of a mass of discrete constituents, unless this unity exists for some other subject, not for the mass itself.[15]

Just so, in the parallelogram of forces, the 'forces' themselves do not combine into the diagonal resultant; a *body* is needed on which they may impinge, to exhibit their resultant effect. No more do musical sounds compound *per se* into concords or discords. Concord and discord are names for their combined effects on that external medium, the *ear*.

Where the elemental units are supposed to be feelings, the case is in no wise altered. Take a hundred of them, shuffle them and pack them as close together as you can (whatever that may mean); still each remains the same feeling it always was, shut in its own skin, windowless, ignorant of what the other feelings are and mean. There would be a 101st feeling there, if, when a group or series of such feelings were set up, a consciousness *belonging to the group as such* should emerge. And this 101st feeling would be a totally new fact; the 100 original feelings might, by a curious physical law, be a signal for its *creation*, when they came together; but they would have no substantial identity with it, nor it with them, and one could never deduce the one from the others, or (in any intelligible sense) say that they *evolved* it.

Take a sentence of a dozen words, and take twelve men and tell to each one word. Then stand the men in a row or jam them in a bunch, and let each think of his word as intently as he will;

---

[15] J. Royce, *Mind*, 6, p. 376.

In defence of the mind-stuff view, see W. K. Clifford, *Mind*, 3, 57 (reprinted in his *Lectures and Essays*, 2, 71); G. T. Fechner, *Psychophysik, Bd.* 2, ch. 45; H. Taine: on Intelligence, Book 3.

nowhere will there be a consciousness of the whole sentence.[16]
We talk of the 'spirit of the age', and the 'sentiment of the
people', and in various ways we hypostatize 'public opinion'.
But we know this to be symbolic speech, and never dream that
the spirit, opinion, sentiment, etc., constitute a consciousness
other than, and additional to, that of the several individuals
whom the words 'age', 'people', or 'public' denote. The private
minds do not agglomerate into a higher compound mind. This
has always been the invincible contention of the spiritualists
against the associationists in psychology – a contention which
we shall take up at greater length in Chapter 10 [*Principles of
Psychology*]. The associationists say the mind is constituted by
a multiplicity of distinct 'ideas' *associated* into a unity. There is,
they say, an idea of *a*, and also an idea of *b*. *Therefore*, they say,
there is an idea of *a* plus *b*, or of *a* and *b* together. Which is like
saying that the mathematical square of *a* plus that of *b* is equal
to the square of *a* plus *b*, a palpable untruth. Idea of *a* plus idea
of *b* is *not* identical with idea of (*a* plus *b*). It is one, they are
two; in it, what knows *a* also knows *b*; in them, what knows *a*
is expressly posited as not knowing *b*; etc. In short, the two
separate ideas can never by any logic be made to figure as one
and the same thing as the 'associated' idea.

This is what the spiritualists keep saying; and since we do, as
a matter of fact, have the 'compounded' idea, and do know *a*
and *b* together, they adopt a farther hypothesis to explain that
fact. The separate ideas exist, they say, but *affect* a third entity,
the soul. *This* has the 'compounded' idea, if you please so to call
it; and the compounded idea is an altogether new psychic fact
to which the separate ideas stand in the relation, not of
constituents, but of occasions of production.

This argument of the spiritualists against the associationists
has never been answered by the latter. It holds good against any
talk about self-compounding amongst feelings, against any

[16] 'Someone might say that although it is true that neither a blind man nor a deaf
man by himself can compare sounds with colours, yet since one hears and the other
sees they might do so both together . . . But whether they are apart or close together
makes no difference; not even if they permanently keep house together; no, not if
they were Siamese twins, or more than Siamese twins, and were inseparably grown
together, would it make the assumption any more possible. Only when sound and
colour are represented in the same reality is it thinkable that they should be compared.'
(Brentano, *Psychologie*, p. 209.)

'blending', or 'complication', or 'mental chemistry', or 'psychic synthesis', which supposes a resultant consciousness to float off from the constituents *per se*, in the absence of a supernumerary principle of consciousness which they may affect. The mind-stuff theory, in short, is unintelligible. Atoms of feeling cannot compose higher feelings, any more than atoms of matter can compose physical things! The 'things', for a clear-headed atomistic evolutionist, are not. Nothing is but the everlasting atoms. When grouped in a certain way, *we* name them this 'thing' or that; but the thing we name has no existence out of our mind. So of the states of mind which are supposed to be compound because they know many different things together. Since indubitably such states do exist, they must exist as single new facts, effects, possibly, as the spiritualists say, on the soul (we will not decide that point here), but at any rate independent and integral, and not compounded of psychic atoms.[17]

[17] The reader must observe that we are reasoning altogether about the *logic* of the mind-stuff theory, about whether it can *explain the constitution* of higher mental states by viewing them as *identical with lower ones* summed together. We say the two sorts of fact are not identical: a higher state *is* not a lot of lower states; it is itself. When, however, a lot of lower states have come together, or when certain brain conditions occur together which, *if they occurred separately, would produce* a lot of lower states, we have not for a moment pretended that a higher state may not emerge. In fact it does emerge under those conditions; and our Chapter 9 [*Principles of Psychology*] will be mainly devoted to the proof of this fact. But such emergence is that of a new psychic entity, and is *toto coelo* different from such an 'integration' of the lower states as the mind-stuff theory affirms.

It may seem strange to suppose that anyone should mistake criticism of a certain theory about a fact for doubt of the fact itself. And yet the confusion is made in high quarters enough to justify our remarks. Mr J. Ward, in his article 'Psychology' in the *Encyclopaedia Britannica*, speaking of the hypothesis that 'a series of feelings can be aware of itself as a series', says (p. 39): 'Paradox is too mild a word for it, even contradiction will hardly suffice.' Whereupon, Professor Bain takes him thus to task: 'As to a series of states being aware of itself, I confess I see no insurmountable difficulty. It may be a fact, or not a fact; it may be a very clumsy expression for what it is applied to; but it is neither paradox nor contradiction. A series merely contradicts an individual, or it may be two or more individuals as coexisting; but that is too general to exclude the possibility of self-knowledge. It certainly does not bring the property of self-knowledge into the foreground, which, however, is not the same as denying it. An algebraic series might know itself, without any contradiction: the only thing against it is the want of evidence of the fact.' (*Mind*, 11, p. 459). Prof. Bain thinks, then, that all the bother is about the difficulty of seeing how a series of feelings can have the knowledge of itself *added to it!!!* As if anybody ever was troubled about that. That, notoriously enough, is a fact: our consciousness is a series of feelings to which every now and then is *added* a retrospective consciousness that they have come and gone. What Mr Ward and I are troubled about is merely the silliness of the mind-stuffists and associationists continuing to say that the 'series of states' *is* the 'awareness

Can States of Mind be Unconscious?

The passion for unity and smoothness is in some minds so insatiate that, in spite of the logical clearness of these reasonings and conclusions, many will fail to be influenced by them. They establish a sort of disjointedness in things which in certain quarters will appear intolerable. They sweep away all chance of 'passing without break' either from the material to the mental, or from the lower to the higher mental; and they thrust us back into a pluralism of consciousnesses — each arising discontinuously in the midst of two disconnected worlds, material and mental — which is even worse than the old notion of the separate creation of each particular soul. But the malcontents will hardly try to refute our reasonings by direct attack. It is more probable that, turning their back upon them altogether, they will devote themselves to sapping and mining the region roundabout until it is a bog of logical liquefaction, into the midst of which all definite conclusions of any sort may be trusted ere long to sink and disappear.

Our reasonings have assumed that the 'integration' of a thousand psychic units must be either just the units over again, simply rebaptized, or else something real, but then other than and additional to those units; that if a certain existing fact is that of a thousand feelings, it cannot at the same time be that of ONE feeling; for the essence of feeling is to be felt, and as a psychic existent *feels*, so it must *be*. If the one feeling feels like no one of the thousand, in what sense can it be said to *be* the thousand? These assumptions are what the monists will seek to undermine. The Hegelizers amongst them will take high ground at once, and say that the glory and beauty of the psychic life is that in it all contradictions find their reconciliation; and that it is just because the facts we are considering *are* facts of the self that they are both one and many at the same time. With this intellectual temper I confess that I cannot contend. As in striking at some unresisting gossamer with a club, one but overreaches one's self, and the thing one aims at gets no harm. So I leave this school to its devices.

---

of itself'; that if the states be posited severally, their collective consciousness is *eo ipso* given; and that we need no farther explanation, or 'evidence of the fact'.

The other monists are of less deliquescent frame, and try to break down distinctness among mental states by *making a distinction*. This sounds paradoxical, but it is only ingenious. The distinction is that *between the unconscious and the conscious being of the mental state*. It is the sovereign means for believing what one likes in psychology, and of turning what might become a science into a tumbling-ground for whimsies.

Difficulty of Stating the Connection Between Mind and Brain

It will be remembered that in our criticism of the theory of the integration of successive conscious units into a feeling of musical pitch, we decided that whatever integration there was was that of the air-pulses into a simpler and simpler sort of physical effect, as the propagations of material change got higher and higher in the nervous system. At last, we said (p. 156, above), there results some simple and massive process in the auditory centres of the hemispherical cortex, to which, *as a whole*, the feeling of musical pitch directly corresponds. Already, in discussing the localization of functions in the brain, I had said that consciousness accompanies the stream of innervation through that organ and varies in quality with the character of the currents, being mainly of things seen if the occipital lobes are much involved, of things heard if the action is focalized in the temporal lobes, etc., etc.; and I had added that a vague formula like this was as much as one could safely venture on in the actual state of physiology. The facts of mental deafness and blindness, of auditory and optical aphasia, show us that the whole brain must act together if certain thoughts are to occur. The consciousness, which is itself an integral thing not made of parts, 'corresponds' to the entire activity of the brain, whatever that may be, at the moment. This is a way of expressing the relation of mind and brain from which I shall not depart during the remainder of the book, because it expresses the bare phenomenal fact with no hypothesis, and is exposed to no such logical objections as we have found to cling to the theory of ideas in combination.

Nevertheless, this formula which is so unobjectionable if taken vaguely, positivistically, or scientifically, as a mere empirical law of concomitance between our thoughts and our brain, tumbles to pieces entirely if we assume to represent anything more intimate or ultimate by it. The ultimate of ultimate problems, of course, in the study of the relations of thought and brain, is to understand why and how such disparate things are connected at all. But before that problem is solved (if it ever is solved) there is a less ultimate problem which must first be settled. Before the connection of thought and brain can be explained, it must at least be *stated* in an elementary form; and there are great difficulties about so stating it. To state it in elementary form one must reduce it to its lowest terms and know which mental fact and which cerebral fact are, so to speak, in immediate juxtaposition. We must find the minimal mental fact whose being reposes directly on a brain-fact; and we must similarly find the minimal brain event which will have a mental counterpart at all. Between the mental and the physical minima thus found there will be an immediate relation, the expression of which, if we had it, would be the elementary psycho-physic law.

Our own formula escapes the unintelligibility of psychic atoms by *taking the entire thought* (even of a complex object) *as the minimum with which it deals on the mental side*. But in taking the entire brain process as its minimal fact on the material side it confronts other difficulties almost as bad.

In the first place, it ignores analogies on which certain critics will insist, those, namely, between the composition of the total brain process and that of the *object* of the thought. The total brain process is composed of parts, of simultaneous processes in the seeing, the hearing, the feeling, and other centres. The object thought of is also composed of parts, some of which are seen, others heard, others perceived by touch and muscular manipulation. 'How then', these critics will say, 'should the thought not itself be composed of parts, each the counterpart of a part of the object and of a part of the brain process?' So natural is this way of looking at the matter that it has given rise to what is on the whole the most flourishing of all psychological systems – that of the Lockean school of associated ideas – of which school the mind-stuff theory is nothing but the last and subtlest offshoot.

The second difficulty is deeper still. *The 'entire brain process' is not a physical fact at all*. It is the appearance to an onlooking mind of a multitude of physical facts. 'Entire brain' is nothing but our name for the way in which a million of molecules arranged in certain positions may affect our sense. On the principles of the corpuscular or mechanical philosophy, the only realities are the separate molecules, or at most the cells. Their aggregation into a 'brain' is a fiction of popular speech. Such a fiction cannot serve as the objectively real counterpart to any psychic state whatever. Only a genuinely physical fact can so serve. But the molecular fact is the only genuine physical fact – whereupon we seem, if we are to have an elementary psychophysic law at all, thrust right back upon something like the mind-stuff theory, for the molecular fact, being an element of the 'brain', would seem naturally to correspond, not to the total thoughts, but to elements in the thought.

What shall we do? Many would find relief at this point in celebrating the mystery of the unknowable and the 'awe' which we should feel at having such a principle to take final charge of our perplexities. Others would rejoice that the finite and separatist view of things with which we started had at last developed its contradictions, and was about to lead us dialectically upwards to some 'higher synthesis' in which inconsistencies cease from troubling and logic is at rest. It may be a constitutional infirmity, but I can take no comfort in such devices for making a luxury of intellectual defeat. They are but spiritual chloroform. Better live on the ragged edge, better gnaw the file forever!

The Material-Monad Theory

The most rational thing to do is to suspect that there may be a third possibility, an alternative supposition which we have not considered. Now there *is* an alternative supposition – a supposition moreover which has been frequently made in the history of philosophy, and which is freer from logical objections than either of the views we have ourselves discussed. It may be called the *theory of polyzoism or multiple monadism*; and it conceives the matter thus:

Every brain cell has its own individual consciousness, which no other cell knows anything about, all individual consciousnesses being 'ejective' to each other. There is, however, among the cells one central or pontifical one to which *our* consciousness is attached. But the events of all the other cells physically influence this arch-cell; and through producing their joint effects on it, these other cells may be said to 'combine'. The arch-cell is, in fact, one of those 'external media' without which we saw that no fusion or integration of a number of things can occur. The physical modifications of the arch-cell thus form a sequence of results in the production whereof every other cell has a share, so that, as one might say, every other cell is represented therein. And similarly, the conscious correlates to these physical modifications form a sequence of thoughts or feelings, each one of which is, as to its substantive being, an integral and uncompounded psychic thing, but each one of which may (in the exercise of its *cognitive* function) be *aware of* THINGS many and complicated in proportion to the number of other cells that have helped to modify the central cell.

By a conception of this sort, one incurs neither of the internal contradictions which we found to beset the other two theories. One has no unintelligible self-combining of psychic units to account for on the one hand; and on the other hand, one need not treat as the physical counterpart of the stream of consciousness under observation, a 'total brain activity' which is non-existent as a genuinely physical fact. But, to offset these advantages, one has physiological difficulties and improbabilities. There is no cell or group of cells in the brain of such anatomical or functional pre-eminence as to appear to be the keystone or centre of gravity of the whole system. And even if there were such a cell, the theory of multiple monadism would, in strictness of thought, have no right to stop at it and treat it as a unit. The cell is no more a unit, materially considered, than the total brain is a unit. It is a compound of molecules, just as the brain is a compound of cells and fibres. And the molecules, according to the prevalent physical theories, are in turn compounds of atoms. The theory in question, therefore, if radically carried out, must set up for its elementary and irreducible psycho-physic couple, not the cell and its consciousness, but the primordial and eternal atom and its consciousness. We are back at Leibnizian monadism, and therewith leave physiology behind us and dive into regions inaccessible to experience and verification; and our doctrine, although not self-contradictory, becomes so remote and unreal as to be almost as bad as if it were. Speculative minds alone will take an interest in it; and metaphysics, not psychology, will be responsible for its career. That the career may be a successful one must be admitted as a possibility – a theory which

Leibniz, Herbart and Lotze have taken under their protection must have some sort of a destiny.

The Soul Theory

But is this my last word? By no means. Many readers have certainly been saying to themselves for the last few pages: 'Why on earth doesn't the poor man say *the soul* and have done with it?' Other readers, of anti-spiritualistic training and prepossessions, advanced thinkers, or popular evolutionists, will perhaps be a little surprised to find this much-despised word now sprung upon them at the end of so physiological a train of thought. But the plain fact is that all the arguments for a 'pontifical cell' or an 'arch-monad' are also arguments for that well-known spiritual agent in which scholastic psychology and common-sense have always believed. And my only reason for beating the bushes so, and not bringing it in earlier as a possible solution of our difficulties, has been that by this procedure I might perhaps force some of these materialistic minds to feel the more strongly the logical respectability of the spiritualistic position. The fact is that one cannot afford to despise any of these great traditional objects of belief. Whether we realize it or not, there is always a great drift of reasons, positive and negative, towing us in their direction. If there be such entities as souls in the universe, they may possibly be affected by the manifold occurrences that go on in the nervous centres. To the state of the entire brain at a given moment they may respond by inward modifications of their own. These changes of state may be pulses of consciousness, cognitive of objects few or many, simple or complex. The soul would be thus a medium upon which (to use our earlier phraseology) the manifold brain processes *combine their effects*. Not needing to consider it as the 'inner aspect' of any arch-molecule or brain cell, we escape that physiological improbability; and as its pulses of consciousness are unitary and integral affairs from the outset, we escape the absurdity of supposing feelings which exist separately and then 'fuse together' by themselves. The separateness is in the brain-world, on this theory, and the unity in the soul-world; and the only trouble that remains to haunt us is the metaphysical one of understanding how one sort of world or existent thing can affect or influence another at all. This trouble, however, since it also exists inside of both worlds, and involves neither physical improbability nor logical contradiction, is relatively small.

I confess, therefore, that to posit a soul influenced in some mysterious way by the brain states and responding to them by conscious affections of its own, seems to me the line of least logical resistance, so far as we have yet attained.

If it does not strictly *explain* anything, it is at any rate less positively objectionable than either mind-stuff or a material-monad creed. *The bare* PHENOMENON, *however, the* IMMEDI-ATELY KNOWN *thing which on the mental side is in apposition with the entire brain-process is the state of consciousness and not the soul itself.* Many of the staunchest believers in the soul admit that we know it only as an inference from experiencing its *states.* In Chapter 12, below, accordingly, we must return to its consideration again, and *ask ourselves whether, after all, the ascertainment of a blank unmediated correspondence, term for term, of the succession of states of consciousness with the succession of total brain-processes, be not the simplest psycho-physic formula, and the last word of a psychology which contents itself with verifiable laws, and seeks only to be clear, and to avoid unsafe hypotheses.* Such a mere admission of the empirical parallelism will there appear the wisest course. By keeping to it, our psychology will remain positivistic and non-metaphysical; and although this is certainly only a provisional halting-place, and things must some day be more thoroughly thought out, we shall abide there in this book, and just as we have rejected mind-dust, we shall take no account of the soul. The spiritualistic reader may nevertheless believe in the soul if he will; whilst the positivistic one who wishes to give a tinge of mystery to the expression of his positivism can continue to say that nature in her unfathomable designs has mixed us of clay and flame, of brain and mind, that the two things hang indubitably together and determine each other's being, but how or why, no mortal may ever know.

11

The Stream of Thought[1]

We now begin our study of the mind from within. Most books start with sensations, as the simplest mental facts, and proceed synthetically, constructing each higher stage from those below it. But this is abandoning the empirical method of investigation. No one ever had a simple sensation by itself. Consciousness, from our natal day, is of a teeming multiplicity of objects and relations, and what we call simple sensations are results of discriminative attention, pushed often to a very high degree. It is astonishing what havoc is wrought in psychology by admitting at the outset apparently innocent suppositions, that nevertheless contain a flaw. The bad consequences develop themselves later on, and are irremediable, being woven through the whole texture of the work. The notion that sensations, being the simplest things, are the first things to take up in psychology is one of these suppositions. The only thing which psychology has a right to postulate at the outset is the fact of thinking itself, and that must first be taken up and analysed. If sensations then prove to be amongst the elements of the thinking, we shall be no worse off as respects them than if we had taken them for granted at the start.

The first fact for us, then, as psychologists, is that thinking of some sort goes on. I use the word thinking, in accordance with what was said [earlier], for every form of consciousness indiscriminately. If we could say in English 'it thinks', as we say 'it rains' or 'it blows', we should be stating the fact most simply and with the minimum of assumption. As we cannot, we must simply say that *thought goes on.*

---

[1] A good deal of this chapter is reprinted from an article 'On some Omissions of Introspective Psychology' which appeared in *Mind* for January 1884.

Five Characters in Thought

How does it go on? We notice immediately five important characters in the process, of which it shall be the duty of the present chapter to treat in a general way:

1 Every thought tends to be part of a personal consciousness.
2 Within each personal consciousness thought is always changing.
3 Within each personal consciousness thought is sensibly continuous.
4 It always appears to deal with objects independent of itself.
5 It is interested in some parts of these objects to the exclusion of others, and welcomes or rejects – *chooses* from among them, in a word – all the while.

In considering these five points successively, we shall have to plunge *in medias res* as regards our vocabulary, and use psychological terms which can only be adequately defined in later chapters of the book. But everyone knows what the terms mean in a rough way; and it is only in a rough way that we are now to take them. This chapter is like a painter's first charcoal sketch upon his canvas, in which no niceties appear.

1 Thought Tends to Personal Form

When I say *every thought is part of a personal consciousness*, 'personal consciousness' is one of the terms in question. Its meaning we know so long as no one asks us to define it, but to give an accurate account of it is the most difficult of philosophic tasks. This task we must confront in the next chapter; here a preliminary word will suffice.

In this room – this lecture room, say – there are a multitude of thoughts, yours and mine, some of which cohere mutually, and some not. They are as little each-for-itself and reciprocally independent as they are all-belonging-together. They are neither: no one of them is separate, but each belongs with certain others and with none beside. My thought belongs with my other thoughts, and your thought with your other thoughts. Whether anywhere in the room there be a mere thought, which is nobody's thought, we have no means of ascertaining, for we have no experience of its like. The only states of consciousness that we naturally deal with are found in personal conscious-nesses, minds, selves, concrete particular I's and you's.

Each of these minds keeps its own thoughts to itself. There is no giving or bartering between them. No thought even comes into direct *sight* of a thought in another personal consciousness than its own. Absolute insulation, irreducible pluralism, is the law. It seems as if the elementary psychic fact were not *thought* or *this thought* or *that thought*, but *my thought*, every thought being *owned*. Neither contemporaneity, nor proximity in space, nor similarity of quality and content are able to fuse thoughts together which are sundered by this barrier of belonging to different personal minds. The breaches between such thoughts are the most absolute breaches in nature. Everyone will recog-nize this to be true, so long as the existence of *something* corresponding to the term 'personal mind' is all that is insisted on, without any particular view of its nature being implied. On these terms the personal self rather than the thought might be treated as the immediate datum in psychology. The universal conscious fact is not 'feelings and thoughts exist', but 'I think' and 'I feel'.[2] No psychology, at any rate, can question the *existence* of personal selves. The worst a psychology can do is so to interpret the nature of these selves as to rob them of their worth. A French writer, speaking of our ideas, says somewhere in a fit of anti-spiritualistic excitement that, misled by certain peculiarities which they display, we 'end by personifying' the procession which they make – such personification being regarded by him as a great philosophic blunder on our part. It could only be a blunder if the notion of personality meant something essentially different from anything to be found in the mental procession. But if that procession be itself the very 'original' of the notion of personality, to personify it cannot possibly be wrong. It is already personified. There are no marks of personality to be gathered *aliunde*, and then found lacking in the train of thought. It has them all already; so that to whatever farther analysis we may subject that form of personal selfhood under which thoughts appear, it is, and must remain, true that

[2] B. P. Bowne, *Metaphysics*, p. 362.

the thoughts which psychology studies do continually tend to appear as parts of personal selves.

I say 'tend to appear' rather than 'appear', on account of those facts of subconscious personality, automatic writings, etc., of which we studied a few in the last chapter. The buried feelings and thoughts proved now to exist in hysterical anaesthetics, in recipients of post-hypnotic suggestion, etc., themselves are parts of *secondary personal selves*. These selves are for the most part very stupid and contracted, and are cut off at ordinary times from communication with the regular and normal self of the individual; but still they form conscious unities, have continuous memories, speak, write, invent distinct names for themselves, or adopt names that are suggested; and, in short, are entirely worthy of that title of secondary personalities which is now commonly given them. According to M. Janet these secondary personalities are always abnormal, and result from the splitting of what ought to be a single complete self into two parts, of which one lurks in the background whilst the other appears on the surface as the only self the man or woman has. For our present purpose it is unimportant whether this account of the origin of secondary selves is applicable to all possible cases of them or not, for it certainly is true of a large number of them. Now although the *size* of a secondary self thus formed will depend on the number of thoughts that are thus split off from the main consciousness, the *form* of it tends to personality, and the later thoughts pertaining to it remember the earlier ones and adopt them as their own. M. Janet caught the actual moment of inspissation (so to speak) of one of these secondary personalities in his anaesthetic somnambulist Lucie. He found that when this young woman's attention was absorbed in conversation with a third party, her anaesthetic hand would write simple answers to questions whispered to her by himself. 'Do you hear?' he asked. '*No*', was the unconsciously written reply. 'But to answer you must hear.' '*Yes, quite so.*' 'Then how do you manage?' '*I don't know.*' 'There must be someone who hears me.' '*Yes.*' 'Who?' '*Someone other than Lucie.*' 'Ah! another person. Shall we give her a name?' '*No.*' 'Yes, it will be more convenient.' '*Well, Adrienne, then.*' 'Once baptized, the subconscious personage', M. Janet continues, 'grows more definitely outlined and displays better her psychological characters. In particular she shows us that she is conscious of the feelings excluded from the consciousness of the primary or normal personage. She it is who tells us that I am pinching the arm or touching the little finger in which Lucie for so long has had no tactile sensations.'[3]

In other cases the adoption of the name by the secondary self is more spontaneous. I have seen a number of incipient automatic writers and mediums as yet imperfectly 'developed', who immediately and of their own accord write and speak in the name of departed spirits. These may be public characters, as Mozart, Faraday, or real persons formerly known to the subject, or altogether imaginary beings. Without prejudicing the question of real 'spirit control' in the more developed sorts of trance-utterance, I incline to think that these (often deplorably unintelligent) rudimentary utterances are the work of an inferior fraction of the subject's own natural mind, set free from control by the rest, and working after a set pattern fixed by the prejudices of the social environment. In a spiritualistic community we get optimistic messages, whilst in an ignorant Catholic village the secondary personage calls itself by the name of a demon, and proffers blasphemies and obscenities, instead of telling us how happy it is in the summer land.

Beneath these tracts of thought, which, however rudimentary, are still organized selves with a memory, habits, and sense of their own identity, M. Janet thinks that the facts of catalepsy in hysteric patients drive us to suppose that there are thoughts quite unorganized and impersonal. A patient in cataleptic trance (which can be produced artificially in certain hypnotized subjects) is without memory on waking, and seems insensible and unconscious as long as the cataleptic condition lasts. If, however, one raises the arm of such a subject it stays in that position, and the whole body can thus be moulded like wax under the hands of the operator, retaining for a considerable time whatever attitude he communicates to it. In hysterics whose arm, for example, is anaesthetic, the same thing may happen. The anaesthetic arm may remain passively in positions which it is made to assume; or if the hand be taken and made to hold a pencil and trace a certain letter, it will continue tracing that letter indefinitely on the paper. These acts, until recently, were supposed to be accompanied by no consciousness at all: they

[3] *L'Automatisme Psychologique*, p. 318.

were physiological reflexes. M. Janet considers with much more plausibility that feeling escorts them. The feeling is probably merely that of the position or movement of the limb, and it produces no more than its natural effects when it discharges into the motor centres which keep the position maintained, or the movement incessantly renewed.[4] Such thoughts as these, says M. Janet, 'are known by *no one*, for disaggregated sensations reduced to a state of mental dust are not synthetized in any personality'.[5] He admits, however, that these very same unutterably stupid thoughts tend to develop memory – the cataleptic ere long moves her arm at a bare hint; so that they form no important exception to the law that all thought tends to assume the form of personal consciousness.

2 *Thought is in Constant Change*

I do not mean necessarily that no one state of mind has any duration – even if true, that would be hard to establish. The change which I have more particularly in view is that which takes place in sensible intervals of time; and the result on which I wish to lay stress is this, that *no state once gone can recur and be identical with what it was before*. Let us begin with Mr Shadworth Hodgson's description:

I go straight to the facts, without saying I go to perception, or sensation, or thought, or any special mode at all. What I find when I look at my consciousness at all is that what I cannot divest myself of, or not have in consciousness, if I have any consciousness at all, is a sequence of different feelings. I may shut my eyes and keep perfectly still, and try not to contribute anything of my own will; but whether I think or do not think, whether I perceive external things or not, I always have a succession of different feelings. Anything else that I may have also, of a more special character, comes in as parts of this succession. Not to have the succession of different feelings is not to be conscious at all . . . The chain of consciousness is a sequence of *differents*.[6]

Such a description as this can awaken no possible protest from anyone. We all recognize as different great classes of our conscious states. Now we are seeing, now hearing; now

[4] For the physiology of this compare the chapter on the Will.
[5] Loc. cit., p. 316.
[6] *The Philosophy of Reflection*, 1, 248, 290.

reasoning, now willing; now recollecting, now expecting; now loving, now hating; and in a hundred other ways we know our minds to be alternately engaged. But all these are complex states. The aim of science is always to reduce complexity to simplicity; and in psychological science we have the celebrated 'theory of *ideas*' which, admitting the great difference among each other of what may be called concrete conditions of mind, seeks to show how this is all the resultant effect of variations in the *combination* of certain simple elements of consciousness that always remain the same. These mental atoms or molecules are what Locke called 'simple ideas'. Some of Locke's successors made out that the only simple ideas were the sensations strictly so called. Which ideas the simple ones may be does not, however, now concern us. It is enough that certain philosophers have thought they could see under the dissolving-view-appearance of the mind elementary facts of *any* sort that remained unchanged amid the flow.

And the view of these philosophers has been called little into question, for our common experience seems at first sight to corroborate it entirely. Are not the sensations we get from the same object, for example, always the same? Does not the same piano key, struck with the same force, make us hear in the same way? Does not the same grass give us the same feeling of green, the same sky the same feeling of blue, and do we not get the same olfactory sensation no matter how many times we put our nose to the same flask of cologne? It seems a piece of metaphysical sophistry to suggest that we do not; and yet a close attention to the matter shows that *there is no proof that the same bodily sensation is ever got by us twice.*

What is got twice is the same OBJECT. We hear the same *note* over and over again; we see the same *quality* of green, or smell the same objective perfume, or experience the same *species* of pain. The realities, concrete and abstract, physical and ideal, whose permanent existence we believe in, seem to be constantly coming up again before our thought, and lead us, in our carelessness, to suppose that our 'ideas' of them are the same ideas. When we come, some time later, to the chapter on perception, we shall see how inveterate is our habit of not attending to sensations as subjective facts, but of simply using them as stepping-stones to pass over to the recognition of the realities whose presence they reveal. The grass out of the window now looks to me of the same green in the sun as in the shade, and yet a painter would have to paint one part of it dark brown, another part bright yellow, to give its real sensational effect. We take no heed, as a rule, of the different way in which the same things look and sound and smell at different distances and under different circumstances. The sameness of the *things* is what we are concerned to ascertain; and any sensations that assure us of that will probably be considered in a rough way to be the same with each other. This is what makes off-hand testimony about the subjective identity of different sensations well-nigh worthless as a proof of the fact. The entire history of sensation is a commentary on our inability to tell whether two sensations received apart are exactly alike. What appeals to our attention far more than the absolute quality or quantity of a given sensation is its ratio to whatever other sensations we may have at the same time. When everything is dark a somewhat less dark sensation makes us see an object white. Helmholtz calculates that the white marble painted in a picture representing an architectural view by moonlight is, when seen by daylight, from ten to twenty thousand times brighter than the real moonlit marble would be.[7]

Such a difference as this could never have been *sensibly* learned; it had to be inferred from a series of indirect considerations. There are facts which make us believe that our sensibility is altering all the time, so that the same object cannot easily give us the same sensation over again. The eye's sensibility to light is at its maximum when the eye is first exposed, and blunts itself with surprising rapidity. A long night's sleep will make it see things twice as brightly on wakening, as simple rest by closure will make it see them later in the day.[8] We feel things differently according as we are sleepy or awake, hungry or full, fresh or tired; differently at night and in the morning, differently in summer and in winter, and above all things differently in childhood, manhood and old age. Yet we never doubt that our feelings reveal the same world, with the same sensible qualities and the same sensible things occupying it. The difference of the sensibility is shown best by the difference of our emotion about the things from one age to another, or when we are in different

[7] *Populäre Wissenschaftliche Vorträge, Drittes Heft,* 1876, p. 72.
[8] Fick, in L. Hermann's *Handb. d. Physiol., Bd.* 3, Th 1, p. 225.

organic moods. What was bright and exciting becomes weary, flat and unprofitable. The bird's song is tedious, the breeze is mournful, the sky is sad.

To these indirect presumptions that our sensations, following the mutations of our capacity for feeling, are always undergoing an essential change, must be added another presumption, based on what must happen in the brain. Every sensation corresponds to some cerebral action. For an identical sensation to recur it would have to occur the second time *in an unmodified brain*. But as this, strictly speaking, is a physiological impossibility, so is an unmodified feeling an impossibility; for to every brain modification, however small, must correspond a change of equal amount in the feeling which the brain subserves.

All this would be true if even sensations came to us pure and single and not combined into 'things'. Even then we should have to confess that, however we might in ordinary conversation speak of getting the same sensation again, we never in strict theoretic accuracy could do so; and that whatever was true of the river of life, of the river of elementary feeling, it would certainly be true to say, like Heraclitus, that we never descend twice into the same stream.

But if the assumption of 'simple ideas of sensation' recurring in immutable shape is so easily shown to be baseless, how much more baseless is the assumption of immutability in the larger masses of our thought!

For there it is obvious and palpable that our state of mind is never precisely the same. Every thought we have of a given fact is, strictly speaking, unique, and only bears a resemblance of kind with our thoughts of the same fact. When the identical fact recurs, we *must* think of it in a fresh manner, see it under a somewhat different angle, apprehend it in different relations from those in which it last appeared. And the thought by which we cognize it is the thought of it-in-those-relations, a thought suffused with the consciousness of all that dim context. Often we are ourselves struck at the strange differences in our successive views of the same thing. We wonder how we ever could have opined as we did last month about a certain matter. We have outgrown the possibility of that state of mind, we know not how. From one year to another we see things in new lights. What was unreal has grown real, and what was exciting is insipid. The friends we used to care the world for are shrunken to shadows; the women, once so divine, the stars, the woods, and the waters, how now so dull and common; the young girls that brought an aura of infinity, at present hardly distinguishable existences; the pictures so empty; and as for the books, what *was* there to find so mysteriously significant in Goethe, or in John Mill so full of weight? Instead of all this, more zestful than ever is the work; and fuller and deeper the import of common duties and of common goods.

But what here strikes us so forcibly on the flagrant scale exists on every scale, down to the imperceptible transition from one hour's outlook to that of the next. Experience is remoulding us every moment, and our mental reaction on every given thing is really a resultant of our experience of the whole world up to that date. The analogies of brain physiology must again be appealed to to corroborate our view.

Our earlier chapters have taught us to believe that, whilst we think, our brain changes, and that, like the aurora borealis, its whole internal equilibrium shifts with every pulse of change. The precise nature of the shifting at a given moment is a product of many factors. The accidental state of local nutrition or blood supply may be among them. But just as one of them certainly is the influence of outward objects on the sense organs during the moment, so is another certainly the very special susceptibility in which the organ has been left at that moment by all it has gone through in the past. Every brain state is partly determined by the nature of this entire past succession. Alter the latter in any part, and the brain state must be somewhat different. Each present brain state is a record in which the eye of Omniscience might read all the foregone history of its owner. It is out of the question, then, that any total brain state should identically recur. Something like it may recur; but to suppose *it* to recur would be equivalent to the absurd admission that all the states that had intervened between its two appearances had been pure nonentities, and that the organ after their passage was exactly as it was before. And (to consider shorter periods) just as, in the senses, an impression feels very differently according to what has preceded it; as one colour succeeding another is modified by the contrast, silence sounds delicious after noise, and a note, when the scale is sung up, sounds unlike itself when the scale is sung down; as the presence of certain lines, and as in music the whole aesthetic effect comes from the manner in which one set of sounds alters our feeling of another; so, in thought, we must admit that those portions of the brain that have just been maximally excited retain a kind of soreness which is a condition of our present consciousness, a codeterminant of how and what we now shall feel.[9]

Ever some tracts are waning in tension, some waxing, whilst others actively discharge. The states of tension have as positive an influence as any in determining the total condition, and in deciding what the *psychosis* shall be. All we know of submaximal nerve irritations, and of the summation of apparently ineffective stimuli, tends to show that *no* changes in the brain are physiologically ineffective, and that presumably none are bare of psychological result. But as the brain tension shifts from one relative state of equilibrium to another, like the gyrations of a kaleidoscope, now rapid and now slow, is it likely that its faithful psychic concomitant is heavier-footed than itself, and that it cannot match each one of the organ's irradiations by a shifting inward iridescence of its own? But if it can do this, its inward iridescences must be infinite, for the brain redistributions are in infinite variety. If so coarse a thing as a telephone-plate can be made to thrill for years and never reduplicate its inward condition, how much more must this be the case with the infinitely delicate brain?

I am sure that this concrete and total manner of regarding the mind's changes is the only true manner, difficult as it may be to carry it out in detail. If anything seems obscure about it, it will grow clearer as we advance. Meanwhile, if it be true, it is certainly also true that no two 'ideas' are ever exactly the same, which is the proposition we started to prove. The proposition is more important theoretically than it at first sight seems. For it makes it already impossible for us to follow obediently in the footprints of either the Lockean or the Herbartian school, schools which have had almost unlimited influence in Germany and among ourselves. No doubt it is often *convenient* to

---

[9] It need of course not follow, because a total brain-state does not recur, that no *point* of the brain can ever be twice in the same condition. That would be as improbable a consequence as that in the sea a wave-crest should never come twice at the same point of space. What can hardly come twice is an identical *combination* of wave forms all with their crests and hollows reoccupying identical places. For such a total combination as this is the analogue of the brain-state to which our actual consciousness at any moment is due.

formulate the mental facts in an atomistic sort of way, and to treat the higher states of consciousness as if they were all built out of unchanging simple ideas. It is convenient often to treat curves as if they were composed of small straight lines, and electricity and nerve-force as if they were fluids. But in the one case as in the other we must never forget that we are talking symbolically, and that there is nothing in nature to answer to our words. *A permanently existing 'idea' or 'Vorstellung' which makes its appearance before the footlights of consciousness at periodical intervals, is as mythological an entity as the Jack of Spades.*

What makes it convenient to use the mythological formulas is the whole organization of speech, which, as was remarked a while ago, was not made by psychologists, but by men who were as a rule only interested in the facts their mental states revealed. They only spoke of their states as *ideas of this or of that thing.* What wonder, then, that the thought is most easily conceived under the law of the thing whose name it bears! If the thing is composed of parts, then we suppose that the thought of the thing must be composed of the thoughts of the parts. If one part of the thing have appeared in the same thing or in other things on former occasions, why then we must be having even now the very same 'idea' of that part which was there on those occasions. If the thing is simple, its thought is simple. If it is multitudinous, it must require a multitude of thoughts to think it. If a succession, only a succession of thoughts can know it. If permanent, its thought is permanent. And so on *ad libitum.* What after all is so natural as to assume that one object, called by one name, should be known by one affection of the mind? But, if language must thus influence us, the agglutinative languages, and even Greek and Latin with their declensions, would be the better guides. Names did not appear in them inalterable, but changed their shape to suit the context in which they lay. It must have been easier then than now to conceive of the same object as being thought of at different times in non-identical conscious states.

This, too, will grow clearer as we proceed. Meanwhile a necessary consequence of the belief in permanent self-identical psychic facts that absent themselves and recur periodically is the Humean doctrine that our thought is composed of separate independent parts and is not a sensibly continuous stream. That

this doctrine entirely misrepresents the natural appearances is
what I next shall try to show.

3 Within each Personal Consciousness, Thought is Sensibly Continuous

I can only define 'continuous' as that which is without breach,
crack or division. I have already said that the breach from one
mind to another is perhaps the greatest breach in nature. The
only breaches that can well be conceived to occur within the
limits of a single mind would either be *interruptions*, *time*-gaps
during which the consciousness went out altogether to come
into existence again at a later moment; or they would be breaks
in the *quality*, or content, of the thought, so abrupt that the
segment that followed had no connection whatever with the one
that went before. The proposition that within each personal
consciousness thought feels continuous, means two things:

1 That even where there is a time-gap the consciousness
   after it feels as if it belonged together with the consciousness before it, as another part of the same self;
2 That the changes from one moment to another in the
   quality of the consciousness are never absolutely abrupt.

The case of the time-gaps, as the simplest, shall be taken first.
And first of all, a word about time-gaps of which the consciousness may not be itself aware.

[Earlier] we saw that such time-gaps existed, and that they
might be more numerous than is usually supposed. If the consciousness is not aware of them, it cannot feel them as interruptions. In the unconsciousness produced by nitrous oxide and
other anaesthetics, in that of epilepsy and fainting, the broken
edges of the sentient life may meet and merge over the gap,
much as the feelings of space of the opposite margins of the
'blind spot' meet and merge over that objective interruption to
the sensitiveness of the eye. Such consciousness as this, whatever
it be for the onlooking psychologist, is for itself unbroken. It
feels unbroken; a waking day of it is sensibly a unit as long as
that day lasts, in the sense in which the hours themselves are
units, as having all their parts next each other, with no intrusive
alien substance between. To expect the consciousness to feel the
interruptions of its objective continuity as gaps, would be like

expecting the eye to feel a gap of silence because it does not hear, or the ear to feel a gap of darkness because it does not see. So much for the gaps that are unfelt.

With the felt gaps the case is different. On waking from sleep, we usually know that we have been unconscious, and we often have an accurate judgment of how long. The judgment here is certainly an inference from sensible signs, and its ease is due to long practice in the particular field.[10] The result of it, however, is that the consciousness is, *for itself*, not what it was in the former case, but interrupted and continuous, in the mere time-sense of the words. But in the other sense of continuity, the sense of the parts being inwardly connected and belonging together because they are parts of a common whole, the consciousness remains sensibly continuous and one. What now is the common whole? The natural name for it is *myself*, *I* or *me*.

When Paul and Peter wake up in the same bed, and recognize that they have been asleep, each one of them mentally reaches back and makes connection with but *one* of the two streams of thought which were broken by the sleeping hours. As the current of an electrode buried in the ground unerringly finds its way to its own similarly buried mate, across no matter how much intervening earth; so Peter's present instantly finds out Peter's past, and never by mistake knits itself on to that of Paul. Paul's thought in turn is as little liable to go astray. The past thought of Peter is appropriated by the present Peter alone. He may have a *knowledge*, and a correct one too, of what Paul's last drowsy states of mind were as he sank into sleep, but it is an entirely different sort of knowledge from that which he has of his own last states. He *remembers* his own states, whilst he only *conceives* Paul's. Remembrance is like direct feeling; its object is suffused with a warmth and intimacy to which no object of mere conception ever attains. This quality of warmth and intimacy and immediacy is what Peter's *present* thought also possesses for itself. So sure as this present is me, is mine, it says, so sure is anything else that comes with the same warmth and intimacy and immediacy, me and mine. What the qualities called warmth and intimacy may in themselves be will have to be matter for future consideration. But whatever past feelings

[10] The accurate registration of the 'how long' is still a little mysterious.

appear with those qualities must be admitted to receive the greeting of the present mental state, to be owned by it, and accepted as belonging together with it in a common self. This community of self is what the time-gap cannot break in twain, and is why a present thought, although not ignorant of the time-gap, can still regard itself as continuous with certain chosen portions of the past.

Consciousness, then, does not appear to itself chopped up in bits. Such words as 'chain' or 'train' do not describe it fitly as it presents itself in the first instance. It is nothing jointed; it flows. A 'river' or a 'stream' are the metaphors by which it is most naturally described. *In talking of it hereafter, let us call it the stream of thought, of consciousness, or of subjective life.*

But now there appears, even within the limits of the same self, and between thoughts all of which alike have this same sense of belonging together, a kind of jointing and separateness among the parts, of which this statement seems to take no account. I refer to the breaks that are produced by sudden *contrasts in the quality* of the successive segments of the stream of thought. If the words 'chain' and 'train' had no natural fitness in them, how came such words to be used at all? Does not a loud explosion rend the consciousness upon which it abruptly breaks, in twain? Does not every sudden shock, appearance of a new object, or change in a sensation, create a real interruption, sensibly felt as such, which cuts the conscious stream across at the moment at which it appears? Do not such interruptions smite us every hour of our lives, and have we the right, in their presence, still to call our consciousness a continuous stream?

This objection is based partly on a confusion and partly on a superficial introspective view.

The confusion is between the thoughts themselves, taken as subjective facts, and the things of which they are aware. It is natural to make this confusion, but easy to avoid it when once put on one's guard. The things are discrete and discontinuous; they do pass before us in a train or chain, making often explosive appearances and rending each other in twain. But their comings and goings and contrasts no more break the flow of the thought that thinks them than they break the time and the space in which they lie. A silence may be broken by a thunder-clap, and we may be so stunned and confused for a moment by the shock as to give no instant account to ourselves of what has happened. But that very confusion is a mental state, and a state that passes us straight over from the silence to the sound. The transition between the thought of one object and the thought of another is no more a break in the *thought* than a joint in a bamboo is a break in the wood. It is a part of the *consciousness* as much as the joint is a part of the *bamboo*.

The superficial introspective view is the overlooking, even when the things are contrasted with each other most violently, of the large amount of affinity that may still remain between the thoughts by whose means they are cognized. Into the awareness of the thunder itself the awareness of the previous silence creeps and continues; for what we hear when the thunder crashes is not thunder *pure*, but thunder-breaking-upon-silence-and-con-trasting-with-it.[11] Our feeling of the same objective thunder, coming in this way, is quite different from what it would be were the thunder a continuation of previous thunder. The thunder itself we believe to abolish and exclude the silence; but the *feeling* of the thunder is also a feeling of the silence as just gone; and it would be difficult to find in the actual concrete consciousness of man a feeling so limited to the present as not to have an inkling of anything that went before. Here, again, language works against our perception of the truth. We name our thoughts simply, each after its thing, as if each knew its own thing and nothing else. What each really knows is clearly the thing it is named for, with dimly perhaps a thousand other things. It ought to be named after all of them, but it never is. Some of them are always things known a moment ago more clearly; others are things to be known more clearly a moment hence.[12] Our own bodily position, attitude, condition, is one of

[11] Cf. Brentano, *Psychologie*, vol. 1, pp. 219–20. Altogether this chapter of Brentano's on the unity of consciousness is as good as anything with which I am acquainted.

[12] Honour to whom honour is due! The most explicit acknowledgement I have anywhere found of all this is in a buried and forgotten paper by the Rev. Jas. Wills, on 'Accidental Association', in the *Transactions of the Royal Irish Academy*, vol. 21, Part I, 1846. Mr Wills writes:

'At every instant of conscious thought there is a certain sum of perceptions, or reflections, or both together, present, and together constituting one whole state of apprehension. Of this some definite portion may be far more distinct than all the rest; and the rest be in consequence proportionably vague, even to the limit of obliteration. But still, within this limit, the most dim shade of perception enters into, and in some infinitesimal degree modifies, the whole existing state. This state will thus be in some

the things of which *some* awareness, however inattentive, invariably accompanies the knowledge of whatever else we know. We think; and as we think we feel our bodily selves as the seat of the thinking. If the thinking be *our* thinking, it must be suffused through all its parts with that peculiar warmth and intimacy that make it come as ours. Whether the warmth and intimacy be anything more than the feeling of the same old body always there, is a matter for the next chapter to decide. *Whatever* the content of the ego may be, it is habitually felt *with* everything else by us humans, and must form a *liaison* between all the things of which we become successively aware.[13]

On this gradualness in the changes of our mental content the principles of nerve-action can throw some more light. When studying, in Chapter 3 [*Principles of Psychology*], the summation of nervous activities, we saw that no state of the brain can be supposed instantly to die away. If a new state comes, the inertia of the old state will still be there and modify the result accordingly. Of course we cannot tell, in our ignorance, what in each instance the modifications ought to be. The commonest modifications in sense perception are known as the phenomena of contrast. In aesthetics they are the feelings of delight or displeasure which certain particular orders in a series of impressions give. In thought, strictly and narrowly so called, they are unquestionably that consciousness of the *whence* and the *whither* that always accompanies its flows. If recently the brain tract *a* was vividly excited, and then *b*, and now vividly *c*,

---

way modified by any sensation or emotion, or act of distinct attention, that may give prominence to any part of it; so that the actual result is capable of the utmost variation, according to the person or the occasion . . . To any portion of the entire scope here described there may be a special direction of the attention, and this special direction is recognized as strictly what is *recognized* as the idea present to the mind. This idea is evidently not commensurate with the entire state of apprehension, and much perplexity has arisen from not observing this fact. However deeply we may suppose the attention to be engaged by any thought, any considerable alteration of the surrounding phenomena would still be perceived; the most abstruse demonstration in this room would not prevent a listener, however absorbed, from noticing the sudden extinction of the lights. Our mental states have always an *essential unity*, such that each state of apprehension, however variously compounded, is a single whole, of which every component is, therefore, strictly apprehended (so far as it is apprehended) as a part. Such is the elementary basis from which all our intellectual operations commence.'

[13] Compare the charming passage in Taine on intelligence (NY edn), 1, 83–4.

the total present consciousness is not produced simply by c's excitement, but also by the dying vibrations of a and b as well. If we want to represent the brain-process we must write it thus: $_{a}{}^{c}_{b}$ — three different processes coexisting, and correlated with them a thought which is no one of the three thoughts which they would have produced had each of them occurred alone. But whatever this fourth thought may exactly be, it seems impossible that it should not be something *like* each of the three other thoughts whose tracts are concerned in its production, though in a fast-waning phase.

It all goes back to what we said in another connection only a few pages ago (p. 180, above). As the total neurosis changes, so does the total psychosis change. But as the changes of neurosis are never absolutely discontinuous, so must the successive psychoses shade gradually into each other, although their *rate* of change may be much faster at one moment than at the next.

This difference in the rate of change lies at the basis of a difference of subjective states of which we ought immediately to speak. When the rate is slow we are aware of the object of our thought in a comparatively restful and stable way. When rapid, we are aware of a passage, a relation, a transition *from* it, or *between* it and something else. As we take, in fact, a general view of the wonderful stream of our consciousness, what strikes us first is this different pace of its parts. Like a bird's life, it seems to be made of an alternation of flights and perchings. The rhythm of language expresses this, where every thought is expressed in a sentence, and every sentence closed by a period. The resting-places are usually occupied by sensorial imaginations of some sort, whose peculiarity is that they can be held before the mind for an indefinite time, and contemplated without changing; the places of flight are filled with thoughts of relations, static or dynamic, that for the most part obtain between the matters contemplated in the periods of comparative rest.

Let us call the resting-places the 'substantive parts', and the places of flight the 'transitive parts', of the stream of thought. It then appears that the main end of our thinking is at all times the attainment of some other substantive part than the one from which we have just been dislodged. And we may say that the main use of the transitive parts is to lead us from one substantive conclusion to another.

Now it is very difficult, introspectively, to see the transitive parts for what they really are. If they are but flights to a conclusion, stopping them to look at them before the conclusion is reached is really annihilating them. Whilst if we wait till the conclusion *be* reached, it so exceeds them in vigour and stability that it quite eclipses and swallows them up in its glare. Let anyone try to cut a thought across in the middle and get a look at its section, and he will see how difficult the introspective observation of the transitive tracts is. The rush of the thought is so headlong that it almost always brings us up at the conclusion before we can arrest it. Or if our purpose is nimble enough and we do arrest it, it ceases forthwith to be itself. As a snowflake crystal caught in the warm hand is no longer a crystal but a drop, so, instead of catching the feeling of relation moving to its term, we find we have caught some substantive thing, usually the last word we were pronouncing, statically taken, and with its function, tendency and particular meaning in the sentence quite evaporated. The attempt at introspective analysis in these cases is in fact like seizing a spinning top to catch its motion, or trying to turn up the gas quickly enough to see how the darkness looks. And the challenge to *produce* these psychoses, which is sure to be thrown by doubting psychologists at anyone who contends for their existence, is as unfair as Zeno's treatment of the advocates of motion, when, asking them to point out in what place an arrow *is* when it moves, he argues the falsity of their thesis from their inability to make to so preposterous a question an immediate reply.

The results of this introspective difficulty are baleful. If to hold fast and observe the transitive parts of thought's stream be so hard, then the great blunder to which all schools are liable must be the failure to register them, and the undue emphasizing of the more substantive parts of the stream. Were we not ourselves a moment since in danger of ignoring any feeling transitive between the silence and the thunder, and of treating their boundary as a sort of break in the mind? Now such ignoring as this has historically worked in two ways. One set of thinkers have been led by it to *sensationalism*. Unable to lay their hands on any coarse feelings corresponding to the innumerable relations and forms of connection between the facts of the world, finding no *named* subjective modifications mirroring such relations, they have for the most part denied that feelings of relation exist, and many of them, like Hume, have gone so far as to deny the reality of most relations *out* of the mind as well as in it. Substantive psychoses, sensations and their copies and derivatives, juxtaposed like dominoes in a game, but really separate, everything else verbal illusion — such is the upshot of this view.[14] The *intellectualists*, on the other hand, unable to give up the reality of relations *extra mentem*, but equally unable to point to any distinct substantive feelings in which they were known, have made the same admission that the feelings do not exist. But they have drawn an opposite conclusion. The relations must be known, they say, in something that is no feeling, no mental modification continuous and consubstantial with the subjective tissue out of which sensations and other substantive states are made. They are known, these relations, by something that lies on an entirely different plane, by an *actus purus* of thought, intellect or reason, all written with capitals and considered to mean something unutterably superior to any fact of sensibility whatever.

But from our point of view both intellectualists and sensationalists are wrong. If there be such things as feelings at all, *then so surely as relations between objects exist in* rerum natura, *so surely, and more surely, do feelings exist to which these relations are known*. There is not a conjunction or a preposition, and hardly an adverbial phrase, a syntactic form or inflection of voice, in human speech, that does not express some shading or other of relation which we at some moment actually feel to exist between the larger objects of our thought. If we speak objectively, it is the real relations that appear revealed; if we speak subjectively, it is the stream of consciousness that matches each of them by an inward colouring of its own. In either case the relations are numberless, and no existing language is capable of doing justice to all their shades.

We ought to say a feeling of *and*, a feeling of *if*, a feeling of *but*, and a feeling of *by*, quite as readily as we say a feeling of *blue* or a feeling of *cold*. Yet we do not: so inveterate has our

---

[14] E.g., 'The stream of thought is not a continuous current, but a series of distinct ideas, more or less rapid in their succession; the rapidity being measurable by the number that pass through the mind in a given time.' (Bain, *E. and W.*, p. 29.)

habit become of recognizing the existence of the substantive parts alone, that language almost refuses to lend itself to any other use. The empiricists have always dwelt on its influence in making us suppose that where we have a separate name, a separate thing must needs be there to correspond with it; and they have rightly denied the existence of the mob of abstract entities, principles and forces, in whose favour no other evidence than this could be brought up. But they have said nothing of that obverse error, of which we said a word in Chapter 13 (p. 243, below), of supposing that where there is *no* name no entity can exist. All *dumb* or anonymous psychic states have, owing to this error, been coolly suppressed; or, if recognized at all, have been named after the substantive perception that led to, as thoughts 'about' this object or 'about' that, the stolid word *about* engulfing all their delicate idiosyncrasies in its monotonous sound. Thus the greater and greater accentuation and isolation of the substantive parts have continually gone on.

Once more take a look at the brain. We believe the brain to be an organ whose internal equilibrium is always in a state of change – the change affecting every part. The pulses of change are doubtless more violent in one place than in another, their rhythm more rapid at this time than at that. As in a kaleidoscope revolving at a uniform rate, although the figures are always rearranging themselves, there are instants during which the transformation seems minute and interstitial and almost absent, followed by others when it shoots with magical rapidity, relatively stable forms thus alternating with forms we should not distinguish if seen again; so in the brain the perpetual rearrangement must result in some forms of tension lingering relatively long, whilst others simply come and pass. But if consciousness corresponds to the fact of rearrangement itself, why, if the rearrangement stop not, should the consciousness ever cease? And if a lingering rearrangement brings with it one kind of consciousness, why should not a swift rearrangement bring another kind of consciousness as peculiar as the rearrangement itself? The lingering consciousnesses, if of simple objects, we call 'sensations' or 'images', according as they are vivid or faint; if of complex objects, we call them 'percepts' when vivid, 'concepts' or 'thoughts' when faint. For the swift consciousnesses we have only those names of 'transitive states', or 'feelings of relation', which we have used. As the brain-changes are continuous, so do all these consciousnesses melt into each other like dissolving views. Properly they are but one protracted consciousness, one unbroken stream.

Feelings of Tendency

So much for the transitive states. But there are other unnamed states or qualities of states that are just as important and just as cognitive as they, and just as much unrecognized by the traditional sensationalist and intellectualist philosophies of mind. The first fails to find them at all, the second finds their *cognitive function*, but denies that anything in the way of *feeling* has a share in bringing it about. Examples will make clear what these inarticulate psychoses, due to waxing and waning excitements of the brain, are like.

Suppose three successive persons say to us: 'Wait!' 'Hark!' 'Look!' Our consciousness is thrown into three quite different attitudes of expectancy, although no definite object is before it in any one of the three cases. Leaving out different actual bodily attitudes, and leaving out the reverberating images of the three words, which are of course diverse, probably no one will deny the existence of a residual conscious affection, a sense of the direction from which an impression is about to come, although no positive impression is yet there. Meanwhile we have no names for the psychoses in question but the names hark, look and wait.

Suppose we try to recall a forgotten name. The state of our consciousness is peculiar. There is a gap therein; but no mere gap. It is a gap that is intensely active. A sort of wraith of the name is in it, beckoning us in a given direction, making us at moments tingle with the sense of our closeness, and then letting us sink back without the longed-for term. If wrong names are proposed to us, this singularly definite gap acts immediately so as to negate them. They do not fit into its mould. And the gap of one word does not feel like the gap of another, all empty of content as both might seem necessarily to be when described as gaps. When I vainly try to recall the name of Spalding, my consciousness is far removed from what it is when I vainly try to recall the name of Bowles. Here some ingenious persons will say: 'How *can* the two consciousnesses be different when the terms which might make them different are not there? All that is there, so long as the effort to recall is vain, is the bare effort itself. How should that differ in the two cases? You are making it seem to differ by prematurely filling it out with the different names, although these, by the hypothesis, have not yet come. Stick to the two efforts as they are, without naming them after facts not yet existent, and you'll be quite unable to designate any point in which they differ.' Designate, truly enough. We can only designate the difference by borrowing the names of objects not yet in the mind. Which is to say that our psychological vocabulary is wholly inadequate to name the differences that exist, even such strong differences as these. But namelessness is compatible with existence. There are innumerable consciousnesses of emptiness, no one of which taken in itself has a name, but all different from each other. The ordinary way is to assume that they are all emptinesses of consciousness, and so the same state. But the feeling of an absence is *toto coelo* other than the absence of a feeling. It is an intense feeling. The rhythm of a lost word may be there without a sound to clothe it; or the evanescent sense of something which is the initial vowel or consonant may mock us fitfully, without growing more distinct. Everyone must know the tantalizing effect of the blank rhythm of some forgotten verse, restlessly dancing in one's mind, striving to be filled out with words.

Again, what is the strange difference between an experience tasted for the first time and the same experience recognized as familiar, as having been enjoyed before, though we cannot name it or say where or when? A tune, an odour, a flavour sometimes carry this inarticulate feeling of their familiarity so deep into our consciousness that we are fairly shaken by its mysterious emotional power. But strong and characteristic as this psychosis is – it probably is due to the submaximal excitement of widespreading associational brain-tracts – the only name we have for all its shadings is 'sense of familiarity'.

When we read such phrases as 'naught but', 'either one or the other', '*a* is *b*, but', 'although it is, nevertheless', 'it is an excluded middle, there is no *tertium quid*', and a host of other verbal skeletons of logical relation, is it true that there is nothing more in our minds than the words themselves as they pass? What then is the meaning of the words which we think we understand as we read? What makes that meaning different in one phrase from what it is in the other? 'Who?' 'When?'

'Where?' Is the difference of felt meaning in these interrogatives nothing more than their difference of sound? And is it not (just like the difference of sound itself) known and understood in an affection of consciousness correlative to it, though so impalpable to direct examination? Is not the same true of such negatives as 'no', 'never', 'not yet'?

The truth is that large tracts of human speech are nothing but *signs of direction* in thought, of which direction we nevertheless have an acutely discriminative sense, though no definite sensorial image plays any part in it whatsoever. Sensorial images are stable psychic facts; we can hold them still and look at them as long as we like. These bare images of logical movement, on the contrary, are psychic transitions, always on the wing, so to speak, and not to be glimpsed except in flight. Their function is to lead from one set of images to another. As they pass, we feel both the waxing and the waning images in a way altogether peculiar and a way quite different from the way of their full presence. If we try to hold fast the feeling of direction, the full presence comes and the feeling of direction is lost. The blank verbal scheme of the logical movement gives us the fleeting sense of the movement as we read it, quite as well as does a rational sentence awakening definite imaginations by its words.

What is that first instantaneous glimpse of someone's meaning which we have, when in vulgar phrase we say we 'twig' it? Surely an altogether specific affection of our mind. And has the reader never asked himself what kind of a mental fact is his *intention of saying a thing* before he has said it? It is an entirely definite intention, distinct from all other intentions, an absolutely distinct state of consciousness, therefore; and yet how much of it consists of definite sensorial images, either of words or of things? Hardly anything! Linger, and the words and things come into the mind; the anticipatory intention, the divination is there no more. But as the words that replace it arrive, it welcomes them successively and calls them right if they agree with it, it rejects them and calls them wrong if they do not. It has therefore a nature of its own of the most positive sort, and yet what can we say about it without using words that belong to the later mental facts that replace it? The intention *to-say-so-and-so* is the only name it can receive. One may admit that a good third of our psychic life consists in these rapid premonitory perspective views of schemes of thought not yet articulate. How comes it about that a man reading something aloud for the first time is able immediately to emphasize all his words aright, unless from the very first he have a sense of at least the form of the sentence yet to come, which sense is fused with his consciousness of the present word, and modifies its emphasis in his mind so as to make him give it the proper accent as he utters it? Emphasis of this kind is almost altogether a matter of grammatical construction. If we read 'no more' we expect presently to come upon a 'than'; if we read 'however' at the outset of a sentence it is a 'yet', a 'still', or a 'nevertheless', that we expect. A noun in a certain position demands a verb in a certain mood and number, in another position it expects a relative pronoun. Adjectives call for nouns, verbs for adverbs, etc., etc. And this foreboding of the coming grammatical scheme combined with each successive uttered word is so practically accurate that a reader incapable of understanding four ideas of the book he is reading aloud, can nevertheless read it with the most delicately modulated expression of intelligence.

Some will interpret these facts by calling them all cases in which certain images, by laws of association, awaken others so very rapidly that we think afterwards we felt the very *tendencies* of the nascent images to arise, before they were actually there. For this school the only possible materials of consciousness are images of a perfectly definite nature. Tendencies exist, but they are facts for the outside psychologist rather than for the subject of the observation. The tendency is thus a *psychical* zero; only its *results* are felt.

Now what I contend for, and accumulate examples to show, is that 'tendencies' are not only descriptions from without, but that they are among the *objects* of the stream, which is thus aware of them from within, and must be described as in very large measure constituted of *feelings* of *tendency*, often so vague that we are unable to name them at all. It is, in short, the reinstatement of the vague to its proper place in our mental life which I am so anxious to press on the attention. Mr Galton and Prof. Huxley have, as we shall see in Chapter 15 [*Principles of Psychology*], made one step in advance in exploding the ridiculous theory of Hume and Berkeley that we can have no images but of perfectly definite things. Another is made in the overthrow of the equally ridiculous notion that, whilst simple objective qualities are revealed to our knowledge in subjective feelings, relations are not. But these reforms are not half sweeping and radical enough. What must be admitted is that the definite images of traditional psychology form but the very smallest part of our minds as they actually live. The traditional psychology talks like one who should say a river consists of nothing but pailsful, spoonsful, quartpotsful, barrelsful and other moulded forms of water. Even were the pails and the pots all actually standing in the stream, still between them the free water would continue to flow. It is just this free water of consciousness that psychologists resolutely overlook. Every definite image in the mind is steeped and dyed in the free water that flows round it. With it goes the sense of its relations, near and remote, the dying echo of whence it came to us, the dawning sense of whither it is to lead. The significance, the value, of the image is all in this halo or penumbra that surrounds and escorts it – or rather that is fused into one with it and has become bone of its bone and flesh of its flesh; leaving it, it is true, an image of the same *thing* it was before, but making it an image of that thing newly taken and freshly understood.

What is that shadowy scheme of the 'form' of an opera, play or book, which remains in our mind and on which we pass judgment when the actual thing is done? What is our notion of a scientific or philosophical system? Great thinkers have vast premonitory glimpses of schemes of relation between terms, which hardly even as verbal images enter the mind, so rapid is the whole process.[15] We all of us have this permanent consciousness of whither our thought is going. It is a feeling like any other, a feeling which ought to have been expressed.[16] In these cases one of two things must have happened: either some local accident of nutrition *blocks* the process that is *due*, so that other processes discharge that ought as yet to be but nascently

[15] Mozart describes thus his manner of composing: First bits and crumbs of the piece come and gradually join together in his mind; then the soul getting warmed to the work, the thing grows more and more, 'and I spread it out broader and clearer, and at last it gets almost finished in my head, even when it is a long piece, so that I can see the whole of it at a single glance in my mind, as if it were a beautiful painting or a handsome human being; in which way I do not hear it in my imagination at all as a succession – the way it must come later – but all at once, as it were. It is a rare feast! All the inventing and making goes on in me as in a beautiful strong dream. But the best of all is the *hearing of it all at once*.'

[16] *Mental Physiology*, s. 236. Dr Carpenter's explanation differs materially from that given in the text.

aroused; or some opposite local accident *furthers* the *latter processes* and makes them explode before their time. In the chapter on association of ideas, numerous instances will come before us of the actual effect on consciousness of neuroses not yet maximally aroused.

It is just like the 'overtones' in music. Different instruments give the 'same note', but each in a different voice, because each gives more than that note, namely, various upper harmonies of it which differ from one instrument to another. They are not separately heard by the ear; they blend with the fundamental note, and suffuse it, and alter it; and even so do the waxing and waning brain processes at every moment blend with and suffuse and alter the psychic effect of the processes which are at their culminating point.

Let us use the words *psychic overtone*, *suffusion* or *fringe*, to designate the influence of a faint brain process upon our thought, as it makes it aware of relations and objects but dimly perceived.[17]

If we then consider the *cognitive function* of different states of mind, we may feel assured that the difference between those that are mere 'acquaintance', and those that are 'knowledges-*about*' is reducible almost entirely to the absence or presence of psychic fringes or overtones. Knowledge *about* a thing is knowledge of its relations. Acquaintance with it is limitation to the bare impression which it makes. Of most of its relations we are only aware in the penumbral nascent way of a 'fringe' of unarticulated affinities about it. And, before passing to the next topic in order, I must say a little of this sense of affinity,

---

[17] Cf. also S. Stricker, *Vorlesungen über allg. u. exp. Pathologie*, 1879, pp. 462–3, 501 and 547; Romanes, *Origin of Human Faculty*, p. 82. It is so hard to make oneself clear that I may advert to a misunderstanding of my views by the late Prof. Thos. Maguire of Dublin (*Lectures on Philosophy*, 1885). This author considers that by the 'fringe' I mean some sort of psychic material by which sensations in themselves separate are made to cohere together, and wittily says that I ought to 'see that uniting sensations by their "fringes" is more vague than to construct the universe out of oysters by platting their beards' (p. 211). But the fringe, as I use the word, means nothing like this; it is part of the *object cognized* – substantive *qualities* and *things* appearing to the mind in a *fringe of relations*. Some parts – the transitive parts – of our stream of thought cognize the relations rather than the things; but both the transitive and the substantive parts form one continuous stream, with no discrete 'sensations' in it such as Prof. Maguire supposes, and supposes me suppose, to be there.

as itself one of the most interesting features of the subjective stream.

In all our voluntary thinking there is some topic or subject about which all the members of the thought revolve. Half the time this topic is a problem, a gap we cannot yet fill with a definite picture, word or phrase, but which, in the manner described some time back, influences us in an intensely active and determinate psychic way. Whatever may be the images and phrases that pass before us, we feel their relation to this aching gap. To fill it up is our thought's destiny. Some bring us nearer to that consummation. Some the gap negates as quite irrelevant. Each swims in a felt fringe of relations of which the aforesaid gap is the term. Or instead of a definite gap we may merely carry a mood of interest about with us. Then, however vague the mood, it will still act in the same way, throwing a mantle of felt affinity over such representations, entering the mind, as suit it, and tingeing with the feeling of tediousness or discord all those with which it has no concern.

Relation, then, to our topic or interest is constantly felt in the fringe, and particularly the relation of harmony and discord, of furtherance or hindrance of the topic. When the sense of furtherance is there, we are 'all right'; with the sense of hindrance we are dissatisfied and perplexed, and cast about us for other thoughts. Now *any* thought the quality of whose fringe lets us feel ourselves 'all right', is an acceptable member of our thinking, whatever kind of thought it may otherwise be. Provided we only feel it to have a place in the scheme of relations in which the interesting topic also lies, that is quite sufficient to make of it a relevant and appropriate portion of our train of ideas.

For the important thing about a train of thought is its conclusion. That is the *meaning*, or, as we say, the topic of the thought. That is what abides when all its other members have faded from memory. Usually this conclusion is a word or phrase or particular image, or practical attitude or resolve, whether rising to answer a problem or fill a pre-existing gap that worried us, or whether accidentally stumbled on in reverie. In either case it stands out from the other segments of the stream by reason of the peculiar interest attaching to it. This interest *arrests* it, makes a sort of crisis of it when it comes, induces attention upon it and makes us treat it in a substantive way.

The parts of the stream that precede these substantive conclusions are but the means of the latter's attainment. And, provided the same conclusion be reached, the means may be as mutable as we like, for the 'meaning' of the stream of thought will be the same. What difference does it make what the means are? '*Qu'importe le flacon, pourvu qu'on ait l'ivresse?*' The relative unimportance of the means appears from the fact that when the conclusion is there, we have always forgotten most of the steps preceding its attainment. When we have uttered a proposition, we are rarely able a moment afterwards to recall our exact words, though we can express it in different words easily enough. The practical upshot of a book we read remains with us, though we may not recall one of its sentences.

The only paradox would seem to lie in supposing that the fringe of felt affinity and discord can be the same in two heterogeneous sets of images. Take a train of words passing through the mind and leading to a certain conclusion on the one hand, and on the other hand an almost wordless set of tactile, visual and other fancies leading to the same conclusion. Can the halo, fringe or scheme in which we feel the words to lie be the same as that in which we feel the images to lie? Does not the discrepancy of terms involve a discrepancy of felt relations among them?

If the terms be taken *qua* mere sensations, it assuredly does. For instance, the words may rhyme with each other – the visual images can have no such affinity as *that*. But *qua* thoughts, *qua* sensations *understood*, the words have contracted by long association fringes of mutual repugnance or affinity with each other and with the conclusion, which run exactly parallel with like fringes in the visual, tactile and other ideas. The most important element of these fringes is, I repeat, the mere feeling of harmony or discord, of a right or wrong direction in the thought.

Many philosophers, however, hold that the reflective consciousness of the self is essential to the cognitive function of thought. They hold that a thought, in order to know a thing at all, must expressly distinguish between the thing and its own self.[18] This is a perfectly wanton assumption, and not the faintest

[18] Kant originated this view. I subjoin a few English statements of it. J. Ferrier, *Institutes of Metaphysic*, Proposition 1: 'Along with whatever any intelligence knows

shadow of reason exists for supposing it true. As well might I contend that I cannot dream without dreaming that I dream, swear without swearing that I swear, deny without denying that I deny, as maintain that I cannot know without knowing that I know. I may have either acquaintance with, or knowledge about, an object O without thinking about myself at all. It suffices for this that I think O, and that it exist. If, in addition to thinking O, I also think that I exist and that I know O, well and good; I then know one more thing, a fact about O, of which I previously was unmindful. That, however, does not prevent me from having already known it a good deal. O *per se*, or O *plus* P, are as good objects of knowledge as O *plus me* is. The philosophers in question simply substitute one particular object for all others, and call it *the* object *par excellence*. It is a case of the 'psychologist's fallacy'. *They* know the object to be one thing and the thought another; and they forthwith foist their own knowledge into that of the thought of which they pretend to give a true account. To conclude, then, *thought may, but need not, in knowing, discriminate between its object and itself.*

We have been using the word Object. *Something must now be said about the proper use of the term Object in psychology.*

In popular parlance the word object is commonly taken without reference to the act of knowledge, and treated as synonymous with individual subject of existence. Thus if anyone ask what is the mind's object when you say 'Columbus discovered America in 1492', most people will reply 'Columbus', or 'America', or, at most, 'the discovery of America'. They will name a substantive kernel or nucleus of the consciousness, and say the thought is 'about' that – as indeed it is – and they will call that your thought's 'object'. Really that is usually only the

---

it must, as the ground or condition of its knowledge, have some knowledge of itself.' Sir Wm. Hamilton, *Discussions*, p. 47: 'We know, and we know that we know – these propositions, logically distinct, are really identical; each implies the other . . . So true is the scholastic brocard: *non sentimus nisi sentiamus nos sentire.*' H. L. Mansel, *Metaphysics*, p. 58: 'Whatever variety of materials may exist within reach of my mind, I can become conscious of them only by recognizing them as mine . . . Relation to the conscious self is thus the permanent and universal feature which every state of consciousness as such must exhibit.' T. H. Green, *Introduction to Hume*, p. 12: 'A consciousness by the man . . . of himself, in negative relation to the thing that is his object, and this consciousness must be taken to go along with the perceptive act itself. Not less than this indeed can be involved in any act that is to be the beginning of knowledge at all. It is the minimum of possible thought or intelligence.'

grammatical object, or more likely the grammatical subject, of your sentence. It is at most your 'fractional object', or you may call it the 'topic' of your thought, or the 'subject of your discourse'. But the *Object* of your thought is really its entire content or deliverance, neither more nor less. It is a vicious use of speech to take out a substantive kernel from its content and call that its object; and it is an equally vicious use of speech to add a substantive kernel not articulately included in its content, and to call that its object. Yet either one of these two sins we commit, whenever we content ourselves with saying that a given thought is simply 'about' a certain topic, or that that topic is its 'object'. The object of my thought in the previous sentence, for example, is strictly speaking neither Columbus, nor America, nor its discovery. It is nothing short of the entire sentence, 'Columbus-discovered-America-in-1492'. And if we wish to speak of it substantively, we must make a substantive of it by writing it out thus with hyphens between all its words. Nothing but this can possibly name its delicate idiosyncrasy. And if we wish to *feel* that idiosyncrasy we must reproduce the thought as it was uttered, with every word fringed and the whole sentence bathed in that original halo of obscure relations, which, like an horizon, then spread about its meaning.

Our psychological duty is to cling as closely as possible to the actual constitution of the thought we are studying. We may err as much by excess as by defect. If the kernel or 'topic', Columbus, is in one way less than the thought's object, so in another way it may be more. That is, when named by the psychologist, it may mean much more than actually is present to the thought of which he is reporter. Thus, for example, suppose you should go on to think: 'He was a daring genius!' An ordinary psychologist would not hesitate to say that the object of your thought was still 'Columbus'. True, your thought is *about* Columbus. It 'terminates' in Columbus, leads from and to the direct idea of Columbus. But for the moment it is not fully and immediately Columbus, it is only 'he', or rather 'he-was-a-daring-genius'; which, though it may be an unimportant difference for conversational purposes, is, for introspective psychology, as great a difference as there can be.

The object of every thought, then, is neither more nor less than all that the thought thinks, exactly as the thought thinks it, however complicated the matter, and however symbolic the manner of the thinking may be. It is needless to say that memory can seldom accurately reproduce such an object, when once it has passed from before the mind. It either makes too little or too much of it. Its best plan is to repeat the verbal sentence, if there was one, in which the object was expressed. But for inarticulate thoughts there is not even this resource, and introspection must confess that the task exceeds her powers. The mass of our thinking vanishes for ever, beyond hope of recovery, and psychology only gathers up a few of the crumbs that fall from the feast.

The next point to make clear is that, *however complex the object may be, the thought of it is one undivided state of consciousness.* As Thomas Brown says:[19]

> I have already spoken too often to require again to caution you against the mistake into which, I confess, that the terms which the poverty of our language obliges us to use might of themselves very naturally lead you; the mistake of supposing that the most complex states of mind are not truly, in their very essence, as much one and indivisible as those which we term simple – the complexity and seeming coexistence which they involve being relative to our feeling[20] only, not to their own absolute nature. I trust I need not repeat to you that, in itself, every notion, however seemingly complex, is, and must be, truly simple – being one state or affection, of one simple substance, mind. Our conception of a whole army, for example, is as truly this one mind existing in this one state, as our conception of any of the individuals that compose an army. Our notion of the abstract numbers, eight, four, two, is as truly one feeling of the mind as our notion of simple unity.

The ordinary associationist psychology supposes, in contrast with this, that whenever an object of thought contains many elements, the thought itself must be made up of just as many ideas, one idea for each element, and all fused together in appearance, but really separate.[21] The enemies of this psychology find (as we have already seen) little trouble in showing that

[19] *Lectures on the Philosophy of the Human Mind*, Lecture 45.
[20] Instead of saying *to our feeling only*, he should have said, to the *object* only.
[21] 'There can be no difficulty in admitting that association does form the ideas of an indefinite number of individuals into one complex idea: because it is an acknowledged fact. Have we not the idea of an army? And is not that precisely the ideas of an indefinite number of men formed into one idea?' (Jas. Mill's *Analysis of the Human Mind* (J. S. Mill's edition), vol. 1, 264.)

such a bundle of separate ideas would never form one thought at all, and they contend that an ego must be added to the bundle to give it unity, and bring the various ideas into relation with each other. We will not discuss the ego just yet, but it is obvious that if things are to be thought in relation, they must be thought together, and in one *something*, be that something ego, psychosis, state of consciousness, or whatever you please. If not thought with each other, things are not thought in relation at all. Now most believers in the ego make the same mistake as the associationists and sensationists whom they oppose. Both agree that the elements of the subjective stream are discrete and separate and constitute what Kant calls a 'manifold'. But while the associationists think that a 'manifold' can form a single knowledge, the egoists deny this, and say that the knowledge comes only when the manifold is subjected to the synthetizing activity of an ego. Both make an identical initial hypothesis; but the egoist, finding it won't express the facts, adds another hypothesis to correct it. Now I do not wish just yet to 'commit myself' about the existence or non-existence of the ego, but I do contend that we need not invoke it for this particular reason – namely, because the manifold of ideas has to be reduced to unity. *There is no manifold of coexisting ideas*; the notion of such a thing is a chimera. *Whatever things are thought in relation are thought from the outset in a unity, in a single pulse of subjectivity, a single psychosis, feeling or state of mind.*

The reason why this fact is so strangely garbled in the books seems to be what on [another] page (see p. 244ff.) I called the psychologist's fallacy. We have the inveterate habit, whenever we try introspectively to describe one of our thoughts, of dropping the thought as it is in itself and talking of something else. We describe the things that appear to the thought, and we describe other thoughts *about* those things – as if these and the original thought were the same. If, for example, the thought be 'the pack of cards is on the table', we say, 'Well, isn't it a thought of the pack of cards? Isn't it of the cards as included in the pack? Isn't it of the table? And of the legs of the table as well? The table has legs – how can you think the table without virtually thinking its legs? Hasn't our thought then, all these parts – one part for the pack and another for the table? And within the pack-part a part for each card, as within the table-part a part for each leg? And isn't each of these parts an idea?

And can our thought, then, be anything but an assemblage or pack of ideas, each answering to some element of what it knows?'

Now not one of these assumptions is true. The thought taken as an example is, in the first place, not of 'a pack of cards'. It is of 'the-pack-of-cards-is-on-the-table', an entirely different subjective phenomenon, whose Object implies the pack, and every one of the cards in it, but whose conscious constitution bears very little resemblance to that of the thought of the pack *per se*. What a thought *is*, and what it may be developed into, or explained to stand for, and be equivalent to, are two things, not one.[22]

Looking back, then, over this review, we see that the mind is at every stage a theatre of simultaneous possibilities. Consciousness consists in the comparison of these with each other, the selection of some, and the suppression of the rest by the reinforcing and inhibiting agency of attention. The highest and most elaborated mental products are filtered from the data chosen by the faculty next beneath, out of the mass offered by the faculty below that, which mass in turn was sifted from a still larger amount of yet simpler material, and so on. The mind, in short, works on his block of stone. In a sense the statue stood there from eternity. But there were a thousand different ones beside it, and the sculptor alone is to thank for having extracted this one from the rest. Just so the world of each of us, howsoever different our several views of it may be, all lay embedded in the primordial chaos of sensations, which gave the mere *matter* to the thought of all of us indifferently. We may, if we like, by our reasonings unwind things back to that black and jointless continuity of space and moving clouds of swarming atoms which science calls the only real world. But all the while the

[22] I know there are readers whom nothing can convince that the thought of a complex object has not as many parts as are discriminated in the object itself. Well, then, let the word parts pass. Only observe that these parts are not the separate 'ideas' of traditional psychology. No one of them can live out of that particular thought, any more than my head can live off of my particular shoulders. In a sense a soap bubble has parts; it is a sum of juxtaposed spherical triangles. But these triangles are not separate realities; neither are the 'parts' of the thought separate realities. Touch the bubble and the triangles are no more. Dismiss the thought and out go its parts. You can no more make a new thought out of 'ideas' that have once served than you can make a new bubble out of old triangles. Each bubble, each thought, is a fresh organic unity, *sui generis*.

world *we* feel and live in will be that which our ancestors and we, by slowly cumulative strokes of choice, have extricated out of this, like sculptors, by simply rejecting certain portions of the given stuff. Other sculptors, other statues from the same stone! Other minds, other worlds from the same monotonous and inexpressive chaos! My world is but one in a million alike embedded, alike real to those who may abstract them. How different must be the worlds in the consciousness of ant, cuttle-fish or crab!

But in my mind and your mind the rejected portions and the selected portions of the original world-stuff are to a great extent the same. The human race as a whole largely agrees as to what it shall notice and name, and what not. And among the noticed parts we select in much the same way for accentuation and preference or subordination and dislike. There is, however, one entirely extraordinary case in which no two men ever are known to choose alike. One great splitting of the whole universe into two halves is made by each of us; and for each of us almost all of the interest attaches to one of the halves; but we all draw the line of division between them in a different place. When I say that we all call the two halves by the same names, and that those names are '*me*' and '*not-me*' respectively, it will at once be seen what I mean. The altogether unique kind of interest which each human mind feels in those parts of creation which it can call *me* or *mine* may be a moral riddle, but it is a fundamental psychological fact. No mind can take the same interest in his neighbour's *me* as in his own. The neighbour's me falls together with all the rest of things in one foreign mass, against which his own *me* stands out in startling relief. Even the trodden worm, as Lotze somewhere says, contrasts his own suffering self with the whole remaining universe, though he have no clear conception either of himself or of what the universe may be. He is for me a mere part of the world; for him it is I who am the mere part. Each of us dichotomizes the Kosmos in a different place.

Descending now to finer work than this first general sketch, let us in the next chapter try to trace the psychology of this fact of self-consciousness to which we have thus once more been led.

12

The Consciousness of Self

Let us begin with the self in its widest acceptation, and follow it up to its most delicate and subtle form, advancing from the study of the empirical, as the Germans call it, to that of the pure, ego.

The Empirical Self or Me

The empirical self of each of us is all that he is tempted to call by the name of *me*. But it is clear that between what a man calls *me* and what he simply calls *mine* the line is difficult to draw. We feel and act about certain things that are ours very much as we feel and act about ourselves. Our fame, our children, the work of our hands, may be as dear to us as our bodies are, and arouse the same feelings and the same acts of reprisal if attacked. And our bodies themselves, are they simply ours, or are they *us*? Certainly men have been ready to disown their very bodies and to regard them as mere vestures, or even as prisons of clay from which they should some day be glad to escape.

We see then that we are dealing with a fluctuating material. The same object being sometimes treated as a part of me, at other times as simply mine, and then again as if I had nothing to do with it at all. *In its widest possible sense*, however, *a man's self is the sum total of all that he* CAN *call his*, not only his body and his psychic powers, but his clothes and his house, his wife and children, his ancestors and friends, his reputation and works, his lands and horses, and yacht and bank account. All these things give him the same emotions. If they wax and prosper, he feels triumphant; if they dwindle and die away, he feels cast down – not necessarily in the same degree for each thing, but in much the same way for all. Understanding the self in this widest sense, we may begin by dividing the history of it into three parts, relating respectively to –

1 Its constituents
2 The feelings and emotions they arouse – *self-feelings*
3 The actions to which they prompt – *self-seeking and self-preservation*.

1 *The constituents of the self* may be divided into two classes, those which make up respectively –

(a) The material self
(b) The social self
(c) The spiritual self
(d) The pure ego.

(a) *The body* is the innermost part of *the material self* in each of us; and certain parts of the body seem more intimately ours than the rest. The clothes come next. The old saying that the human person is composed of three parts – soul, body and clothes – is more than a joke. We so appropriate our clothes and identify ourselves with them that there are few of us who, if asked to choose between having a beautiful body clad in raiment perpetually shabby and unclean, and having an ugly and blemished form always spotlessly attired, would not hesitate a moment before making a decisive reply. Next, our immediate family is a part of ourselves. Our father and mother, our wife and babes, are bone of our bone and flesh of our flesh. When they die, a part of our very selves is gone. If they do anything wrong, it is our shame. If they are insulted, our anger flashes forth as readily as if we stood in their place. Our home comes next. Its scenes are part of our life; its aspects awaken the tenderest feelings of affection; and we do not easily forgive the stranger who, in visiting it, finds fault with its arrangements or treats it with contempt. All these different things are the objects of instinctive preferences coupled with the most important practical interests of life. We all have a blind impulse to watch over our body, to deck it with clothing of an ornamental sort, to cherish parents, wife and babes, and to find for ourselves a home of our own which we may live in and 'improve'.

An equally instinctive impulse drives us to collect property; and the collections thus made become, with different degrees of intimacy, parts of our empirical selves. The parts of our wealth most intimately ours are those which are saturated with our labour. There are few men who would not feel personally annihilated if a lifelong construction of their hands or brains – say an entomological collection or an extensive work in manuscript – were suddenly swept away. The miser feels similarly towards his gold, and although it is true that a part of our depression at the loss of possessions is due to our feeling that we must now go without certain goods that we expected the possessions to bring in their train, yet in every case there remains, over and above this, a sense of the shrinkage of our personality, a partial conversion of ourselves to nothingness, which is a psychological phenomenon by itself. We are all at once assimilated to the tramps and poor devils whom we so despise, and at the same time removed farther than ever away from the happy sons of earth who lord it over land and sea and men in the fullblown lustihood that wealth and power can give, and before whom, stiffen ourselves as we will by appealing to anti-snobbish first principles, we cannot escape an emotion, open or sneaking, of respect and dread.

(b) *A man's social self* is the recognition which he gets from his mates. We are not only gregarious animals, liking to be in sight of our fellows, but we have an innate propensity to get ourselves noticed, and noticed favourably, by our kind. No more fiendish punishment could be devised, were such a thing physically possible, than that one should be turned loose in society and remain absolutely unnoticed by all the members thereof. If no one turned round when we entered, answered when we spoke, or minded what we did, but if every person we met 'cut us dead', and acted as if we were non-existing things, a kind of rage and impotent despair would ere long well up in us, from which the cruellest bodily tortures would be a relief; for these would make us feel that, however bad might be our plight, we had not sunk to such a depth as to be unworthy of attention at all.

Properly speaking, *a man has as many social selves as there are individuals who recognize him* and carry an image of him in their mind. To wound any one of these his images is to wound him.[1] But as the individuals who carry the images fall naturally into classes, we may practically say that he has as many different

---

[1] 'Who filches from me my good name', etc.

social selves as there are distinct *groups* of persons about whose opinion he cares. He generally shows a different side of himself to each of these different groups. Many a youth who is demure enough before his parents and teachers, swears and swaggers like a pirate among his 'tough' young friends. We do not show ourselves to our children as to our club-companions, to our customers as to the labourers we employ, to our own masters and employers as to our intimate friends. From this there results what practically is a division of the man into several selves; and this may be a discordant splitting, as where one is afraid to let one set of his acquaintances know him as he is elsewhere; or it may be a perfectly harmonious division of labour, as where one tender to his children is stern to the soldiers or prisoners under his command.

The most peculiar social self which one is apt to have is in the mind of the person one is in love with. The good or bad fortunes of this self cause the most intense elation and dejection – unreasonable enough as measured by every other standard than that of the organic feeling of the individual. To his own consciousness he *is* not, so long as this particular social self fails to get recognition, and when it is recognized his contentment passes all bounds.

A man's *fame*, good or bad, and his *honour* or dishonour, are names for one of his social selves. The particular social self of a man called his honour is usually the result of one of those splittings of which we have spoken. It is his image in the eyes of his own 'set', which exalts or condemns him as he conforms or not to certain requirements that may not be made of one in another walk of life. Thus a layman may abandon a city infected with cholera; but a priest or a doctor would think such an act incompatible with his honour. A soldier's honour requires him to fight or to die under circumstances where another man can apologize or run away with no stain upon his social self. A judge, a statesman, are in like manner debarred by the honour of their cloth from entering into pecuniary relations perfectly honourable to persons in private life. Nothing is commoner than to hear people discriminate between their different selves of this sort: 'As a man I pity you, but as an official I must show you no mercy; as a politician I regard him as an ally, but as a moralist I loathe him'; etc., etc. What may be called 'club-opinion' is one of the very strongest forces in life.[2] The thief must not steal from other thieves; the gambler must pay his gambling debts, though he pay no other debts in the world. The code of honour of fashionable society has throughout history been full of permissions as well as of vetoes, the only reason for following either of which is that so we best serve one of our social selves. You must not lie in general, but you may lie as much as you please if asked about your relations with a lady; you must accept a challenge from an equal, but if challenged by an inferior you may laugh him to scorn: these are examples of what is meant.

(c) *By the spiritual self*, so far as it belongs to the empirical Me, I mean a man's inner or subjective being, his psychic faculties or dispositions, taken concretely; not the bare principle of personal unity, or 'pure' ego, which remains still to be discussed. These psychic dispositions are the most enduring and intimate part of the self, that which we most verily seem to be. We take a purer self-satisfaction when we think of our ability to argue and discriminate, of our moral sensibility and conscience, of our indomitable will, than when we survey any of our other possessions. Only when these are altered is a man said to be *alienatus a se*.

Now this spiritual self may be considered in various ways. We

[2] 'He who imagines commendation and disgrace not to be strong motives on men . . . seems little skilled in the nature and history of mankind: the greatest part whereof he shall find to govern themselves chiefly, if not solely, by this law of fashion; and so they do that which keeps them in reputation with their company, little regard the laws of God or the magistrate. The penalties that attend the breach of God's laws some, nay, most, men seldom seriously reflect on; and amongst those that do, many whilst they break the laws, entertain thoughts of future reconciliation, and making their peace for such breaches: and as to the punishments due from the laws of the commonwealth, they frequently flatter themselves with the hope of impunity. But no man escapes the punishment of *their* censure and dislike who offends against the fashion and opinion of the company he keeps, and would recommend himself to. Nor is there one in ten thousand who is stiff and insensible enough to bear up under the constant dislike and condemnation of his own club. He must be of a strange and unusual constitution who can content himself to live in constant disgrace and disrepute with his own particular society. Solitude many men have sought and been reconciled to; but nobody that has the least thought or sense of a man about him can live in society under the constant dislike and ill opinion of his familiars and those he converses with. This is a burden too heavy for human sufferance: and he must be made up of irreconcilable contradictions who can take pleasure in company and yet be insensible of contempt and disgrace from his companions.' (Locke's *Essay*, Book 2, ch. 28, s. 12.)

may divide it into faculties, as just instanced, isolating them one from another, and identifying ourselves with either in turn. This is an *abstract* way of dealing with consciousness, in which, as it actually presents itself, a plurality of such faculties are always to be simultaneously found; or we may insist on a concrete view, and then the spiritual self in us will be either the entire stream of our personal consciousness, or the present 'segment' or 'section' of that stream, according as we take a broader or a narrower view – both the stream and the section being concrete existences in time, and each being a unity after its own peculiar kind. But whether we take it abstractly or concretely, our considering the spiritual self at all is a reflective process, is the result of our abandoning the outward-looking point of view, and of our having become able to think of subjectivity as such, to *think ourselves as thinkers*.

This attention to thought as such, and the identification of ourselves with it rather than with any of the objects which it reveals, is a momentous and in some respects a rather mysterious operation, of which we need here only say that as a matter of fact it exists; and that in everyone, at an early age, the distinction between thought as such, and what it is 'of' or 'about', has become familiar to the mind. The deeper grounds for this discrimination may possibly be hard to find; but superficial grounds are plenty and near at hand. Almost anyone will tell us that thought is a different sort of existence from things, because many sorts of thought are of no things – e.g. pleasures, pains and emotions; others are of non-existent things – errors and fictions; others again of existent things, but in a form that is symbolic and does not resemble them – abstract ideas and concepts; whilst in the thoughts that do resemble the things they are 'of' (percepts, sensations), we can feel, alongside of the thing known, the thought of it going on as an altogether separate act and operation in the mind.

Now this subjective life of ours, distinguished as such so clearly from the objects known by its means, may, as aforesaid, be taken by us in a concrete or in an abstract way. Of the concrete way I will say nothing just now, except that the actual 'section' of the stream will ere long, in our discussion of the nature of the principle of *unity* in consciousness, play a very important part. The abstract way claims our attention first. If the stream as a whole is identified with the self far more than any outward thing, a *certain portion of the stream abstracted from the rest* is so identified in an altogether peculiar degree, and is felt by all men as a sort of innermost centre within the circle, of sanctuary within the citadel, constituted by the subjective life as a whole. Compared with this element of the stream, the other parts, even of the subjective life, seem transient external possessions, of which each in turn can be disowned, whilst that which disowns them remains. Now, *what is this self of all the other selves?*

Probably all men would describe it in much the same way up to a certain point. They would call it the *active* element in all consciousness; saying that whatever qualities a man's feelings may possess, or whatever content his thought may include, there is a spiritual something in him which seems to *go out* to meet these qualities and contents, whilst they seem to *come in* to be received by it. It is what welcomes or rejects. It presides over the perception of sensations, and by giving or withholding its assent it influences the movements they tend to arouse. It is the home of interest – not the pleasant or the painful, not even pleasure or pain, as such, but that within us to which pleasure and pain, the pleasant and the painful, speak. It is the source of effort and attention, and the place from which appear to emanate the fiats of the will. A physiologist who should reflect upon it in his own person could hardly help, I should think, connecting it more or less vaguely with the process by which ideas or incoming sensations are 'reflected' or pass over into outward acts. Not necessarily that it should *be* this process or the mere feeling of this process, but that it should be in some close way *related* to this process; for it plays a part analogous to it in the psychic life, being a sort of junction at which sensory ideas terminate and from which motor ideas proceed, and forming a kind of link between the two. Being more incessantly there than any other single element of the mental life, the other elements end by seeming to accrete round it and to belong to it. It becomes opposed to them as the permanent is opposed to the changing and inconstant.

One may, I think, without fear of being upset by any future Galtonian circulars, believe that all men must single out from the rest of what they call themselves some central principle of which each would recognize the foregoing to be a fair general description – accurate enough, at any rate, to denote what it meant, and keep it unconfused with other things. The moment, however, they came to closer quarters with it, trying to define more accurately its precise nature, we should find opinions beginning to diverge. Some would say that it is a simple active substance, the soul, of which they are thus conscious; others, that it is nothing but a fiction, the imaginary being denoted by the pronoun I; and between these extremes of opinion all sorts of intermediaries would be found.

Later we must ourselves discuss them all, and sufficient to that day will be the evil thereof. *Now*, let us try to settle for ourselves as definitely as we can, just how this central nucleus of the self may *feel*, no matter whether it be a spiritual substance or only a delusive word.

For this central part of the self is *felt*. It may be all that transcendentalists say it is, and all that empiricists say it is into the bargain, but it is at any rate no *mere ens rationis*, cognized only in an intellectual way, and no *mere* summation of memories or *mere* sound of a word in our ears. It is something with which we also have direct sensible acquaintance, and which is as fully present at any moment of consciousness in which it *is* present, as in a whole lifetime of such moments. When, just now, it was called an abstraction, that did not mean that, like some general notion, it could not be presented in a particular experience. It only meant that in the stream of consciousness it never was found all alone. But when it is found, it is *felt*; just as the body is felt, the feeling of which is also an abstraction, because never is the body felt all alone, but always together with other things. *Now can we tell more precisely in what the feeling of this central active self consists* − not necessarily as yet what the active self *is*, as a being or principle, but what we *feel* when we become aware of its existence?

I think I can in my own case; and as what I say will be likely to meet with opposition if generalized (as indeed it may be in part inapplicable to other individuals), I had better continue in the first person, leaving my description to be accepted by those to whose introspection it may commend itself as true, and confessing my inability to meet the demands of others, if others there be.

First of all, I am aware of a constant play of furtherances and hindrances in my thinking, of checks and releases, tendencies which run with desire, and tendencies which run the other way.

Among the matters I think of, some range themselves on the side of the thought's interests, whilst others play an unfriendly part thereto. The mutual inconsistencies and agreements, reinforcements and obstructions, which obtain amongst these objective matters reverberate backwards and produce what seem to be incessant reactions of my spontaneity upon them, welcoming or opposing, appropriating or disowning, striving with or against, saying yes or no. This palpitating inward life is, in me, that central nucleus which I just tried to describe in terms that all men might use.

But when I forsake such general descriptions and grapple with particulars, coming to the closest possible quarters with the facts, *it is difficult for me to detect in the activity any purely spiritual element at all. Whenever my introspective glance succeeds in turning round quickly enough to catch one of these manifestations of spontaneity in the act, all it can ever feel distinctly is some bodily process, for the most part taking place within the head.* Omitting for a moment what is obscure in these introspective results, let me try to state those particulars which to my own consciousness seem indubitable and distinct.

In the first place, the acts of attending, assenting, negating, making an effort, are felt as movements of something in the head. In many cases it is possible to describe these movements quite exactly. In attending to either an idea or a sensation belonging to a particular sense-sphere, the movement is the adjustment of the sense organ, felt as it occurs. I cannot think in visual terms, for example, without feeling a fluctuating play of pressures, convergences, divergences and accommodations in my eyeballs. The direction in which the object is conceived to lie determines the character of these movements, the feeling of which becomes, for my consciousness, identified with the manner in which I make myself ready to receive the visible thing. My brain appears to me as if all shot across with lines of direction, of which I have become conscious as my attention has shifted from one sense organ to another, in passing to successive outer things, or in following trains of varying sense-ideas.

When I try to remember or reflect, the movements in question, instead of being directed towards the periphery, seem to come from the periphery inwards and feel like a sort of *withdrawal* from the outer world. As far as I can detect, these feelings are due to an actual rolling outwards and upwards of the eyeballs, such as I believe occurs in me in sleep, and is the exact opposite of their action in fixating a physical thing. In reasoning, I find that I am apt to have a kind of vaguely localized diagram in my mind, with the various fractional objects of the thought disposed at particular points thereof; and the oscillations of my attention from one of them to another are most distinctly felt as alternations of direction in movements occurring inside the head.[3]

In consenting and negating, and in making a mental effort, the movements seem more complex, and I find them harder to describe. The opening and closing of the glottis play a great part in these operations, and, less distinctly, the movements of the soft palate, etc., shutting off the posterior nares from the mouth. My glottis is like a sensitive valve, intercepting my breath instantaneously at every mental hesitation or felt aversion to the objects of my thought, and as quickly opening, to let the air pass through my throat and nose, the moment the repugnance is overcome. The feeling of the movement of this air is, in me, one strong ingredient of the feeling of assent. The movements of the muscles of the brow and eyelids also respond very sensitively to every fluctuation in the agreeableness or disagreeableness of what comes before my mind.

In *effort* of any sort, contractions of the jaw-muscles and of those of respiration are added to those of the brow and glottis, and thus the feeling passes out of the head properly so called. It passes out of the head whenever the welcoming or rejecting of the object is *strongly* felt. Then a set of feelings pour in from many bodily parts, all 'expressive' of my emotion, and the head-feelings proper are swallowed up in this larger mass.

In a sense, then, it may be truly said that, in one person at least, *the 'self of the selves', when carefully examined, is found to consist mainly of the collection of these peculiar motions in the head or between the head and throat*. I do not for a moment say that this is *all* it consists of, for I fully realize how desperately hard is introspection in this field. But I feel quite sure that these cephalic motions are the portions of my innermost activity of which I am *most distinctly aware*. If the dim portions which I cannot yet define should prove to be like unto these distinct

[3] For some farther remarks on these feelings of movement see the next chapter.

portions in me, and I like other men, *it would follow that our entire feeling of spiritual activity, or what commonly passes by that name, is really a feeling of bodily activities whose exact nature is by most men overlooked.*

Now, without pledging ourselves in any way to adopt this hypothesis, let us dally with it for a while to see to what consequences it might lead if it were true.

In the first place, the nuclear part of the self, intermediary between ideas and overt acts, would be a collection of activities physiologically in no essential way different from the overt acts themselves. If we divide all possible physiological acts into *adjustments* and *executions*, the nuclear self would be the adjustments collectively considered; and the less intimate, more shifting self, so far as it was active, would be the executions. But both adjustments and executions would obey the reflex type. Both would be the result of sensorial and ideational processes discharging either into each other within the brain, or into muscles and other parts outside. The peculiarity of the adjustments would be that they are minimal reflexes, few in number, incessantly repeated, constant amid great fluctuations in the rest of the mind's content, and entirely unimportant and uninteresting except through their uses in furthering or inhibiting the presence of various things, and actions before consciousness. These characters would naturally keep us from introspectively paying much attention to them in detail, whilst they would at the same time make us aware of them as a coherent group of processes, strongly contrasted with all the other things consciousnesses contained – even with the other constituents of the 'self', material, social or spiritual, as the case might be. They are reactions, and they are *primary* reactions. Everything arouses them; for objects which have no other effects will for a moment contract the brow and make the glottis close. It is as if all that visited the mind had to stand an entrance examination, and just show its face so as to be either approved or sent back. These primary reactions are like the opening or the closing of the door. In the midst of psychic change they are the permanent core of turnings-towards and turnings-from, of yieldings and arrests, which naturally seem central and interior in comparison with the foreign matters, *apropos* to which they occur, and hold a sort of arbitrating, decisive position, quite unlike that held by any of the other constituents of the Me. It would not be surprising, then, if we were to feel them as the birthplace of conclusions and the starting point of acts, or if they came to appear as what we called a while back the 'sanctuary within the citadel' of our personal life.

If they really were the innermost sanctuary, the *ultimate* one of all the selves whose being we can ever directly experience, it would follow that *all* that is experienced is, strictly considered, *objective*; that this Objective falls asunder into two contrasted parts, one realized as 'self', the other as 'not-self'; and that over and above these parts there *is* nothing save the fact that they are known, the fact of the stream of thought being there as the indispensable subjective condition of their being experienced at all. But this *condition* of the experience is not one of the *things experienced* at the moment; this knowing is not immediately *known*. It is only known in subsequent reflection. Instead, then, of the stream of thought being one of *con*-sciousness, 'thinking its own existence along with whatever else it thinks' (as Ferrier says), it might be better called a stream of *scious*ness pure and simple, thinking objects of some of which it makes what it calls a 'Me', and only aware of its 'pure' self in abstract, hypothetic or conceptual way. Each 'section' of the stream would then be a bit of sciousness or knowledge of this sort, including and contemplating its 'me' and its 'not-me' as objects which work out their drama together, but not yet including or contemplating its own subjective being. The sciousness in question would be the *thinker*, and the existence of this thinker would be given to us rather as a logical postulate than as that direct inner perception of spiritual activity which we naturally believe ourselves to have. 'Matter', as something behind physical phenomena, is a postulate of this sort. Between the postulated matter and the postulated thinker, the sheet of phenomena would then swing, some of them (the 'realities') pertaining more to the matter, others (the fictions, opinions and errors) pertaining more to the thinker. But *who* the thinker would be, or how many distinct thinkers we ought to suppose in the universe, would all be subjects for an ulterior metaphysical inquiry.

Speculations like this traverse common-sense; and not only do they traverse common-sense (which in philosophy is no insuperable objection) but they contradict the fundamental assumption of *every* philosophic school. Spiritualists, transcendentalists and empiricists alike admit in us a continual direct perception of the thinking activity in the concrete. However they may otherwise disagree, they vie with each other in the cordiality of their recognition of our *thoughts* as the one sort of existent which scepticism cannot touch. I will therefore treat the last few pages as a parenthetical digression, and from now to the end of the volume revert to the path of common-sense again. I mean by this that I will continue to assume (as I have assumed all along, especially in the last chapter) a direct awareness of the process of our thinking as such, simply insisting on the fact that it is an even more inward and subtle phenomenon than most of us suppose. At the conclusion of the volume, however, I may permit myself to revert again to the doubts here provisionally mooted, and will indulge in some metaphysical reflections suggested by them.

At present, then, the only conclusion I come to is the following: That (in some persons at least) the part of the innermost self which is most vividly felt turns out to consist for the most part of a collection of cephalic movements of 'adjustments' which, for want of attention and reflection, usually fail to be perceived and classed as what they are; that over and above these there is an obscurer feeling of something more; but whether it be of fainter physiological processes, or of nothing objective at all, but rather of subjectivity as such, of thought become 'its own object', must at present remain an open question — like the question whether it be an indivisible active soul-substance, or the question whether it be a personification of the pronoun I, or any other of the guesses as to what its nature may be.

Farther than this we cannot as yet go clearly in our analysis of the self's constituents . . .

The Pure Ego

Having summed up [. . .] the principal results of the chapter thus far, I have said all that need be said of the constituents of the phenomenal self [. . .] Our decks are consequently cleared for the struggle with that pure principle of personal identity which has met us all along our preliminary exposition, but which we have always shied from and treated as a difficulty to be postponed. Ever since Hume's time, it has been justly regarded as the most puzzling puzzle with which psychology has to deal; and whatever view one may espouse, one has to hold his position against heavy odds. If, with the spiritualists, one contend for a substantial soul, or transcendental principle of unity, one can give no positive account of what that may be. And if, with the Humeans, one deny such a principle and say that the stream of passing thoughts is all, one runs against the entire common-sense of mankind, of which the belief in a distinct principle of selfhood seems an integral part. Whatever solution be adopted in the pages to come, we may as well make up our minds in advance that it will fail to satisfy the majority of those to whom it is addressed. The best way of approaching the matter will be to take up first –

The Sense of Personal Identity

In that last chapter it was stated in as radical a way as possible that the thoughts which we actually know to exist do not fly about loose, but seem each to belong to some one thinker and not to another. Each thought, out of a multitude of other thoughts of which it may think, is able to distinguish those which belong to its own ego from those which do not. The former have a warmth and intimacy about them of which the latter are completely devoid, being merely conceived, in a cold and foreign fashion, and not appearing as blood relatives, bringing their greetings to us from out of the past.

Now this consciousness of personal sameness may be treated either as a subjective phenomenon or as an objective deliverance, as a feeling, or as a truth. We may explain how one bit of thought can come to judge other bits to belong to the same ego with itself; or we may criticize its judgment and decide how far it may tally with the nature of things.

As a mere subjective phenomenon the judgment presents no difficulty or mystery peculiar to itself. It belongs to the great class of judgments of sameness; and there is nothing more remarkable in making a judgment of sameness in the first person than in the second or the third. The intellectual operations seem essentially alike, whether I say 'I am the same', or whether I say 'the pen is the same, as yesterday'. It is as easy to think this as to think the opposite and say 'neither I nor the pen is the same'. This sort of *bringing of things together into the object of a single judgment* is of course essential to all thinking. The things are conjoined *in* the thought, whatever may be the relation in which they appear to the thought. The thinking them is *thinking* them together, even if only with the result of judging that they do not *belong* together. This sort of *subjective synthesis*, essential to knowledge as such (whenever it has a complex object), must not be confounded with *objective synthesis* or union instead of difference or disconnection, known among the things.[4] The subjective synthesis is involved in thought's mere existence. Even a really disconnected world could only be *known* to be such by having its parts temporarily united in the Object of some pulse of consciousness.[5]

The sense of personal identity is not, then, this mere synthetic form essential to all thought. It is the sense of a sameness perceived *by* thought and predicated of things *thought-about*. These things are a present self and a self of yesterday. The thought not only thinks them both, but thinks that they are identical. The psychologist, looking on and playing the critic, might prove the thought wrong, and show there was no real identity – there might have been no yesterday, or, at any rate, no self of yesterday; or, if there were, the sameness predicated might not obtain, or might be predicated on insufficient grounds. In either case the personal identity would not exist as a *fact*; but it would exist as a *feeling* all the same; the consciousness of it by the thought would be there, and the psychologist would still

---

[4] *Also nur dadurch, dass ich ein Mannigfaltiges gegebener Vorstellungen in* EINEM BEWUSSTSEIN *verbinden kann, ist es möglich dass ich die* IDENTITÄT DES BEWUSSTSEINS *in diesen* VORSTELLUNGEN *selbst vorstelle, d. h. die analytische Einheit der Apperception ist nur unter der Voraussetzung irgend einer synthetischen möglich.*' [So it is only because I can unite a manifold of given ideas *in one consciousness* that I represent to myself the identity of consciousness in those ideas; that is to say, the analytic unity of apperception is possible only on the presupposition of a synthetic unity.] In this passage (*Kritik der reinen Vernunft*, 2nd edn, s. 16) Kant calls by the names of analytic and synthetic apperception what we here mean by objective and subjective synthesis respectively. It were much to be desired that someone might invent a good pair of terms in which to record the distinction – those used in the text are certainly very bad, but Kant's seem to me still worse. 'Categorical unity' and 'transcendental synthesis' would also be good Kantian, but hardly good human, speech.

[5] So that we might say, by a sort of bad pun, 'only a connected world can be known as disconnected'. I say bad pun, because the point of view shifts between the connectedness and the disconnectedness. The disconnectedness is of the realities known; the connectedness is of the knowledge of them; and reality and knowledge of it are, from the psychological point of view held fast to in these pages, two different facts.

have to analyse that, and show where its illusoriness lay. Let us now be the psychologist and see whether it be right or wrong when it says, *I am the same self that I was yesterday.*

We may immediately call it right and intelligible so far as it posits a past time with past thoughts or selves contained therein – these were data which we assumed at the outset of the book. Right also and intelligible so far as it thinks of a present self – that present self we have just studied in its various forms. The only question for us is as to what the consciousness may mean when it calls the present self the *same* with one of the past selves which it has in mind.

We spoke a moment since of warmth and intimacy. This leads us to the answer sought. For, whatever the thought we are criticizing may think about its present self, that self comes to its acquaintance, or is actually felt, with warmth and intimacy. Of course this is the case with the *bodily* part of it; we feel the whole cubic mass of our body all the while, it gives us an unceasing sense of personal existence. Equally do we feel the inner 'nucleus of the spiritual self', either in the shape of yon faint physiological adjustments, or (adopting the universal psychological belief), in that of the pure activity of our thought taking place as such. Our remoter spiritual, material and social selves, so far as they are realized, come also with a glow and a warmth; for the thought of them infallibly brings some degree of organic emotion in the shape of quickened heartbeats, oppressed breathing, or some other alteration, even though it be a slight one, in the general bodily tone. The character of 'warmth', then, in the present self, reduces itself to either of two things – something in the feeling which we have of the thought itself, as thinking, or else the feeling of the body's actual existence at the moment – or finally to both. We cannot realize our present self without simultaneously feeling one or other of these two things. Any other fact which brings these two things with it into consciousness will be thought with a warmth and an intimacy like those which cling to the present self.

Any *distant* self which fulfils this condition will be thought with such warmth and intimacy. But which distant selves *do* fulfil the condition, when represented?

Obviously those, and only those, which fulfilled it when they were alive. *Then* we shall imagine with the animal warmth upon them, to them may possibly cling the aroma, the echo of the thinking taken in the act. And by a natural consequence, we shall assimilate them to each other and to the warm and intimate self we now feel within us as we think, and separate them as a collection from whatever selves have not this mark, much as out of a herd of cattle let loose for the winter on some wide western prairie the owner picks out and sorts together when the time for the round-up comes in the spring, all the beasts on which he finds his own particular brand.

The various members of the collection thus set apart are felt to belong with each other whenever they are thought at all. The animal warmth, etc., is their herd-mark, the brand from which they can never more escape. It runs through them all like a thread through a chaplet and makes them into a whole, which we treat as a unit, no matter how much in other ways the parts may differ *inter se*. Add to this character the farther one that the distant selves appear to our thought as having for hours of time been *continuous* with each other, and the most recent ones of them continuous with the self of the present moment, melting into it by slow degrees; and we get a still stronger bond of union. As we think we see an identical bodily thing when, in spite of changes of structure, it exists continuously before our eyes, or when, however interrupted its presence, its quality returns unchanged; so here we think we experience an identical *self* when it appears to us in an analogous way. Continuity makes us unite what dissimilarity might otherwise separate; similarity makes us unite what discontinuity might hold apart. And thus it is, finally, that Peter, awakening in the same bed with Paul, and recalling what both had in mind before they went to sleep, reidentifies and appropriates the 'warm' ideas as his, and is never tempted to confuse them with those cold and pale-appearing ones which he ascribes to Paul. As well might he confound Paul's body, which he only sees, with his own body, which he sees but also feels. Each of us when he awakens says, Here's the same old self again, just as he says, Here's the same old bed, the same old room, the same old world.

The sense of our own personal identity, then, is exactly like any one of our other perceptions of sameness among phenomena. It is a conclusion grounded either on the resemblance in a fundamental respect, or on the continuity before the mind, of the phenomena compared.

And it must not be taken to mean more than these grounds warrant, or treated as a sort of metaphysical or absolute unity in which all differences are overwhelmed. The past and present selves compared are the same just so far as they *are* the same, and no farther. A uniform feeling of 'warmth', of bodily existence (or an equally uniform feeling of pure psychic energy?) pervades them all; and this is what gives them a *generic* unity, and makes them the same in *kind*. But this generic unity coexists with generic differences just as real as the unity. And if from the one point of view they are one self, from others they are as truly not one but many selves. And similarly of the attribute of continuity; it gives its own kind of unity to the self – that of mere connectedness, or unbrokenness, a perfectly definite phenomenal thing – but it gives not a jot or tittle more. And this unbrokenness in the stream of selves, like the unbrokenness in an exhibition of 'dissolving views', in no wise implies any farther unity or contradicts any amount of plurality in other respects.

And accordingly we find that, where the resemblance and the continuity are no longer felt, the sense of personal identity goes too. We hear from our parents various anecdotes about our infant years, but we do not appropriate them as we do our own memories. Those breaches of decorum awaken no blush, those bright sayings no self-complacency. That child is a foreign creature with which our present self is no more identified in feeling than it is with some stranger's living child today. Why? Partly because great time-gaps break up all these early years – we cannot ascend to them by continuous memories; and partly because no representation of how the child *felt* comes up with the stories. We know what he said and did; but no sentiment of his little body, of his emotions, of his psychic strivings as they felt to him, comes up to contribute an element of warmth and intimacy to the narrative we hear, and the main bond of union with our present self thus disappears. It is the same with certain of our dimly recollected experiences. We hardly know whether to appropriate them or to disown them as fancies, or things read or heard and not lived through. Their animal heat has evaporated; the feelings that accompanied them are so lacking in the recall, or so different from those we now enjoy, that no judgment of identity can be decisively cast.

Resemblance among the parts of a continuum of feelings (especially bodily feelings) experienced along with things widely different in all other regards, *thus constitutes the real and verifiable 'personal identity' which we feel*. There is no other identity than this in the 'stream' of subjective consciousness which we described in the last chapter. Its parts differ, but under all their differences they are knit in these two ways; and if either way of knitting disappears, the sense of unity departs. If a man wakes up some fine day unable to recall any of his past experiences, so that he has to learn his biography afresh, or if he only recalls the facts of it in a cold abstract way as things that he is sure once happened; or if, without this loss of memory, his bodily and spiritual habits all change during the night, each organ giving a different tone, and the act of thought becoming aware of itself in a different way; he *feels*, and he *says*, that he is a changed person. He disowns his former me, gives himself a new name, identifies his present life with nothing from out of the older time. Such cases are not rare in mental pathology; but, as we still have some reasoning to do, we had better give no concrete account of them until the end of the chapter.

This description of personal identity will be recognized by the instructed reader as the ordinary doctrine professed by the empirical school. Associationists in England and France, Herbartians in Germany, all describe the self as an aggregate of which each part, as to its *being*, is a separate fact. So far so good, then; thus much is true whatever farther things may be true; and it is to the imperishable glory of Hume and Herbart and their successors to have taken so much of the meaning of personal identity out of the clouds and made of the self an empirical and verifiable thing.

But in leaving the matter here, and saying that this sum of passing things is all, these writers have neglected certain more subtle aspects of the unity of consciousness, to which we next must turn.

Our recent simile of the herd of cattle will help us. It will be remembered that the beasts were brought together into one herd because their owner found on each of them his brand. The 'owner' symbolizes here that 'section' of consciousness, or pulse of thought, which we have all along represented as the vehicle of the judgment of identity; and the 'brand' symbolizes the characters of warmth and continuity, by reason of which the judgment is made. There is found a *self*-brand, just as there is found a herd-brand. Each brand, so far, is the mark, or cause of our knowing, that certain things belong-together. But if the brand is the *ratio cognoscendi* of the belonging, the belonging, in the case of the herd, is in turn the *ratio existendi* of the brand. No beast would be so branded unless he belonged to the owner of the herd. They are not his because they are branded; they are branded because they are his. So that it seems as if our description of the belonging-together of the various selves, as a belonging-together which is merely *represented*, in a later pulse of thought, had knocked the bottom out of the matter, and omitted the most characteristic one of all the features found in the herd — a feature which common-sense finds in the phenomenon of personal identity as well, and for our omission of which also will hold us to a strict account. For common-sense insists that the unity of all the selves is not a mere appearance of similarity or continuity, ascertained after the fact. She is sure that it involves a real belonging to a real owner, to a pure spiritual entity of some kind. Relation to this entity is what makes the self's constituents stick together as they do for thought. The individual beasts do not stick together, for all that they wear the same brand. Each wanders with whatever accidental mates it finds. The herd's unity is only potential, its centre ideal, like the 'centre of gravity' in physics, until the herdsman or owner comes. He furnishes a real centre of accretion to which the beasts are driven and by which they are held. The beasts stick together by sticking severally to him. Just so, common-sense insists, there must be a real proprietor in the case of the selves, or else their actual accretion into a 'personal consciousness' would never have taken place. To the usual empirical explanation of personal consciousness this is a formidable reproof, because all the individual thoughts and feelings which have succeeded each other 'up to date' are represented by ordinary associationism as in some inscrutable way 'integrating' or gumming themselves together on their own account, and thus fusing into a stream. All the incomprehensibilities which in Chapter 10, above, we saw to attach to the idea of things fusing without a *medium* apply to the empiricist description of personal identity.

But in our own account the medium is fully assigned, the herdsman is there, in the shape of something not among the things collected, but superior to them all, namely, the real, present onlooking, remembering, 'judging thought' or identify-ing 'section' of the stream. This is what collects – 'owns' some of the past facts which it surveys, and disowns the rest – and so makes a unity that is actualized and anchored and does not merely float in the blue air of possibility. And the reality of such pulses of thought, with their function of knowing, it will be remembered that we did not seek to deduce or explain, but simply assumed them as the ultimate kind of fact that the psychologist must admit to exist.

But this assumption, though it yields much, still does not yield all that common-sense demands. The unity into which the Thought – as I shall for a time proceed to call, with a capital T, the present mental state – binds the individual past facts with each other and with itself, does not exist until the Thought is there. It is as if wild cattle were lassoed by a newly created settler and then owned for the first time. But the essence of the matter to common-sense is that the past thoughts never were wild cattle, they were always owned. The Thought does not capture them, but as soon as it comes into existence it finds them already its own. How is this possible unless the Thought have a *substantial* identity with a former owner – not a mere continuity or a resemblance, as in our account, but a *real unity*? Common-sense in fact would drive us to admit what we may for the moment call an arch-ego, dominating the entire stream of thought and all the selves that may be represented in it, as the ever self-same and changeless principle implied in their union. The 'soul' of metaphysics and the 'transcendental ego' of the Kantian philosophy, are, as we shall soon see, but attempts to satisfy this urgent demand of common-sense. But, for a time at least, we can still express without any such hypotheses that appearance of never-lapsing ownership for which common-sense contends.

For how would it be if the Thought, the present judging Thought, instead of being in any way substantially or transcen-dentally identical with the former owner of the past self, merely inherited his 'title', and thus stood as his legal representative now? It would then, if its birth coincided exactly with the death of another owner, *find* the past self already its own as soon as it found it at all, and the past self would thus never be wild, but always owned, by a title that never lapsed. We can imagine a long succession of herdsmen coming rapidly into possession of the same cattle by transmission of an original title by bequest. May not the 'title' of a collective self be passed from one Thought to another in some analogous way?

It is a patent fact of consciousness that a transmission like this actually occurs. Each pulse of cognitive consciousness, each Thought, dies away and is replaced by another. The other, among the things it knows, knows its own predecessor, and finding it 'warm', in the way we have described, greets it, saying: 'Thou art *mine*, and part of the same self with me.' Each later Thought, knowing and including thus the Thoughts which went before, is the final receptacle – and appropriating them is the final owner – of all that they contain and own. Each Thought is thus born an owner, and dies owned, transmitting whatever it realized as its self to its own later proprietor. As Kant says, it is as if elastic balls were to have not only motion but knowledge of it, and a first ball were to transmit both its motion and its consciousness to a second, which took both up into *its* consciousness and passed them to a third, until the last ball held all that the other balls had held, and realized it as its own. It is this trick which the nascent thought has of immediately taking up the expiring thought and 'adopting' it, which is the foundation of the appropriation of most of the remoter constituents of the self. Who owns the last self owns the self before the last, for what possesses the possessor possesses the possessed.

It is impossible to discover any *verifiable* features in personal identity, which this sketch does not contain, impossible to imagine how any transcendent non-phenomenal sort of an arch ego, were he there, could shape matters to any other result, or be known in time by any other fruit, than just this production of a stream of consciousness each 'section' of which should know, and knowing, hug to itself and adopt, all those that went before – thus standing as the *representative* of the entire past stream; and which should similarly adopt the objects already adopted by any portion of this spiritual stream. Such standing-as-representative, and such adopting, are perfectly clear phenomenal relations. The Thought which, whilst it knows another Thought and the Object of that Other, appropriates the Other and the Object which the Other appropriated, is still a perfectly distinct phenomenon from that Other; it may hardly resemble it; it may be far removed from it in space and time.

The only point that is obscure is the *act of appropriation* itself. Already in enumerating the constituents of the self and their rivalry, I had to use the word appropriate. And the quick-witted reader probably noticed at the time, in hearing how one constituent was let drop and disowned and another one held fast to and espoused, that the phrase was meaningless unless the constituents were objects in the hands of something else. A thing cannot appropriate itself: it *is* itself; and still less can it disown itself. There must be an agent of the appropriating and disowning; but that agent we have already named. It is the Thought to whom the various 'constituents' are known. That Thought is a vehicle of choice as well as of cognition; and among the choices it makes are these appropriations, or repudiations of its 'own'. But the Thought never is an object in its own hands, it never appropriates or disowns itself. It appropriates *to* itself, it is the actual focus of accretion, the hook from which the chain of past selves dangles, planted firmly in the present, which alone passes for real, and thus keeping the chain from being a purely ideal thing. Anon the book itself will drop into the past with all it carries, and then be treated as an object and appropriated by a new Thought in the new present which will serve as living hook in turn. The present moment of consciousness is thus, as Mr Hodgson says, the darkest in the whole series. It may feel its own immediate existence – we have all along admitted the possibility of this, hard as it is by direct introspection to ascertain the fact – but nothing can be known *about* it till it be dead and gone. Its appropriations are therefore less to *itself* than to the most intimately felt *part of its present Object, the body, and the central adjustments*, which accompany the act of thinking, in the head. *These are the real nucleus of our personal identity*, and it is their actual existence, realized as a solid present fact, which makes us say 'as sure *as I exist*, those past facts were part of myself'. They are the kernel to which the *represented* parts of the self are assimilated, accreted and knit on; and even were Thought entirely unconscious of itself in the act of thinking, these 'warm' parts of its present object would be a firm basis on which the consciousness of personal identity would rest.[6] Such consciousness, then, as a psychologic fact, can

---

[6] Some subtle reader will object that the Thought cannot call any part of its Object 'I' and knit other parts to it, without first knitting that part on to *Itself*; and that it

be fully described without supposing any other agent than a succession of perishing thoughts, endowed with the functions of appropriation and rejection, and of which some can know and appropriate or reject objects already known, appropriated or rejected by the rest.

The passing Thought then seems to be the Thinker; and though there *may* be another non-phenomenal Thinker behind that, so far we do not seem to need him to express the facts. But we cannot definitively make up our mind about him until we have heard the reasons that have historically been used to prove his reality.

The Pure Self or Inner Principle of Personal Unity

To a brief survey of the theories of the ego let us then next proceed. They are three in number, as follows:

1 The spiritualist theory
2 The associationist theory
3 The transcendentalist theory.

The Theory of the Soul

In Chapter 10, above, we were led ourselves to the spiritualist theory of the 'soul', as a means of escape from the unintelligibilities of mind-stuff 'integrating' with itself, and from the physiological improbability of a material monad, with thought attached to it, in the brain. But at the end of the chapter we said

---

cannot knit it on to Itself without knowing itself – so that our supposition that the Thought may conceivably have no immediate knowledge of Itself is thus overthrown. To which the reply is that we must take care not to be duped by words. The words *I* and *me* signify nothing mysterious and unexampled – they are at bottom only names of *emphasis*; and Thought is always emphasizing something. Within a tract of space which it cognizes, it contrasts a *here* with a *there*; within a tract of time a *now* and *then*: of a pair of things calls one *this*, the other *that*. I and *thou*, I and *it*, are distinctions exactly on a par with these – distinctions possible in an exclusively *objective* field of knowledge, the 'I' meaning for the Thought nothing but the bodily life which it momentarily feels. The sense of my bodily existence, however obscurely recognized as such, *may* then be the absolute original of my conscious selfhood, the fundamental perception that *I am*. All appropriations *may* be made *to* it, *by* a Thought not at the moment immediately cognized by itself. Whether these are not only logical possibilities but actual facts is something not yet dogmatically decided in the text.

we should examine the 'soul' critically in a later place, to see whether it had any other advantages as a theory over the simple phenomenal notion of a stream of thought accompanying a stream of cerebral activity, by a law yet unexplained.

The theory of the soul is the theory of popular philosophy and of scholasticism, which is only popular philosophy made systematic. It declares that the principle of individuality within us must be *substantial*, for psychic phenomena are activities, and there can be no activity without a concrete agent. This substantial agent cannot be the brain but must be something *immaterial*; for its activity, thought, is both immaterial, and takes cognizance of immaterial things, and of material things in general and intelligible, as well as in particular and sensible ways – all which powers are incompatible with the nature of matter, of which the brain is composed. Thought moreover is simple, whilst the activities of the brain are compounded of the elementary activities of each of its parts. Furthermore, thought is spontaneous or free, whilst all material activity is determined *as extra*; and the will can turn itself against all corporeal goods and appetites, which would be impossible were it a corporeal function. For these objective reasons the principle of psychic life must be both immaterial and simple as well as substantial, must be what is called a *soul*. The same consequence follows from subjective reasons. Our consciousness of personal identity assures us of our essential simplicity: the owner of the various constituents of the self, as we have seen them, the hypothetical arch-ego whom we provisionally conceived as possible, is a real entity of whose existence self-consciousness makes us directly aware. No material agent could thus turn round and grasp *itself* – material activities always grasp something else than the agent. And if a brain *could* grasp itself and be self-conscious, it would be conscious of itself *as* a brain and not as something of an altogether different kind. The soul then exists as a simple spiritual substance in which the various psychic faculties, operations and affections inhere . . .

Summary

To sum up now this long chapter. The consciousness of self involves a stream of thought, each part of which as 'I' can (1) remember those which went before, and know the things they knew; and (2) emphasize and care paramountly for certain ones among them as '*me*', and *appropriate to these* the rest. The nucleus of the '*me*' is always the bodily existence felt to be present at the time. Whatever remembered-past-feelings *resemble* this present feeling are deemed to belong to the same *me* with it. Whatever other things are perceived to be *associated* with this feeling are deemed to form part of that me's *experience*; and of them certain ones (which fluctuate more or less) are reckoned to be themselves *constituents* of the me in a larger sense – such are the clothes, the material possessions, the friends, the honours and esteem which the person receives or may receive. This me is an empirical aggregate of things objectively known. The *I* which knows them cannot itself be an aggregate, neither for psychological purposes need it be considered to be an unchanging metaphysical entity like the soul, or a principle like the pure ego, viewed as 'out of time'. It is a *Thought*, at each moment different from that of the last moment, but *appropriative* of the latter, together with all that the latter called its own. All the experiential facts find their place in this description, unencumbered with any hypothesis save that of the existence of passing thoughts or states of mind. The same brain may subserve many conscious selves, either alternate or coexisting; but by what modifications in its action, or whether ultra-cerebral conditions may intervene, are questions which cannot now be answered.

If anyone urge that I assign no *reason* why the successive passing thoughts should inherit each other's possessions, or why they and the brain states should be functions (in the mathematical sense) of each other, I reply that the reason, if there be any, must lie where all real reasons lie, in the total sense or meaning of the world. If there be such a meaning, or any approach to it (as we are bound to trust there is), it alone can make clear to us why such finite human streams of thought are called into existence in such functional dependence upon brains. This is as much as to say that the special natural science of *psychology* must stop with the mere functional formula. *If the passing thought be the directly verifiable existent which no school has hitherto doubted it to be, then that thought is itself the thinker*, and psychology need not look beyond. The only pathway that I can discover for bringing in a more transcendental thinker would be to *deny* that we have any *direct* knowledge of the thought as such. The latter's existence would then be reduced to a postulate, an assertion that there *must be* a *knower* correlative to all this known; and the problem *who that knower is* would have become a metaphysical problem. With the question once stated in these terms, the spiritualist and transcendentalist solutions must be considered as *prima facie* on a par with our own psychological one, and discussed impartially. But that carries us beyond the psychological or naturalistic point of view.

13

The Methods and Snares of Psychology

We have now finished the physiological preliminaries of our subject and must in the remaining chapters study the mental states themselves whose cerebral conditions and concomitants we have been considering hitherto. Beyond the brain, however, there is an outer world to which the brain-states themselves 'correspond'. And it will be well, ere we advance farther, to say a word about the relation of the mind to this larger sphere of physical fact.

Psychology is a Natural Science

That is, the mind which the psychologist studies is the mind of distinct individuals inhabiting definite portions of a real space and of a real time. With any other sort of mind, absolute intelligence, mind unattached to a particular body, or mind not subject to the course of time, the psychologist as such has nothing to do. 'Mind', in his mouth, is only a class name for *minds*. Fortunate will it be if his more modest inquiry result in any generalizations which the philosopher devoted to absolute intelligence as such can use.

To the psychologist, then, the minds he studies are *objects*, in a world of other objects. Even when he introspectively analyses his own mind, and tells what he finds there, he talks about it in an objective way. He says, for instance, that under certain circumstances the colour grey appears to him green, and calls the appearance an illusion. This implies that he compares two objects, a real colour seen under certain conditions, and a mental perception which he believes to represent it, and that he declares the relation between them to be of a certain kind. In making this critical judgment, the psychologist stands as much outside of the perception which he criticizes as he does of the colour. Both are his objects. And if this is true of him when he reflects on his own conscious states, how much truer is it when he treats of those of others! In German philosophy since Kant the word *Erkenntnisstheorie*, criticism of the faculty of knowledge, plays a great part. Now the psychologist necessarily becomes such an *Erkenntnisstheoretiker*. But the knowledge he theorizes about is not the bare function of knowledge which Kant criticizes – he does not inquire into the possibility of knowledge *überhaupt*. He assumes it to be possible, he does not doubt its presence in himself at the moment he speaks. The knowledge he criticizes is the knowledge of particular men about the particular things that surround them. This he may, upon occasion, in the light of his *own* unquestioned knowledge, pronounce true or false, and trace the reasons by which it has become one or the other.

It is highly important that this natural-science point of view should be understood at the outset. Otherwise more may be demanded of the psychologist than he ought to be expected to perform.

A diagram will exhibit more emphatically what the assumptions of psychology must be:

1 The Psychologist	2 The Thought Studied	3 The Thought's Object	4 The Psychologist's Reality

These four squares contain the irreducible data of psychology. No. 1, the psychologist, believes Nos 2, 3 and 4, which together form *his* total object, to be realities, and reports them and their mutual relations as truly as he can without troubling himself with the puzzle of how he can report them at all. About such *ultimate* puzzles he in the main need trouble himself no more than the geometer, the chemist or the botanist do, who make precisely the same assumptions as he.[1]

Of certain fallacies to which the psychologist is exposed by reason of his peculiar point of view – that of being a reporter of subjective as well as of objective facts, we must presently speak.

---

[1] On the relation between psychology and general philosophy, see G. C. Robertson, *Mind*, vol. 8, p. 1.

But not until we have considered the methods he uses for ascertaining what the facts in question are.

The Methods of Investigation

Introspective observation is what we have to rely on first and foremost and always. The word introspection need hardly be defined – it means, of course, the looking into our own minds and reporting what we there discover. *Everyone agrees that we there discover states of consciousness.* So far as I know, the existence of such states has never been doubted by any critic, however sceptical in other respects he may have been. That we have *cogitations* of some sort is the *inconcussum* in a world most of whose other facts have at some time tottered in the breath of philosophic doubt. All people unhesitatingly believe that they feel themselves thinking, and that they distinguish the mental state as an inward activity or passion, from all the objects with which it may cognitively deal. *I regard this belief as the most fundamental of all the postulates of psychology,* and shall discard all curious inquiries about its certainty as too metaphysical for the scope of this book.

A question of nomenclature. We ought to have some general term by which to designate all states of consciousness merely as such, and apart from their particular quality or cognitive function. Unfortunately most of the terms in use have grave objections. 'Mental state', 'state of consciousness', 'conscious modification', are cumbrous and have no kindred verbs. The same is true of 'subjective condition'. 'Feeling' has the verb 'to feel', both active and neuter, and such derivatives as 'feelingly', 'felt', 'feltness', etc., which make it extremely convenient. But on the other hand it has specific meanings as well as its generic one, sometimes standing for pleasure and pain, and being sometimes a synonym of *'sensation'* as opposed to *thought*; whereas we wish a term to cover sensation and thought indifferently. Moreover, 'feeling' has acquired in the hearts of Platonizing thinkers a very opprobrious set of implications; and since one of the great obstacles to mutual understanding in philosophy is the use of words eulogistically and disparagingly, impartial terms ought always, if possible, to be preferred. The word *psychosis* has been proposed by Mr Huxley. It has the advantage of being correlative to *neurosis* (the name applied by the same author to the corresponding nerve process), and is moreover technical and devoid of partial implications. But it has no verb or other grammatical form allied to it. The expressions 'affection of the soul', 'modification of the ego', are clumsy, like 'state of consciousness', and they implicitly assert theories which it is not well to embody in terminology before they have been openly discussed and approved. 'Idea' is a good vague neutral word, and was by Locke employed in the broadest generic way; but notwithstanding his authority it has not domesticated itself in the language so as to cover bodily sensations, and it moreover has no verb. 'Thought' would be by far the best word to use if it could be made to cover sensations. It has no opprobrious connotation such as 'feeling' has, and it immediately suggests the omnipresence of cognition (or reference to an object other than the mental state itself), which we shall soon see to be of the mental life's essence. But can the expression 'thought of a toothache' ever suggest to the reader the actual present pain itself? It is hardly possible; and we thus seem about to be forced back on some *pair* of terms like Hume's 'impression and idea', or Hamilton's 'presentation and representation', or the ordinary 'feeling and thought', if we wish to cover the whole ground.

In this quandary we can make no definitive choice, but must, according to the convenience of the context, use sometimes one, sometimes another of the synonyms that have been mentioned. *My own partiality is for either* FEELING *or* THOUGHT. I shall probably often use both words in a wider sense than usual, and alternately startle two classes of readers by their unusual sound; but if the connection makes it clear that mental states at large, irrespective of their kind, are meant, this will do no harm, and may even do some good.[2]

The inaccuracy of introspective observation has been made a subject of debate. It is important to gain some fixed ideas on this point before we proceed.

The commonest spiritualistic opinion is that the soul or *subject* of the mental life is a metaphysical entity, inaccessible to direct knowledge, and that the various mental states and operations of which we reflectively become aware are objects of an

[2] Compare some remarks in Mill's *Logic*, Book 1, ch. 3, s. 2 and 3.

inner sense which does not lay hold of the real agent in itself, any more than sight or hearing gives us direct knowledge of matter in itself. From this point of view introspection is, of course, incompetent to lay hold of anything more than the soul's *phenomena*. But even then the question remains, How well can it know the phenomena themselves?

Some authors take high ground here and claim for it a sort of infallibility. Thus Ueberweg:

> When a mental image, as such, is the object of my apprehension, there is no meaning in seeking to distinguish its existence in my consciousness (in me) from its existence out of my consciousness (in itself); for the object apprehended is, in this case, one which does not even exist, as the objects of external perception do, in itself outside of my consciousness. It exists only within me.[3]

And Brentano:

> The phenomena inwardly apprehended are true in themselves. As they appear – of this the evidence with which they are apprehended is a warrant – so they are in reality. Who, then, can deny that in this a great superiority of psychology over the physical sciences comes to light?

And again:

> No one can doubt whether the psychic condition he apprehends in himself *be*, and be *so*, as he apprehends it. Whoever should doubt this would have reached that *finished* doubt which destroys itself in destroying every fixed point from which to make an attack upon knowledge.[4]

Others have gone to the opposite extreme, and maintained that we can have no introspective cognition of our own minds at all. A deliverance of Auguste Comte to this effect has been so often quoted as to be almost classical; and some reference to it seems therefore indispensable here.

Philosophers, says Comte,[5] have

> in these latter days imagined themselves able to distinguish, by a very singular subtlety, two sorts of observation of equal import-ance, one external, the other internal, the latter being solely destined for the study of intellectual phenomena . . . I limit myself

[3] *Logic*, s. 40.
[4] *Psychologie*, Book 2, ch. 3, s. 1 and 2.
[5] *Cours de Philosophie Positive*, 1, 34–8.

to pointing out the principal consideration which proves clearly that this pretended direct contemplation of the mind itself is a pure illusion . . . It is in fact evident that, by an invincible necessity, the human mind can observe directly all phenomena except its own proper states. For by whom shall the observation of these be made? It is conceivable that a man might observe himself with respect to the *passions* that animate him, for the anatomical organs of passion are distinct from those whose function is observation. Though we have all made such observations on ourselves, they can never have much scientific value, and the best mode of knowing the passions will always be that of observing them from without; for every strong state of passion . . . is necessarily incompatible with the state of observation. But, as for observing in the same way *intellectual* phenomena at the time of their actual presence, that is a manifest impossibility. The thinker cannot divide himself into two, of whom one reasons whilst the other observes him reason. The organ observed and the organ observing being, in this case, identical, how could observation take place? This pretended psychological method is then radically null and void. On the one hand, they advise you to isolate yourself, as far as possible, from every external sensation, especially every intellectual work – for if you were to busy yourself even with the simplest calculation, what would become of *internal* observation? – on the other hand, after having with the utmost care attained this state of intellectual slumber, you must begin to contemplate the operations going on in your mind, when nothing there takes place! Our descendants will doubtless see such pretensions some day ridiculed upon the stage. The results of so strange a procedure harmonize entirely with its principle. For all the two thousand years during which metaphysicians have thus cultivated psychology, they are not agreed about one intelligible and established proposition. '*Internal observation*' gives almost as many divergent results as there are individuals who think they practise it.

Comte hardly could have known anything of the English, and nothing of the German, empirical psychology. The 'results' which he had in mind when writing were probably scholastic ones, such as principles of internal activity, the faculties, the ego, the *liberum arbitrium indifferentiae*, etc. John Mill, in replying to him,[6] says:

It might have occurred to M. Comte that a fact may be studied through the medium of memory, not at the very moment of our

[6] *Auguste Comte and Positivism*, 3rd edn, 1882, p. 64.

perceiving it, but the moment after: and this is really the mode in which our best knowledge of our intellectual acts is generally acquired. We reflect on what we have been doing when the act is past, but when its impression in the memory is still fresh. Unless in one of these ways, we could not have acquired the knowledge which nobody denies us to have, of what passes in our minds, M. Comte would scarcely have affirmed that we are not aware of our own intellectual operations. We know of our observings and our reasonings, either at the very time, or by memory the moment after; in either case, by direct knowledge, and not (like things done by us in a state of somnambulism) merely by their results. This simple fact destroys the whole of M. Comte's argument. Whatever we are directly aware of, we can directly observe.

Where now does the truth lie? Our quotation from Mill is obviously the one which expresses the most of *practical* truth about the matter. Even the writers who insist upon the absolute veracity of our immediate inner apprehension of a conscious state have to contrast with this the fallibility of our *memory* or *observation* of it, a moment later. No one has emphasized more sharply than Brentano himself the difference between the immediate *feltness* of a feeling, and its perception by a subsequent reflective act. But which mode of consciousness of it is that which the psychologist must depend on? If to *have* feelings or thoughts in their immediacy were enough, babies in the cradle would be psychologists, and infallible ones. But the psychologist must not only *have* his mental states in their absolute veritableness, he must report them and write about them, name them, classify and compare them and trace their relations to other things. Whilst alive they are their own property; it is only *postmortem* that they become his prey.[7] And as in the naming, classing and knowing of things in general we are notoriously fallible, why not also here? Comte is quite right in laying stress on the fact that a feeling, to be named, judged or perceived, must be already past. No subjective state, whilst present, is its

[7] Wundt says: 'The first rule for utilizing inward observation consists in taking, as far as possible, experiences that are accidental, unexpected, and not intentionally brought about ... *First* it is best as far as possible to rely on *memory* and not on immediate apprehension ... *Second*, internal observation is better fitted to grasp clearly conscious states, especially voluntary mental acts: such inner processes as are obscurely conscious and involuntary will almost entirely elude it, because the effort to observe interferes with them, and because they seldom abide in memory.' (*Logik*, 2, 432.)

own object; its object is always something else. There are, it is true, cases in which we appear to be naming our present feeling, and so to be experiencing and observing the same inner fact at a single stroke, as when we say 'I feel tired', 'I am hungry', etc. But these are illusory, and a little attention unmasks the illusion. The present conscious state, when I say 'I feel tired', is not the direct state of tire; when I say 'I feel angry', it is not the direct state of anger. It is the state of *saying-I-feel-tired*, of *saying-I-feel-angry* — entirely different matters, so different that the fatigue and anger apparently included in them are considerable modifications of the fatigue and anger directly felt the previous instant. The act of naming them has momentarily detracted from their force.[8]

The only sound grounds on which the infallible veracity of the introspective judgment might be maintained are empirical. If we had reason to think it has never yet deceived us, we might continue to trust it. This is the ground actually maintained by Herr Mohr.

> The illusions of our senses have undermined our belief in the reality of the outer world; but in the sphere of inner observation our confidence is intact, for we have never found ourselves to be in error about the reality of an act of thought or feeling. We have never been misled into thinking we were *not* in doubt or in anger when these conditions were really states of our consciousness.[9]

But sound as the reasoning here would be, were the premises correct, I fear the latter cannot pass. However it may be with such strong feelings as doubt or anger, about weaker feelings, and about the *relations to each other* of all feelings, we find ourselves in continual error and uncertainty so soon as we are called on to name and class, and not merely to feel. Who can be sure of the exact *order* of his feelings when they are excessively rapid? Who can be sure, in his sensible perception of a chair,

---

[8] In cases like this, where the state outlasts the act of naming it, exists before it, and recurs when it is past, we probably run little practical risk of error when we talk as if the state knew itself. The state of feeling and the state of naming the feeling are continuous, and the infallibility of such prompt introspective judgments is probably great. But even here the certainty of our knowledge ought not to be argued on the *a priori* ground that *percipi* and *esse* are in psychology the same. The states are really two; the naming state and the named state are apart; *percipi* is *esse* is not the principle that applies.

[9] J. Mohr, *Grundlage der Empirischen Psychologie*, Leipzig, 1882, p. 47.

how much comes from the eye and how much is supplied out of the previous knowledge of the mind? Who can compare with precision the *quantities* of disparate feelings even where the feelings are very much alike. For instance, where an object is felt now against the back and now against the cheek, which feeling is most extensive? Who can be sure that two given feelings are or are not exactly the same? Who can tell which is briefer or longer than the other when both occupy but an instant of time? Who knows, of many actions, for what motive they were done, or if for any motive at all? Who can enumerate all the distinct ingredients of such a complicated feeling as *anger*? and who can tell off-hand whether or no a perception of *distance* be a compound or a simple state of mind. The whole mind-stuff controversy would stop if we could decide conclusively by introspection that what seem to us elementary feelings are really elementary and not compound.

Mr Sully, in his work on illusions, has a chapter on those of introspection from which we might now quote. But, since the rest of this volume will be little more than a collection of illustrations of the difficulty of discovering by direct introspection exactly what our feelings and their relations are, we need not anticipate our own future details, but just state our general conclusion that *introspection is difficult and fallible; and that the difficulty is simply that of all observation of whatever kind.* Something is before us; we do our best to tell what it is, but in spite of our good will we may go astray, and give a description more applicable to some other sort of thing. The only safeguard is in the final *consensus* of our farther knowledge about the thing in question, later views correcting earlier ones, until at last the harmony of a consistent system is reached. Such a system, gradually worked out, is the best guarantee the psychologist can give for the soundness of any particular psychologic observation which he may report. Such a system we ourselves must strive, as far as may be, to attain.

The English writers on psychology, and the school of Herbart in Germany, have in the main contented themselves with such results as the immediate introspection of single individuals gave, and shown what a body of doctrine they may make. The works of Locke, Hume, Reid, Hartley, Stewart, Brown, the Mills, will always be classics in this line; and in Professor Bain's treatises we have probably the last word of what this method taken mainly by itself can do – the last monument of the youth of our science, still untechnical and generally intelligible, like the chemistry of Lavoisier, or anatomy before the microscope was used.

The experimental method. But psychology is passing into a less simple phase. Within a few years what one may call a microscopic psychology has arisen in Germany, carried on by experimental methods, asking of course every moment for introspective data, but eliminating their uncertainty by operating on a large scale and taking statistical means. This method taxes patience to the utmost, and could hardly have arisen in a country whose natives could be *bored*. Such Germans as Weber, Fechner, Vierordt and Wundt obviously cannot; and their success has brought into the field an array of younger experimental psychologists, bent on studying the *elements* of the mental life, dissecting them out from the gross results in which they are embedded, and as far as possible reducing them to quantitative scales. The simple and open method of attack having done what it can, the method of patience, starving out, and harassing to death is tried; the mind must submit to a regular *siege*, in which minute advantages gained night and day by the forces that hem her in must sum themselves up at last into her overthrow. There is little of the grand style about these new prism, pendulum, and chronograph-philosophers. They mean business, not chivalry. What generous divination, and that superiority in virtue which was thought by Cicero to give a man the best insight into nature, have failed to do, their spying and scraping, their deadly tenacity and almost diabolic cunning, will doubtless some day bring about.

No general description of the methods of experimental psychology would be instructive to one unfamiliar with the instances of their application, so we will waste no words upon the attempt. *The principal fields of experimentation* so far have been: (1) the connection of conscious states with their physical conditions, including the whole of brain physiology, and the recent minutely cultivated physiology of the sense-organs, together with what is technically known as 'psycho-physics', or the laws of correlation between sensations and the outward stimuli by which they are aroused; (2) the analysis of space-perception into its sensational elements; (3) the measurement of the *duration* of the simplest mental processes; (4) that of the *accuracy of reproduction* in the memory of sensible experiences and of intervals of space and time; (5) that of the manner in which simple mental states *influence each other*, call each other up, or inhibit each other's reproduction; (6) that of the *number of facts* which consciousness can simultaneously discern; finally, (7) that of the elementary laws of oblivescence and retention. It must be said that in some of these fields the results have as yet borne little theoretic fruit commensurate with the great labour expended in their acquisition. But facts are facts, and if we only get enough of them they are sure to combine. New ground will from year to year be broken, and theoretic results will grow. Meanwhile the experimental method has quite changed the face of the science so far as the latter is a record of mere work done.

The comparative method, finally, supplements the introspective and experimental methods. This method presupposes a normal psychology of introspection to be established in its main features. But where the origin of these features, or their dependence upon one another, is in question, it is of the utmost importance to trace the phenomenon considered through all its possible variations of type and combination. So it has come to pass that instincts of animals are ransacked to throw light on our own; and that the reasoning faculties of bees and ants, the minds of savages, infants, madmen, idiots, the deaf and blind, criminals, and eccentrics, are all invoked in support of this or that special theory about some part of our own mental life. The history of sciences, moral and political institutions, and languages, as types of mental product, are pressed into the same service. Messrs Darwin and Galton have set the example of circulars of questions sent out by the hundred to those supposed able to reply. The custom has spread, and it will be well for us in the next generation if such circulars be not ranked among the common pests of life. Meanwhile information grows, and results emerge. There are great sources of error in the comparative method. The interpretation of the 'psychoses' of animals, savages and infants is necessarily wild work, in which the personal equation of the investigator has things very much its own way. A savage will be reported to have no moral or religious feeling if his actions shock the observer unduly. A child will be assumed without self-consciousness because he talks of himself in the third person, etc., etc. No rules can be laid down in advance. Comparative observations, to be definite, must usually be made to test some pre-existing hypothesis; and the only thing then is to use as much sagacity as you possess, and to be as candid as you can.

The Sources of Error in Psychology

The first of them arises from the misleading influence of speech. Language was originally made by men who were not psychologists, and most men today employ almost exclusively the vocabulary of outward things. The cardinal passions of our life, anger, love, fear, hate, hope, and the most comprehensive divisions of our intellectual activity, to remember, expect, think, know, dream, with the broadest genera of aesthetic feeling, joy, sorrow, pleasure, pain, are the only facts of a subjective order which this vocabulary deigns to note by special words. The elementary qualities of sensation, bright, loud, red, blue, hot, cold, are, it is true, susceptible of being used in both an objective and a subjective sense. They stand for outer qualities and for the feelings which these arouse. But the objective sense is the original sense; and still today we have to describe a large number of sensations by the name of the object from which they have most frequently been got. An orange colour, an odour of violets, a cheesy taste, a thunderous sound, a fiery smart, etc., will recall what I mean. This absence of a special vocabulary for subjective facts hinders the study of all but the very coarsest of them. Empiricist writers are very fond of emphasizing one great set of delusions which language inflicts on the mind. Whenever we have made a word, they say, to denote a certain group of phenomena, we are prone to suppose a substantive entity existing beyond the phenomena, of which the word shall be the name. But the *lack* of a word quite as often leads to the directly opposite error. We are then prone to suppose that no entity can be there; and so we come to overlook phenomena whose existence would be patent to us all, had we only grown up to hear it familiarly recognized in speech.[10] It is hard to focus our attention on the nameless, and so there results a certain vacuousness in the descriptive parts of most psychologies.

[10] In English we have not even the generic distinction between the-thing-thought-of and the-thought-thinking-it, which in German is expressed by the opposition between *Gedachtes* and *Gedanke*, in Latin by that between *cogitatum* and *cogitatio*.

But a worse defect than vacuousness comes from the dependence of psychology on common speech. Naming our thought by its own objects, we almost all of us assume that as the objects are, so the thought must be. The thought of several distinct things can only consist of several distinct bits of thought, or 'ideas'; that of an abstract or universal object can only be an abstract or universal idea. As each object may come and go, be forgotten and then thought of again, it is held that the thought of it has a precisely similar independence, self-identity and mobility. The thought of the object's recurrent identity is regarded as the identity of its recurrent thought; and the perceptions of multiplicity, of coexistence, of succession, are severally conceived to be brought about only through a multiplicity, a coexistence, a succession, of perceptions. The continuous flow of the mental stream is sacrificed, and in its place an atomism, a brickbat plan of construction, is preached, for the existence of which no good introspective grounds can be brought forward, and out of which presently grow all sorts of paradoxes and contradictions, the heritage of woe of students of the mind.

These words are meant to impeach the entire English psychology derived from Locke and Hume, and the entire German psychology derived from Herbart, so far as they both treat 'ideas' as separate subjective entities that come and go. Examples will soon make the matter clearer. Meanwhile our psychologic insight is vitiated by still other snares.

The psychologist's fallacy. The *great* snare of the psychologist is the *confusion of his own standpoint with that of the mental fact* about which he is making his report. I shall hereafter call this the 'psychologist's fallacy' *par excellence.* For some of the mischief, here too, language is to blame. The psychologist, as we remarked above (p. 199, above), stands outside of the mental state he speaks of. Both itself and its object are objects for him. Now when it is a *cognitive* state (percept, thought, concept, etc.), he ordinarily has no other way of naming it than as the thought, percept, etc., *of that object.* He himself, meanwhile, knowing the self-same object in *his* way, gets easily led to suppose that the thought, which is *of* it, knows it in the same way in which he knows it, although this is often very far from being the case.[11]

[11] Compare B. P. Bowne's *Metaphysics*, 1882, p. 408.

The most fictitious puzzles have been introduced into our science by this means. The so-called question of presentative or representative perception, of whether an object is present to the thought that thinks it by a counterfeit image of itself, or directly and without any intervening image at all; the question of nominalism and conceptualism, of the shape in which things are present when only a general notion of them is before the mind; are comparatively easy questions when once the psychologist's fallacy is eliminated from their treatment — as we shall ere long see (in Chapter 12 [*Principles of Psychology*]).

Another variety of the psychologist's fallacy is the assumption that the mental state studied must be conscious of itself as the psychologist is conscious of it. The mental state is aware of itself only from within it; it grasps what we call its own content, and nothing more. The psychologist, on the contrary, is aware of it from without, and knows its relations with all sorts of other things. What the thought sees is only its own object; what the psychologist sees is the thought's object, plus the thought itself, plus possibly all the rest of the world. We must be very careful therefore, in discussing a state of mind from the psychologist's point of view, to avoid foisting into its own ken matters that are only there for ours. We must avoid substituting what we know the consciousness *is*, for what it is a consciousness *of*, and counting its outward, and so to speak physical, relations with other facts of the world, in among the objects of which we set it down as aware. Crude as such a confusion of standpoints seems to be when abstractly stated, it is nevertheless a snare into which no psychologist has kept himself at all times from falling, and which forms almost the entire stock-in-trade of certain schools. We cannot be too watchful against its subtly corrupting influence.

Summary. To sum up the chapter, psychology assumes that thoughts successively occur, and that they know objects in a world which the psychologist also knows. *These thoughts are the subjective data of which he treats, and their relations to their objects, to the brain, and to the rest of the world constitute the subject-matter of psychologic science.* Its methods are introspection, experimentation and comparison. But introspection is no sure guide to truths *about* our mental states; and in particular the poverty of the psychological vocabulary leads us to drop out certain states from our consideration, and to treat others as if they knew themselves and their objects as the psychologist knows both, which is a disastrous fallacy in the science.

MORAL PHILOSOPHY

14
The Will to Believe[1]

In the recently published life by Leslie Stephen of his brother, Fitz-James, there is an account of a school to which the latter went when he was a boy. The teacher, a certain Mr Guest, used to converse with his pupils in this wise: 'Guerney, what is the difference between justification and sanctification? – Stephen, prove the omnipotence of God!' etc. In the midst of our Harvard freethinking and indifference we are prone to imagine that here at your good old orthodox college conversation continues to be somewhat upon this order; and to show you that we at Harvard had not lost all interest in these vital subjects, I have brought with me tonight something like a sermon on justification by faith to read to you – I mean an essay in justification *of* faith, a defence of our right to adopt a believing attitude in religious matters, in spite of the fact that our merely logical intellect may not have been coerced. 'The Will to Believe', accordingly, is the title of my paper.

I have long defended to my own students the lawfulness of voluntarily adopted faith; but as soon as they have got well imbued with the logical spirit, they have as a rule refused to admit my contention to be lawful philosophically, even though in point of fact they were personally all the time chockfull of some faith or other themselves. I am all the while, however, so profoundly convinced that my own position is correct, that your invitation has seemed to me a good occasion to make my statements more clear. Perhaps your minds will be more open than those with which I have hitherto had to deal. I will be as little technical as I can, though I must begin by setting up some technical distinctions that will help us in the end.

[1] An address to the Philosophical Clubs of Yale and Brown Universities. Published in the *New World*, June 1896.

I

Let us give the name of *hypothesis* to anything that may be proposed to our belief; and just as the electricians speak of live and dead wires, let us speak of any hypothesis as either *live* or *dead*. A live hypothesis is one which appeals as a real possibility to him to whom it is proposed. If I ask you to believe in the Mahdi, the notion makes no electric connection with your nature – it refuses to scintillate with any credibility at all. As an hypothesis it is completely dead. To an Arab, however (even if he be not one of the Mahdi's followers), the hypothesis is among the mind's possibilities: it is alive. This shows that deadness and liveness in an hypothesis are not intrinsic properties, but relations to the individual thinker. They are measured by his willingness to act. The maximum of liveness in an hypothesis means willingness to act irrevocably. Practically, that means belief; but there is some believing tendency wherever there is willingness to act at all.

Next, let us call the decision between two hypotheses an *option*. Options may be of several kinds. They may be – (1) *living* or *dead*; (2) *forced* or *avoidable*; (3) *momentous* or *trivial*; and for our purposes we may call an option a genuine option when it is of the forced, living and momentous kind.

(1) A living option is one in which both hypotheses are live ones. If I say to you: 'Be a theosophist or be a Mohammedan', it is probably a dead option, because for you neither hypothesis is likely to be alive. But if I say: 'Be an agnostic or be a Christian', it is otherwise: trained as you are, each hypothesis makes some appeal, however small, to your belief.

(2) Next, if I say to you: 'Choose between going out with your umbrella or without it', I do not offer you a genuine option, for it is not forced. You can easily avoid it by not going out at all. Similarly, if I say, 'Either love me or hate me', 'Either call my theory true or call it false', your option is avoidable. You may remain indifferent to me, neither loving nor hating, and you may decline to offer any judgment as to my theory. But if I say, 'Either accept this truth or go without it', I put on you a forced option, for there is no standing place outside of the alternative. Every dilemma based on a complete logical disjunction, with no possibility of not choosing, is an option of this forced kind.

(3) Finally, if I were Dr Nansen and proposed to you to join my North Pole expedition, your option would be momentous; for this would probably be your only similar opportunity, and your choice now would either exclude you from the North Pole sort of immortality altogether or put at least the chance of it into your hands. He who refuses to embrace a unique opportunity loses the prize as surely as if he tried and failed. *Per contra*, the option is trivial when the opportunity is not unique, when the stake is insignificant, or when the decision is reversible if it later prove unwise. Such trivial options abound in the scientific life. A chemist finds an hypothesis live enough to spend a year in its verification: he believes in it to that extent. But if his experiments prove inconclusive either way, he is quit for his loss of time, no vital harm being done.

It will facilitate our discussion if we keep all these distinctions well in mind.

2

The next matter to consider is the actual psychology of human opinion. When we look at certain facts, it seems as if our passional and volitional nature lay at the root of all our convictions. When we look at others, it seems as if they could do nothing when the intellect had once said its say. Let us take the latter facts up first.

Does it not seem preposterous on the very face of it to talk of our opinions being modifiable at will? Can our will either help or hinder our intellect in its perceptions of truth? Can we, by just willing it, believe that Abraham Lincoln's existence is a myth, and that the portraits of him in *McClure's Magazine* are all of someone else? Can we, by any effort of our will, or by any strength of wish that it were true, believe ourselves well and about when we are roaring with rheumatism in bed, or feel certain that the sum of the two one-dollar bills in our pocket must be a hundred dollars? We can *say* any of these things, but we are absolutely impotent to believe them; and of just such things is the whole fabric of the truths that we do believe in made up – matters of fact, immediate or remote, as Hume said, and relations between ideas, which are either there or not there for us if we see them so, and which if not there cannot be put there by any action of our own.

In Pascal's *Thoughts* there is a celebrated passage known in literature as Pascal's wager. In it he tries to force us into Christianity by reasoning as if our concern with truth resembled our concern with the stakes in a game of chance. Translated freely his words are these: You must either believe or not believe that God is — which will you do? Your human reason cannot say. A game is going on between you and the nature of things which at the day of judgment will bring out either heads or tails. Weigh what your gains and your losses would be if you should stake all you have on heads, or God's existence: if you win in such case, you gain eternal beatitude; if you lose, you lose nothing at all. If there were an infinity of chances, and only one for God in this wager, still you ought to stake your all on God; for though you surely risk a finite loss by this procedure, any finite loss is reasonable, even a certain one is reasonable, if there is but the possibility of infinite gain. Go, then, and take holy water, and have masses said; belief will come and stupefy your scruples — *Cela vous fera croire et vous abêtira.* Why should you not? At bottom, what have you to lose?

You probably feel that when religious faith expresses itself thus, in the language of the gaming-table, it is put to its last trumps. Surely Pascal's own personal belief in masses and holy water had far other springs; and this celebrated page of his is but an argument for others, a last desperate snatch at a weapon against the hardness of the unbelieving heart. We feel that a faith in masses and holy water adopted wilfully after such a mechanical calculation would lack the inner soul of faith's reality; and if we were ourselves in the place of the deity, we should probably take particular pleasure in cutting off believers of this pattern from their infinite reward. It is evident that unless there be some pre-existing tendency to believe in masses and holy water, the option offered to the will by Pascal is not a living option. Certainly no Turk ever took to masses and holy water on its account; and even to us Protestants these means of salvation seem such foregone impossibilities that Pascal's logic, invoked for them specifically, leaves us unmoved. As well might the Mahdi write to us, saying, 'I am the Expected One whom God has created in his effulgence. You shall be infinitely happy if you confess me; otherwise you shall be cut off from the light of the sun. Weigh, then, your infinite gain if I am genuine against your finite sacrifice if I am not!' His logic would be that of

Pascal; but he would vainly use it on us, for the hypothesis he offers us is dead. No tendency to act on it exists in us to any degree.

The talk of believing by our volition seems, then, from one point of view, simply silly. From another point of view it is worse than silly, it is vile. When one turns to the magnificent edifice of the physical sciences, and sees how it was reared; what thousands of disinterested moral lives of men lie buried in its mere foundations; what patience and postponement, what choking down of preference, what submission to the icy laws of outer fact are wrought into its very stones and mortar; how absolutely impersonal it stands in its vast augustness — then how besotted and contemptible seems every little sentimentalist who comes blowing his voluntary smoke-wreaths, and pretending to decide things from out of his private dream! Can we wonder if those bred in the rugged and manly school of science should feel like spewing such subjectivism out of their mouths? The whole system of loyalties which grow up in the schools of science go dead against its toleration; so that it is only natural that those who have caught the scientific fever should pass over to the opposite extreme and write sometimes as if the incorruptibly truthful intellect ought positively to prefer bitterness and unacceptableness to the heart in its cup.

> It fortifies my soul to know
> That, though I perish, Truth is so —

sings Clough, while Huxley exclaims: 'My only consolation lies in the reflection that, however bad our posterity may become, so far as they hold by the plain rule of not pretending to believe what they have no reason to believe, because it may be to their advantage so to pretend [the word 'pretend' is surely here redundant], they will not have reached the lowest depth of immorality.' And that delicious *enfant terrible* Clifford writes:

Belief is desecrated when given to unproved and unquestioned statements for the solace and private pleasure of the believer ... Whoso would deserve well of his fellows in this matter will guard the purity of his belief with a very fanaticism of jealous care, lest at any time it should rest on an unworthy object, and catch a stain which can never be wiped away ... If [a] belief has been accepted on insufficient evidence [even though the belief be true, as Clifford on the same page explains] the pleasure is a stolen one ... It is sinful because it is stolen in defiance of our duty to mankind. That duty is to guard ourselves from such beliefs as from a pestilence which may shortly master our own body and then spread to the rest of the town ... It is wrong always, everywhere, and for everyone, to believe anything upon insufficient evidence.

3

All this strikes one as healthy, even when expressed, as by Clifford, with somewhat too much of robustious pathos in the voice. Free-will and simple wishing do seem, in the matter of our credences, to be only fifth wheels to the coach. Yet if anyone should thereupon assume that intellectual insight is what remains after wish and will and sentimental preference have taken wing, or that pure reason is what then settles our opinions, he would fly quite as directly in the teeth of the facts.

It is only our already dead hypotheses that our willing nature is unable to bring to life again. But what has made them dead for us is for the most part a previous action of our willing nature of an antagonistic kind. When I say 'willing nature', I do not mean only such deliberate volitions as may have set up habits of belief that we cannot now escape from – I mean all such factors of belief as fear and hope, prejudice and passion, imitation and partisanship, the circumpressure of our caste and set. As a matter of fact we find ourselves believing, we hardly know how or why. Mr Balfour gives the name of 'authority' to all those influences, born of the intellectual climate, that make hypotheses possible or impossible for us, alive or dead. Here in this room, we all of us believe in molecules and the conservation of energy, in democracy and necessary progress, in Protestant Christianity and the duty of fighting for 'the doctrine of the immortal Monroe', all for no reasons worthy of the name. We see into these matters with no more inner clearness, and probably with much less, than any disbeliever in them might possess. His unconventionality would probably have some grounds to show for its conclusions; but for us, not insight, but the *prestige* of the opinions, is what makes the spark shoot from them and light up our sleeping magazines of faith. Our reason is quite satisfied, in nine hundred and ninety-nine cases out of every thousand of us, if it can find a few arguments that will do to recite in case our credulity is criticized by someone else. Our faith is faith in someone else's faith, and in the greatest matters this is most the case. Our belief in truth itself, for instance, that there is a truth, and that our minds and it are made for each other – what is it but a passionate affirmation of desire, in which our social system backs us up? We want to have a truth; we want to believe that our experiments and studies and discussions must put us in a continually better and better position towards it; and on this line we agree to fight out our thinking lives. But if a pyrrhonistic sceptic asks us *how we know* all this, can our logic find a reply? No! Certainly it cannot. It is just one volition against another – we willing to go in for life upon a trust or assumption which he, for his part, does not care to make.[2]

As a rule, we disbelieve all facts and theories for which we have no use. Clifford's cosmic emotions find no use for Christian feelings. Huxley belabours the bishops because there is no use for sacerdotalism in his scheme of life. Newman, on the contrary, goes over to Romanism, and finds all sorts of reasons good for staying there, because a priestly system is for him an organic need and delight. Why do so few 'scientists' even look at the evidence for telepathy, so called? Because they think, as a leading biologist, now dead, once said to me, that even if such a thing were true, scientists ought to band together to keep it suppressed and concealed. It would undo the uniformity of nature and all sorts of other things without which scientists cannot carry on their pursuits. But if this very man had been shown something which as a scientist he might *do* with telepathy, he might not only have examined the evidence, but even have found it good enough. This very law which the logicians would impose upon us – if I may give the name of logicians to those who would rule out our willing nature here – is based on nothing but their own natural wish to exclude all elements for which they, in their professional quality of logicians, can find no use.

Evidently, then, our non-intellectual nature does influence our convictions. There are passional tendencies and volitions which run before and others which come after belief, and it is only the latter that are too late for the fair; and they are not too late when the previous passional work has been already in their own

---

[2] Compare the admirable page 310 in S. H. Hodgson's *Time and Space*, London, 1865.

direction. Pascal's argument, instead of being powerless, then seems a regular clincher, and is the last stroke needed to make our faith in masses and holy water complete. The state of things is evidently far from simple; and pure insight and logic, whatever they might do ideally, are not the only things that really do produce our creeds.

4

Our next duty, having recognized this mixed-up state of affairs, is to ask whether it be simply reprehensible and pathological, or whether, on the contrary, we must treat it as a normal element in making up our minds. The thesis I defend is, briefly stated, this: *Our passional nature not only lawfully may, but must, decide an option between propositions, whenever it is a genuine option that cannot by its nature be decided on intellectual grounds; for to say, under such circumstances, 'Do not decide, but leave the question open', is itself a passional decision – just like deciding yes or no – and is attended with the same risk of losing the truth.* The thesis thus abstractly expressed will, I trust, soon become quite clear. But I must first indulge in a bit more of preliminary work.

5

It will be observed that for the purposes of this discussion we are on 'dogmatic' ground – ground, I mean, which leaves systematic philosophical scepticism altogether out of account. The postulate that there is truth, and that it is the destiny of our minds to attain it, we are deliberately resolving to make, though the sceptic will not make it. We part company with him, therefore, absolutely, at this point. But the faith that truth exists, and that our minds can find it, may be held in two ways. We may talk of the *empiricist* way and of the *absolutist* way of believing in truth. The absolutists in this matter say that we not only can attain to knowing truth, but we can *know when* we have attained to knowing it; while the empiricists think that although we may attain it, we cannot infallibly know when. To *know* is one thing, and to know for certain *that* we know is another. One may hold to the first being possible without the second; hence the empiricists and the absolutists, although neither of them is a sceptic in the usual philosophic sense of the term, show very different degrees of dogmatism in their lives.

If we look at the history of opinions, we see that the empiricist tendency has largely prevailed in science, while in philosophy the absolutist tendency has had everything its own way. The characteristic sort of happiness, indeed, which philosophies yield has mainly consisted in the conviction felt by each successive school or system that by it bottom-certitude had been attained. 'Other philosophies are collections of opinions, mostly false; *my* philosophy gives standing-ground forever' – who does not recognize in this the keynote of every system worthy of the name? A system, to be a system at all, must come as a *closed* system, reversible in this or that detail, perchance, but in its essential features never!

Scholastic orthodoxy, to which one must always go when one wishes to find perfectly clear statement, has beautifully elaborated this absolutist conviction in a doctrine which it calls that of 'objective evidence'. If, for example, I am unable to doubt that I now exist before you, that two is less than three, or that if all men are mortal then I am mortal too, it is because these things illumine my intellect irresistibly. The final ground of this objective evidence possessed by certain propositions is the *adaequatio intellectus nostri cum re*. The certitude it brings involves an *aptitudinem ad extorquendum certum assensum* on the part of the truth envisaged, and on the side of the subject a *quietem in cognitione*, when once the object is mentally received, that leaves no possibility of doubt behind; and in the whole transaction nothing operates but the *entitas ipsa* of the object and the *entitas ipsa* of the mind. We slouchy modern thinkers dislike to talk in Latin – indeed, we dislike to talk in set terms at all; but at bottom our own state of mind is very much like this whenever we uncritically abandon ourselves: You believe in objective evidence, and I do. Of some things we feel that we are certain: we know, and we know that we do know. There is something that gives a click inside of us, a bell that strikes twelve, when the hands of our mental clock have swept the dial and meet over the meridian hour. The greatest empiricists among us are only empiricists on reflection: when left to their instincts, they dogmatize like infallible popes. When the Cliffords tell us how sinful it is to be Christians on such 'insufficient evidence', insufficiency is really the last thing they have in mind. For them the evidence is absolutely sufficient, only it makes the other way. They believe so completely in an anti-Christian order of the universe that there is no living option: Christianity is a dead hypothesis from the start.

6

But now, since we are all such absolutists by instinct, what in our quality of students of philosophy ought we to do about the fact? Shall we espouse and endorse it? Or shall we treat it as a weakness of our nature from which we must free ourselves, if we can?

I sincerely believe that the latter course is the only one we can follow as reflective men. Objective evidence and certitude are doubtless very fine ideals to play with, but where on this moonlit and dream-visited planet are they found? I am, therefore, myself a complete empiricist so far as my theory of human knowledge goes. I live, to be sure, by the practical faith that we must go on experiencing and thinking over our experience, for only thus can our opinions grow more true; but to hold any one of them – I absolutely do not care which – as if it never could be reinterpretable or corrigible, I believe to be a tremendously mistaken attitude, and I think that the whole history of philosophy will bear me out. There is but one indefectibly certain truth, and that is the truth that pyrrhonistic scepticism itself leaves standing – the truth that the present phenomenon of consciousness exists. That, however, is the bare starting point of knowledge, the mere admission of a stuff to be philosophized about. The various philosophies are but so many attempts at expressing what this stuff really is. And if we repair to our libraries what disagreement do we discover! Where is a certainly true answer found? Apart from abstract propositions of comparison (such as two and two are the same as four), propositions which tell us nothing by themselves about concrete reality, we find no proposition ever regarded by anyone as evidently certain that has not either been called a falsehood, or at least had its truth sincerely questioned by someone else. The transcending of the axioms of geometry, not in play but in earnest, by certain of our contemporaries (as Zöllner and Charles H. Hinton), and the rejection of the whole Aristotelian logic by the Hegelians, are striking instances in point.

No concrete test of what is really true has ever been agreed upon. Some make the criterion external to the moment of perception, putting it either in revelation, the *consensus gentium*, the instincts of the heart, or the systematized experience of the race. Others make the perceptive moment its own test – Descartes, for instance, with his clear and distinct ideas guaranteed by the veracity of God; Reid with his 'common-sense'; and Kant with his forms of synthetic judgment *a priori*. The inconceivability of the opposite; the capacity to be verified by sense; the possession of complete organic unity or self-relation, realized when a thing is its own other – are standards which, in turn, have been used. The much lauded objective evidence is never triumphantly there; it is a mere aspiration or *Grenzbegriff*, marking the infinitely remote ideal of our thinking life. To claim that certain truths now possess it, is simply to say that when you think them true and they *are* true, then their evidence is objective, otherwise it is not. But practically one's conviction that the evidence one goes by is of the real objective brand, is only one more subjective opinion added to the lot. For what a contradictory array of opinions have objective evidence and absolute certitude been claimed! The world is rational through and through – its existence is an ultimate brute fact; there is a personal God – a personal God is inconceivable; there is an extra-mental physical world immediately known – the mind can only know its own ideas; a moral imperative exists – obligation is only the resultant of desires; a permanent spiritual principle is in everyone – there are only shifting states of mind; there is an endless chain of causes – there is an absolute first cause; an eternal necessity – a freedom; a purpose – no purpose; a primal One – a primal Many; a universal continuity – an essential discontinuity in things; an infinity – no infinity. There is this – there is that; there is indeed nothing which someone has not thought absolutely true, while his neighbour deemed it absolutely false; and not an absolutist among them seems ever to have considered that the trouble may all the time be essential, and that the intellect, even with truth directly in its grasp, may have no infallible signal for knowing whether it be truth or no. When indeed, one remembers that the most striking practical application to life of the doctrine of objective certitude has been the conscientious labours of the Holy Office of the Inquisition, one feels less tempted than ever to lend the doctrine a respectful ear.

But please observe, now, that when as empiricists we give up the doctrine of objective certitude, we do not thereby give up the quest or hope of truth itself. We still pin our faith on its existence, and still believe that we gain an ever better position towards it by systematically continuing to roll up experiences and think. Our great difference from the scholastic lies in the way we face. The strength of his system lies in the principles, the origin, the *terminus a quo* of his thought; for us the strength is in the outcome, the upshot, the *terminus ad quem*. Not where it comes from but what it leads to is to decide. It matters not to an empiricist from what quarter an hypothesis may come to him: he may have acquired it by fair means or by foul; passion may have whispered or accident suggested it; but if the total drift of thinking continues to confirm it, that is what he means by its being true.

7

One more point, small but important, and our preliminaries are done. There are two ways of looking at our duty in the matter of opinion – ways entirely different, and yet ways about whose difference the theory of knowledge seems hitherto to have shown very little concern. *We must know the truth*; and *we must avoid error* – these are our first and great commandments as would-be knowers; but they are not two ways of stating an identical commandment, they are two separable laws. Although it may indeed happen that when we believe the truth A, we escape as an incidental consequence from believing the falsehood B, it hardly ever happens that by merely disbelieving B we necessarily believe A. We may in escaping B fall into believing other falsehoods, C or D, just as bad as B; or we may escape B by not believing anything at all, not even A.

Believe truth! Shun error! – these, we see, are two materially different laws; and by choosing between them we may end by colouring differently our whole intellectual life. We may regard the chase for truth as paramount, and the avoidance of error as secondary; or we may, on the other hand, treat the avoidance of error as more imperative, and let truth take its chance. Clifford, in the instructive passage which I have quoted, exhorts us to the latter course. Believe nothing, he tells us, keep your mind in suspense forever, rather than by closing it on insufficient evidence incur the awful risk of believing lies. You, on the other hand, may think that the risk of being in error is a very small matter when compared with the blessings of real knowledge, and be ready to be duped many times in your investigation rather than postpone indefinitely the chance of guessing true. I myself find it impossible to go with Clifford. We must remember that these feelings of our duty about either truth or error are in any case only expressions of our passional life. Biologically considered, our minds are as ready to grind out falsehood as veracity, and he who says, 'Better go without belief forever than believe a lie!' merely shows his own preponderant private horror of becoming a dupe. He may be critical of many of his desires and fears, but this fear he slavishly obeys. He cannot imagine anyone questioning its binding force. For my own part, I have also a horror of being duped; but I can believe that worse things than being duped may happen to a man in this world: so Clifford's exhortation has to my ears a thoroughly fantastic sound. It is like a general informing his soldiers that it is better to keep out of battle forever than to risk a single wound. Not so are victories either over enemies or over nature gained. Our errors are surely not such awfully solemn things. In a world where we are so certain to incur them in spite of all our caution, a certain lightness of heart seems healthier than this excessive nervousness on their behalf. At any rate, it seems the fittest thing for the empiricist philosopher.

8

And now, after all this introduction, let us go straight at our question. I have said, and now repeat it, that not only as a matter of fact do we find our passional nature influencing us in our opinions, but that there are some options between opinions in which this influence must be regarded both as an inevitable and as a lawful determinant of our choice.

I fear that some of you my hearers will begin to scent danger, and lend an inhospitable ear. Two first steps of passion you have indeed had to admit as necessary — we must think so as to avoid dupery, and we must think so as to gain truth; but the surest path to those ideal consummations, you will probably consider, is from now onwards to take no further passional step.

Well, of course, I agree as far as the facts will allow. Wherever the option between losing truth and gaining it is not momentous, we can throw the chance of *gaining truth* away, and at any rate save ourselves from any chance of *believing falsehood*, by not making up our minds at all till objective evidence has come. In scientific questions, this is almost always the case; and even in human affairs in general, the need of acting is seldom so urgent that a false belief to act on is better than no belief at all. Law courts, indeed, have to decide on the best evidence attainable for the moment, because a judge's duty is to make law as well as to ascertain it, and (as a learned judge once said to me) few cases are worth spending much time over: the great thing is to have them decided on *any* acceptable principle, and got out of the way. But in our dealings with objective nature we obviously are recorders, not makers, of the truth; and decisions for the mere sake of deciding promptly and getting on to the next business would be wholly out of place. Throughout the breadth of physical nature facts are what they are quite independently of us, and seldom is there any such hurry about them that the risks of being duped by believing a premature theory need be faced. The questions here are always trivial options, the hypotheses are hardly living (at any rate not living for us spectators), the choice between believing truth or falsehood is seldom forced. The attitude of sceptical balance is therefore the absolutely wise one if we would escape mistakes. What difference, indeed, does it make to most of us whether we have or have not a theory of the Röntgen rays, whether we believe or not in mind-stuff, or have a conviction about the causality of conscious states? It makes no difference. Such options are not forced on us. On every account it is better not to make them, but still keep weighing reasons *pro et contra* with an indifferent hand.

I speak, of course, here of the purely judging mind. For purposes of discovery such indifference is to be less highly recommended, and science would be far less advanced than she is if the passionate desires of individuals to get their own faiths confirmed had been kept out of the game. See for example the sagacity which Spencer and Weismann now display. On the other hand, if you want an absolute duffer in an investigation, you must, after all, take the man who has no interest whatever in its results: he is the warranted incapable, the positive fool. The most useful investigator, because the most sensitive observer, is always he whose eager interest in one side of the question is balanced by an equally keen nervousness lest he become deceived.[3] Science has organized this nervousness into a regular *technique*, her so-called method of verification; and she has fallen so deeply in love with the method that one may even say she has ceased to care for truth by itself at all. It is only truth as technically verified that interests her. The truth of truths might come in merely affirmative form, and she would decline to touch it. Such truth as that, she might repeat with Clifford, would be stolen in defiance of her duty to mankind. Human passions, however, are stronger than technical rules. '*Le coeur a ses raisons*', as Pascal says, '*que la raison ne connaît pas*'; and however indifferent to all but the bare rules of the game the umpire, the abstract intellect, may be, the concrete players who furnish him the materials to judge of are usually, each one of them, in love with some pet 'live hypothesis' of his own. Let us agree, however, that wherever there is no forced option, the dispassionately judicial intellect with no pet hypothesis, saving us, as it does, from dupery at any rate, ought to be our ideal.

The question now arises: Are there not somewhere forced options in our speculative questions, and can we (as men who may be interested at least as much in positively gaining truth as in merely escaping dupery) always wait with impunity till the coercive evidence shall have arrived? It seems *a priori* improbable that the truth should be so nicely adjusted to our needs and powers as that. In the great boarding-house of nature, the cakes and the butter and the syrup seldom come out so even and leave the plates so clean. Indeed, we should view them with scientific suspicion if they did.

9

Moral questions immediately present themselves as questions whose solution cannot wait for sensible proof. A moral question is a question not of what sensibly exists, but of what is good, or would be good if it did exist. Science can tell us what exists; but

---

[3] Compare Wilfrid Ward's essay, 'The Wish to Believe', in his *Witnesses to the Unseen*. Macmillan and Co., 1893.

to compare the *worths*, both of what exists and of what does not exist, we must consult not science, but what Pascal calls our heart. Science herself consults her heart when she lays it down that the infinite ascertainment of fact and correction of false belief are the supreme goods for man. Challenge the statement, and science can only repeat it oracularly, or else prove it by showing that such ascertainment and correction bring man all sorts of other goods which man's heart in turn declares. The question of having moral beliefs at all or not having them is decided by our will. Are our moral preferences true or false, or are they only odd biological phenomena, making things good or bad for *us*, but in themselves indifferent? How can your pure intellect decide? If your heart does not *want* a world or moral reality, your head will assuredly never make you believe in one. Mephistophelian scepticism, indeed, will satisfy the head's play-instincts much better than any rigorous idealism can. Some men (even at the student age) are so naturally cool-hearted that the moralistic hypothesis never has for them any pungent life, and in their supercilious present the hot young moralist always feels strangely ill at ease. The appearance of knowingness is on their side, of naivety and gullibility on his. Yet, in the inarticulate heart of him, he clings to it that he is not a dupe, and that there is a realm in which (as Emerson says) all their wit and intellectual superiority is no better than the cunning of a fox. Moral scepticism can no more be refuted or proved by logic than intellectual scepticism can. When we stick to it that there *is* truth (be it of either kind), we do so with our whole nature, and resolve to stand or fall by the results. The sceptic with his whole nature adopts the doubting attitude; but which of us is the wiser, Omniscience only knows.

Turn now from these wide questions of good to a certain class of questions of fact, questions concerning personal relations, states of mind between one man and another. *Do you like me or not?* – for example. Whether you do or not depends, in countless instances, on whether I meet you halfway, am willing to assume that you must like me, and show you trust and expectation. The previous faith on my part in your liking's existence is in such cases what makes your liking come. But if I stand aloof, and refuse to budge an inch until I have objective evidence, until you shall have done something apt, as the absolutists say, *ad extorquendum assensum meum*, ten to one your liking never comes. How many women's hearts are vanquished by the mere sanguine insistence of some man that they *must* love him! he will not consent to the hypothesis that they cannot. The desire for a certain kind of truth here brings about that special truth's existence; and so it is in innumerable cases of other sorts. Who gains promotions, boons, appointments, but the man in whose life they are seen to play the part of live hypotheses, who discounts them, sacrifices other things for their sake before they come, and takes risks for them in advance? His faith acts on the powers above him as a claim, and creates its own verification.

A social organism of any sort whatever, large or small, is what it is because each member proceeds to his own duty with a trust that the other members will simultaneously do theirs. Wherever a desired result is achieved by the co-operation of many independent persons, its existence as a fact is a pure consequence of the precursive faith in one another of those immediately concerned. A government, an army, a commercial system, a ship, a college, an athletic team, all exist on this condition, without which not only is nothing achieved, but nothing is even attempted. A whole train of passengers (individually brave enough) will be looted by a few highwaymen, simply because the latter can count on one another, while each passenger fears that if he makes a movement of resistance, he will be shot before any one else backs him up. If we believed that the whole car-full would rise at once with us, we should each severally rise, and train-robbing would never even be attempted. There are, then, cases where a fact cannot come at all unless a preliminary faith exists in its coming. *And where faith in a fact can help create the fact*, that would be an insane logic which should say that faith running ahead of scientific evidence is the 'lowest kind of immorality' into which a thinking being can fall. Yet such is the logic by which our scientific absolutists pretend to regulate our lives!

10

In truths dependent on our personal action, then, faith based on desire is certainly a lawful and possibly an indispensable thing.

But now, it will be said, these are all childish human cases, and have nothing to do with great cosmical matters, like the question of religious faith. Let us then pass on to that. Religions differ so much in their accidents that in discussing the religious question we must make it very generic and broad. What then do we now mean by the religious hypothesis? Science says things are; morality says some things are better than other things; and religion says essentially two things.

First, she says that the best things are the more eternal things, the overlapping things, the things in the universe that throw the last stone, so to speak, and say the final word. 'Perfection is eternal' – this phrase of Charles Secrétan seems a good way of putting this first affirmation of religion, an affirmation which obviously cannot yet be verified scientifically at all.

The second affirmation of religion is that we are better off even now if we believe her first affirmation to be true.

Now, let us consider what the logical elements of this situation are *in case the religious hypothesis in both its branches be really true*. (Of course, we must admit that possibility at the outset. If we are to discuss the question at all, it must involve a living option. If for any of you religion be a hypothesis that cannot, by any living possibility be true, then you need go no farther. I speak to the 'saving remnant' alone.) So proceeding, we see, first, that religion offers itself as a *momentous* option. We are supposed to gain, even now, by our belief, and to lose by our non-belief, a certain vital good. Secondly, religion is a *forced* option, so far as that good goes. We cannot escape the issue by remaining sceptical and waiting for more light, because, although we do avoid error in that way *if religion be untrue*, we lose the good, *if it be true*, just as certainly as if we positively chose to disbelieve. It is as if a man should hesitate indefinitely to ask a certain woman to marry him because he was not perfectly sure that she would prove an angel after he brought her home. Would he not cut himself off from that particular angel-possibility as decisively as if he went and married someone else? Scepticism, then, is not avoidance of option; it is option of a certain particular kind of risk. *Better risk loss of truth than chance of error* – that is your faith-vetoer's exact position. He is actively playing his stake as much as the believer is; he is backing the field against the religious hypothesis, just as the believer is backing the religious hypothesis against the field. To preach scepticism to us as a duty until 'sufficient evidence' for religion be found, is tantamount therefore to telling us, when in presence of the religious hypothesis, that to yield to our fear of its being error is wiser and better than to yield to our hope that it may be true. It is not intellect against all passions, then; it is only intellect with one passion laying down its law. And by what, forsooth, is the supreme wisdom of this passion warranted? Dupery for dupery, what proof is there that dupery through hope is so much worse than dupery through fear? I, for one, can see no proof; and I simply refuse obedience to the scientist's command to imitate his kind of option, in a case where my own stake is important enough to give me the right to choose my own form of risk. If religion be true and the evidence for it be still insufficient, I do not wish, by putting your extinguisher upon my nature (which feels to me as if it had after all some business in this matter), to forfeit my sole chance in life of getting upon the winning side — that chance depending, of course, on my willingness to run the risk of acting as if my passional need of taking the world religiously might be prophetic and right.

All this is on the supposition that it really may be prophetic and right, and that, even to us who are discussing the matter, religion is a live hypothesis which may be true. Now, to most of us religion comes in a still further way that makes a veto on our active faith even more illogical. The more perfect and more eternal aspect of the universe is represented in our religions as having personal form. The universe is no longer a mere *It* to us, but a *Thou*, if we are religious; and any relation that may be possible from person to person might be possible here. For instance, although in one sense we are passive portions of the universe, in another we show a curious autonomy, as if we were small active centres on our own account. We feel, too, as if the appeal of religion to us were made to our own active goodwill, as if evidence might be forever withheld from us unless we met the hypothesis halfway. To take a trivial illustration: just as a man who in a company of gentlemen made no advances, asked a warrant for every concession, and believed no one's word without proof, would cut himself off by such churlishness from all the social rewards that a more trusting spirit would earn — so here, one who should shut himself up in snarling logicality and try to make the gods extort his recognition willy-nilly, or not get it at all, might cut himself off forever from his only opportunity of making the gods' acquaintance. This feeling, forced on us we know not whence, that by obstinately believing that there are gods (although not to do so would be so easy both for our logic and our life) we are doing the universe the deepest service we can, seems part of the living essence of the religious hypothesis. If the hypothesis *were* true in all its parts, including this one, then pure intellectualism, with its veto on our making willing advances, would be an absurdity; and some participation of our sympathetic nature would be logically required. I, therefore, for one, cannot see my way to accepting the agnostic rules for truthseeking, or wilfully agree to keep my willing nature out of the game. I cannot do so for this plain reason, that a *rule of thinking which would absolutely prevent me from acknowledging certain kinds of truth if those kinds of truth were really there, would be an irrational rule.* That for me is the long and short of the formal logic of the situation, no matter what the kinds of truth might materially be.

I confess I do not see how this logic can be escaped. But sad experience makes me fear that some of you may still shrink from radically saying with me, *in abstracto*, that we have the right to believe at our own risk any hypothesis that is live enough to tempt our will. I suspect, however, that if this is so, it is because you have got away from the abstract logical point of view altogether, and are thinking (perhaps without realizing it) of some particular religious hypothesis which for you is dead. The freedom to 'believe what we will' you apply to the case of some patent superstition; and the faith you think of is the faith defined by the schoolboy when he said, 'Faith is when you believe something that you know ain't true.' I can only repeat that this is misapprehension. *In concreto*, the freedom to believe can only cover living options which the intellect of the individual cannot by itself resolve; and living options never seem absurdities to him who has them to consider. When I look at the religious question as it really puts itself to concrete men, and when I think of all the possibilities which both practically and theoretically it involves, then this command that we shall put a stopper on our heart, instincts and courage, and *wait* – acting of course meanwhile more or less as if religion were *not* true[4] – till

---

[4] Since belief is measured by action, he who forbids us to believe religion to be true, necessarily also forbids us to act as we should if we did believe it to be true. The

doomsday, or till such time as our intellect and senses working together may have raked in evidence enough – this command, I say, seems to me the queerest idol ever manufactured in the philosophic cave. Were we scholastic absolutists, there might be more excuse. If we had an infallible intellect with its objective certitudes, we might feel ourselves disloyal to such a perfect organ of knowledge in not trusting to it exclusively, in not waiting for its releasing word. But if we are empiricists, if we believe that no bell in us tolls to let us know for certain when truth is in our grasp, then it seems a piece of idle fantasticality to preach so solemnly our duty of waiting for the bell. Indeed we *may* wait if we will – I hope you do not think that I am denying that – but if we do so, we do so at our peril as much as if we believed. In either case we *act*, taking our life in our hands. No one of us ought to issue vetoes to the other, nor should we bandy words of abuse. We ought, on the contrary, delicately and profoundly to respect one another's mental freedom: then only shall we bring about the intellectual republic; then only shall we have that spirit of inner tolerance without which all our outer tolerance is soulless, and which is empiricism's glory; then only shall we live and let live, in speculative as well as in practical things.

I began by a reference to Fitz-James Stephen; let me end by a quotation from him

What do you think of yourself? What do you think of the world? . . . These are questions with which all must deal as it seems good to them. They are riddles of the Sphinx, and in some way or other we must deal with them . . . In all important transactions of life we have to take a leap in the dark . . . If we decide to leave the riddles unanswered, that is a choice; if we waver in our answer, that, too, is a choice: but whatever choice we make, we make it at our peril. If a man chooses to turn his back altogether on God and the future, no one can prevent him; no one can show beyond reasonable doubt that he is mistaken. If a man thinks otherwise

---

whole defence of religious faith hinges upon action. If the action required or inspired by the religious hypothesis is in no way different from that dictated by the naturalistic hypothesis, then religious faith is a pure superfluity, better pruned away, and controversy about its legitimacy is a piece of idle trifling, unworthy of serious minds. I myself believe, of course, that the religious hypothesis gives to the world an expression which specifically determines our reactions, and makes them in a large part unlike what they might be on a purely naturalistic scheme of belief.

and acts as he thinks, I do not see that anyone can prove that *he* is mistaken. Each must act as he thinks best; and if he is wrong, so much the worse for him. We stand on a mountain pass in the midst of a whirling snow and blinding mist, through which we get glimpses now and then of paths which may be deceptive. If we stand still we shall be frozen to death. If we take the wrong road we shall be dashed to pieces. We do not certainly know whether there is any right one. What must we do? 'Be strong and of a good courage.' Act for the best, hope for the best, and take what comes . . . If death ends all, we cannot meet death better.[5]

[5] *Liberty, Equality, Fraternity*, 2nd edn, London, 1874, p. 353.

15

The Dilemma of Determinism[1]

A common opinion prevails that the juice has ages ago been pressed out of the free-will controversy, and that no new champion can do more than warm up stale arguments which everyone has heard. This is a radical mistake. I know of no subject less worn out, or in which inventive genius has a better chance of breaking open new ground – not, perhaps, of forcing a conclusion or of coercing assent, but of deepening our sense of what the issue between the two parties really is, of what the ideas of fate and of free-will imply. At our very side almost, in the past few years, we have seen falling in rapid succession from the press works that present the alternative in entirely novel lights. Not to speak of the English disciples of Hegel, such as Green and Bradley; not to speak of Hinton and Hodgson, nor of Hazard here – we see in the writings of Renouvier, Fouillée and Delboeuf[2] how completely changed and refreshed is the form of all the old disputes. I cannot pretend to vie in originality with any of the masters I have named, and my ambition limits itself to just one little point. If I can make two of the necessarily implied corollaries of determinism clearer to you than they have been made before, I shall have made it possible for you to decide for or against that doctrine with a better understanding of what you are about. And if you prefer not to decide at all, but to remain doubters, you will at least see more plainly what the subject of your hesitation is. I thus disclaim openly on the threshold all pretension to prove to you that the freedom of the will is true. The most I hope is to induce some of you to follow my own example in assuming it true, and acting as if it were true. If it be true, it seems to me that this is involved in the strict logic of the case. Its truth ought not to be forced willy-nilly

---

[1] An address to the Harvard divinity students, published in the *Unitarian Review* for September 1884.

[2] And I may now say Charles S. Peirce – see the *Monist* for 1892–3.

down our indifferent throats. It ought to be freely espoused by men who can equally well turn their backs upon it. In other words, our first act of freedom, if we are free, ought in all inward propriety to be to affirm that we are free. This should exclude, it seems to me, from the free-will side of the question all hope of a coercive demonstration — a demonstration which I, for one, am perfectly contented to go without.

With thus much understood at the outset, we can advance. But not without one more point understood as well. The arguments I am about to urge all proceed on two suppositions: first, when we make theories about the world and discuss them with one another, we do so in order to attain a conception of things which shall give us subjective satisfaction; and, second, if there be two conceptions, and the one seems to us, on the whole, more rational than the other, we are entitled to suppose that the more rational one is the truer of two. I hope that you are willing to make these suppositions with me; for I am afraid that if there be any of you here who are not, they will find little education in the rest of what I have to say. I cannot stop to argue the point; but I myself believe that all the magnificent achievements of mathematical and physical science — our doctrines of evolution, of uniformity of law, and the rest — proceed from our indomitable desire to cast the world into a more rational shape in our minds than the shape into which it is thrown there by the crude order of our experience. The world has shown itself, to a great extent, plastic to this demand of ours for rationality. How much farther it will show itself plastic no one can say. Our only means of finding out is to try; and I, for one, feel as free to try conceptions of moral as of mechanical or of logical rationality. If a certain formula for expressing the nature of the world violates my moral demand, I shall feel as free to throw it overboard, or at least to doubt it, as if it disappointed my demand for uniformity of sequence, for example; the one demand being, so far as I can see, quite as subjective and emotional as the other is. The principle of causality, for example — what is it but a postulate, an empty name covering simply a demand that the sequence of events shall some day manifest a deeper kind of belonging of one thing with another than the mere arbitrary juxtaposition which now phenomenally appears? It is as much an altar to an unknown god as the one that Saint

Paul found at Athens. All our scientific and philosophic ideals are altars to unknown gods. Uniformity is as much so as is free-will. If this be admitted, we can debate on even terms. But if anyone pretends that while freedom and variety are, in the first instance, subjective demands, necessity and uniformity are something altogether different, I do not see how we can debate at all.[3]

To begin, then, I must suppose you acquainted with all the usual arguments on the subject. I cannot stop to take up the old proofs from causation, from statistics, from the certainty with which we can foretell one another's conduct, from the fixity of character, and all the rest. But there are two *words* which usually encumber these classical arguments, and which we must immediately dispose of if we are to make any progress. One is the eulogistic word *freedom*, and the other is the opprobrious word *chance*. The word 'chance' I wish to keep, but I wish to get rid of the word 'freedom'. Its eulogistic associations have so far overshadowed all the rest of its meaning that both parties claim the sole right to use it, and determinists today insist that they alone are freedom's champions. Old-fashioned determinism

---

[3] 'The whole history of popular beliefs about Nature refutes the notion that the thought of a universal physical order can possibly have arisen from the purely passive reception and association of particular perceptions. Indubitable as it is that men infer from known cases to unknown, it is equally certain that this procedure, if restricted to the phenomenal materials that spontaneously offer themselves, would never have led to the belief in a general uniformity, but only to the belief that law and lawlessness rule the world in motley alternation. From the point of view of strict experience, nothing exists but the sum of particular perceptions, with their coincidences on the one hand, their contradictions on the other.

'That there is more order in the world than appears at first sight is not discovered *till the order is looked for*. The first impulse to look for it proceeds from practical needs: where ends must be attained, we must know trustworthy means which infallibly possess a property, or produce a result. But the practical need is only the first occasion for our reflection on the conditions of true knowledge; and even were there no such need, motives would still be present for carrying us beyond the stage of mere association. For not with an equal interest, or rather with an equal lack of interest, does man contemplate those natural processes in which a thing is linked with its former mate, and those in which it is linked to something else. *The former processes harmonize with the conditions of his own thinking*: the latter do not. In the former, his *concepts*, *general judgments* and *inferences* apply to reality: in the latter, they have no such application. And thus the intellectual satisfaction which at first comes to him without reflection, at last excites in him the conscious wish to find realized throughout the entire phenomenal world those rational continuities, uniformities, and necessities which are the fundamental element and guiding principle of his own thought.' (Sigwart, *Logik*, Bd. 2, s. 382.)

was what we may call *hard* determinism. It did not shrink from such words as fatality, bondage of the will, necessitation, and the like. Nowadays, we have a *soft* determinism which abhors harsh words, and, repudiating fatality, necessity, and even predetermination, says that its real name is freedom; for freedom is only necessity understood, and bondage to the highest is identical with true freedom. Even a writer as little used to making capital out of soft words as Mr Hodgson hesitates not to call himself a 'free-will determinist'.

Now, all this is a quagmire of evasion under which the real issue of fact has been entirely smothered. Freedom in all these senses presents simply no problem at all. No matter what the soft determinist mean by it — whether he mean the acting without external constraint; whether he mean the acting rightly, or whether he mean the acquiescing in the law of the whole — who cannot answer him that sometimes we are free and sometimes we are not? But there *is* a problem, an issue of fact and not of words, an issue of the most momentous importance, which is often decided without discussion in one sentence — nay, in one clause of a sentence — by those very writers who spin out whole chapters in their efforts to show what 'true' freedom is; and that is the question of determinism, about which we are to talk tonight.

Fortunately, no ambiguities hang about this word or about its opposite indeterminism. Both designate an outward way in which things may happen, and their cold and mathematical sound has no sentimental associations that can bribe our partiality either way in advance. Now, evidence of an external kind to decide between determinism and indeterminism is, as I intimated a while back, strictly impossible to find. Let us look at the difference between them and see for ourselves. What does determinism profess?

It professes that those parts of the universe already laid down absolutely appoint and decree what the other parts shall be. The future has no ambiguous possibilities hidden in its womb: the part we call the present is compatible with only one totality. Any other future complement than the one fixed from eternity is impossible. The whole is in each and every part, and welds it with the rest into an absolute unity, an iron block, in which there can be no equivocation or shadow of turning.

With earth's first clay they did the last man knead,
And there of the last harvest sowed the seed.
And the first morning of creation wrote
What the last dawn of reckoning shall read.

Indeterminism, on the contrary, says that the parts have a certain amount of loose play on one another, so that the laying down of one of them does not necessarily determine what the others shall be. It admits that possibilities may be in excess of actualities, and that things not yet revealed to our knowledge may really in themselves be ambiguous. Of two alternative futures which we conceive, both may now be really possible; and the one become impossible only at the very moment when the other excludes it by becoming real itself. Indeterminism thus denies the world to be one unbending unit of fact. It says there is a certain ultimate pluralism in it; and, so saying, it corroborates our ordinary unsophisticated view of things. To that view, actualities seem to float in a wider sea of possibilities from out of which they are chosen; and, *somewhere*, indeterminism says, such possibilities exist, and form a part of truth.

Determinism, on the contrary, says they exist *nowhere*, and that necessity on the one hand and impossibility on the other are the sole categories of the real. Possibilities that fail to get realized are, for determinism, pure illusions: they never were possibilities at all. There is nothing inchoate, it says, about this universe of ours, all that was or is or shall be actual in it having been from eternity virtually there. The cloud of alternatives our minds escort this mass of actuality withal is a cloud of sheer deceptions, to which 'impossibilities' is the only name that rightfully belongs.

The issue, it will be seen, is a perfectly sharp one, which no eulogistic terminology can smear over or wipe out. The truth *must* lie with one side or the other, and its lying with one side makes the other false.

The question relates solely to the existence of possibilities, in the strict sense of the term, as things that may, but need not, be. Both sides admit that a volition, for instance, has occurred. The indeterminists say another volition might have occurred in its place: the determinists swear that nothing could possibly have occurred in its place. Now, can science be called in to tell us which of these two point-blank contradicters of each other is right? Science professes to draw no conclusions but such as are based on matters of fact, things that have actually happened; but how can any amount of assurance that something actually happened give us the least grain of information as to whether another thing might or might not have happened in its place? Only facts can be proved by other facts. With things that are possibilities and not facts, facts have no concern. If we have no other evidence than the evidence of existing facts, the possibility-question must remain a mystery never to be cleared up.

And the truth is that facts practically have hardly anything to do with making us either determinists or indeterminists. Sure enough, we make a flourish of quoting facts this way or that; and if we are determinists, we talk about the infallibility with which we can predict one another's conduct; while if we are indeterminists, we lay great stress on the fact that it is just because we cannot foretell one another's conduct, either in war or statecraft or in any of the great and small intrigues and businesses of men, that life is so intensely anxious and hazardous a game. But who does not see the wretched insufficiency of this so-called objective testimony on both sides? What fills up the gaps in our minds is something not objective, not external. What divides us into possibility men and anti-possibility men is different faiths or postulates — postulates of rationality. To this man the world seems more rational with possibilities in it — to that man more rational with possibilities excluded; and talk as we will about having to yield to evidence, what makes us monists or pluralists, determinists or indeterminists, is at bottom always some sentiment like this.

The stronghold of the deterministic sentiment is the antipathy to the idea of chance. As soon as we begin to talk indeterminism to our friends, we find a number of them shaking their heads. This notion of alternative possibility, they say, this admission that any one of several things may come to pass, is, after all, only a roundabout name for chance; and chance is something the notion of which no sane mind can for an instant tolerate in the world. What is it, they ask, but barefaced crazy unreason, the negation of intelligibility and law? And if the slightest particle of it exist anywhere, what is to prevent the whole fabric from falling together, the stars from going out, and chaos from recommencing her topsy-turvy reign?

Remarks of this sort about chance will put an end to discussion as quickly as anything one can find. I have already told you that 'chance' was a word I wished to keep and use. Let us then examine exactly what it means, and see whether it ought to be such a terrible bugbear to us. I fancy that squeezing the thistle bodily will rob it of its sting.

The sting of the word 'chance' seems to lie in the assumption that it means something positive, and that if anything happens by chance, it must needs be something of an intrinsically irrational and preposterous sort. Now, chance means nothing of the kind. It is a purely negative and relative term,[4] giving us no information about that of which it is predicated, except that it happens to be disconnected with something else — not controlled, secured or necessitated by other things in advance of its own actual presence. As this point is the most subtle one of the whole lecture, and at the same time the point on which all the rest hinges, I beg you to pay particular attention to it. What I say is that it tells us nothing about what a thing may be in itself to call it 'chance'. It may be a bad thing, it may be a good thing. It may be lucidity, transparency, fitness incarnate, matching the whole system of other things, when it has once befallen, in an unimaginably perfect way. All you mean by calling it 'chance' is that this is not guaranteed, that it may also fall out otherwise. For the system of other things has no positive hold on the chance-thing. Its origin is in a certain fashion negative: it escapes, and says, Hands off! coming, when it comes, as a free gift, or not at all.

This negativeness, however, and this opacity of the chance-thing when thus considered *ab extra*, or from the point of view of previous things or distant things, do not preclude its having any amount of positiveness and luminosity from within, and at its own place and moment. All that its chance character asserts about it is that there is something in it really of its own, something that is not the unconditional property of the whole. If the whole wants this property, the whole must wait till it can get it, if it be a matter of chance. That the universe may actually be a sort of joint-stock society of this sort, in which the sharers

[4] Speaking technically, it is a word with a positive denotation, but a connotation that is negative. Other things must be silent about *what* it is: it alone can decide that point at the moment in which it reveals itself.

have both limited liabilities and limited powers, is of course a simple and conceivable notion.

Nevertheless, many persons talk as if the minutest dose of disconnectedness of one part with another, the smallest modicum of independence, the faintest tremor of ambiguity about the future, for example, would ruin everything, and turn this goodly universe into a sort of insane sand-heap or nulliverse, no universe at all. Since future human volitions are as a matter of fact the only ambiguous things we are tempted to believe in, let us stop for a moment to make ourselves sure whether their independent and accidental character need be fraught with such direful consequences to the universe as these.

What is meant by saying that my choice of which way to walk home after the lecture is ambiguous and matter of chance as far as the present moment is concerned? It means that both Divinity Avenue and Oxford Street are called; but that only one, and that one *either* one, shall be chosen. Now, I ask you seriously to suppose that this ambiguity of my choice is real; and then to make the impossible hypothesis that the choice is made twice over, and each time falls on a different street. In other words, imagine that I first walk through Divinity Avenue, and then imagine that the powers governing the universe annihilate ten minutes of time with all that it contained, and set me back at the door of this hall just as I was before the choice was made. I imagine then that, everything else being the same, I now make a different choice and traverse Oxford Street. You, as passive spectators, look on and see the two alternative universes – one of them with me walking through Divinity Avenue in it, the other with the same me walking through Oxford Street. Now, if you are determinists you believe one of these universes to have been from eternity impossible: you believe it to have been impossible because of the intrinsic irrationality or accidentality somewhere involved in it. But looking outwardly at these universes, can you say which is the impossible and accidental one, and which the rational and necessary one? I doubt if the most ironclad determinist among you could have the slightest glimmer of light on this point. In other words, either universe *after the fact* and once there would, to our means of observation and understanding, appear just as rational as the other. There would be absolutely no criterion by which we might judge one necessary and the other matter of chance. Suppose now we relieve the gods of their hypothetical task and assume my choice, once made, to be made forever. I go through Divinity Avenue for good and all. If, as good determinists, you now begin to affirm, what all good determinists punctually do affirm, that in the nature of things I *couldn't* have gone through Oxford Street – had I done so it would have been chance, irrationality, insanity, a horrid gap in nature – I simply call your attention to this, that your affirmation is what the Germans call a *Machtspruch*, a mere conception fulminated as a dogma and based on no insight into details. Before my choice, either street seemed as natural to you as to me. Had I happened to take Oxford Street, Divinity Avenue would have figured in your philosophy as the gap in nature; and you would have so proclaimed it with the best deterministic conscience in the world.

But what a hollow outcry, then, is this against a chance which, if it were present to us, we could by no character whatever distinguish from a rational necessity! I have taken the most trivial of examples, but no possible example could lead to any different result. For what are the alternatives which, in point of fact, offer themselves to human volition? What are those futures that now seem matters of chance? Are they not one and all like the Divinity Avenue and Oxford Street of our example? Are they not all of them *kinds* of things already here and based in the existing frame of nature? Is anyone ever tempted to produce an *absolute* accident, something utterly irrelevant to the rest of the world? Do not all the motives that assail us, all the futures that offer themselves to our choice, spring equally from the soil of the past; and would not either one of them, whether realized through chance or through necessity, the moment it was realized, seem to us to fit that past, and in the completest and most continuous manner to interdigitate with the phenomena already there?[5]

---

[5] A favourite argument against free-will is that if it be true, a man's murderer may as probably be his best friend as his worst enemy, a mother be as likely to strangle as to suckle her first born, and all of us be as ready to jump from fourth-storey windows as to go out of front doors, etc. Users of this argument should properly be excluded from debate till they learn what the real question is. 'Free-will' does not say that everything that is physically conceivable is also morally possible. It merely says that of alternatives that really *tempt* our will more than one is really possible. Of course, the alternatives that do thus tempt our will are vastly fewer than the physical possibilities we can coldly fancy. Persons really tempted often do murder their best friends, mothers do strangle their first born, people do jump out of fourth-storey windows, etc.

The more one thinks of the matter, the more one wonders that so empty and gratuitous a hubbub as this outcry against chance should have found so great an echo in the hearts of men. It is a word which tells us absolutely nothing about what chances, or about the *modus operandi* of the chancing; and the use of it as a war-cry shows only a temper of intellectual absolutism, a demand that the world shall be a solid block, subject to one control – which temper, which demand, the world may not be bound to gratify at all. In every outwardly verifiable and practical respect, a world in which the alternatives that now actually distract *your* choice were decided by pure chance would be by *me* absolutely undistinguished from the world in which I now live. I am, therefore, entirely willing to call it, so far as your choices go, a world of chance for me. To *yourselves*, it is true, those very acts of choice, which to me are so blind, opaque and external, are the opposites of this, for you are within them and effect them. To you they appear as decisions; and decisions, for him who makes them, are altogether peculiar psychic facts. Self-luminous and self-justifying at the living moment at which they occur, they appeal to no outside moment to put its stamp upon them or make them continuous with the rest of nature. Themselves it is rather who seem to make nature continuous; and in their strange and intense function of granting consent to one possibility and withholding it from another, to transform an equivocal and double future into an inalterable and simple past.

But with the psychology of the matter we have no concern this evening. The quarrel which determinism has with chance fortunately has nothing to do with this or that psychological detail. It is a quarrel altogether metaphysical. Determinism denies the ambiguity of future volitions, because it affirms that nothing future can be ambiguous. But we have said enough to meet the issue. Indeterminate future volitions *do* mean chance. Let us not fear to shout it from the house-tops if need be; for we now know that the idea of chance is, at bottom, exactly the same thing as the idea of gift – the one simply being a disparaging, and the other a eulogistic, name for anything on which we have no effective *claim*. And whether the world be the better or the worse for having either chances or gifts in it will depend altogether on *what* these uncertain and unclaimable things turn out to be.

*

And this at last brings us within sight of our subject. We have seen what determinism means: we have seen that indeterminism is rightly described as meaning chance; and we have seen that chance, the very name of which we are urged to shrink from as from a metaphysical pestilence, means only the negative fact that no part of the world, however big, can claim to control absolutely the destinies of the whole. But although, in discussing the word 'chance', I may at moments have seemed to be arguing for its real existence, I have not meant to do so yet. We have not yet ascertained whether this be a world of chance or no; at most, we have agreed that it seems so. And I now repeat what I said at the outset, that, from any strict theoretical point of view, the question is insoluble. To deepen our theoretic sense of the *difference* between a world with chances in it and a deterministic world is the most I can hope to do; and this I may now at last begin upon, after all our tedious clearing of the way.

I wish first of all to show you just what the notion that this is a deterministic world implies. The implications I call your attention to are all bound up with the fact that it is a world in which we constantly have to make what I shall, with your permission, call judgments of regret. Hardly an hour passes in which we do not wish that something might be otherwise; and happy indeed are those of us whose hearts have never echoed the wish of Omar Khayam —

> That we might clasp, ere closed, the book of fate,
>   And make the writer on a fairer leaf
> Inscribe our names, or quite obliterate.
>
> Ah! Love, could you and I with fate conspire
> To mend this sorry scheme of things entire,
>   Would we not shatter it to bits, and then
> Remould it nearer to the heart's desire?

Now, it is undeniable that most of these regrets are foolish, and quite on a par in point of philosophic value with the criticism on the universe of that friend of our infancy, the hero of the fable 'The Atheist and the Acorn' —

> Fool! had that bough a pumpkin bore,
> Thy whimsies would have worked no more, etc.

Even from the point of view of our own ends, we should probably make a botch of remodelling the universe. How much more then from the point of view of ends we cannot see! Wise men therefore regret as little as they can. But still some regrets are pretty obstinate and hard to stifle – regrets for acts of wanton cruelty or treachery, for example, whether performed by others or by ourselves. Hardly anyone can remain *entirely* optimistic after reading the confession of the murderer at Brockton the other day: how, to get rid of the wife whose continued existence bored him, he inveigled her into a desert spot, shot her four times, and then, as she lay on the ground and said to him, 'You didn't do it on purpose, did you, dear?' replied, 'No, I didn't do it on purpose', as he raised a rock and smashed her skull. Such an occurrence, with the mild sentence and self-satisfaction of the prisoner, is a field for a crop of regrets, which one need not take up in detail. We feel that, although a perfect mechanical fit to the rest of the universe, it is a bad moral fit, and that something else would really have been better in its place.

But for the deterministic philosophy the murder, the sentence, and the prisoner's optimism were all necessary from eternity; and nothing else for a moment had a ghost of a chance of being put into their place. To admit such a chance, the determinists tell us, would be to make a suicide of reason; so we must steel our hearts against the thought. And here our plot thickens, for we see the first of those difficult implications of determinism and monism which it is my purpose to make you feel. If this Brockton murder was called for by the rest of the universe, if it had to come at its preappointed hour, and if nothing else would have been consistent with the sense of the whole, what are we to think of the universe? Are we stubbornly to stick to our judgment of regret, and say, though it *couldn't* be, yet it *would* have been a better universe with something different from this Brockton murder in it? That, of course, seems the natural and spontaneous thing for us to do; and yet it is nothing short of deliberately espousing a kind of pessimism. The judgment of regret calls the murder bad. Calling a thing bad means, if it mean anything at all, that the thing ought not to be, that something else ought to be in its stead. Determinism, in denying that anything else can be in its stead, virtually defines the universe as a place in which what ought to be is impossible – in other words, as an organism whose constitution is afflicted with an incurable taint, an irremediable flaw. The pessimism of a

Schopenhauer says no more than this — that the murder is a symptom; and that it is a vicious symptom because it belongs to a vicious whole, which can express its nature no otherwise than by bringing forth just such a symptom as that at this particular spot. Regret for the murder must transform itself, if we are determinists and wise, into a larger regret. It is absurd to regret the murder alone. Other things being what they are, *it* could not be different. What we should regret is that whole frame of things of which the murder is one member. I see no escape whatever from this pessimistic conclusion, if, being determinists, our judgment of regret is to be allowed to stand at all.

The only deterministic escape from pessimism is everywhere to abandon the judgment of regret. That this can be done, history shows to be not impossible. The devil, *quoad existentiam*, may be good. That is, although he be a *principle* of evil, yet the universe, with such a principle in it, may practically be a better universe than it could have been without. On every hand, in a small way, we find that a certain amount of evil is a condition by which a higher form of good is bought. There is nothing to prevent anybody from generalizing this view, and trusting that if we could but see things in the largest of all ways, even such matters as this Brockton murder would appear to be paid for by the uses that follow in their train. An optimism *quand même*, a systematic and infatuated optimism like that ridiculed by Voltaire in his *Candide*, is one of the possible ideal ways in which a man may train himself to look on life. Bereft of dogmatic hardness and lit up with the expression of a tender and pathetic hope, such an optimism has been the grace of some of the most religious characters that ever lived.

> Throb thine with Nature's throbbing breast,
> And all is clear from east to west.

Even cruelty and treachery may be among the absolutely blessed fruits of time, and to quarrel with any of their details may be blasphemy. The only real blasphemy, in short, may be that pessimistic temper of the soul which lets it give way to such things as regrets, remorse and grief.

Thus, our deterministic pessimism may become a deterministic optimism at the price of extinguishing our judgments of regret.

But does not this immediately bring us into a curious logical predicament? Our determinism leads us to call our judgments of regret wrong, because they are pessimistic in implying that what is impossible yet ought to be. But how then about the judgments of regret themselves? If they are wrong, other judgments, judgments of approval presumably, ought to be in their place. But as they are necessitated, nothing else *can* be in their place; and the universe is just what it was before – namely, a place in which what ought to be appears impossible. We have got one foot out of the pessimistic bog, but the other one sinks all the deeper. We have rescued our actions from the bonds of evil, but our judgments are now held fast. When murders and treacheries cease to be sins, regrets are theoretic absurdities and errors. The theoretic and the active life thus play a kind of seesaw with each other on the ground of evil. The rise of either sends the other down. Murder and treachery cannot be good without regret being bad: regret cannot be good without treachery and murder being bad. Both, however, are supposed to have been fore-doomed; so something must be fatally unreasonable, absurd and wrong in the world. It must be a place of which either sin or error forms a necessary part. From this dilemma there seems at first sight no escape. Are we then so soon to fall back into the pessimism from which we thought we had emerged? And is there no possible way by which we may, with good intellectual consciences, call the cruelties and the treacheries, the reluctances and the regrets, *all* good together?

Certainly there is such a way, and you are probably most of you ready to formulate it yourselves. But, before doing so, remark how inevitably the question of determinism and indeterminism slides us into the question of optimism and pessimism, or, as our fathers called it, 'the question of evil'. The theological form of all these disputes is the simplest and the deepest, the form from which there is the least escape – not because, as some have sarcastically said, remorse and regret are clung to with a morbid fondness by the theologians as spiritual luxuries, but because they are existing facts of the world, and as such must be taken into account in the deterministic interpretation of all that is fated to be. If they are fated to be error, does not the bat's wing of irrationality still cast its shadow over the world?

The refuge from the quandary lies, as I said, not far off. The necessary acts we erroneously regret may be good, and yet our error in so regretting them may be also good, on one simple condition; and that condition is this: The world must not be regarded as a machine whose final purpose is the making real of any outward good, but rather as a contrivance for deepening the theoretic consciousness of what goodness and evil in their intrinsic natures are. Not the doing either of good or of evil is what nature cares for, but the knowing of them. Life is one long eating of the fruit of the tree of *knowledge*. I am in the habit, in thinking to myself, of calling this point of view the *gnostical* point of view. According to it, the world is neither an optimism nor a pessimism, but a *gnosticism*. But as this term may perhaps lead to some misunderstandings, I will use it as little as possible here, and speak rather of *subjectivism*, and the *subjectivistic* point of view.

Subjectivism has three great branches — we may call them scientificism, sentimentalism and sensualism, respectively. They all agree essentially about the universe, in deeming that what happens there is subsidiary to what we think or feel about it. Crime justifies its criminality by awakening our intelligence of that criminality, and eventually our remorses and regrets; and the error included in remorses and regrets, the error of supposing that the past could have been different, justifies itself by its use. Its use is to quicken our sense of *what* the irretrievably lost is. When we think of it as that which might have been ('the saddest words of tongue or pen'), the quality of its worth speaks to us with a wilder sweetness; and, conversely, the dissatisfaction wherewith we think of what seems to have driven it from its natural place gives us the severer pang. Admirable artifice of nature! we might be tempted to exclaim — deceiving us in order the better to enlighten us, and leaving nothing undone to accentuate to our consciousness the yawning distance of those opposite poles of good and evil between which creation swings.

We have thus clearly revealed to our view what may be called the dilemma of determinism, so far as determinism pretends to think things out at all. A merely mechanical determinism, it is true, rather rejoices in not thinking them out. It is very sure that the universe must satisfy its postulate of a physical continuity and coherence, but it smiles at anyone who comes forward with a postulate of moral coherence as well. I may suppose, however, that the number of purely mechanical or hard determinists among you this evening is small. The determinism to whose seductions you are most exposed is what I have called soft determinism — the determinism which allows considerations of good and bad to mingle with those of cause and effect in deciding what sort of a universe this may rationally be held to be. The dilemma of this determinism is one whose left horn is pessimism and whose right horn is subjectivism. In other words, if determinism is to escape pessimism, it must leave off looking at the good and ills of life in a simple objective way, and regard them as materials, indifferent in themselves, for the production of consciousness, scientific and ethical, in us.

To escape pessimism is, as we all know, no easy task. Your own studies have sufficiently shown you the almost desperate difficulty of making the notion that there is a single principle of things, and that principle absolute perfection, rhyme together with our daily vision of the facts of life. If perfection be the principle, how comes there any imperfection here? If God be good, how came he to create — or, if he did not create, how comes he to permit — the devil? The evil facts must be explained as seeming: the devil must be whitewashed, the universe must be disinfected, if neither God's goodness nor his unity and power are to remain impugned. And of all the various ways of operating the disinfection, and making bad seem less bad, the way of subjectivism appears by far the best.[6]

For, after all, is there not something rather absurd in our ordinary notion of external things being good or bad in themselves? Can murders and treacheries, considered as mere outward happenings, or motions of matter, be bad without anyone to feel their badness? And could paradise properly be good in the absence of a sentient principle by which the goodness was perceived? Outward goods and evils seem practically indistinguishable except insofar as they result in getting moral judgments made about them. But then the moral judgments seem the main thing, and the outward facts mere perishing

---

[6] To a reader who says he is satisfied with a pessimism, and has no objection to thinking the whole bad, I have no more to say: he makes fewer demands on the world than I, who, making them, wish to look a little further before I give up all hope of having them satisfied. If, however, all he means is that the badness of some parts does not prevent his acceptance of a universe whose *other* parts give him satisfaction, I welcome him as an ally. He has abandoned the notion of the *whole*, which is the essence of deterministic monism, and views things as a pluralism, just as I do in this paper.

instruments for their production. This is subjectivism. Everyone must at some time have wondered at that strange paradox of our moral nature, that, though the pursuit of outward good is the breath of its nostrils, the attainment of outward good would seem to be in suffocation and death. Why does the painting of any paradise or utopia, in heaven or in earth, awaken such yawnings for nirvana and escape? The white-robed harp-playing heaven of our sabbath-schools and the ladylike tea-table elysium represented in Mr Spencer's *Data of Ethics*, as the final consummation of progress, are exactly on a par in this respect — lubberlands, pure and simple, one and all.[7] We look upon them from this delicious mess of insanities and realities, strivings and deadnesses, hopes and fears, agonies and exultations, which forms our present state, and *tedium vitae* is the only sentiment they awaken in our breasts. To our crepuscular natures, born for the conflict, the Rembrandtesque moral chiaroscuro, the shifting struggle of the sunbeam in the gloom, such pictures of light upon light are vacuous and expressionless, and neither to be enjoyed nor understood. If *this* be the whole fruit of the victory, we say; if the generations of mankind suffered and laid down their lives; if prophets confessed and martyrs sang in the fire, and all the sacred tears were shed for no other end than that a race of creatures of such unexampled insipidity should succeed, and protract *in saecula saeculorum* their contented and inoffensive lives — why, at such a rate, better lose than win the battle, or at all events better ring down the curtain before the last of the play, so that a business that began so importantly may be saved from so singularly flat a winding-up.

All this is what I should instantly say, were I called on to plead for gnosticism; and its real friends, of whom you will presently perceive I am not one, would say without difficulty a great deal more. Regarded as a stable finality, every outward good becomes a mere weariness to the flesh. It must be menaced, be occasionally lost, for its goodness to be fully felt as such. Nay, more than occasionally lost. No one knows the worth of innocence till he knows it is gone forever, and that money cannot buy it back. Not the saint, but the sinner that repenteth, is he to whom the full length and breadth, and height and depth,

---

[7] Compare Sir James Stephen's *Essays by a Barrister*, London, 1862, pp. 138 and 318.

of life's meaning is revealed. Not the absence of vice, but vice there, and virtue holding her by the throat, seems the ideal human state. And there seems no reason to suppose it not a permanent human state. There is a deep truth in what the school of Schopenhauer insists on – the illusoriness of the notion of moral progress. The more brutal forms of evil that go are replaced by others more subtle and more poisonous. Our moral horizon moves with us as we move, and never do we draw nearer to the far-off line where the black waves and the azure meet. The final purpose of our reaction seems most plausibly to be the greatest possible enrichment of our ethical consciousness, through the intensest play of contrasts and the widest diversity of characters. This of course obliges some of us to be vessels of wrath, while it calls others to be vessels of honour. But the subjectivist point of view reduces all these outward distinctions to a common denominator. The wretch languishing in the felon's cell may be drinking draughts of the wine of truth that will never pass the lips of the so-called favourite of fortune. And the peculiar consciousness of each of them is an indispensable note in the great ethical concert which the centuries as they roll are grinding out of the living heart of man.

So much for subjectivism! If the dilemma of determinism be to choose between it and pessimism, I see little room for hesitation from the strictly theoretical point of view. Subjectivism seems the more rational scheme. And the world may, possibly, for aught I know, be nothing else. When the healthy love of life is on one, and all its forms and its appetites seem so unutterably real; when the most brutal and the most spiritual things are lit by the same sun, and each is an integral part of the total richness – why, then it seems a grudging and sickly way of meeting so robust a universe to shrink from any of its facts and wish them not to be. Rather take the strictly dramatic point of view, and treat the whole thing as a great unending romance which the spirit of the universe, striving to realize its own content, is eternally thinking out and representing to itself.

No one, I hope, will accuse me, after I have said all this, of underrating the reasons in favour of subjectivism. And now that I proceed to say why those reasons, strong as they are, fail to convince my own mind, I trust the presumption may be that my objections are stronger still.

I frankly confess that they are of a practical order. If we practically take up subjectivism in a sincere and radical manner and follow its consequences, we meet with some that make us pause. Let a subjectivism begin in never so severe and intellectual a way, it is forced by the law of its nature to develop another side of itself and end with the corruptest curiosity. Once dismiss the notion that certain duties are good in themselves, and that we are here to do them, not matter how we feel about them; once consecrate the opposite notion that our performances and our violations of duty are for a common purpose, the attainment of subjective knowledge and feeling, and that the deepening of these is the chief end of our lives – and at what point on the downward slope are we to stop? In theology, subjectivism develops as its 'left-wing' antinomianism. In literature, its left wing is romanticism. And in practical life it is either a nerveless sentimentality or a sensualism without bounds.

Everywhere it fosters the fatalistic mood of mind. It makes those who are already too inert more passive still; it renders wholly reckless those whose energy is already in excess. All through history we find how subjectivism, as soon as it has a free career, exhausts itself in every sort of spiritual, moral and practical licence. Its optimism turns to an ethical indifference, which infallibly brings dissolution in its train. It is perfectly safe to say now that if the Hegelian gnosticism, which has begun to show itself here and in Great Britain, were to become a popular philosophy, as it once was in Germany, it would certainly develop its left wing here as there, and produce a reaction of disgust. Already I have heard a graduate of this very school express in the pulpit his willingness to sin like David, if only he might repent like David. You may tell me he was only sowing his wild, or rather his tame, oats; and perhaps he was. But the point is that in the subjectivistic or gnostical philosophy oat sowing, wild or tame, becomes a systematic necessity and the chief function of life. After the pure and classic truths, the exciting and rancid ones must be experienced; and if the stupid virtues of the philistine herd do not then come in and save society from the influence of the children of light, a sort of inward putrefaction becomes its inevitable doom.

Look at the last runnings of the romantic school, as we see them in that strange contemporary Parisian literature, with which we of the less clever countries are so often driven to rinse out our minds after they have become clogged with the dullness and heaviness of our native pursuits. The romantic school began with the worship of subjective sensibility and the revolt against legality of which Rousseau was the first great prophet: and through various fluxes and refluxes, right wings and left wings, it stands today with two men of genius, M. Renan and M. Zola, as its principal exponents – one speaking with its masculine, and the other with what might be called its feminine, voice. I prefer not to think now of less noble members of the school, and the Renan I have in mind is of course the Renan of latest dates. As I have used the term gnostic, both he and Zola are gnostics of the most pronounced sort. Both are athirst for the facts of life, and both think the facts of human sensibility to be of all facts the most worthy of attention. Both agree, moreover, that sensibility seems to be there for no higher purpose – certainly not, as the philistines say, for the sake of bringing mere outward rights to pass and frustrating outward wrongs. One dwells on the sensibilities for their energy, the other for their sweetness; one speaks with a voice of bronze, the other with that of an aeolian harp; one ruggedly ignores the distinction of good and evil, the other plays the coquette between the craven unmanliness of his *Philosophic Dialogues* and the butterfly optimism of his *Souvenirs de Jeunesse*. But under the pages of both there sounds incessantly the hoarse bass of *vanitas vanitatum, omnia vanitas*, which the reader may hear, whenever he will, between the lines. No writer of this French romantic school has a word of rescue from the hour of satiety with the things of life – the hour in which we say, 'I take no pleasure in them' – or from the hour of terror at the world's vast meaningless grinding, if perchance such hours should come. For terror and satiety are facts of sensibility like any others; and at their own hour they reign in their own right. The heart of the romantic utterances, whether poetical, critical or historical, is this inward remedilessness, what Carlyle calls this far-off whimpering of wail and woe. And from this romantic state of mind there is absolutely no possible *theoretic* escape. Whether, like Renan, we look upon life in a more refined way, as a romance of the spirit; or whether, like the friends of M. Zola, we pique ourselves on our 'scientific' and 'analytic' character, and prefer to be cynical, and call the world a '*roman experimental*' on an infinite scale – in either case the world appears to us potentially as what the same

Carlyle once called it, a vast, gloomy, solitary Golgotha and mill of death.

The only escape is by the practical way. And since I have mentioned the nowadays much-reviled name of Carlyle, let me mention it once more, and say it is the way of his teaching. No matter for Carlyle's life, no matter for a great deal of his writing. What was the most important thing he said to us? He said: 'Hang your sensibilities! Stop your snivelling complaints, and your equally snivelling raptures! Leave off your general emotional tomfoolery, and get to WORK like men!' But this means a complete rupture with the subjectivist philosophy of things. It says conduct, and not sensibility, is the ultimate fact for our recognition. With the vision of certain works to be done, of certain outward changes to be wrought or resisted, it says our intellectual horizon terminates. No matter how we succeed in doing these outward duties, whether gladly and spontaneously, or heavily and unwillingly, do them we somehow must; for the leaving of them undone is perdition. No matter how we feel; if we are only faithful in the outward act and refuse to do wrong, the world will in so far be safe, and we quit of our debt toward it. Take, then, the yoke upon our shoulders; bend our neck beneath the heavy legality of its weight; regard something else than our feeling as our limit, our master, and our law; be willing to live and die in its service — and, at a stroke, we have passed from the subjective into the objective philosophy of things, much as one awakens from some feverish dream, full of bad lights and noises, to find one's self bathed in the sacred coolness and quiet of the air of the night.

But what is the essence of this philosophy of objective conduct, so old-fashioned and finite, but so chaste and sane and strong, when compared with its romantic rival? It is the recognition of limits, foreign and opaque to our understanding. It is the willingness, after bringing about some external good, to feel at peace; for our responsibility ends with the performance of that duty, and the burden of the rest we may lay on higher powers.[8]

> Look to thyself, O Universe,
> Thou art better and not worse,

[8] The burden, for example, of seeing to it that the *end* of all our righteousness be some positive universal gain.

we may say in that philosophy, the moment we have done our stroke of conduct, however small. For in the view of that philosophy the universe belongs to a plurality of semi-independent forces, each one of which may help or hinder, and be helped or hindered by, the operations of the rest.

But this brings us right back, after such a long detour, to the question of indeterminism and to the conclusion of all I came here to say tonight. For the only consistent way of representing a pluralism and a world whose parts may affect one another through their conduct being either good or bad is the indeterministic way. What interest, zest or excitement can there be in achieving the right way, unless we are enabled to feel that the wrong way is also a possible and a natural way — nay, more, a menacing and an imminent way? And what sense can there be in condemning ourselves for taking the wrong way, unless we need have done nothing of the sort, unless the right way was open to us as well? I cannot understand the willingness to act, no matter how we feel, without the belief that acts are really good and bad. I cannot understand the belief that an act is bad, without regret at its happening. I cannot understand regret without the admission of real, genuine possibilities in the world. Only *then* is it other than a mockery to feel, after we have failed to do our best, that an irreparable opportunity is gone from the universe, the loss of which it must forever after mourn.

If you insist that this is all superstition, that possibility is in the eye of science and reason impossibility, and that if I act badly it is that the universe was foredoomed to suffer this defect, you fall right back into the dilemma, the labyrinth, of pessimism and subjectivism, from out of whose toils we have just wound our way.

Now, we are of course free to fall back, if we please. For my own part, though, whatever difficulties may beset the philosophy of objective right and wrong, and the indeterminism it seems to imply, determinism, with its alternative of pessimism or romanticism, contains difficulties that are greater still. But you will remember that I expressly repudiated a while ago the pretension to offer any arguments which could be coercive in a so-called scientific fashion in this matter. And I consequently find myself, at the end of this long talk, obliged to state my conclusions in an altogether personal way. This personal method of appeal seems to be among the very conditions of the problem; and the most anyone can do is to confess as candidly as he can the grounds for the faith that is in him, and leave his example to work on others as it may.

Let me, then, without circumlocution say just this. The world is enigmatical enough in all conscience, whatever theory we may take up toward it. The indeterminism I defend, the free-will theory of popular sense based on the judgment of regret, represents that world as vulnerable, and liable to be injured by certain of its parts if they act wrong. And it represents their acting wrong as a matter of possibility or accident, neither inevitable nor yet to be infallibly warded off. In all this, it is a theory devoid either of transparency or of stability. It gives us a pluralistic, restless universe, in which no single point of view can ever take in the whole scene; and to a mind possessed of the love of unity at any cost, it will, no doubt, remain forever unacceptable. A friend with such a mind once told me that the thought of my universe made him sick, like the sight of the horrible motion of a mass of maggots in their carrion bed.

But while I freely admit that the pluralism and the restlessness are repugnant and irrational in a certain way, I find that every alternative to them is irrational in a deeper way. The indeterminism with its maggots, if you please to speak so about it, offends only the native absolutism of my intellect — an absolutism which, after all, perhaps, deserves to be snubbed and kept in check. But the determinism with its necessary carrion, to continue the figure of speech, and with no possible maggots to eat the latter up, violates my sense of moral reality through and through. When, for example, I imagine such carrion as the Brockton murder, I cannot conceive it as an act by which the universe, as a whole, logically and necessarily expresses its nature without shrinking from complicity with such a whole. And I deliberately refuse to keep on terms of loyalty with the universe by saying blankly that the murder, since it does flow from the nature of the whole, is not carrion. There are *some* instinctive reactions which I, for one, will not tamper with. The only remaining alternative, the attitude of gnostical romanticism, wrenches my personal instincts in quite as violent a way. It falsifies the simple objectivity of their deliverance. It makes the goose-flesh the murder excites in me a sufficient reason for the perpetration of the crime. It transforms life from a tragic reality into an insincere melodramatic exhibition, as foul or as tawdry as anyone's diseased curiosity pleases to carry it out. And with its consecration of the '*roman naturaliste*' state of mind, and its enthronement of the baser crew of Parisian *littérateurs* among the eternally indispensable organs by which the infinite spirit of things attains to that subjective illumination which is the task of its life, it leaves me in presence of a sort of subjective carrion considerably more noisome than the objective carrion I called it in to take away.

No! better a thousand times, than such systematic corruption of our moral sanity, the plainest pessimism, so that it be straightforward; but better far than that the world of chance. Make as great an uproar about chance as you please, I know that chance means pluralism and nothing more. If some of the members of the pluralism are bad, the philosophy of pluralism, whatever broad views it may deny me, permits me, at least, to turn to the other members with a clean breast of affection and an unsophisticated moral sense. And if I still wish to think of the world as a totality, it lets me feel that a world with a *chance* in it of being altogether good, even if the chance never come to pass, is better than a world with no such chance at all. That 'chance' whose very notion I am exhorted and conjured to banish from my view of the future as the suicide of reason concerning it, that 'chance' is – what? Just this – the chance that in moral respects the future may be other and better than the past has been. This is the only chance we have any motive for supposing to exist. Shame, rather, on its repudiation and its denial! For its presence is the vital air which lets the world live, the salt which keeps it sweet.

And here I might legitimately stop, having expressed all I care to see admitted by others tonight. But I know that if I do stop here, misapprehensions will remain in the minds of some of you, and keep all I have said from having its effect; so I judge it best to add a few more words.

In the first place, in spite of all my explanations, the word 'chance' will still be giving trouble. Though you may yourselves be adverse to the deterministic doctrine, you wish a pleasanter word than 'chance' to name the opposite doctrine by; and you very likely consider my preference for such a word a perverse sort of a partiality on my part. It certainly *is* a bad word to make converts with; and you wish I had not thrust it so butt-foremost at you – you wish to use a milder term.

Well, I admit there may be just a dash of perversity in its choice. The spectacle of the mere word-grabbing game played by the soft determinists has perhaps driven me too violently the other way; and, rather than be found wrangling with them for the good words, I am willing to take the first bad one which comes along, provided it be unequivocal. The question is of things, not of eulogistic names for them; and the best word is the one that enables men to know the quickest whether they disagree or not about the things. But the word 'chance', with its singular negativity, is just the word for this purpose. Whoever uses it instead of 'freedom', squarely and resolutely gives up all pretence to control the things he says are free. For *him*, he confesses that they are no better than mere chance would be. It is a word of *impotence*, and is therefore the only sincere word we can use, if, in granting freedom to certain things, we grant it honestly, and really risk the game. 'Who chooses me must give and forfeit all he hath.' Any other word permits of quibbling, and lets us, after the fashion of the soft determinists, make a pretence of restoring the caged bird to liberty with one hand, while with the other we anxiously tie a string to its leg to make sure it does not get beyond our sight.

But now you will bring up your final doubt. Does not the admission of such an unguaranteed chance or freedom preclude utterly the notion of a Providence governing the world? Does it not leave the fate of the universe at the mercy of the chance-possibilities, and so far insecure? Does it not, in short, deny the craving of our nature for an ultimate peace behind all tempests, for a blue zenith above all clouds?

To this my answer must be very brief. The belief in free-will is not in the least incompatible with the belief in Providence, provided you do not restrict the Providence to fulminating nothing but *fatal* decrees. If you allow him to provide possibilities as well as actualities to the universe, and to carry on his own thinking in those two categories just as we do ours, chances may be there, uncontrolled even by him, and the course of the universe be really ambiguous; and yet the end of all things may be just what he intended it to be from all eternity.

An analogy will make the meaning of this clear. Suppose two men before a chessboard – the one a novice, the other an expert player of the game. The expert intends to beat. But he cannot foresee exactly what any one actual move of his adversary may be. He knows, however, all the *possible* moves of the latter; and he knows in advance how to meet each of them by a move of his own which leads in the direction of victory. And the victory infallibly arrives, after no matter how devious a course, in the one predestined form of checkmate to the novice's king.

Let now the novice stand for us finite free agents, and the expert for the infinite mind in which the universe lies. Suppose the latter to be thinking out his universe before he actually creates it. Suppose him to say, I will lead things to a certain end, but I will not *now*[9] decide on all the steps thereto. At various points, ambiguous possibilities shall be left open, *either* of which, at a given instant, may become actual. But whichever branch of these bifurcations become real, I know what I shall do at the *next* bifurcation to keep things from drifting away from the final result I intend.[10]

The Creator's plan of the universe would thus be left blank as to many of its actual details, but all possibilities would be

---

[9] This of course leaves the creative mind subject to the law of time. And to anyone who insists on the timelessness of that mind I have no reply to make. A mind to whom all time is simultaneously present must see all things under the form of actuality, or under some form to us unknown. If he thinks certain moments as ambiguous in their content while future, he must simultaneously know how the ambiguity will have been decided when they are past. So that none of his mental judgments can possibly be called hypothetical, and his world is one from which chance is excluded. Is not, however, the timeless mind rather a gratuitous fiction? And is not the notion of eternity being given at a stroke to omniscience only just another way of whacking upon us the block-universe, and of denying that possibilities exist? – just the point to be proved. To say that time is an illusory appearance is only a roundabout manner of saying there is no real plurality, and that the frame of things is an absolute unit. Admit plurality, and time may be its form.

[10] And this of course means 'miraculous' interposition, but not necessarily of the gross sort our fathers took such delight in representing, and which has so lost its magic for us. Emerson quotes some Eastern sage as saying that if evil were really done under the sun, the sky would incontinently shrivel to a snakeskin and cast it out in spasms. But, says Emerson, the spasms of Nature are years and centuries; and it will tax man's patience to wait so long. We may think of the reserved possibilities God keeps in his own hand, under as invisible and molecular and slowly self-summating a form as we please. We may think of them as counteracting human agencies which he inspires *ad hoc*. In short, signs and wonders and convulsions of the earth and sky are not the only neutralizers of obstruction to a god's plans of which it is possible to think.

marked down. The realization of some of these would be left absolutely to chance; that is, would only be determined when the moment of realization came. Other possibilities would be *contingently* determined; that is, their decision would have to wait till it was seen how the matters of absolute chance fell out. But the rest of the plan, including its final upshot, would be rigorously determined once for all. So the creator himself would not need to know *all* the details of actuality until they came; and at any time his own view of the world would be a view partly of facts and partly of possibilities, exactly as ours is now. Of one thing, however, he might be certain; and that is that his world was safe, and that no matter how much it might zigzag he could surely bring it home at last.

Now, it is entirely immaterial, in this scheme, whether the Creator leave the absolute chance-possibilities to be decided by himself, each when its proper moment arrives, or whether, on the contrary, he alienate this power from himself, and leave the decision out and out to finite creatures such as we men are. The great point is that the possibilities are really *here*. Whether it be we who solve them, or he working through us, at those soul-trying moments when fate's scales seem to quiver, and good snatches the victory from evil or shrinks nerveless from the fight, is of small account, so long as we admit that the issue is decided nowhere else than *here* and *now*. *That* is what gives the palpitating reality to our moral life and makes it tingle, as Mr Mallock says, with so strange and elaborate an excitement. This reality, this excitement, are what the determinisms, hard and soft alike, suppress by their denial that *anything* is decided here and now, and their dogma that all things were foredoomed and settled long ago. If it be so, may you and I then have been foredoomed to the error of continuing to believe in liberty.[11] It is fortunate for the winding up of controversy that in every discussion with determinism this *argumentum ad hominem* can be its adversary's last word.

[11] As long as languages contain a future perfect tense, determinists, following the bent of laziness or passion, the lines of least resistance, can reply in that tense saying, 'It will have been fated', to the still small voice which urges an opposite course; and thus excuse themselves from effort in a quite unanswerable way.

16

The Moral Philosopher and the Moral Life[1]

The main purpose of this paper is to show that there is no such thing possible as an ethical philosophy dogmatically made up in advance. We all help to determine the content of ethical philosophy so far as we contribute to the race's moral life. In other words, there can be no final truth in ethics any more than in physics, until the last man has had his experience and said his say. In the one case as in the other, however, the hypotheses which we now make while waiting, and the acts to which they prompt us, are among the indispensable conditions which determine what that 'say' shall be.

First of all, what is the position of him who seeks an ethical philosophy? To begin with, he must be distinguished from all those who are satisfied to be ethical sceptics. He *will* not be a sceptic; therefore, so far from ethical scepticism being one possible fruit of ethical philosophizing, it can only be regarded as that residual alternative to all philosophy which from the outset menaces every would-be philosopher who may give up the quest discouraged, and renounce his original aim. That aim is to find an account of the moral relations that obtain among things, which will weave them into the unity of a stable system, and make of the world what one may call a genuine universe from the ethical point of view. So far as the world resists reduction to the form of unity, so far as ethical propositions seem unstable, so far does the philosopher fail of his ideal. The subject-matter of his study is the ideals he finds existing in the world; the purpose which guides him is this ideal of his own, of getting them into a certain form. This ideal is thus a factor in ethical philosophy whose legitimate presence must never be overlooked; it is a positive contribution which the philosopher

[1] An address to the Yale Philosophical Club, published in the *International Journal of Ethics*, April 1891.

himself necessarily makes to the problem. But it is his only positive contribution. At the outset of his inquiry he ought to have no other ideals. Were he interested peculiarly in the triumph of any one kind of good, he would *pro tanto* cease to be a judicial investigator, and become an advocate for some limited element of the case.

There are three questions in ethics which must be kept apart. Let them be called respectively the *psychological* question, the *metaphysical* question, and the *casuistic* question. The psychological question asks after the historical *origin* of our moral ideas and judgments; the metaphysical question asks what the very *meaning* of the words 'good', 'ill' and 'obligation' are; the casuistic question asks what is the *measure* of the various goods and ills which men recognize, so that the philosopher may settle the true order of human obligations.

I

The psychological question is for most disputants the only question. When your ordinary doctor of divinity has proved to his own satisfaction that an altogether unique faculty called 'conscience' must be postulated to tell us what is right and what is wrong, or when your popular-science enthusiast has proclaimed that 'apriorism' is an exploded superstition, and that our moral judgments have gradually resulted from the teaching of the environment, each of these persons thinks that ethics is settled and nothing more is to be said. The familiar pair of names, intuitionist and evolutionist, so commonly used now to connote all possible differences in ethical opinion, really refer to the psychological question alone. The discussion of this question hinges so much upon particular details that it is impossible to enter upon it at all within the limits of this paper. I will therefore only express dogmatically my own belief, which is this – that the Benthams, the Mills and the Bains have done a lasting service in taking so many of our human ideals and showing how they must have arisen from the association with acts of simple bodily pleasures and reliefs from pain. Association with many remote pleasures will unquestionably make a thing significant of goodness in our minds; and the more vaguely the goodness is conceived of, the more mysterious will its source appear to be.

But it is surely impossible to explain all our sentiments and preferences in this simple way. The more minutely psychology studies human nature, the more clearly it finds there traces of secondary affections, relating the impressions of the environment with one another and with our impulses in quite different ways from those mere associations of coexistence and succession which are practically all that pure empiricism can admit. Take the love of drunkenness; take bashfulness, the terror of high places, the tendency to seasickness, to faint at the sight of blood, the susceptibility to musical sounds; take the emotion of the comical, the passion for poetry, for mathematics, or for metaphysics — no one of these things can be wholly explained by either association or utility. They *go with* other things that can be so explained, no doubt; and some of them are prophetic of future utilities, since there is nothing in us for which some use may not be found. But their origin is in incidental complications to our cerebral structure, a structure whose original features arose with no reference to the perception of such discords and harmonies as these.

Well, a vast number of our moral perceptions also are certainly of this secondary and brain-born kind. They deal with directly felt fitnesses between things, and often fly in the teeth of all the prepossessions of habit and presumptions of utility. The moment you get beyond the coarser and more commonplace moral maxims, the Decalogues and *Poor Richard's Almanacs*, you fall into schemes and positions which to the eye of commonsense are fantastic and overstrained. The sense for abstract justice which some persons have is as eccentric a variation, from the natural-history point of view, as is the passion for music or for the higher philosophical consistencies which consumes the soul of others. The feeling of the inward dignity of certain spiritual attitudes, as peace, serenity, simplicity, veracity; and of the essential vulgarity of others, as querulousness, anxiety, egoistic fussiness, etc. — are quite inexplicable except by an innate preference of the more ideal attitude for its own pure sake. The nobler thing *tastes* better, and that is all that we can say. 'Experience' of consequences may truly teach us what things are *wicked*, but what have consequences to do with what is *mean* and *vulgar*? If a man has shot his wife's paramour, by reason of what subtle repugnancy in things is it that we are so disgusted when we hear that the wife and the husband have made it up and are living comfortably together again? Or if the hypothesis were offered us of a world in which Messrs Fourier's and Bellamy's and Morris's utopias should all be outdone, and millions kept permanently happy on the one simple condition that a certain lost soul on the far-off edge of things should lead a life of lonely torture, what except a specifical and independent sort of emotion can it be which would make us immediately feel, even though an impulse arose within us to clutch at the happiness so offered, how hideous a thing would be its enjoyment when deliberately accepted as the fruit of such a bargain? To what, once more, but subtle brain-born feelings of discord can be due all these recent protests against the entire race-tradition of retributive justice? – I refer to Tolstoy with his ideas of non-resistance, to Mr Bellamy with his substitution of oblivion for repentance (in his novel of *Dr Heidenhain's Process*), to M. Guyau with his radical condemnation of the punitive ideal. All these subtleties of the moral sensibility go as much beyond what can be ciphered out from the 'laws of association' as the delicacies of sentiment possible between a pair of young lovers go beyond such precepts of the 'etiquette to be observed during engagement' as are printed in manuals of social form.

No! Purely inward forces are certainly at work here. All the higher, more penetrating ideals are revolutionary. They present themselves far less in the guise of effects of past experience than in that of probable causes of future experience, factors to which the environment and the lessons it has so far taught us must learn to bend.

This is all I can say of the psychological question now. In the last chapter of a recent work[2] I have sought to prove in a general way the existence, in our thought, of relations which do not merely repeat the couplings of experience. Our ideals have certainly many sources. They are not all explicable as signifying corporeal pleasures to be gained, and pains to be escaped. And for having so constantly perceived this psychological fact, we must applaud the intuitionist school. Whether or not such applause must be extended to that school's other characteristics will appear as we take up the following questions.

The next one in order is the metaphysical question, of what we mean by the words 'obligation', 'good' and 'ill'.

---

[2] *The Principles of Psychology*, New York, H. Holt and Co., 1890.

2

First of all, it appears that such words can have no application or relevancy in a world in which no sentient life exists. Imagine an absolutely material world, containing only physical and chemical facts, and existing from eternity without a god, without even an interested spectator: would there be any sense in saying of that world that one of its states is better than another? Or if there were two such worlds possible, would there be any rhyme or reason in calling one good and the other bad – good or bad positively, I mean, and apart from the fact that one might relate itself better than the other to the philosopher's private interests? But we must leave these private interests out of the account, for the philosopher is a mental fact, and we are asking whether goods and evils and obligations exist in physical facts *per se*. Surely there is no *status* for good and evil to exist in, in a purely insentient world. How can one physical fact, considered simply as a physical fact, be 'better' than another? Betterness is not a physical relation. In its mere material capacity, a thing can no more be good or bad than it can be pleasant or painful. Good for what? Good for the production of another physical fact, do you say? But what in a purely physical universe demands the production of that other fact? Physical facts simply *are* or are *not*; and neither when present or absent, can they be supposed to make demands. If they do, they can only do so by having desires; and then they have ceased to be purely physical facts, and have become facts of conscious sensibility. Goodness, badness and obligation must be *realized* somewhere in order really to exist; and the first step in ethical philosophy is to see that no merely inorganic 'nature of things' can realize them. Neither moral relations nor the moral law can swing *in vacuo*. Their only habitat can be a mind which feels them; and no world composed of merely physical facts can possibly be a world to which ethical propositions apply.

The moment one sentient being, however, is made a part of the universe, there is a chance for goods and evils really to exist. Moral relations now have their *status*, in that being's consciousness. So far as he feels anything to be good, he *makes* it good. It *is* good, for him; and being good for him, is absolutely good, for he is the sole creator of values in that universe, and outside of his opinion things have no moral character at all.

In such a universe as that it would of course be absurd to raise the question of whether the solitary thinker's judgments of good and ill are true or not. Truth supposes a standard outside of the thinker to which he must conform; but here the thinker is a sort of divinity, subject to no higher judge. Let us call the supposed universe which he inhabits a *moral solitude*. In such a moral solitude it is clear that there can be no outward obligation, and that the only trouble the god-like thinker is liable to have will be over the consistency of his own several ideals with one another. Some of these will no doubt be more pungent and appealing than the rest; their goodness will have a profounder, more penetrating taste; they will return to haunt him with more obstinate regrets if violated. So the thinker will have to order his life with them as its chief determinants, or else remain inwardly discordant and unhappy. Into whatever equilibrium he may settle, though, and however he may straighten out his system, it will be a right system; for beyond the facts of his own subjectivity there is nothing moral in the world.

If now we introduce a second thinker with his likes and dislikes into the universe, the ethical situation becomes much more complex, and several possibilities are immediately seen to obtain.

One of these is that the thinkers may ignore each other's attitude about good and evil altogether, and each continue to indulge his own preferences, indifferent to what the other may feel or do. In such a case we have a world with twice as much of the ethical quality in it as our moral solitude, only it is without ethical unity. The same object is good or bad there, according as you measure it by the view which this one or that one of the thinkers takes. Nor can you find any possible ground in such a world for saying that one thinker's opinion is more correct than the other's, or that either has the truer moral sense. Such a world, in short, is not a moral universe but a moral dualism. Not only is there no single point of view within it from which the values of things can be unequivocally judged, but there is not even a demand for such a point of view, since the two thinkers are supposed to be indifferent to each other's thoughts and acts. Multiply the thinkers into a pluralism, and we find realized for us in the ethical sphere something like that world which the antique sceptics conceived of – in which individual minds are the measures of all things, and in which no one 'objective' truth, but only a multitude of 'subjective' opinions, can be found.

But this is the kind of world with which the philosopher, so long as he holds to the hope of a philosophy, will not put up. Among the various ideals represented, there must be, he thinks, some which have the more truth or authority; and to these the others *ought* to yield, so that system and subordination may reign. Here in the word 'ought' the notion of *obligation* comes emphatically into view, and the next thing in order must be to make its meaning clear.

Since the outcome of the discussion so far has been to show us that nothing can be good or right except so far as some consciousness feels it to be good or thinks it to be right, we perceive on the very threshold that the real superiority and authority which are postulated by the philosopher to reside in some of the opinions, and the really inferior character which he supposes must belong to others, cannot be explained by any abstract moral 'nature of things' existing antecedently to the concrete thinkers themselves with their ideals. Like the positive attributes good and bad, the comparative ones better and worse must be *realized* in order to be real. If one ideal judgment be objectively better than another, that betterness must be made flesh by being lodged concretely in someone's actual perception. It cannot float in the atmosphere, for it is not a sort of meteorological phenomenon, like the aurora borealis or the zodiacal light. Its *esse* is *percipi*, like the *esse* of the ideals themselves between which it obtains. The philosopher, therefore, who seeks to know which ideal ought to have supreme weight and which one ought to be subordinated, must trace the *ought* itself to the *de facto* constitution of some existing consciousness, behind which, as one of the data of the universe, he as a purely ethical philosopher is unable to go. This consciousness must make the one ideal right by feeling it to be right, the other wrong by feeling it to be wrong. But now what particular consciousness in the universe *can* enjoy this prerogative of obliging others to conform to a rule which it lays down?

If one of the thinkers were obviously divine, while all the rest were human, there would probably be no practical dispute about the matter. The divine thought would be the model, to which the others should conform. But still the theoretic question would remain, What is the ground of the obligation, even here?

In our first essays at answering this question, there is an inevitable tendency to slip into an assumption which ordinary men follow when they are disputing with one another about questions of good and bad. They imagine an abstract moral order in which the objective truth resides; and each tries to prove that this pre-existing order is more accurately reflected in his own ideas than in those of his adversary. It is because one disputant is backed by this overarching abstract order that we think the other should submit. Even so, when it is a question no longer of two finite thinkers, but of God and ourselves – we follow our usual habit, and imagine a sort of *de jure* relation, which antedates and overarches the mere facts, and would make it right that we should conform our thoughts to God's thoughts, even though he made no claim to that effect, and though we preferred *de facto* to go on thinking for ourselves.

But the moment we take a steady look at the question, *we see not only that without a claim actually made by some concrete person there can be no obligation, but that there is some obligation wherever there is a claim*. Claim and obligation are, in fact, coextensive terms; they cover each other exactly. Our ordinary attitude of regarding ourselves as subject to an over-arching system of moral relations, true 'in themselves', is therefore either an out-and-out superstition, or else it must be treated as a merely provisional abstraction from that real Thinker in whose actual demand upon us to think as he does our obligation must be ultimately based. In a theistic-ethical philosophy that thinker in question is, of course, the deity to whom the existence of the universe is due.

I know well how hard it is for those who are accustomed to what I have called the superstitious view, to realize that every *de facto* claim creates in so far forth an obligation. We inveterately think that something which we call the 'validity' of the claim is what gives to it its obligatory character, and that this validity is something outside of the claim's mere existence as a matter of fact. It rains down upon the claim, we think, from some sublime dimension of being, which the moral law inhabits, much as upon the steel of the compass-needle the influence of the Pole rains down from out of the starry heavens. But again, how can such an inorganic abstract character of imperativeness, additional to the imperativeness which is in the concrete claim itself, *exist*? Take any demand, however slight, which any creature, however weak, may make. Ought it not, for its own sole sake, to be satisfied? If not, prove why not. The only possible kind of proof you could adduce would be the exhibition of another creature who should make a demand that ran the other way. The only possible reason there can be why any phenomenon ought to exist is that such a phenomenon actually is desired. Any desire is imperative to the extent of its amount; it *makes* itself valid by the fact that it exists at all. Some desires, truly enough, are small desires; they are put forward by insignificant persons, and we customarily make light of the obligations which they bring. But the fact that such personal demands as these impose small obligations does not keep the largest obligations from being personal demands.

If we must talk impersonally, to be sure we can say that 'the universe' requires, exacts, or makes obligatory such or such an action, whenever it expresses itself through the desires of such or such a creature. But it is better not to talk about the universe in this personified way, unless we believe in a universal or divine consciousness which actually exists. If there be such a consciousness, then its demands carry the most of obligation simply because they are the greatest in amount. But it is even then not *abstractly* right that we should respect them. It is only *concretely* right – or right after the fact, and by virtue of the fact, that they are actually made. Suppose we do not respect them, as seems largely to be the case in this queer world. That ought not to be, we say; that is wrong. But in what way is this fact of wrongness made more acceptable or intelligible when we imagine it to consist rather in the laceration of an *a priori* ideal order than in the disappointment of a living personal god? Do we, perhaps, think that we cover God and protect him and make his impotence over us less ultimate, when we back him up with this *a priori* blanket from which he may draw some warmth of further appeal? But the only force of appeal to *us*, which either a living god or an abstract ideal order can wield, is found in the 'everlasting ruby vaults' of our own human hearts, as they happen to beat responsive and not irresponsive to the claim. So far as they do feel it when made by a living consciousness, it is life answering to life. A claim thus livingly acknowledged is acknowledged with a solidity and fullness which no thought of an 'ideal' backing can render more complete; while if, on the other hand, the heart's response is withheld, the stubborn phenomenon is there of an impotence in the claims which the universe embodies, which no talk about an eternal nature of things can gloze over or dispel. An ineffective *a priori* order is as impotent a thing as an ineffective God; and in the eye of philosophy, it is as hard a thing to explain.

We may now consider that what we distinguished as the metaphysical question in ethical philosophy is sufficiently answered, and that we have learned what the words 'good', 'bad' and 'obligation' severally mean. They mean no absolute natures, independent of personal support. They are objects of feeling and desire, which have no foothold or anchorage in Being, apart from the existence of actually living minds.

Wherever such minds exist, with judgments of good and ill, and demands upon one another, there is an ethical world in its essential features. Were all other things, gods and men and starry heavens, blotted out from this universe, and were there left but one rock with two loving souls upon it, that rock would have as thoroughly moral a constitution as any possible world which the eternities and immensities could harbour. It would be a tragic constitution, because the rock's inhabitants would die. But while they lived, there would be real good things and real bad things in the universe; there would be obligations, claims and expectations; obediences, refusals and disappointments; compunctions and longings for harmony to come again, and inward peace of conscience when it was restored; there would, in short, be a moral life, whose active energy would have no limit but the intensity of interest in each other with which the hero and heroine might be endowed.

We, on this terrestrial globe, so far as the visible facts go, are just like the inhabitants of such a rock. Whether a god exist, or whether no god exist, in yon blue heaven above us bent, we form at any rate an ethical republic here below. And the first reflection which this leads to is that ethics have as genuine and real a foothold in a universe where the highest consciousness is human, as in a universe where there is a god as well. 'The religion of humanity' affords a basis for ethics as well as theism does. Whether the purely human system can gratify the philosopher's demand as well as the other is a different question, which we ourselves must answer ere we close.

3

The last fundamental question in ethics was, it will be remembered, the *casuistic* question. Here we are, in a world where the existence of a divine thinker has been and perhaps always will be doubted by some of the lookers-on, and where, in spite of the presence of a large number of ideals in which human beings agree, there are a mass of others about which no general consensus obtains. It is hardly necessary to present a literary picture of this, for the facts are too well known. The wars of the flesh and the spirit in each man, the concupiscences of different individuals pursuing the same unshareable material or social prizes, the ideals which contrast so according to races, circumstances, temperaments, philosophical beliefs, etc. – all form a maze of apparently inextricable confusion with no obvious Ariadne's thread to lead one out. Yet the philosopher, just because he is a philosopher, adds his own peculiar ideal to the confusion (with which if he were willing to be a sceptic he would be passably content), and insists that over all these individual opinions there is a *system of truth* which he can discover if he only takes sufficient pains.

We stand ourselves at present in the place of that philosopher, and must not fail to realize all the features that the situation comports. In the first place we will not be sceptics; we hold to it that there is a truth to be ascertained. But in the second place we have just gained the insight that that truth cannot be a self-proclaiming set of laws, or an abstract 'moral reason', but can only exist in act, or in the shape of an opinion held by some thinker really to be found. There is, however, no visible thinker invested with authority. Shall we then simply proclaim our own ideals as the lawgiving ones? No; for if we are true philosophers we must throw our own spontaneous ideals, even the dearest, impartially in with that total mass of ideals which are fairly to be judged. But how then can we as philosophers ever find a test; how avoid complete moral scepticism on the one hand, and on the other escape bringing a wayward personal standard of our own along with us, on which we simply pin faith?

The dilemma is a hard one, nor does it grow a bit more easy

as we revolve it in our minds. The entire undertaking of the philosopher obliges him to seek an impartial test. That test, however, must be incarnated in the demand of some actually existent person; and how can he pick out the person save by an act in which his own sympathies and prepossessions are implied?

One method indeed presents itself, and has as a matter of history been taken by the more serious ethical schools. If the heap of things demanded proved on inspection less chaotic than at first they seemed, if they furnished their own relative test and measure, then the casuistic problem would be solved. If it were found that all goods *qua* goods contained a common essence, then the amount of this essence involved in any one good would show its rank in the scale of goodness, and order could be quickly made; for this essence would be *the* good upon which all thinkers were agreed, the relatively objective and universal good that the philosopher seeks. Even his own private ideals would be measured by their share of it, and find their rightful place among the rest.

Various essences of good have thus been found and proposed as bases of the ethical system. Thus, to be a mean between two extremes; to be recognized by a special intuitive faculty; to make the agent happy for the moment; to make others as well as him happy in the long run; to add to his perfection or dignity; to harm no one; to follow from reason or flow from universal law; to be in accordance with the will of God; to promote the survival of the human species on this planet – are so many tests, each of which has been maintained by somebody to constitute the essence of all good things or actions so far as they are good.

No one of the measures that have been actually proposed has, however, given general satisfaction. Some are obviously not universally present in all cases – e.g., the character of harming no one, or that of following a universal law; for the best course is often cruel; and many acts are reckoned good on the sole condition that they be exceptions, and serve not as examples of a universal law. Other characters, such as following the will of God, are unascertainable, and vague. Others again, like survival, are quite indeterminate in their consequences, and leave us in the lurch where we most need their help: a philosopher of the Sioux nation, for example, will be certain to use the survival-criterion in a very different way from ourselves. The best, on the whole, of these marks and measures of goodness seems to be the capacity to bring happiness. But in order not to break down fatally, this test must be taken to cover innumerable acts and impulses that never *aim* at happiness; so that, after all, in seeking for a universal principle we inevitably are carried onward to the *most* universal principle — that *the essence of good is simply to satisfy demand*. The demand may be for anything under the sun. There is really no more ground for supposing that all our demands can be accounted for by one universal underlying kind of motive than there is ground for supposing that all physical phenomena are cases of a single law. The elementary forces in ethics are probably as plural as those of physics are. The various ideals have no common character apart from the fact that they are ideals. No single abstract principle can be so used as to yield to the philosopher anything like a scientifically accurate and genuinely useful casuistic scale.

A look at another peculiarity of the ethical universe, as we find it, will still further show us the philosopher's perplexities. As a purely theoretic problem, namely, the casuistic question would hardly ever come up at all. If the ethical philosopher were only asking after the best *imaginable* system of goods he would indeed have an easy task; for all demands as such are *prima facie* respectable, and the best simply imaginary world would be one in which *every* demand was gratified as soon as made. Such a world would, however, have to have a physical constitution entirely different from that of the one which we inhabit. It would need not only a space, but a time, 'of *n*-dimensions', to include all the acts and experiences incompatible with one another here below, which would then go on in conjunction — such as spending our money, yet growing rich; taking our holiday, yet getting ahead with our work; shooting and fishing, yet doing no hurt to the beasts; gaining no end of experience, yet keeping our youthful freshness of heart; and the like. There can be no question that such a system of things, however brought about, would be the absolutely ideal system; and that if a philosopher could create universes *a priori*, and provide all the mechanical conditions, that is the sort of universe which he should unhesitatingly create.

But this world of ours is made on an entirely different pattern, and the casuistic question here is most tragically practical. The actually possible in this world is vastly narrower than all that is demanded; and there is always a *pinch* between the ideal and the actual which can only be got through by leaving part of the ideal behind. There is hardly a good which we can imagine except as competing for the possession of the same bit of space and time with some other imagined good. Every end of desire that presents itself appears exclusive of some other end of desire. Shall a man drink and smoke, *or* keep his nerves in condition? – he cannot do both. Shall he follow his fancy for Amelia, *or* for Henrietta? – both cannot be the choice of his heart. Shall he have the dear old Republican Party, *or* a spirit of unsophistication in public affairs? – he cannot have both, etc. So that the ethical philosopher's demand for the right scale of subordination in ideals is the fruit of an altogether practical need. Some part of the ideal must be butchered, and he needs to know which part. It is a tragic situation, and no mere speculative conundrum, with which he has to deal.

Now *we* are blinded to the real difficulty of the philosopher's task by the fact that we are born into a society whose ideals are largely ordered already. If we follow the ideal which is conventionally highest, the others which we butcher either die and do not return to haunt us; or if they come back and accuse us of murder, everyone applauds us for turning to them a deaf ear. In other words, our environment encourages us not to be philosophers but partisans. The philosopher, however, cannot, so long as he clings to his own ideal of objectivity, rule out any ideal from being heard. He is confident, and rightly confident, that the simple taking counsel of his own intuitive preferences would be certain to end in a mutilation of the fullness of the truth. The poet Heine is said to have written 'Bunsen' in the place of 'Gott' in his copy of that author's work entitled *God in History*, so as to make it read *Bunsen in der Geschichte*. Now, with no disrespect to the good and learned Baron, is it not safe to say that any single philosopher, however wide his sympathies, must be just such a Bunsen in der Geschichte of the moral world, so soon as he attempt to put his own ideas of order into that howling mob of desires, each struggling to get breathing-room for the ideal to which it clings? The very best of men must not only be insensible, but be ludicrously and peculiarly insensible, to many goods. As a militant, fighting free-handed that the goods to which he *is* sensible may not be submerged and lost from out of life, the philosopher, like every other human being, is in a natural position. But think of Zeno and of Epicurus, think of Calvin and of Paley, think of Kant and Schopenhauer, of Herbert Spencer and John Henry Newman, no longer as one-sided champions of special ideals, but as schoolmasters deciding what all must think – and what more grotesque topic could a satirist wish for on which to exercise his pen? The fabled attempt of Mrs Partington to arrest the rising ride of the North Atlantic with her broom was a reasonable spectacle compared with their effort to substitute the content of their clean-shaven systems for that exuberant mass of goods with which all human nature is in travail, and groaning to bring to the light of day. Think, furthermore, of such individual moralists, no longer as mere schoolmasters, but as pontiffs armed with the temporal power, and having authority in every concrete case of conflict to order which good shall be butchered and which shall be suffered to survive – and the notion really turns one pale. All one's slumbering revolutionary instincts waken at the thought of any single moralist wielding such powers of life and death. Better chaos forever than an order based on any closet-philosopher's rule, even though he were the most enlightened possible member of his tribe. No! if the philosopher is to keep his judicial position, he must never become one of the parties to the fray.

What can he do, then, it will now be asked, except to fall back on scepticism and give up the notion of being a philosopher at all?

But do we not already see a perfectly definite path of escape which is open to him just because he is a philosopher, and not the champion of one particular ideal? Since everything which is demanded is by that fact a good, must not the guiding principle for ethical philosophy (since all demands conjointly cannot be satisfied in this poor world) be simply to satisfy at all times *as many demands as we can*? That act must be the best act, accordingly, which makes for the *best whole*, in the sense of awakening the least sum of dissatisfactions. In the casuistic scale, therefore, those ideals must be written highest which *prevail at the least cost*, or by whose realization the least possible number of other ideals are destroyed. Since victory and defeat there must be, the victory to be philosophically prayed for is that of the more inclusive side – of the side which even in the hour of triumph will to some degree do justice to the ideals in which the vanquished party's interests lay. The course of history is nothing but the story of men's struggles from generation to generation to find the more and more inclusive order. *Invent some manner* of realizing your own ideals which will also satisfy the alien demands – that and that only is the path of peace! Following the path, society has shaken itself into one sort of relative equilibrium after another by a series of social discoveries quite analogous to those of science. Polyandry and polygamy and slavery, private warfare and liberty to kill, judicial torture and arbitrary royal power have slowly succumbed to actually aroused complaints; and though someone's ideals are unquestionably the worse off for each improvement, yet a vastly greater total number of them find shelter in our civilized society than in the older savage ways. So far then, and up to date, the casuistic scale is made for the philosopher already far better than he can ever make it for himself. An experiment of the most searching kind has proved that the laws and usages of land are what yield the maximum of satisfaction to the thinkers taken all together. The presumption in cases of conflict must always be in favour of the conventionally recognized good. The philosopher must be a conservative, and in the construction of his casuistic scale must put the things most in accordance with the customs of the community on top.

And yet if he be a true philosopher he must see that there is nothing final in any actual given equilibrium of human ideals, but that as our present laws and customs have fought and conquered other past ones, so they will in their turn be overthrown by any newly discovered order which will hush up the complaints that they still give rise to, without producing others louder still. 'Rules are made for man, not man for rules' – that one sentence is enough to immortalize Green's *Prolegomena to Ethics*. And although a man always risks much when he breaks away from established rules and strives to realize a larger ideal whole than they permit, yet the philosopher must allow that it is at all times open to anyone to make the experiment, provided he fear not to stake his life and character upon the throw. The pinch is always here. Pent in under every system of moral rules are innumerable persons whom it weighs upon, and goods which it represses; and these are always rumbling and grumbling in the background, and ready for any issue by which they may get free. See the abuses which the institution of private property covers, so that even today it is shamelessly asserted among us that one of the prime functions of the national government is to help the adroiter citizens to grow rich. See the unnamed and unnamable sorrows which the tyranny, on the whole so beneficent, of the marriage institution brings to so many, both of the married and the unwed. See the wholesale loss of opportunity under our regime of so-called equality and industrialism, with the drummer and the counter-jumper in the saddle, for so many faculties and graces which could flourish in the feudal world. See our kindliness for the humble and the outcast, how it wars with that stern weeding-out which until now has been the condition of every perfection in the breed. See everywhere the struggle and the squeeze; and everlastingly the problem how to make them less. The anarchists, nihilists and free-lovers; the free-silverites, socialists and single-tax men; the free-traders and civil-service reformers; the prohibitionists and anti-vivisectionists; the radical Darwinians with their idea of the suppression of the weak — these and all the conservative sentiments of society arrayed against them, are simply deciding through actual experiment by what sort of conduct the maximum amount of good can be gained and kept in this world. These experiments are to be judged, not *a priori*, but by actually finding, after the fact of their making, how much more outcry or how much appeasement comes about. What closet-solutions can possibly anticipate the result of trials made on such a scale? Or what can any superficial theorist's judgment be worth, in a world where every one of hundreds of ideals has its special champion already provided in the shape of some genius expressly born to feel it, and to fight to death in its behalf? The pure philosopher can only follow the windings of the spectacle, confident that the line of least resistance will always be towards the richer and the more inclusive arrangement, and that by one tack after another some approach to the kingdom of heaven is incessantly made.

4

All this amounts to saying that, so far as the casuistic question goes, ethical science is just like physical science, and instead of being deducible all at once from abstract principles, must simply bide its time, and be ready to revise its conclusions from day to day. The presumption of course, in both sciences, always is that the vulgarly accepted opinions are true, and the right casuistic order that which public opinion believes in; and surely it would be folly quite as great, in most of us, to strike out independently and to aim at originality in ethics as in physics. Every now and then, however, someone is born with the right to be original, and his revolutionary thought or action may bear prosperous fruit. He may replace old 'laws of nature' by better ones; he may, by breaking old moral rules in a certain place, bring in a total condition of things more ideal than would have followed had the rules been kept.

On the whole, then, we must conclude that no philosophy of ethics is possible in the old-fashioned absolute sense of the term. Everywhere the ethical philosopher must wait on facts. The thinkers who create the ideals come he knows not whence, their sensibilities are evolved he knows not how; and the question as to which of two conflicting ideals will give the best universe then and there, can be answered by him only through the aid of the experience of other men. I said some time ago, in treating of the 'first' question, that the intuitional moralists deserve credit for keeping most clearly to the psychological facts. They do much to spoil this merit on the whole, however, by mixing with it that dogmatic temper which, by absolute distinctions and unconditional 'thou shalt nots', changes a growing, elastic and continuous life into a superstitious system of relics and dead bones. In point of fact, there are no absolute evils, and there are no non-moral goods; and the *highest* ethical life – however few may be called to bear its burdens – consists at all times in the breaking of rules which have grown too narrow for the actual case. There is but one unconditional commandment, which is that we should seek incessantly, with fear and trembling, so to vote and to act as to bring about the very largest total universe of good which we can see. Abstract rules indeed can help; but they help the less in proportion as our intuitions are more piercing, and our vocation is the stronger for the moral life. For every real dilemma is in literal strictness a unique situation; and the exact combination of ideals realized and ideals disappointed which each decision creates is always a universe without a precedent, and for which no adequate previous rule exists. The philosopher, then, *qua* philosopher, is no better able to determine the best universe in the concrete emergency than other men. He sees, indeed, somewhat better than most men what the question always is – not a question of this good or that good simply taken, but of the two total universes with which these goods respectively belong. He knows that he must vote always for the richer universe, for the good which seems most organizable, most fit to enter into complex combinations, most apt to be a member of a more inclusive whole. But which particular universe this is he cannot know for certain in advance; he only knows that if he makes a bad mistake the cries of the wounded will soon inform him of the fact. In all this the philosopher is just like the rest of us non-philosophers, so far as we are just and sympathetic instinctively, and so far as we are open to the voice of complaint. His function is in fact indistinguishable from that of the best kind of statesman at the present day. His books upon ethics, therefore, so far as they truly touch the moral life, must more and more ally themselves with a literature which is confessedly tentative and suggestive rather than dogmatic – I mean with novels and dramas of the deeper sort, with sermons, with books on statecraft and philanthropy and social and economical reform. Treated in this way ethical treatises may be voluminous and luminous as well; but they never can be *final*, except in their abstractest and vaguest feature; and they must more and more abandon the old-fashioned, clear-cut and would-be 'scientific' form.

5

The chief of all the reasons why concrete ethics cannot be final is that they have to wait on metaphysical and theological beliefs. I said some time back that real ethical relations existed in a purely human world. They would exist even in what we called a moral solitude if the thinker had various ideals which took hold of him in turn. His self of one day would make demands on his self of another; and some of the demands might be urgent and tyrannical, while others were gentle and easily put aside. We call the tyrannical demands *imperatives*. If we ignore these we do not hear the last of it. The good which we have wounded returns to plague us with interminable crops of consequential damages, compunctions and regrets. Obligation can thus exist inside a single thinker's consciousness; and perfect peace can abide with him only so far as he lives according to some sort of a casuistic scale which keeps his more imperative goods on top. It is the nature of these goods to be cruel to their rivals. Nothing shall avail when weighed in the balance against them. They call out all the mercilessness in our disposition, and do not easily forgive us if we are so soft-hearted to shrink from sacrifice in their behalf.

The deepest difference, practically, in the moral life of man is the difference between the easygoing and the strenuous mood. When in the easygoing mood the shrinking from present ill is our ruling consideration. The strenuous mood, on the contrary, makes us quite indifferent to present ill, if only the greater ideal be attained. The capacity for the strenuous mood probably lies slumbering in every man, but it has more difficulty in some than in others in waking up. It needs the wilder passions to arouse it, the big fears, loves and indignations; or else the deeply penetrating appeal of some one of the higher fidelities, like justice, truth or freedom. Strong relief is a necessity of its vision; and a world where all the mountains are brought down and all the valleys are exalted is no congenial place for its habitation. This is why in a solitary thinker this mood might slumber on forever without waking. His various ideals, known to him to be mere preferences of his own, are too nearly of the same denominational value: he can play fast or loose with them at will. This too is why, in a merely human world without a god, the appeal to our moral energy falls short of its maximal stimulating power. Life, to be sure, is even in such a world a genuinely ethical symphony; but it is played in the compass of a couple of poor octaves, and the infinite scale of values fails to open up. Many of us, indeed — like Sir James Stephen in those eloquent *Essays by a Barrister* — would openly laugh at the very idea of the strenuous mood being awakened in us by those claims of remote posterity which constitute the last appeal of the religion of humanity. We do not love these men of the future keenly enough; and we love them perhaps the less the more we hear of their evolutionized perfection, their high average longevity and education, their freedom from war and crime, their relative immunity from pain and zymotic disease, and all their other negative superiorities. This is all too finite, we say; we see too well the vacuum beyond. It lacks the note of infinitude and mystery, and may all be dealt with in the don't-care mood. No need of agonizing ourselves or making others agonize for these good creatures just at present.

When, however, we believe that a God is there, and that he is one of the claimants, the infinite perspective opens out. The scale of the symphony is incalculably prolonged. The more imperative ideals now begin to speak with an altogether new objectivity and significance, and to utter the penetrating, shattering, tragically challenging note of appeal. They ring out like the call of Victor Hugo's alpine eagle, '*qui parle au précipice et que le gouffre entend*', and the strenuous mood awakens at the sound. It saith among the trumpets, ha, ha! it smelleth the battle afar off, the thunder of the captains and the shouting. Its blood is up; and cruelty to the lesser claims, so far from being a deterrent element, does but add to the stern joy with which it leaps to answer to the greater. All through history, in the periodical conflicts of Puritanism with the don't-care temper, we see the antagonism of the strenuous and genial moods, and the contrast between the ethics of infinite and mysterious obligation from on high, and those of prudence and the satisfaction of merely finite need.

The capacity of the strenuous mood lies so deep down among our natural human possibilities that even if there were no metaphysical or traditional grounds for believing in a God, men would postulate one simply as a pretext for living hard, and getting out of the game of existence its keenest possibilities of zest. Our attitude towards concrete evils is entirely different in a world where we believe there are none but finite demanders, from what it is in one where we joyously face tragedy for an infinite demander's sake. Every sort of energy and endurance of courage and capacity for handling life's evils, is set free in those who have religious faith. For this reason the strenuous type of character will on the battlefield of human history always outwear the easy-going type, and religion will drive irreligion to the wall.

It would seem, too – and this is my final conclusion – that the stable and systematic moral universe for which the ethical philosopher asks is fully possible only in a world where there is a divine thinker with all-enveloping demands. If such a thinker existed, his way of subordinating the demands to one another would be the finally valid casuistic scale; his claims would be the most appealing; his ideal universe would be the most inclusive realizable whole. If he now exist, then actualized in his thought already must be that ethical philosophy which we seek as the pattern which our own must evermore approach.[3] In the interests of our own ideal of systematically unified moral truth, therefore, we, as would-be philosophers, must postulate a divine thinker, and pray for the victory of the religious cause. Meanwhile, exactly what the thought of the infinite thinker may be is hidden from us even were we sure of his existence; so that our postulation of him after all serves only to let loose in us the strenuous mood. But this is what it does in all men, even those who have no interest in philosophy. The ethical philosopher, therefore, whenever he ventures to say which course of action is the best, is on no essentially different level from the common man. 'See, I have set before thee this day life and good, and death and evil; therefore, choose life that thou and thy seed may live — when this challenge comes to us, it is simply our total character and personal genius that are on trial; and if we invoke any so-called philosophy, our choice and use of that also are but revelations of our personal aptitude or incapacity for moral life. From this unsparing practical ordeal no professor's lectures and no array of books can save us. The solving word, for the learned and the unlearned man alike, lies in the last resort in the dumb willingnesses and unwillingnesses of their interior characters, and nowhere else. It is not in heaven, neither is it beyond the sea; but the word is very nigh unto thee, in thy mouth and in thy heart, that thou mayest do it.

[3] All this is set forth with great freshness and force in the work of my colleague, Professor Josiah Royce, *The Religious Aspect of Philosophy*, Boston, 1885.

17

On a Certain Blindness in Human Beings

Our judgments concerning the worth of things, big or little, depend on the *feelings* the things arouse in us. Where we judge a thing to be precious in consequence of the *idea* we frame of it, this is only because the idea is itself associated already with a feeling. If we were radically feelingless, and if ideas were the only things our mind could entertain, we should lose all our likes and dislikes at a stroke, and be unable to point to any one situation or experience in life more valuable or significant than any other.

Now the blindness in human beings, of which this discourse will treat, is the blindness with which we all are afflicted in regard to the feelings of creatures and people different from ourselves.

We are practical beings, each of us with limited functions and duties to perform. Each is bound to feel intensely the importance of his own duties and the significance of the situations that call these forth. But this feeling is in each of us a vital secret, for sympathy with which we vainly look to others. The others are too much absorbed in their own vital secrets to take an interest in ours. Hence the stupidity and injustice of our opinions, so far as they deal with the significance of alien lives. Hence the falsity of our judgments, so far as they presume to decide in an absolute way on the value of other persons' conditions or ideals.

Take our dogs and ourselves, connected as we are by a tie more intimate than most ties in this world; and yet, outside of that tie of friendly fondness, how insensible, each of us, to all that makes life significant for the other — we to the rapture of bones under hedges, or smells of trees and lamp-posts, they to the delights of literature and art. As you sit reading the most moving romance you ever fell upon, what sort of a judge is your fox-terrier of your behaviour? With all his goodwill toward you, the nature of your conduct is absolutely excluded from his comprehension. To sit there like a senseless statue, when you might be taking him to walk and throwing sticks for him to catch! What queer disease is this that comes over you every day, of holding things and staring at them like that for hours together, paralysed of motion and vacant of all conscious life? The African savages came nearer the truth; but they, too, missed it, when they gathered wonderingly round one of our American travellers who, in the interior, had just come into possession of a stray copy of the New York *Commercial Advertiser*, and was devouring it column by column. When he got through, they offered him a high price for the mysterious object; and, being asked for what they wanted it, they said: 'For an eye medicine' – that being the only reason they could conceive of for the protracted bath which he had given his eyes upon its surface.

The spectator's judgment is sure to miss the root of the matter, and to possess no truth. The subject judged knows a part of the world of reality which the judging spectator fails to see, knows more while the spectator knows less; and, wherever there is conflict of opinion and difference of vision, we are bound to believe that the truer side is the side that feels the more, and not the side that feels the less.

Let me take a personal example of the kind that befalls each one of us daily:

Some years ago, while journeying in the mountains of North Carolina, I passed by a large number of 'coves', as they call them there, or heads of small valleys between the hills, which had been newly cleared and planted. The impression on my mind was one of unmitigated squalor. The settler had in every case cut down the more manageable trees, and left their charred stumps standing. The larger trees he had girdled and killed, in order that their foliage should not cast a shade. He had then built a log cabin, plastering its chinks with clay, and had set up a tall zigzag rail fence around the scene of his havoc, to keep the pigs and cattle out. Finally, he had irregularly planted the intervals between the stumps and trees with Indian corn, which grew among the chips; and there he dwelt with his wife and babes – an axe, a gun, a few utensils and some pigs and chickens feeding in the woods, being the sum total of his possessions.

The forest had been destroyed; and what had 'improved' it out of existence was hideous, a sort of ulcer, without a single element of artificial grace to make up for the loss of Nature's beauty. Ugly, indeed, seemed the life of the squatter, scudding,

as the sailors say, under bare poles, beginning again away back
where our first ancestors started, and by hardly a single item the
better off for all the achievements of the intervening generations.

Talk about going back to nature! I said to myself, oppressed
by the dreariness, as I drove by. Talk of a country life for one's
old age and for one's children! Never thus, with nothing but the
bare ground and one's bare hands to fight the battle! Never,
without the best spoils of culture woven in! The beauties and
commodities gained by the centuries are sacred. They are our
heritage and birthright. No modern person ought to be willing
to live a day in such a state of rudimentariness and denudation.

Then I said to the mountaineer who was driving me, 'What
sort of people are they who have to make these new clearings?'
'All of us', he replied. 'Why, we ain't happy here, unless we are
getting one of these coves under cultivation.' I instantly felt that
I had been losing the whole inward significance of the situation.
Because to me the clearings spoke of naught but denudation, I
thought that to those whose sturdy arms and obedient axes had
made them they could tell no other story. But, when *they* looked
on the hideous stumps, what they thought of was personal
victory. The chips, the girdled trees and the vile split rails spoke
of honest sweat, persistent toil and final reward. The cabin was
a warrant of safety for self and wife and babes. In short, the
clearing, which to me was a mere ugly picture on the retina, was
to them a symbol redolent with moral memories and sang a very
paean of duty, struggle, and success.

I had been as blind to the peculiar ideality of their conditions
as they certainly would also have been to the ideality of mine,
had they had a peep at my strange indoor academic ways of life
at Cambridge.

Wherever a process of life communicates an eagerness to him
who lives it, there the life becomes genuinely significant. Sometimes the eagerness is more knit up with the motor activities,
sometimes with the perceptions, sometimes with the imagination, sometimes with reflective thought. But, wherever it is
found, there is the zest, the tingle, the excitement of reality; and
there *is* 'importance' in the only real and positive sense in which
importance ever anywhere can be.

Robert Louis Stevenson has illustrated this by a case, drawn
from the sphere of the imagination, in an essay which I really

think deserves to become immortal, both for the truth of its matter and the excellence of its form.

Toward the end of September, when schooltime was drawing near, and the nights were already black, we would begin to sally from our respective villas, each equipped with a tin bull's-eye lantern. The thing was so well known that it had worn a rut in the commerce of Great Britain; and the grocers, about the due time, began to garnish their windows with our peculiar brand of luminary. We wore them buckled to the waist upon a cricket belt, and over them, such was the rigour of the game, a buttoned top-coat. They smelled noisomely of blistered tin. They never burned aright, though they would always burn our fingers. Their use was naught, the pleasure of them merely fanciful, and yet a boy with a bull's-eye under his top-coat asked for nothing more. The fishermen used lanterns about their boats, and it was from them, I suppose, that we had got the hint; but theirs were not bull's-eyes, nor did we ever play at being fishermen. The police carried them at their belts, and we had plainly copied them in that; yet we did not pretend to be policemen. Burglars, indeed, we may have had some haunting thought of; and we had certainly an eye to past ages when lanterns were more common, and to certain story-books in which we had found them to figure very largely. But take it for all in all, the pleasure of the thing was substantive; and to be a boy with a bull's-eye under his top-coat was good enough for us.

When two of these asses met, there would be an anxious 'Have you got your lantern?' and a gratified 'Yes!' That was the shibboleth, and very needful, too; for, as it was the rule to keep our glory contained, none could recognize a lantern-bearer unless (like the polecat) by the smell. Four or five would sometimes climb into the belly of a ten-man lugger, with nothing but the thwarts above them — for the cabin was usually locked — or choose out some hollow of the links where the wind might whistle overhead. Then the coats would be unbuttoned, and the bull's-eyes discovered; and in the chequering glimmer, under the huge, windy hall of the night, and cheered by a rich steam of toasting tinware, these fortunate young gentlemen would crouch together in the cold sand of the links, or on the scaly bilges of the fishing boat, and delight them with inappropriate talk. Woe is me that I cannot give some specimens! . . . But the talk was but a condiment, and these gatherings themselves only accidents in the career of the lantern-bearer. The essence of this bliss was to walk by yourself in the black night, the slide shut, the top-coat buttoned, not a ray escaping, whether to conduct your footsteps or to make your glory public – a mere pillar of darkness in the dark; and all the while, deep down in the privacy of your fool's heart, to know you had a bull's-eye at your belt, and to exult and sing over the knowledge.

It is said that a poet has died young in the breast of the most stolid. It may be contended rather that a (somewhat minor) bard in almost every case survives, and is the spice of life to his possessor. Justice is not done to the versatility and the unplumbed childishness of man's imagination. His life from without may seem but a rude mound of mud: there will be some golden chamber at the heart of it, in which he dwells delighted; and for as dark as his pathway seems to the observer, he will have some kind of bull's-eye at his belt.

. . . There is one fable that touches very near the quick of life – the fable of the monk who passed into the woods, heard a bird break into song, hearkened for a trill or two, and found himself at his return a stranger at his convent gates; for he had been absent fifty years, and of all his comrades there survived but one to recognize him. It is not only in the woods that this enchanter carols, though perhaps he is native there. He sings in the most doleful places. The miser hears him and chuckles, and his days are moments. With no more apparatus than an evil-smelling lantern, I have evoked him on the naked links. All life that is not merely mechanical is spun out of two strands – seeking for that bird and hearing him. And it is just this that makes life so hard to value, and the delight of each so incommunicable. And it is just a knowledge of this, and a remembrance of those fortunate hours in which the bird *has* sung to *us*, that fills us with such wonder when we turn to the pages of the realist. There, to be sure, we find a picture of life in so far as it consists of mud and of old iron, cheap desires and cheap fears, that which we are ashamed to remember and that which we are careless whether we forget; but of the note of that time-devouring nightingale we hear no news.

. . . Say that we came [in such a realistic romance] on some such business as that of my lantern-bearers on the links, and described the boys as very cold, spat upon by flurries of rain, and drearily surrounded, all of which they were; and their talk as silly and indecent, which it certainly was. To the eye of the observer they *are* wet and cold and drearily surrounded; but ask themselves, and they are in the heaven of a recondite pleasure, the ground of which is an ill-smelling lantern.

For, to repeat, the ground of a man's joy is often hard to hit. It may hinge at times upon a mere accessory, like the lantern; it may reside in the mysterious inwards of psychology . . . It has so little bond with externals . . . that it may even touch them not, and the man's true life, for which he consents to live, lie together in the field of fancy ... In such a case the poetry runs underground. The observer (poor soul, with his documents!) is all abroad. For to look at the man is but to court deception. We shall see the trunk from which he draws his nourishment; but he himself is above and abroad in the green dome of foliage, hummed through by winds and nested in by nightingales. And the true realism were that of the poets, to climb after him like a squirrel, and catch some glimpse of the heaven in which he lives. And the true realism, always and everywhere, is that of the poets: to find out where joy resides, and give it a voice far beyond singing.

For to miss the joy is to miss all. In the joy of the actors lies the sense of any action. That is the explanation, that the excuse. To one who has not the secret of the lanterns the scene upon the links is meaningless. And hence the haunting and truly spectral unreality of realistic books ... In each we miss the personal poetry, the enchanted atmosphere, that rainbow work of fancy that clothes what is naked and seems to ennoble what is base; in each, life falls dead like dough, instead of soaring away like a balloon into the colours of the sunset; each is true, each inconceivable; for no man lives in the external truth among salts and acids, but in the warm, phantasmagoric chamber of his brain, with the painted windows and the storied wall.[1]

These paragraphs are the best thing I know in all Stevenson. 'To miss the joy is to miss all.' Indeed, it is. Yet we are but finite, and each one of us has some single specialized vocation of his own. And it seems as if energy in the service of its particular duties might be got only by hardening the heart toward everything unlike them. Our deadness toward all but one particular kind of joy would thus be the price we inevitably have to pay for being practical creatures. Only in some pitiful dreamer, some philosopher, poet or romancer, or when the common practical man becomes a lover, does the hard externality give way, and a gleam of insight into the ejective world, as Clifford called it, the vast world of inner life beyond us, so different from that of outer seeming, illuminate our mind. Then the whole scheme of our customary values gets confounded, then our self is riven and its narrow interests fly to pieces, then a new centre and a new perspective must be found.

The change is well described by my colleague, Josiah Royce:

[1] 'The Lantern-bearers', in the volume entitled *Across the Plains*. Abridged in the quotation.

What, then, is our neighbour? Thou hast regarded his thought, his feeling, as somehow different from thine. Thou hast said, 'A pain in him is not like a pain in me, but something far easier to bear.' He seems to thee a little less living than thou; his life is dim, it is cold, it is a pale fire beside thy own burning desires . . . So, dimly and by instinct hast thou lived with thy neighbour, and hast known him not, being blind. Thou hast made [of him] a thing, no Self at all. Have done with this illusion, and simply try to learn the truth. Pain is pain, joy is joy, everywhere, even as in thee. In all the songs of the forest birds; in all the cries of the wounded and dying, struggling in the captor's power; in the boundless sea where the myriads of water-creatures strive and die; amid all the countless hordes of savage men; in all sickness and sorrow; in all exultation and hope, everywhere, from the lowest to the noblest, the same conscious, burning, wilful life is found, endlessly manifold as the forms of the living creatures, unquenchable as the fires of the sun, real as these impulses that even now throb in thine own little selfish heart. Lift up thy eyes, behold that life, and then turn away, and forget it as thou canst; but, if thou hast *known* that, thou hast begun to know thy duty.[2]

This higher vision of an inner significance in what, until then, we had realized only in the dead external way, often comes over a person suddenly; and, when it does so, it makes an epoch in his history. As Emerson says, there is a depth in those moments that constrains us to ascribe more reality to them than to all other experiences. The passion of love will shake one like an explosion, or some act will awaken a remorseful compunction that hangs like a cloud over all one's later day.

This mystic sense of hidden meaning starts upon us often from non-human natural things. I take this passage from *Obermann*, a French novel that had some vogue in its day:

Paris, March 7 – It was dark and rather cold. I was gloomy, and walked because I had nothing to do. I passed by some flowers placed breast-high upon a wall. A jonquil in bloom was there. It is the strongest expression of desire: it was the first perfume of the year. I felt all the happiness destined for man. This unutterable harmony of souls, the phantom of the ideal world, arose in me complete. I never felt anything so great or so instantaneous. I know not what shape, what analogy, what secret of relation it

---

[2] *The Religious Aspect of Philosophy*, pp. 157–62 (abridged).

was that made me see in this flower a limitless beauty ... I shall never enclose in a conception this power, this immensity that nothing will express; this form that nothing will contain; this ideal of a better world which one feels, but which it would seem that nature has not made.[3]

Wordsworth and Shelley are similarly full of this sense of a limitless significance in natural things. In Wordsworth it was a somewhat austere and moral significance – a 'lonely cheer'.

> To every natural form, rock, fruit, or flower,
> Even the loose stones that cover the highway,
> I gave a moral life: I saw them feel
> Or linked them to some feeling: the great mass
> Lay bedded in some quickening soul, and all
> That I beheld respired with inward meaning.[4]

'Authentic tidings of invisible things!' Just what this hidden presence in nature was, which Wordsworth so rapturously felt, and in the light of which he lived, tramping the hills for days together, the poet never could explain logically or in articulate conceptions. Yet to the reader who may himself have had gleaming moments of a similar sort the verses in which Wordsworth simply proclaims the fact of them come with a heart-satisfying authority:

> Magnificent
> The morning rose, in memorable pomp,
> Glorious as ere I had beheld. In front
> The sea lay laughing at a distance; near
> The solid mountains shone, bright as the clouds,
> Grain-tinctured, drenched in empyrean light;
> And in the meadows and the lower grounds
> Was all the sweetness of a common dawn –
> Dews, vapours, and the melody of birds,
> And labourers going forth to till the fields.
>
> Ah! need I say, dear Friend, that to the brim
> My heart was full; I made no vows, but vows
> Were then made for me; bond unknown to me
> Was given, that I should be, else sinning greatly,
> A dedicated Spirit. On I walked,
> In thankful blessedness, which yet survives.[5]

[3] De Sénancour, *Obermann*, Letter 30.
[4] *The Prelude*, Book 3.
[5] *The Prelude*, Book 4.

As Wordsworth walked, filled with his strange inner joy, responsive thus to the secret life of nature round about him, his rural neighbours, tightly and narrowly intent upon their own affairs, their crops and lambs and fences, must have thought him a very insignificant and foolish personage. It surely never occurred to any one of them to wonder what was going on inside of *him* or what it might be worth. And yet that inner life of his carried the burden of a significance that has fed the souls of others, and fills them to this day with inner joy.

Richard Jefferies has written a remarkable autobiographic document entitled *The Story of my Heart*. It tells, in many pages, of the rapture with which in youth the sense of the life of nature filled him. On a certain hill-top he says:

> I was utterly alone with the sun and the earth. Lying down on the grass, I spoke in my soul to the earth, the sun, the air, and the distant sea, far beyond sight ... With all the intensity of feeling which exalted me, all the intense communion I held with the earth, the sun and sky, the stars hidden by the light, with the ocean – in no manner can the thrilling depth of these feelings be written – with these I prayed as if they were the keys of an instrument ... The great sun, burning with light, the strong earth – dear earth – the warm sky, the pure air, the thought of ocean, the inexpressible beauty of all filled me with a rapture, an ecstasy, an inflatus. With this inflatus, too, I prayed ... The prayer, this soul-emotion, was in itself, not for an object: it was a passion. I hid my face in the grass. I was wholly prostrated, I lost myself in the wrestle, I was rapt and carried away ... Had any shepherd accidentally seen me lying on the turf, he would only have thought I was resting a few minutes. I made no outward show. Who could have imagined the whirlwind of passion that was going on in me as I reclined there![6]

Surely, a worthless hour of life, when measured by the usual standards of commercial value. Yet in what other *kind* of value can the preciousness of any hour, made precious by any standard, consist, if it consist not in feelings of excited significance like these, engendered in someone, by what the hour contains?

Yet so blind and dead does the clamour of our own practical interests make us to all other things, that it seems almost as if it were necessary to become worthless as a practical being, if one

[6] Op. cit., Boston, Roberts, 1883, pp. 5 and 6.

is to hope to attain to any breadth of insight into the impersonal world of worths as such, to have any perception of life's meaning on a large objective scale. Only your mystic, your dreamer, or your insolvent tramp or loafer, can afford so sympathetic an occupation, an occupation which will change the usual standards of human value in the twinkling of an eye, giving to foolishness a place ahead of power, and laying low in a minute the distinctions which it takes a hard-working conventional man a lifetime to build up. You may be a prophet, at this rate; but you cannot be a worldly success.

Walt Whitman, for instance, is accounted by many of us a contemporary prophet. He abolishes the usual human distinctions, brings all conventionalisms into solution, and loves and celebrates hardly any human attributes save those elementary ones common to all members of the race. For this he becomes a sort of ideal tramp, a rider on omnibus-tops and ferry-boats, and, considered either practically or academically, a worthless, unproductive being. His verses are but ejaculations – things mostly without subject or verb, a succession of interjections on an immense scale. He felt the human crowd as rapturously as Wordsworth felt the mountains, felt it as an overpoweringly significant presence, simply to absorb one's mind in which should be business sufficient and worthy to fill the days of a serious man. As he crosses Brooklyn ferry, this is what he feels:

Flood-tide below me! I watch you, face to face;
Clouds of the west! sun there half an hour high! I see you also face
    to face.
Crowds of men and women attired in the usual costumes! how
    curious you are to me!
On the ferry-boats, the hundreds and hundreds that cross, returning
    home, are more curious to me than you suppose;
And you that shall cross from shore to shore years hence, are more
    to me, and more in my meditations, than you might suppose.
Others will enter the gates of the ferry, and cross from shore to shore;
    Others will watch the run of the flood-tide;
Others will see the shipping of Manhattan north and west, and the
    heights of Brooklyn to the south and east;
Others will see the islands large and small;
Fifty years hence, others will see them as they cross, the sun half an
    hour high.
A hundred years hence, or ever so many hundred years hence, others
    will see them.

Will enjoy the sunset, the pouring in of the flood-tide, the falling
　　back to the sea of the ebb-tide.
It avails not, neither time or place – distance avails not.
Just as you feel when you look on the river and sky, so I felt;
Just as any of you is one of a living crowd, I was one of a crowd;
Just as you are refresh'd by the gladness of the river and the bright
　　flow, I was refresh'd;
Just as you stand and lean on the rail, yet hurry with the swift
　　current, I stood, yet was hurried;
Just as you look on the numberless masts of ships, and the thick-
　　stemmed pipes of steamboats, I looked.
I too many and many a time cross'd the river, the sun half an hour
　　high;
I watched the Twelfth-month sea-gulls – I saw them high in the air,
　　with motionless wings, oscillating their bodies,
I saw how the glistening yellow lit up parts of their bodies, and left
　　the rest in strong shadow,
I saw the slow-wheeling circles, and the gradual edging toward the
　　south.
Saw the white sails of schooners and sloops, saw the ships at anchor,
The sailors at work in the rigging, or out astride the spars;
The scallop-edged waves in the twilight, the ladled cups, the
　　frolicsome crests and glistening;
The stretch afar growing dimmer and dimmer, the grey walls of the
　　granite store-houses by the docks;
On the neighbouring shores, the fires from the foundry chimneys
　　burning high . . . into the night,
Casting their flicker of black . . . into the clefts of streets.
These, and all else, were to me the same as they are to you.[7]

And so on, through the rest of a divinely beautiful poem. And,
if you wish to see what this hoary loafer considered the most
worthy way of profiting by life's heaven-sent opportunities, read
the delicious volume of his letters to a young car-conductor who
had become his friend:

New York
Oct. 9, 1868

DEAR PETE,
　It is splendid here this forenoon – bright and cool. I was out early
taking a short walk by the river only two squares from where I
live . . . Shall I tell you about [my life] just to fill up? I generally
spend the forenoon in my room writing, etc., then take a bath, fix

[7] *Crossing Brooklyn Ferry* (abridged).

up and go out about twelve and loaf somewhere or call on someone down town or on business, or perhaps if it is very pleasant and I feel like it ride a trip with some driver friend on Broadway from 23rd Street to Bowling Green, three miles each way. (Every day I find I have plenty to do, every hour is occupied with something.) You know it is a never ending amusement and study and recreation to me to ride a couple of hours on a pleasant afternoon on a Broadway stage in this way. You see everything as you pass, a sort of living, endless panorama – shops and splendid buildings and great windows: on the broad sidewalks crowds of women richly dressed continually passing, altogether different, superior in style and looks from any to be seen anywhere else – in fact a perfect stream of people – men too dressed in high style, and plenty of foreigners – and then in the streets the thick crowd of carriages, stages, carts, hotel and private coaches, and in fact all sorts of vehicles and many first class teams, mile after mile, and the splendour of such a great street and so many tall, ornamental, noble buildings many of them of white marble, and the gaiety and motion on every side: you will not wonder how much attraction all this is on a fine day, to a great loafer like me, who enjoys so much seeing the busy world move by him, and exhibiting itself for his amusement, while he takes it easy and just looks on and observes.[8]

Truly a futile way of passing the time, some of you may say, and not altogether creditable to a grown-up man. And yet, from the deepest point of view, who knows the more of truth, and who knows the less – Whitman on his omnibus-top, full of the inner joy with which the spectacle inspires him, or you, full of the disdain which the futility of his occupation excites?

When your ordinary Brooklynite or New Yorker, leading a life replete with too much luxury, or tired and careworn about his personal affairs, crosses the ferry or goes up Broadway, *his* fancy does not thus 'soar away into the colours of the sunset' as did Whitman's, nor does he inwardly realize at all the indisputable fact that this world never did anywhere or at any time contain more of essential divinity, or of eternal meaning, than is embodied in the fields of vision over which his eyes so carelessly pass. There is life; and there, a step away, is death. There is the only kind of beauty there ever was. There is the old human struggle and its fruits together. There is the text and the sermon, the real and the ideal in one. But to the jaded and unquickened

[8] *Calamus*, Boston, 1897, pp. 41–2.

eye it is all dead and common, pure vulgarism, flatness and disgust. 'Heck! it is a sad sight!' says Carlyle, walking at night with someone who appeals to him to note the splendour of the stars. And that very repetition of the scene to new generations of men *in secula seculorum*, that eternal recurrence of the common order, which so fills a Whitman with mystic satisfaction, is to a Schopenhauer, with the emotional anaesthesia, the feeling of 'awful inner emptiness' from out of which he views it all, the chief ingredient of the tedium it instils. What is life on the largest scale, he asks, but the same recurrent inanities, the same dog barking, the same fly buzzing, forevermore? Yet of the kind of fibre of which such inanities consist is the material woven of all the excitements, joys and meanings that ever were, or ever shall be, in this world.

To be rapt with satisfied attention, like Whitman, to the mere spectacle of the world's presence, is one way, and the most fundamental way, of confessing one's sense of its unfathomable significance and importance. But how can one attain to the feeling of the vital significance of an experience, if one have it not to begin with? There is no receipt which one can follow. Being a secret and a mystery, it often comes in mysteriously unexpected ways. It blossoms sometimes from out of the very grave wherein we imagined that our happiness was buried. Benvenuto Cellini, after a life in the outer sunshine, made of adventures and artistic excitements, suddenly finds himself cast into a dungeon in the Castle of San Angelo. The place is horrible. Rats and wet and mould possess it. His leg is broken and his teeth fall out, apparently with scurvy. But his thoughts turn to God as they have never turned before. He gets a Bible, which he reads during the one hour in the twenty-four in which a wandering ray of daylight penetrates his cavern. He has religious visions. He sings psalms to himself, and composes hymns. And thinking, on the last day of July, of the festivities customary on the morrow in Rome, he says to himself:

All these past years I celebrated this holiday with the vanities of the world: from this year henceforward I will do it with the divinity of God. And then I said to myself, 'Oh, how much more happy I am for this present life of mine than for all those things remembered!'[9]

[9] *Vita, lib.* 2, ch. 4.

But the great understander of these mysterious ebbs and flows is Tolstoy. They throb all through his novels. In his *War and Peace*, the hero, Peter, is supposed to be the richest man in the Russian empire. During the French invasion he is taken prisoner, and dragged through much of the retreat. Cold, vermin, hunger and every form of misery assail him, the result being a revelation to him of the real scale of life's values.

Here only, and for the first time, he appreciated, because he was deprived of it, the happiness of eating when he was hungry, of drinking when he was thirsty, of sleeping when he was sleepy, and of talking when he felt the desire to exchange some words ... Later in life he always recurred with joy to this month of captivity, and never failed to speak with enthusiasm of the powerful and ineffaceable sensations, and especially of the moral calm which he had experienced at this epoch. When at daybreak, on the morrow of his imprisonment, he saw [I abridge here Tolstoy's description] the mountains with their wooded slopes disappearing in the greyish mist; when he felt the cool breeze caress him; when he saw the light drive away the vapours, and the sun rise majestically behind the clouds and cupolas, and the crosses, the dew, the distance, the river, sparkle in the splendid, cheerful rays – his heart overflowed with emotion. This emotion kept continually with him, and increased a hundredfold as the difficulties of his situation grew graver ... He learnt that man is meant for happiness, and that this happiness is in him, in the satisfaction of the daily needs of existence, and that unhappiness is the fatal result, not of our need, but of our abundance ... When calm reigned in the camp, and the embers paled, and little by little went out, the full moon had reached the zenith. The woods and the fields roundabout lay clearly visible; and, beyond the inundation of light which filled them, the view plunged into the limitless horizon. Then Peter cast his eyes upon the firmament, filled at that hour with myriads of stars. 'All that is mine', he thought. 'All that is in me, is me! And that is what they think they have taken prisoner! That is what they have shut up in a cabin!' So he smiled, and turned in to sleep among his comrades.[10]

The occasion and the experience, then, are nothing. It all depends on the capacity of the soul to be grasped, to have its life-currents absorbed by what is given. 'Crossing a bare common', says Emerson, 'in snow puddles, at twilight, under a clouded sky, without having in my thoughts any occurrence of

[10] *La Guerre et la Paix*, vol. 3, Paris, 1884, pp. 268, 275 and 316.

special good fortune, I have enjoyed a perfect exhilaration. I am glad to the brink of fear.'

Life is always worth living, if one have such responsive sensibilities. But we of the highly educated classes (so called) have most of us got far, far away from Nature. We are trained to seek the choice, the rare, the exquisite exclusively, and to overlook the common. We are stuffed with abstract conceptions, and glib with verbalities, and verbosities; and in the culture of these higher functions the peculiar sources of joy connected with our simpler functions often dry up, and we grow stone-blind and insensible to life's more elementary and general goods and joys.

The remedy under such conditions is to descend to a more profound and primitive level. To be imprisoned or shipwrecked or forced into the army would permanently show the good of life to many an over-educated pessimist. Living in the open air and on the ground, the lop-sided beam of the balance slowly rises to the level line; and the over-sensibilities and insensibilities even themselves out. The good of all the artificial schemes and fevers fades and pales; and that of seeing, smelling, tasting, sleeping, and daring and doing with one's body, grows and grows. The savages and children of nature, to whom we deem ourselves so much superior, certainly are alive where we are often dead, along these lines; and, could they write as glibly as we do, they would read us impressive lectures on our impatience for improvement and on our blindness to the fundamental static goods of life. 'Ah! my brother,' said a chieftain to his white guest,

> thou wilt never know the happiness of both thinking of nothing and doing nothing. This, next to sleep, is the most enchanting of all things. Thus we were before our birth, and thus we shall be after death. Thy people, . . . when they have finished reaping one field, they begin to plough another; and, if the day were not enough, I have seen them plough by moonlight. What is their life to ours – the life that is as naught to them? Blind that they are, they lose it all! But we live in the present.[11]

The intense interest that life can assume when brought down to the non-thinking level, the level of pure sensorial perception, has been beautifully described by a man who *can* write – Mr W. H. Hudson, in his volume, *Idle Days in Patagonia*,

[11] Quoted by Lotze, *Microcosmus*, English translation, vol. II, p. 240.

I spent the greater part of one winter at a point on the Rio Negro, seventy or eighty miles from the sea.

... It was my custom to go out every morning on horseback with my gun, and, followed by one dog, to ride away from the valley; and no sooner would I climb the terrace, and plunge into the grey, universal thicket, than I would find myself as completely alone as if five hundred instead of only five miles separated me from the valley and river. So wild and solitary and remote seemed that grey waste, stretching away into infinitude, a waste untrodden by man, and where the wild animals are so few that they have made no discoverable path in the wilderness of thorns ... Not once nor twice nor thrice, but day after day I returned to this solitude, going to it in the morning as if to attend a festival, and leaving it only when hunger and thirst and the westering sun compelled me. And yet I had no object in going – no motive which could be put into words; for, although I carried a gun, there was nothing to shoot – the shooting was all left behind in the valley ... Sometimes I would pass a whole day without seeing one mammal, and perhaps not more than a dozen birds of any size. The weather at that time was cheerless, generally with a grey film of cloud spread over the sky, and a bleak wind, often cold enough to make my bridle-hand quite numb ... At a slow pace, which would have seemed intolerable under other circumstances, I would ride about for hours together at a stretch. On arriving at a hill, I would slowly ride to its summit, and stand there to survey the prospect. On every side it stretched away in great undulations, wild and irregular. How grey it all was! Hardly less so near at hand than on the haze-wrapped horizon where the hills were dim and the outline obscured by distance. Descending from my out-look, I would take up my aimless wanderings again, and visit other elevations to gaze on the same landscape from another point; and so on for hours. And at noon I would dismount, and sit or lie on my folded poncho for an hour or longer. One day in these rambles I discovered a small grove composed of twenty or thirty trees, growing at a convenient distance apart, that had evidently been resorted to by a herd of deer or other wild animals. This grove was on a hill differing in shape from other hills in its neighbourhood; and, after a time, I made a point of finding and using it as a resting-place every day at noon. I did not ask myself why I made choice of that one spot, sometimes going out of my way to sit there, instead of sitting down under any one of the millions of trees and bushes on any other hillside. I thought nothing about it, but acted unconsciously. Only afterward it seemed to me that, after having rested there once, each time I wished to rest again, the wish came associated with the image of that particular clump of trees, with polished stems and clean bed of sand beneath; and in a short time I formed a habit of returning, animal like, to repose at that same spot.

It was, perhaps, a mistake to say that I would sit down and rest, since I was never tired; and yet, without being tired, that noon-day pause, during which I sat for an hour without moving, was strangely grateful. All day there would be no sound, not even the rustling of a leaf. One day, while *listening* to the silence, it occurred to my mind to wonder what the effect would be if I were to shout aloud. This seemed at the time a horrible suggestion, which almost made me shudder. But during those solitary days it was a rare thing for any thought to cross my mind. In the state of mind I was in, thought had become impossible. My state was one of *suspense* and *watchfulness*; yet I had no expectation of meeting an adventure, and felt as free from apprehension as I feel now while sitting in a room in London. The state seemed familiar rather than strange, and accompanied by a strong feeling of elation; and I did not know that something had come between me and my intellect until I returned to my former self – to thinking, and the old insipid existence [again].

I had undoubtedly *gone back*; and that state of intense watch-fulness or alertness, rather, with suspension of the higher intellec-tual faculties, represented the mental state of the pure savage. He thinks little, reasons little, having a surer guide in his [mere sensory perceptions]. He is in perfect harmony with nature, and is nearly on a level, mentally, with the wild animals he preys on, and which in their turn sometimes prey on him.[12]

For the spectator, such hours as Mr Hudson writes of form a mere tale of emptiness, in which nothing happens, nothing is gained, and there is nothing to describe. They are meaningless and vacant tracts of time. To him who feels their inner secret, they tingle with an importance that unutterably vouches for itself. I am sorry for the boy or girl, or man or woman, who has never been touched by the spell of this mysterious sensorial life, with its irrationality, if so you like to call it, but its vigilance and its supreme felicity. The holidays of life are its most vitally significant portions, because they are, or at least should be, covered with just this kind of magically irresponsible spell.

And now what is the result of all these considerations and quotations? It is negative in one sense, but positive in another.

[12] Op. cit., pp. 210–22 (abridged).

It absolutely forbids us to be forward in pronouncing on the meaninglessness of forms of existence other than our own; and it commands us to tolerate, respect and indulge those whom we see harmlessly interested and happy in their own ways, however unintelligible these may be to us. Hands off: neither the whole of truth nor the whole of good is revealed to any single observer, although each observer gains a partial superiority of insight from the peculiar position in which he stands. Even prisons and sick-rooms have their special revelations. It is enough to ask of each of us that he should be faithful to his own opportunities and make the most of his own blessings, without presuming to regulate the rest of the vast field.

PHILOSOPHY OF RELIGION

18

Lecture 20
Conclusions

The material of our study of human nature is now spread before us; and in this parting hour, set free from the duty of description, we can draw our theoretical and practical conclusions. In my first lecture, defending the empirical method, I foretold that whatever conclusions we might come to could be reached by spiritual judgments only, appreciations of the significance for life of religion, taken 'on the whole'. Our conclusions cannot be as sharp as dogmatic conclusions would be, but I will formulate them, when the time comes, as sharply as I can.

Summing up in the broadest possible way the characteristics of the religious life, as we have found them, it includes the following beliefs:

1 That the visible world is part of a more spiritual universe from which it draws its chief significance;
2 That union or harmonious relation with that higher universe is our true end;
3 That prayer or inner communion with the spirit thereof – be that spirit 'God' or 'law' – is a process wherein work is really done, and spiritual energy flows in and produces effects, psychological or material, within the phenomenal world.

Religion includes also the following psychological characteristics:

4 A new zest which adds itself like a gift to life, and takes the form either of lyrical enchantment or of appeal to earnestness and heroism.
5 An assurance of safety and a temper of peace, and, in relation to others, a preponderance of loving affections.

In illustrating these characteristics by documents, we have been literally bathed in sentiment. In re-reading my manuscript, I am almost appalled at the amount of emotionality which I find in it. After so much of this, we can afford to be dryer and less sympathetic in the rest of the work that lies before us.

The sentimentality of many of my documents is a consequence of the fact that I sought them among the extravagances of the subject. If any of you are enemies of what our ancestors used to brand as enthusiasm, and are, nevertheless, still listening to me now, you have probably felt my selection to have been sometimes almost perverse, and have wished I might have stuck to soberer examples. I reply that I took these extremer examples as yielding the profounder information. To learn the secrets of any science we go to expert specialists, even though they may be eccentric persons, and not to commonplace pupils. We combine what they tell us with the rest of our wisdom, and form our final judgment independently. Even so with religion. We who have pursued such radical expressions of it may now be sure that we know its secrets as authentically as anyone can know them who learns them from another; and we have next to answer, each of us for himself, the practical question: what are the dangers in this element of life? and in what proportion may it need to be restrained by other elements, to give the proper balance?

But this question suggests another one which I will answer immediately and get it out of the way, for it has more than once already vexed us. Ought it to be assumed that in all men the mixture of religion with other elements should be identical? Ought it, indeed, to be assumed that the lives of all men should show identical religious elements? In other words, is the existence of so many religious types and sects and creeds regrettable?

To these questions I answer 'No' emphatically. And my reason is that I do not see how it is possible that creatures in such different positions and with such different powers as human individuals are, should have exactly the same functions and the same duties. No two of us have identical difficulties, nor should we be expected to work out identical solutions. Each, from his peculiar angle of observation, takes in a certain sphere of fact and trouble, which each must deal with in a unique manner. One of us must soften himself, another must harden himself; one must yield a point, another must stand firm – in order the better to defend the position assigned him. If an Emerson were forced to be a Wesley, or a Moody forced to be a Whitman, the total human consciousness of the divine would suffer. The divine can mean no single quality, it must mean a group of qualities, by being champions of which in alternation, different men may all find worthy missions. Each attitude being a syllable in human nature's total message, it takes the whole of us to spell the meaning out completely. So a 'god of battles' must be allowed to be the god for one kind of person, a god of peace and heaven and home the god for another. We must frankly recognize the fact that we live in partial systems, and that parts are not interchangeable in the spiritual life. If we are peevish and jealous, destruction of the self must be an element of our religion; why need it be one if we are good and sympathetic from the outset? If we are sick souls, we require a religion of deliverance; but why think so much of deliverance if we are healthy minded? Unquestionably, some men have the completer experience and the higher vocation, here just as in the social world; but for each man to stay in his own experience, whate'er it be, and for others to tolerate him there, is surely best.

But, you may now ask, would not this one-sidedness be cured if we should all espouse the science of religions as our own religion? In answering this question I must open again the general relations of the theoretic to the active life.

Knowledge about a thing is not the thing itself. You remember what Al-Ghazzali told us in the 'Lecture on Mysticism' – that to understand the causes of drunkenness, as a physician understands them, is not to be drunk. A science might come to understand everything about the causes and elements of religion, and might even decide which elements were qualified, by their general harmony with other branches of knowledge, to be considered true; and yet the best man at this science might be the man who found it hardest to be personally devout. *Tout savoir c'est tout pardonner*. The name of Renan would doubtless occur to many persons as an example of the way in which breadth of knowledge may make one only a dilettante in possibilities, and blunt the acuteness of one's living faith. If religion be a function by which either God's cause or man's cause is to be really advanced, then he who lives the life of it, however narrowly, is a better servant than he who merely knows about it, however much. Knowledge about life is one thing; effective occupation of a place in life, with its dynamic currents passing through your being, is another.

For this reason, the science of religions may not be an

equivalent for living religion; and if we turn to the inner difficulties of such a science, we see that a point comes when she must drop the purely theoretic attitude, and either let her knots remain uncut or have them cut by active faith. To see this, suppose that we have our science of religions constituted as a matter of fact. Suppose that she has assimilated all the necessary historical material and distilled out of it as its essence the same conclusions which I myself a few moments ago pronounced. Suppose that she agrees that religion, wherever it is an active thing, involves a belief in ideal presences, and a belief that in our prayerful communion with them, work is done, and something real comes to pass. She has now to exert her critical activity, and to decide how far, in the light of other sciences and in that of general philosophy, such beliefs can be considered *true*.

Dogmatically to decide this is an impossible task. Not only are the other sciences and the philosophy still far from being completed, but in their present state we find them full of conflicts. The sciences of nature know nothing of spiritual presences, and on the whole hold no practical commerce whatever with the idealistic conceptions towards which general philosophy inclines. The so-called scientist is, during his scientific hours at least, so materialistic that one may well say that on the whole the influence of science goes against the notion that religion should be recognized at all. And this antipathy to religion finds an echo within the very science of religions itself. The cultivator of this science has to become acquainted with so many grovelling and horrible superstitions that a presumption easily arises in his mind that any belief that is religious probably is false. In the 'prayful communion' of savages with such mumbo-jumbos of deities as they acknowledge, it is hard for us to see what genuine spiritual work – even though it were work relative only to their dark savage obligations – can possibly be done.

The consequence is that the conclusions of the science of religions are as likely to be adverse as they are to be favourable to the claim that the essence of religion is true. There is a notion in the air about us that religion is probably only an anachronism, a case of 'survival', an atavistic relapse into a mode of thought which humanity in its more enlightened examples has outgrown;

and this notion our religious anthropologists at present do little to counteract.

This view is so widespread at the present day that I must consider it with some explicitness before I pass to my own conclusions. Let me call it the 'survival theory' for brevity's sake.

The pivot round which the religious life, as we have traced it, revolves, is the interest of the individual in his private personal destiny. Religion, in short, is a monumental chapter in the history of human egotism. The gods believed in – whether by crude savages or by men disciplined intellectually – agree with each other in recognizing personal calls. Religious thought is carried on in terms of personality, this being, in the world of religion, the one fundamental fact. Today, quite as much as at any previous age, the religious individual tells you that the divine meets him on the basis of his personal concerns.

Science, on the other hand, has ended by utterly repudiating the personal point of view. She catalogues her elements and records her laws, indifferent as to what purpose may be shown forth by them, and constructs her theories quite careless of their bearing on human anxieties and fates. Though the scientist may individually nourish a religion and be a theist in his irresponsible hours, the days are over when it could be said that for Science herself the heavens declare the glory of God and the firmament showeth his handiwork. Our solar system, with its harmonies, is seen now as but one passing case of a certain sort of moving equilibrium in the heavens, realized by a local accident in an appalling wilderness of worlds where no life can exist. In a span of time which as a cosmic interval will count but as an hour it will have ceased to be. The Darwinian notion of chance production, and subsequent destruction, speedy or deferred, applies to the largest as well as to the smallest facts. It is impossible, in the present temper of the scientific imagination, to find in the driftings of the cosmic atoms, whether they work on the universal or on the particular scale, anything but a kind of aimless weather, doing and undoing, achieving no proper history, and leaving no result. Nature has no one distinguishable ultimate tendency with which it is possible to feel a sympathy. In the vast rhythm of her processes, as the scientific mind now follows them, she appears to cancel herself. The books of natural theology which satisfied the intellects of our grandfathers seem to us quite grotesque, representing, as they did, a God who conformed the largest things of nature to the paltriest of our private wants. The god whom science recognizes must be a god of universal laws exclusively, a god who does a wholesale, not a retail business. He cannot accommodate his processes to the convenience of individuals. The bubbles on the foam which coats a stormy sea are floating episodes, made and unmade by the forces of the wind and water. Our private selves are like those bubbles – epiphenomena, as Clifford, I believe, ingeniously called them; their destinies weigh nothing and determine nothing in the world's irremediable currents of events.

You see how natural it is, from this point of view, to treat religion as a mere survival, for religion does in fact perpetuate the traditions of the most primeval thought. To coerce the spiritual powers, or to square them and get them on our side, was, during enormous tracts of time, the one great object in our dealings with the natural world. For our ancestors, dreams, hallucinations, revelations, and cock-and-bull stories were inextricably mixed with facts. Up to a comparatively recent date such distinctions as those between what has been verified and what is only conjectured, between the impersonal and the personal aspects of existence, were hardly suspected or conceived. Whatever you imagined in a lively manner, whatever you thought fit to be true, you affirmed confidently; and whatever you affirmed, your comrades believed. Truth was what had not yet been contradicted, most things were taken into the mind from the point of view of their human suggestiveness, and the attention confined itself exclusively to the aesthetic and dramatic aspects of events.

How indeed could it be otherwise? The extraordinary value, for explanation and prevision, of those mathematical and mechanical modes of conception which science uses, was a result that could not possibly have been expected in advance. Weight, movement, velocity, direction, position, what thin, pallid, uninteresting ideas! How could the richer animistic aspects of Nature, the peculiarities and oddities that make phenomena picturesquely striking or expressive, fail to have been first singled out and followed by philosophy as the more promising avenue to the knowledge of Nature's life? Well, it is still in these richer animistic and dramatic aspects that religion delights to dwell. It is the terror and beauty of phenomena, the 'promise' of the dawn and of the rainbow, the 'voice' of the thunder, the 'gentleness' of the summer rain, the 'sublimity' of the stars, and not the physical laws which these things follow, by which the religious mind still continues to be most impressed; and just as of yore, the devout man tells you that in the solitude of his room or of the fields he still feels the divine presence, that inflowings of help come in reply to his prayers, and that sacrifices to this unseen reality fill him with security and peace.

Pure anachronism! says the survival theory – anachronism for which deanthropomorphization of the imagination is the remedy required. The less we mix the private with the cosmic, the more we dwell in universal and impersonal terms, the truer heirs of science we become.

In spite of the appeal which this impersonality of the scientific attitude makes to a certain magnanimity of temper, I believe it to be shallow, and I can now state my reason in comparatively few words. That reason is that, so long as we deal with the cosmic and the general, we deal only with the symbols of reality, but *as soon as we deal with private and personal phenomena as such, we deal with realities in the completest sense of the term.* I think I can easily make clear what I mean by these words.

The world of our experience consists at all times of two parts, an objective and a subjective part, of which the former may be incalculably more extensive than the latter, and yet the latter can never be omitted or suppressed. The objective part is the sum total of whatsoever at any given time we may be thinking of, the subjective part is the inner 'state' in which the thinking comes to pass. What we think of may be enormous – the cosmic times and spaces, for example – whereas the inner state may be the most fugitive and paltry activity of mind. Yet the cosmic objects, so far as the experience yields them, are but ideal pictures of something whose existence we do not inwardly possess but only point at outwardly, while the inner state is our very experience itself; its reality and that of our experience are one. A conscious field *plus* its object as felt or thought of *plus* an attitude towards the object *plus* the sense of a self to whom the attitude belongs – such a concrete bit of personal experience may be a small bit, but it is a solid bit as long as it lasts; not hollow, not a mere abstract element of experience, such as the 'object' is when taken all alone. It is a *full* fact, even though it be an insignificant fact; it is of the *kind* to which all realities whatsoever must belong; the motor currents of the world run through the like of it; it is on the line connecting real events with real events. That unsharable feeling which each one of us has of the pinch of his individual destiny as he privately feels it rolling out on fortune's wheel may be disparaged for its egotism, may be sneered at as unscientific, but it is the one thing that fills up the measure of our concrete actuality, and any would-be existent that should lack such a feeling, or its analogue, would be a piece of reality only half made up.

If this be true, it is absurd for science to say that the egotistic elements of experience should be suppressed. The axis of reality runs solely through the egotistic places – they are strung upon it like so many beads. To describe the world with all the various feelings of the individual pinch of destiny, all the various spiritual attitudes, left out from the description – they being as describable as anything else – would be something like offering a printed bill of fare as the equivalent for a solid meal. Religion makes no such blunder. The individual's religion may be egotistic, and those private realities which it keeps in touch with may be narrow enough; but at any rate it always remains infinitely less hollow and abstract, as far as it goes, than a science which prides itself on taking no account of anything private at all.

A bill of fare with one real raisin on it instead of the word 'raisin', with one real egg instead of the word 'egg', might be an inadequate meal, but it would at least be a commencement of reality. The contention of the survival theory that we ought to stick to non-personal elements exclusively seems like saying that we ought to be satisfied forever with reading the naked bill of fare. I think, therefore, that however particular questions connected with our individual destinies may be answered, it is only by acknowledging them as genuine questions, and living in the sphere of thought which they open up, that we become profound. But to live thus is to be religious; so I unhesitatingly repudiate the survival theory of religion as being founded on an egregious mistake. It does not follow, because our ancestors made so many errors of fact and mixed them with their religion, that we should therefore leave off being religious at all.[1] By

---

[1] Even the errors of fact may possibly turn out not to be as wholesale as the scientist assumes. We saw in Lecture 4 how the religious conception of the universe seems to many mind-curers 'verified' from day to day by their experience of fact. 'Experience of fact' is a field with so many things in it that the sectarian scientist,

being religious we establish ourselves in possession of ultimate reality at the only points at which reality is given us to guard. Our responsible concern is with our private destiny after all.

You see now why I have been so individualistic throughout these lectures, and why I have seemed so bent on rehabilitating the element of feeling in religion and subordinating its intellectual part. Individuality is founded in feeling; and the recesses of feeling, the darker, blinder strata of character, are the only places in the world in which we catch real fact in the making, and directly perceive how events happen, and how work is actually done. Compared with this world of living individualized feelings, the world of generalized objects which the intellect contemplates is without solidity or life. As in stereoscopic or kinetoscopic pictures seen outside the instrument, the third dimension, the movement, the vital element, are not there. We get a beautiful picture of an express train supposed to be moving, but where in the picture, as I have heard a friend say, is the energy or the fifty miles an hour?

Let us agree, then, that Religion, occupying herself with

---

methodically declining, as he does, to recognize such 'facts' as mind-curers and others like them experience, otherwise than by such rude heads of classification as 'bosh', 'rot', 'folly', certainly leaves out a mass of raw fact which, save for the industrious interest of the religious in the more personal aspects of reality, would never have succeeded in getting itself recorded at all. We know this to be true already in certain cases; it may, therefore, be true in others as well. Miraculous healings have always been part of the supernaturalist stock in trade, and have always been dismissed by the scientist as figments of the imagination. But the scientist's tardy education in the facts of hypnotism has recently given him an apperceiving mass for phenomena of this order, and he consequently now allows that the healings may exist, provided you expressly call them effects of 'suggestion'. Even the stigmata of the cross on Saint Francis's hands and feet may on these terms not be a fable. Similarly, the time-honoured phenomenon of diabolical possession is on the point of being admitted by the scientist as a fact, now that he has the name of 'hystero-demonopathy' by which to apperceive it. No one can foresee just how far this legitimation of occultist phenomena under newly found scientist [sic] titles may proceed – even 'prophecy', even 'levitation', might creep into the pale.

Thus the divorce between scientist [sic] facts and religious facts may not necessarily be as eternal as it at first sight seems, nor the personalism and romanticism of the world, as they appeared to primitive thinking, be matters so irrevocably outgrown. The final human opinion may, in short, in some manner now impossible to foresee, revert to the more personal style, just as any path of progress may follow a spiral rather than a straight line. If this were so, the rigorously impersonal view of science might one day appear as having been a temporarily useful eccentricity rather than the definitively triumphant position which the sectarian scientist at present so confidently announces it to be.

personal destinies and keeping thus in contact with the only
absolute realities which we know, must necessarily play an
eternal part in human history. The next thing to decide is what
she reveals about those destinies, or whether indeed she reveals
anything distinct enough to be considered a general message to
mankind. We have done, as you see, with our preliminaries, and
our final summing up can now begin.

I am well aware that after all the palpitating documents which
I have quoted, and all the perspectives of emotion-inspiring
institution and belief that my previous lectures have opened, the
dry analysis to which I now advance may appear to many of
you like an anticlimax, a tapering-off and flattening-out of the
subject, instead of a crescendo of interest and result. I said
awhile ago that the religious attitude of Protestants appears
poverty-stricken to the Catholic imagination. Still more poverty-
stricken, I fear, may my final summing up of the subject appear
at first to some of you. On which account I pray you now to
bear this point in mind, that in the present part of it I am
expressly trying to reduce religion to its lowest admissible terms,
to that minimum, free from individualistic excrescences, which
all religions contain as their nucleus, and on which it may be
hoped that all religious persons may agree. That established, we
should have a result which might be small but would at least be
solid; and on it and round it the ruddier additional beliefs on
which the different individuals make their venture might be
grafted, and flourish as richly as you please. I shall add my own
over-belief (which will be, I confess, of a somewhat pallid kind,
as befits a critical philosopher), and you will, I hope, also add
your over-beliefs, and we shall soon be in the varied world of
concrete religious constructions once more. For the moment let
me dryly pursue the analytic part of the task.

Both thought and feeling are determinants of conduct, and
the same conduct may be determined either by feeling or by
thought. When we survey the whole field of religion, we find a
great variety in the thoughts that have prevailed there; but the
feelings on the one hand and the conduct on the other are
almost always the same, for Stoic, Christian and Buddhist saints
are practically indistinguishable in their lives. The theories which
Religion generates, being thus variable, are secondary; and if
you wish to grasp her essence you must look to the feelings and
the conduct as being the more constant elements. It is between

these two elements that the short circuit exists on which she carries on her principal business, while the ideas and symbols and other institutions form loop-lines which may be perfections and improvements, and may even some day all be united into one harmonious system, but which are not to be regarded as organs with an indispensable function, necessary at all times for religious life to go on. This seems to me the first conclusion which we are entitled to draw from the phenomena we have passed in review.

The next step is to characterize the feelings. To what psychological order do they belong?

The resultant outcome of them is in any case what Kant calls a 'sthenic' affection, an excitement of the cheerful, expansive, 'dynamogenic' order which, like any tonic, freshens our vital powers. In almost every lecture, but especially in the lectures on Conversion [Chapters IX–X] and on Saintliness [Chapters XI–XIII], we have seen how this emotion overcomes temperamental melancholy and imparts endurance to the subject, or a zest, or a meaning, or an enchantment and glory to the common objects of life. The name of 'faith-state', by which Professor Leuba designates it, is a good one. It is a biological as well as a psychological condition, and Tolstoy is absolutely accurate in classing faith among the forces *by which men live*. The total absence of it, anhedonia, means collapse.

The faith-state may hold a very minimum of intellectual content. We saw examples of this in those sudden raptures of the divine presence, or in such mystical seizures as Dr Bucke described. It may be a mere vague enthusiasm, half spiritual, half vital, a courage, and a feeling that great and wondrous things are in the air.[2]

When, however, a positive intellectual content is associated with a faith-state, it gets invincibly stamped in upon belief, and

---

[2] Example: Henri Perreyve writes to Gratry: 'I do not know how to deal with the happiness which you aroused in me this morning. It overwhelms me; I want to *do* something, yet I can do nothing and am fit for nothing . . . I would fain do *great things*.' Again, after an inspiring interview, he writes: 'I went homewards intoxicated with joy, hope, and strength. I wanted to feed upon my happiness in solitude, far from all men. It was late; but, unheeding that, I took a mountain path and went on like a madman, looking at the heavens, regardless of earth. Suddenly an instinct made me draw hastily back – I was on the very edge of a precipice, one step more and I must have fallen. I took fright and gave up my nocturnal promenade.' – A. Gratry, *Henri Perreyve*, London, 1872, pp. 89 and 92.

this explains the passionate loyalty of religious persons everywhere to the minutest details of their so widely differing creeds.
Taking creeds and faith-states together, as forming 'religions',
and treating these as purely subjective phenomena, without
regard to the question of their 'truth', we are obliged, on account
of their extraordinary influence upon action and endurance, to
class them amongst the most important biological functions of
mankind. Their stimulant and anaesthetic effect is so great that
Professor Leuba, in a recent article, goes so far as to say that so
long as men can *use* their god, they care very little who he is, or
even whether he is at all. 'The truth of the matter can be put',
says Leuba,

> in this way: *God is not known, he is not understood; he is used* —
> sometimes as meat-purveyor, sometimes as moral support, some-
> times as friend, sometimes as an object of love. If he proves himself
> useful, the religious consciousness asks for no more than that.
> Does God really exist? How does he exist? What is he? are so
> many irrelevant questions. Not God, but life, more life, a larger,
> richer, more satisfying life, is, in the last analysis, the end of
> religion. The love of life, at any and every level of development, is
> the religious impulse.

At this purely subjective rating, therefore, Religion must be
considered vindicated in a certain way from the attacks of her
critics. It would seem that she cannot be a mere anachronism
and survival, but must exert a permanent function, whether she
be with or without intellectual content, and whether, if she have
any, it be true or false.

We must next pass beyond the point of view of merely
subjective utility, and make inquiry into the intellectual content
itself.

First, is there, under all the discrepancies of the creeds, a
common nucleus to which they bear their testimony
unanimously?

And second, ought we to consider the testimony true? I will
take up the first question first, and answer it immediately in the
affirmative. The warring gods and formulas of the various
religions do indeed cancel each other, but there is a certain
uniform deliverance in which religions all appear to meet. It
consists of two parts:

1 An uneasiness; and
2 Its solution.
1 The uneasiness, reduced to its simplest terms, is a sense that there is *something wrong about us* as we naturally stand.
2 The solution is a sense that *we are saved from the wrongness* by making proper connection with the higher powers.

In those more developed minds which alone we are studying, the wrongness takes a moral character, and the salvation takes a mystical tinge. I think we shall keep well within the limits of what is common to all such minds if we formulate the essence of their religious experience in terms like these:

The individual, so far as he suffers from his wrongness and criticizes it, is to that extent consciously beyond it and in at least possible touch with something higher, if anything higher exist. Along with the wrong part there is thus a better part of him, even though it may be but a most helpless germ. With which part he should identify his real being is by no means obvious at this stage; but when stage two (the stage of solution or salvation) arrives, the man identifies his real being with the germinal higher part of himself; and does so in the following way. He becomes conscious that this higher part is conterminous and continuous with a MORE of the same quality, which is operative in the universe outside of him, and which he can keep in working touch with, and in a fashion get on board of and save himself when all his lower being has gone to pieces in the wreck.

It seems to me that all the phenomena are accurately describable in these very simple general terms. They allow for the divided self and the struggle; they involve the change of personal centre and the surrender of the lower self; they express the appearance of exteriority of the helping power and yet account for our sense of union with it; and they fully justify our feelings of security and joy. There is probably no autobiographic document, among all those which I have quoted, to which the description will not well apply. One need only add such specific details as will adapt it to various theologies and various personal temperaments, and one will then have the various experiences reconstructed in their individual forms.

So far, however, as this analysis goes, the experiences are only psychological phenomena. They possess, it is true, enormous biological worth. Spiritual strength really increases in the subject when he has them, a new life opens for him, and they seem to him a place of conflux where the forces of two universes meet; and yet this may be nothing but his subjective way of feeling things, a mood of his own fancy, in spite of the effects produced. I now turn to my second question: What is the objective 'truth' of their content?

The part of the content concerning which the question of truth most pertinently arises is that 'MORE of the same quality' with which our own higher self appears in the experience to come into harmonious working relation. Is such a 'more' merely our own notion, or does it really exist? If so, in what shape does it exist? Does it act, as well as exist? And in what form should we conceive of that 'union' with it of which religious geniuses are so convinced?

It is in answering these questions that the various theologies perform their theoretic work, and that their divergencies most come to light. They all agree that the 'more' really exists; though some of them hold it to exist in the shape of a personal god or gods, while others are satisfied to conceive it as a stream of ideal tendency embedded in the eternal structure of the world. They all agree, moreover, that it acts as well as exists, and that something really is effected for the better when you throw your life into its hands. It is when they treat of the experience of 'union' with it that their speculative differences appear most clearly. Over this point pantheism and theism, nature and second birth, works and grace and karma, immortality and reincarnation, rationalism and mysticism, carry on inveterate disputes.

At the end of my lecture on philosophy I held out the notion that an impartial science of religions might sift out from the midst of their discrepancies a common body of doctrine which she might also formulate in terms to which physical science need not object. This, I said, she might adopt as her own reconciling hypothesis, and recommend it for general belief. I also said that in my last lecture I should have to try my own hand at framing such an hypothesis.

The time has now come for this attempt. Who says 'hypothesis' renounces the ambition to be coercive in his arguments. The most I can do is, accordingly, to offer something that may fit the facts so easily that your scientific logic will find no plausible pretext for vetoing your impulse to welcome it as true.

The 'more', as we called it, and the meaning of our 'union' with it, form the nucleus of our inquiry. Into what definite description can these words be translated, and for what definite facts do they stand? It would never do for us to place ourselves off-hand at the position of a particular theology, the Christian theology, for example, and proceed immediately to define the 'more' as Jehovah, and the 'union' as his imputation to us of the righteousness of Christ. That would be unfair to other religions, and, from our present standpoint at least, would be an over-belief.

We must begin by using less particularized terms; and, since one of the duties of the science of religions is to keep religion in connection with the rest of science, we shall do well to seek first of all a way of describing the 'more', which psychologists may also recognize as real. The *subconscious self* is nowadays a well-accredited psychological entity; and I believe that in it we have exactly the mediating term required. Apart from all religious considerations, there is actually and literally more life in our total soul than we are at any time aware of. The exploration of the transmarginal field has hardly yet been seriously undertaken, but what Mr Myers said in 1892 in his essay on the subliminal consciousness[3] is as true as when it was first written:

> Each of us is in reality an abiding psychical entity far more extensive than he knows – an individuality which can never express itself completely through any corporeal manifestation. The Self manifests through the organism; but there is always some part of the Self unmanifested; and always, as it seems, some power of organic expression in abeyance or reserve.

Much of the content of this larger background against which our conscious being stands out in relief is insignificant. Imperfect memories, silly jingles, inhibitive timidities, 'dissolutive' phenomena of various sorts, as Myers calls them, enter into it for a large part. But in it many of the performances of genius seem also to have their origin; and in our study of conversion, of mystical experiences, and of prayer, we have seen how striking a part invasions from this region play in the religious life.

[3] *Proceedings of the Society for Psychical Research*, vol. 7, p. 305.

Let me then propose, as an hypothesis, that whatever it may be on its *farther* side, the 'more' with which in religious experience we feel ourselves connected is on its *hither* side the subconscious continuation of our conscious life. Starting thus with a recognized psychological fact as our basis, we seem to preserve a contact with 'science' which the ordinary theologian lacks. At the same time the theologian's contention that the religious man is moved by an external power is vindicated, for it is one of the peculiarities of invasions from the subconscious region to take on objective appearances, and to suggest to the subject an external control. In the religious life the control is felt as 'higher'; but since on our hypothesis it is primarily the higher faculties of our own hidden mind which are controlling, the sense of union with the power beyond us is a sense of something, not merely apparently but literally true.

This doorway into the subject seems to me the best one for a science of religions, for it mediates between a number of different points of view. Yet it is only a doorway, and difficulties present themselves as soon as we step through it, and ask how far our transmarginal consciousness carries us if we follow it on its remoter side. Here the over-beliefs begin: here mysticism and the conversion-rapture and Vedantism and transcendental idealism bring in their monistic interpretations and tell us that the finite self rejoins the absolute self, for it was always one with God and identical with the soul of the world. Here the prophets of all the different religions come with their visions, voices, raptures and other openings, supposed by each to authenticate his own peculiar faith.

Those of us who are not personally favoured with such specific revelations must stand outside of them altogether and, for the present at least, decide that, since they corroborate incompatible theological doctrines, they neutralize one another and leave no fixed result. If we follow any one of them, or if we follow philosophical theory and embrace monistic pantheism on non-mystical grounds, we do so in the exercise of our individual freedom, and build out our religion in the way most congruous with our personal susceptibilities. Among these susceptibilities intellectual ones play a decisive part. Although the religious question is primarily a question of life, of living or not living in the higher union which opens itself to us as a gift, yet the spiritual excitement in which the gift appears a real one will often fail to be aroused in an individual until certain particular intellectual beliefs or ideas which, as we say, come home to him, are touched. These ideas will thus be essential to that individual's religion – which is as much as to say that over-beliefs in various directions are absolutely indispensable, and that we should treat them with tenderness and tolerance so long as they are not intolerant themselves. As I have elsewhere written, the most interesting and valuable things about a man are usually his over-beliefs.

Disregarding the over-beliefs, and confining ourselves to what is common and generic, we have in *the fact that the conscious person is continuous with a wider self through which saving experiences come*, a positive content of religious experience which, it seems to me, *is literally and objectively true as far as it goes*. If I now proceed to state my own hypothesis about the farther limits of this extension of our personality, I shall be offering my own over-belief – though I know it will appear a sorry under-belief to some of you – for which I can only bespeak the same indulgence which in a converse case I should accord to yours.

The farther limits of our being plunge, it seems to me, into an altogether other dimension of existence from the sensible and merely 'understandable' world. Name it the mystical region, or the supernatural region, whichever you choose. So far as our ideal impulses originate in this region (and most of them do originate in it, for we find them possessing us in a way for which we cannot articulately account), we belong to it in a more intimate sense than that in which we belong to the visible world, for we belong in the most intimate sense wherever our ideals belong. Yet the unseen region in question is not merely ideal, for it produces effects in this world. When we commune with it, work is actually done upon our finite personality, for we are turned into new men, and consequences in the way of conduct follow in the natural world upon our regenerative change. But that which produces effects within another reality must be termed a reality itself, so I feel as if we had no philosophic excuse for calling the unseen or mystical world unreal.

God is the natural appellation, for us Christians at least, for the supreme reality, so I will call this higher part of the universe by the name of God. We and God have business with each other; and in opening ourselves to his influence our deepest destiny is fulfilled. The universe, at those parts of it which our personal being constitutes, takes a turn genuinely for the worse or for the better in proportion as each one of us fulfils or evades God's demands. As far as this goes, I probably have you with me, for I only translate into schematic language what I may call the instinctive belief of mankind: God is real since he produces real effects.

The real effects in question, so far as I have as yet admitted them, are exerted on the personal centres of energy of the various subjects, but the spontaneous faith of most of the subjects is that they embrace a wider sphere than this. Most religious men believe (or 'know', if they be mystical) that not only they themselves, but the whole universe of beings to whom the god is present, are secure in his parental hands. There is a sense, a dimension, they are sure, in which we are *all* saved, in spite of the gates of hell and all adverse terrestrial appearances. God's existence is the guarantee of an ideal order that shall be permanently preserved. This world may indeed, as science assures us, some day burn up or freeze; but if it is part of his order, the old ideals are sure to be brought elsewhere to fruition, so that where God is, tragedy is only provisional and partial, and shipwreck and dissolution are not the absolutely final things. Only when this farther step of faith concerning God is taken, and remote objective consequences are predicted, does religion, as it seems to me, get wholly free from the first immediate subjective experience, and bring a *real hypothesis* into play. A good hypothesis in science must have other properties than those of the phenomenon it is immediately invoked to explain, otherwise it is not prolific enough. God, meaning only what enters into the religious man's experience of union, falls short of being an hypothesis of this more useful order. He needs to enter into wider cosmic relations in order to justify the subject's absolute confidence and peace.

That the god with whom, starting from the hither side of our own extra-marginal self, we come at its remoter margin into commerce should be the absolute world-ruler, is of course a very considerable over-belief. Over-belief as it is, though, it is an article of almost everyone's religion. Most of us pretend in some way to prop it upon our philosophy, but the philosophy itself is really propped upon this faith. What is this but to say that Religion, in her fullest exercise of function, is not a mere illumination of facts already elsewhere given, not a mere passion, like love, which views things in a rosier light? It is indeed that, as we have seen abundantly. But it is something more, namely, a postulator of new *facts* as well. The world interpreted religiously is not the materialistic world over again, with an altered expression; it must have, over and above the altered expression, a natural constitution different at some point from that which a materialistic world would have. It must be such that different events can be expected in it, different conduct must be required.

This thoroughly 'pragmatic' view of religion has usually been taken as a matter of course by common men. They have interpolated divine miracles into the field of nature, they have built a heaven out beyond the grave. It is only transcendentalist metaphysicians who think that, without adding any concrete details to Nature, or subtracting any, but by simply calling it the expression of absolute spirit, you make it more divine just as it stands. I believe the pragmatic way of taking religion to be the deeper way. It gives it body as well as soul, it makes it claim, as everything real must claim, some characteristic realm of fact as its very own. What the more characteristically divine facts are, apart from the actual inflow of energy in the faith-state and the prayer-state, I know not. But the over-belief on which I am ready to make my personal venture is that they exist. The whole drift of my education goes to persuade me that the world of our present consciousness is only one out of many worlds of consciousness that exist, and that those other worlds must contain experiences which have a meaning for our life also; and that although in the main their experiences and those of this world keep discrete, yet the two become continuous at certain points, and higher energies filter in. By being faithful in my poor measure to this over-belief, I seem to myself to keep more sane and true. I *can*, of course, put myself into the sectarian scientist's attitude, and imagine vividly that the world of sensations and of scientific laws and objects may be all. But whenever I do this, I hear that inward monitor of which W. K. Clifford once wrote, whispering the word 'bosh!' Humbug is humbug, even though it bear the scientific name, and the total expression of human experience, as I view it objectively, invincibly urges me beyond the narrow 'scientific' bounds. Assuredly, the real world is of a different temperament – more intricately built than physical science allows. So my objective and my subjective conscience both hold me to the over-belief which I express. Who knows whether the faithfulness of individuals here below to their own poor over-beliefs may not actually help God in turn to be more effectively faithful to his own greater tasks?

19

Postscript

TO THE VARIETIES OF RELIGIOUS EXPERIENCE

In writing my concluding lecture I had to aim so much at simplification that I fear that my general philosophic position received so scant a statement as hardly to be intelligible to some of my readers. I therefore add this epilogue, which must also be so brief as possibly to remedy but little the defect. In a later work I may be enabled to state my position more amply and consequently more clearly.

Originality cannot be expected in a field like this, where all the attitudes and tempers that are possible have been exhibited in literature long ago, and where any new writer can immediately be classed under a familiar head. If one should make a division of all thinkers into naturalists and supernaturalists, I should undoubtedly have to go, along with most philosophers, into the supernaturalist branch. But there is a crasser and a more refined supernaturalism, and it is to the refined division that most philosophers at the present day belong. If not regular transcendental idealists, they at least obey the Kantian direction enough to bar out ideal entities from interfering causally in the course of phenomenal events. Refined supernaturalism is universalistic supernaturalism; for the 'crasser' variety 'piecemeal' supernaturalism would perhaps be the better name. It went with that older theology which today is supposed to reign only among uneducated people, or to be found among the few belated professors of the dualisms which Kant is thought to have displaced. It admits miracles and providential leadings, and finds no intellectual difficulty in mixing the ideal and the real worlds together by interpolating influences from the ideal region among the forces that causally determine the real world's details. In this the refined supernaturalists think that it muddles disparate dimensions of existence. For them the world of the ideal has no efficient causality, and never bursts into the world of phenomena at particular points. The ideal world, for them, is not a world of facts, but only of the meaning of facts; it is a point of view for judging facts. It appertains to a different '-ology', and inhabits a different dimension of being altogether from that in which existential propositions obtain. It cannot get down upon the flat level of experience and interpolate itself piecemeal between distinct portions of nature, as those who believe, for example, in divine aid coming in response to prayer, are bound to think it must.

Notwithstanding my own inability to accept either popular Christianity or scholastic theism, I suppose that my belief that in communion with the Ideal new force comes into the world, and new departures are made here below, subjects me to being classed among the supernaturalists of the piecemeal or crasser type. Universalistic supernaturalism surrenders, it seems to me, too easily to naturalism. It takes the facts of physical science at their face value, and leaves the laws of life just as naturalism finds them, with no hope of remedy, in case their fruits are bad. It confines itself to sentiments about life as a whole, sentiments which may be admiring and adoring, but which need not be so, as the existence of systematic pessimism proves. In this universalistic way of taking the ideal world, the essence of practical religion seems to me to evaporate. Both instinctively and for logical reasons, I find it hard to believe that principles can exist which make no difference in facts.[1] But all facts are particular facts, and the whole interest of the question of God's existence seems to me to lie in the consequences for particulars which that existence may be expected to entail. That no concrete particular of experience should alter its complexion in consequence of a god being there seems to me an incredible proposition, and yet it is the thesis to which (implicitly at any rate) refined supernaturalism seems to cling. It is only with experience *en bloc,* it says,

---

[1] Transcendental idealism, of course, insists that its ideal world makes *this* difference, that facts *exist.* We owe it to the absolute that we have a world of fact at all. 'A world' of fact – that exactly is the trouble. An entire world is the smallest unit with which the absolute can work, whereas to our finite minds work for the better ought to be done within this world, setting in at single points. Our difficulties and our ideals are all piecemeal affairs, but the absolute can do no piecework for us; so that all the interests which our poor souls compass raise their heads too late. We should have spoken earlier, prayed for another world absolutely, before this world was born. It is strange, I have heard a friend say, to see this blind corner into which Christian thought has worked itself at last, with its God who can raise no particular weight whatever, who can help us with no private burden, and who is on the side of our enemies as much as he is on our own. Odd evolution from the God of David's psalms!

that the absolute maintains relations. It condescends to no transactions of detail.

I am ignorant of Buddhism and speak under correction, and merely in order the better to describe my general point of view; but as I apprehend the Buddhistic doctrine of karma, I agree in principle with that. All supernaturalists admit that facts are under the judgment of higher law; but for Buddhism as I interpret it, and for religion generally so far as it remains unweakened by transcendentalistic metaphysics, the word 'judgment' here means no such bare academic verdict or Platonic appreciation as it means in Vedantic or modern absolutist systems; it carries, on the contrary, *execution* with it, is *in rebus* as well as *post rem*, and operates 'causally' as partial factor in the total fact. The universe becomes a gnosticism[2] pure and simple on any other terms. But this view that judgment and execution go together is that of the crasser supernaturalist way of thinking, so the present volume must on the whole be classed with the other expressions of that creed.

I state the matter thus bluntly, because the current of thought in academic circles runs against me, and I feel like a man who must set his back against an open door quickly if he does not wish to see it closed and locked. In spite of its being so shocking to the reigning intellectual tastes, I believe that a candid consideration of piecemeal supernaturalism and a complete discussion of all its metaphysical bearings will show it to be the hypothesis by which the largest number of legitimate requirements are met. That of course would be a programme for other books than this; what I now say sufficiently indicates to the philosophic reader the place where I belong.

If asked just where the differences in fact which are due to God's existence come in, I should have to say that in general I have no hypothesis to offer beyond what the phenomenon of 'prayerful communion', especially when certain kinds of incursion from the subconscious region take part in it, immediately suggests. The appearance is that in this phenomenon something ideal, which in one sense is part of ourselves and in another sense is not ourselves, actually exerts an influence, raises our centre of personal energy, and produces regenerative effects unattainable in other ways. If, then, there be a wider world of

[2] See my *Will to Believe*, p. 285, above.

being than that of our everyday consciousness, if in it there be forces whose effects on us are intermittent, if one facilitating condition of the effects be the openness of the 'subliminal' door, we have the elements of a theory to which the phenomena of religious life lend plausibility. I am so impressed by the importance of these phenomena that I adopt the hypothesis which they so naturally suggest. At these places at least, I say, it would seem as though transmundane energies, God, if you will, produced immediate effects within the natural world to which the rest of our experience belongs.

The difference in natural 'fact' which most of us would assign as the first difference which the existence of a God ought to make would, I imagine, be personal immortality. Religion, in fact, for the great majority of our own race *means* immortality, and nothing else. God is the producer of immortality; and whoever has doubts of immortality is written down as an atheist without farther trial. I have said nothing in my lectures about immortality or the belief therein, for to me it seems a secondary point. If our ideals are only cared for in 'eternity', I do not see why we might not be willing to resign their care to other hands than ours. Yet I sympathize with the urgent impulse to be present ourselves, and in the conflict of impulses, both of them so vague yet both of them noble, I know not how to decide. It seems to me that it is eminently a case for facts to testify. Facts, I think, are yet lacking to prove 'spirit-return', though I have the highest respect for the patient labours of Messrs Myers, Hodgson and Hyslop, and am somewhat impressed by their favourable conclusions. I consequently leave the matter open, with this brief word to save the reader from a possible perplexity as to why immortality got no mention in the body of this book.

The ideal power with which we feel ourselves in connection, the 'God' of ordinary men, is, both by ordinary men and by philosophers, endowed with certain of those metaphysical attributes which in the lecture on philosophy I treated with such disrespect. He is assumed as a matter of course to be 'one and only' and to be 'infinite'; and the notion of many finite gods is one which hardly anyone thinks it worth while to consider, and still less to uphold. Nevertheless, in the interests of intellectual clearness, I feel bound to say that religious experience, as we have studied it, cannot be cited as unequivocally supporting the infinitist belief. The only thing that it unequivocally testifies to is that we can experience union with *something* larger than ourselves and in that union find our greatest peace. Philosophy, with its passion for unity, and mysticism with its monoideistic bent, both 'pass to the limit' and identify the something with a unique God who is the all-inclusive soul of the world. Popular opinion, respectful to their authority, follows the example which they set.

Meanwhile the practical needs and experiences of religion seem to me sufficiently met by the belief that beyond each man and in a fashion continuous with him there exists a larger power which is friendly to him and to his ideals. All that the facts require is that the power should be both other and larger than our conscious selves. Anything larger will do, if only it be large enough to trust for the next step. It need not be infinite, it need not be solitary. It might conceivably even be only a larger and more god-like self, of which the present self would then be but the mutilated expression, and the universe might conceivably be a collection of such selves, of different degrees of inclusiveness, with no absolute unity realized in it at all.[3] Thus would a sort of polytheism return upon us – a polytheism which I do not on this occasion defend, for my only aim at present is to keep the testimony of religious experience clearly within its proper bounds.

Upholders of the monistic view will say to such a polytheism (which, by the way, has always been the real religion of common people, and is so still today) that unless there be one all-inclusive God, our guarantee of security is left imperfect. In the absolute, and in the absolute only, *all* is saved. If there be different gods, each caring for his part, some portion of some of us might not be covered with divine protection, and our religious consolation would thus fail to be complete. It goes back to what was said on pages 348–52, above, about the possibility of there being portions of the universe that may irretrievably be lost. Commonsense is less sweeping in its demands than philosophy or mysticism have been wont to be, and can suffer the notion of this world being partly saved and partly lost. The ordinary moralistic state of mind makes the salvation of the world conditional upon the success with which each unit does its part.

[3] Such a notion is suggested in my Ingersoll Lecture, *On Human Immortality*, Boston and London, 1899.

Partial and conditional salvation is in fact a most familiar notion when taken in the abstract, the only difficulty being to determine the details. Some men are even disinterested enough to be willing to be in the unsaved remnant as far as their persons go, if only they can be persuaded that their cause will prevail – all of us are willing, whenever our activity-excitement rises sufficiently high. I think, in fact, that a final philosophy of religion will have to consider the pluralistic hypothesis more seriously than it has hitherto been willing to consider it. For practical life at any rate, the *chance* of salvation is enough. No fact in human nature is more characteristic than its willingness to live on a chance. The existence of the chance makes the difference, as Edmund Gurney says, between a life of which the keynote is resignation and a life of which the keynote is hope.[4] But all these statements are unsatisfactory from their brevity, and I can only say that I hope to return to the same questions in another book.

[4] *Tertium Quid*, 1887, p. 99. See also pp. 148 and 149.

SUGGESTIONS FOR FURTHER READING

Biographical Material

The following books give accounts of William James and his family.

Allen, G. W., *William James: A Biography*, New York: Viking Press, 1967. The most up-to-date biography of William James. It is concise, readable and informative.

Lewis, R. W. B., *The Jameses*, London: Andre Deutsch, 1991. A longer and more informal account of the James family, from William James's grandparents to his own children. It is particularly useful in the information it gives of the less well-known members of the family.

Matthiessen, F. O., *The James Family*, New York: Alfred Knopf, 1948. An older biography of the James family; it is more scholarly than Lewis's book but also shorter.

William James's Philosophy

Two of the most recent general accounts of James's philosophy are:

Bird, G., *William James*, London: Routledge, 1986. An examination of, and introduction to, the central aspects of James's philosophy. It considers his pragmatism, empiricism and philosophical psychology, as well as his moral philosophy and philosophy of religion.

Myers, G. E., *William James: His Life and Thought*, New Haven: Yale University Press, 1986. A substantial and scholarly account of James's work, with an emphasis on the links between his philosophy and psychology. It contains a comprehensive critical discussion of James's ideas.

Other useful commentaries on James are:

Dooley, P. K., *Pragmatism as Humanism: The Philosophy of William James*, Chicago: Nelson-Hall, 1974. An account of James's thought with special reference to its emphasis on human interests and human problems. It focusses on James's subordination of purely intellectual issues to the demands and problems of practical life.

Gavin, W. J., *William James and the Reinstatement of the Vague*, Philadelphia: Temple University Press, 1992. A short, readable account of James's views, focussing on his resistance to analytic, problem-solving aspects of philosophy. It compares James's ideas with those of some post-modern philosophers.

Perry, R. B., *The Thought and Character of William James*, 2 vols, Boston: Little, Brown and Co., 1935. An early survey of James's thought and its development, written by a close associate of James. It is long, informative, but rather unsystematic.

Suckiel, E. K., *The Pragmatic Philosophy of William James*, Notre Dame: Notre Dame University Press, 1982. Provides a concise, comprehensive account of James's philosophical method, his philosophical psychology, and his theories of meaning, truth and moral values.

Pragmatism in General

The following books offer a general picture of the development of American pragmatism.

Rorty, R., *The Consequences of Pragmatism*, Brighton: Harvester Press, 1982. A philosophical discussion of selected themes from pragmatism, not confined to William James's philosophy. It is especially interesting in indicating the impact of pragmatism on the development of Rorty's own philosophy.

Scheffler, I., *Four Pragmatists*, New York: Routledge, 1974. A concise account of the philosophical development of Peirce, James, Dewey and Mead. A readable short introduction to these philosophers, with a critical discussion of their ideas.

Smith, J. E., *The Spirit of American Philosophy*, New York: Oxford University Press, 1963. A survey of the 'golden age' of American philosophy exemplified in the work of Peirce, James, Dewey, Royce and Whitehead. Although not all these philosophers were pragmatists there is an emphasis on pragmatism as a distinctively American philosophy.

Thayer, H. S., *Meaning and Action: A Critical History of Pragmatism*, Indianapolis: Bobbs-Merrill, 1968. A detailed scholarly account of the development of pragmatism, with some philosophical criticism of the views of its exponents.

White, M., *Pragmatism and the American Mind*, Oxford: Oxford University Press, 1973. A philosophical assessment of the central themes of pragmatism in their relation to American life and thought. A valuable complement to Smith's book.

The following provide more detailed accounts of specific pragmatist philosophers.

Hookway, C., *Peirce*, London: Routledge, 1985. A comprehensive and detailed discussion of the philosophy of C. S. Peirce, particularly valuable in bringing together central ideas which are relatively inaccessible in Peirce's own publications.

Tiles, J., *Dewey*, London: Routledge, 1988. A valuable survey of the main themes in Dewey's philosophy, with a critical discussion of their relevance to current issues in philosophy.

INDEX